Sakai Courseware Management

The Official Guide

A comprehensive and pragmatic guide to using, managing, and maintaining Sakai in the real world

Alan Berg

Michael Korcuska

PACKT PUBLISHING

BIRMINGHAM - MUMBAI

Sakai Courseware Management
The Official Guide

Copyright © 2009 Packt Publishing

First published: June 2009

Production Reference: 2120609

Published by Packt Publishing Ltd.
32 Lincoln Road
Olton
Birmingham, B27 6PA, UK.

ISBN 978-1-84719-940-9

www.packtpub.com

Cover Image by Vinayak Chittar (vinayak.chittar@gmail.com)

Credits

Authors
Alan Berg
Michael Korcuska

Reviewers
Aaron Zeckoski
Ian Boston
Margaret Wagner
Tony Atkins

Acquisition Editor
James Lumsden

Development Editor
Siddharth Mangarole

Technical Editor
Ajay Shanker

Editorial Team Leader
Akshara Aware

Project Team Leader
Lata Basantani

Project Coordinator
Srimoyee Ghoshal

Indexer
Monica Ajmera

Proofreader
Chris Smith

Production Coordinator
Dolly Dasilva

Cover Work
Dolly Dasilva

Foreword

In 2004, the Mellon Foundation provided seed funding for a group of four top universities in the United States — University of Michigan, Indiana University, Massachusetts Institute of Technology, and Stanford University — to collaborate to create an open source teaching, learning, and academic collaboration software platform. The University of California at Berkeley joined the effort, soon thereafter. And, so, Sakai was born. Today, hundreds of individuals of universities, schools, and corporations all around the world are involved in building Sakai. And millions more use Sakai as an everyday part of their teaching, learning, and research at educational institutions around the world.

This book is primarily a practical guide to installing, configuring, and using the Sakai Collaboration and Learning Environment (CLE). You will learn a lot about the Sakai CLE as you read this book and will begin to understand why so many top universities have chosen to deploy Sakai. But there is more to the story than just an enterprise software application. Before diving into the practical material it is worth spending a few minutes familiarizing yourself with the other three ingredients that make up the Sakai project: the Sakai community, the open source license that Sakai uses, and the Sakai Foundation.

This information is not simply interesting background material. As you begin to use Sakai you will undoubtedly be drawn to the Sakai email lists, Wiki, and blogs written by Sakai contributors. Understanding this context will aide your interactions with members of the Sakai community.

The Sakai Community

Open Source software efforts are organized in a variety of different ways. Some, like MySQL, are driven primarily by a single commercial organization. Others, like Linux, are built from the diverse contributions of many individuals and organizations and often led by a "benevolent dictator". The Sakai community fits neither of these descriptions exactly but, instead, is a co-operation amongst educational institutions, commercial organizations, and independent individuals all working collaboratively to build the Sakai CLE. Often an organization will commit the time of its staff members to participate in Sakai. In other cases, individuals volunteer their time to contribute something of value.

The Sakai community as a whole, not a single organization or individual, is responsible for all aspects of evolving the Sakai CLE. There is no central decision maker, which places a premium on communication and determining the best way forward based on the merits of the idea. The Sakai CLE is truly designed by education, for education. These community members, who generally work at educational institutions around the world, sit extremely close to the end users of Sakai. Members of the Sakai community believe this community-driven development model inevitably leads to the best product for use on campus. So when you interact with the Sakai community you should keep in mind that nobody is "in charge" — your contributions will be accepted based on their value and the time and effort you have to contribute.

This community is fundamental to Sakai's value. Sharing product development, academic, and e-learning best practices with peers around the world is a unique aspect of Sakai, a rare cross-institutional collaboration in higher education information technology. For many organizations and individuals, this aspect of Sakai is as important as the functionality of the software itself.

Educational Community License

Sakai is distributed as free and open source software. Access to this code is extremely valuable to those who want to customize their on-campus instance or wish to develop innovative new tools. But open source code is important to the entire Sakai community. The ability to make that one change to the code for your campus can be crucially important and that change can be added to the Sakai code base, removing the need for customization as you upgrade. And the source code serves as the ultimate insurance policy, ensuring that you aren't locked into a single vendor.

Sakai uses the Educational Community License (ECL), a minor variant of the Apache License. This licence is commercial friendly because it allows the Sakai code to be extended and bundled with proprietary code and re-distributed—it allows use of the source code for the development of proprietary software as well as free and open source software (of course the original Sakai code in any such commercial re-distribution remains free and open source). This distinguishes Sakai from open source projects that use the GPL license, which requires that any released extensions to the software also be free and open source. In part because of this license, Sakai has attracted a variety of well-known commercial partners including IBM and Oracle.

The Sakai Foundation

The Sakai Foundation is a member supported non-profit corporation with a small staff and modest budget. It was created in 2006 when the original Mellon funding for Sakai had run its course. Those involved in the Sakai effort wanted a small organization to continue to coordinate the activities of the community.

While membership in the Foundation is optional, approximately 100 organizations around the world support the foundation so that it can continue its important community activities. These include managing the intellectual property of Sakai, organizing conferences and planning meetings, maintaining the Sakai technology infrastructure including the bug tracking system and project Wiki, coordinating development activities and quality assurance, publishing the Sakai CLE releases and functioning as a public advocate for Sakai.

Getting started

It is time to get started. Chapter 1 provides a good overview of the Sakai software and a little more detail on the history of Sakai and the Sakai community. After that it's feet first into the software itself—you'll have a Sakai demo up and running by the end of Chapter 2. From that point it's up to you. Readers with a technology background will certainly be interested in the chapters, *Setting up Sakai* and *The Administration Workspace*. *Tools, Tools, Tools* is important information about the wide variety of tools that are available in Sakai and is important for getting the most out of Sakai. *Using Sakai For Teaching and Collaboration* will be of special interest to anyone using Sakai or supporting Sakai end-users. And *Sakai at its Best* provides many case studies and examples of Sakai in use. In many ways that is the most important chapter in the book because it demonstrates that so much of the value of using Sakai comes from being part of the community. By reading this book your taking a first (or another) step into that community. Welcome aboard!

About the authors

Alan Mark Berg BSc. MSc. PGCE, has been a lead developer at the Central Computer Services at the Universiteit van Amsterdam for the last ten years. In his famously scarce spare time, he writes computer articles (`http://home.uva.nl/a.m.berg`). Alan has a degree, two masters, and a teaching qualification. In previous incarnations, he was a technical writer, an Internet/Linux course writer, a product line development officer, and a teacher. He likes to get his hands dirty with the building and gluing of systems. He remains agile by playing computer games with his kids who sadly consistently beat him physically, mentally, and morally.

I am lucky to be working for understanding employers, the Informatiseringscentrum at the Universiteit van Amsterdam (`http://ic.uva.nl`), who have allowed me to work in company time on this book, and Léon Raijmann my current boss who gave me the space I needed when I needed it.

Let's not forget the Sakai community, which responded positively to my requests for help, as it always has done, with thought-out text and advice that enhanced the value of this book. Parts of this book are written by specific members of the community; their biographies reside next to their work.

I would particularly like to acknowledge Margaret Wagner of Sakai Newsletter fame for her hard work and attention to detail while turning my words into sentences.

Thank you Tony Mobily, owner and editor of the FreeSoftware Magazine (`http://www.freesoftwaremagazine.com/`), your wise words at complex moments helped.

Finally, I felt supported and occasionally understood by my family; yes you may pretend you don't know me, but you do. Hester, Lawrence, and Nelson, without your unwritten understanding that 2 A.M. is a normal time to work and a constant supply of sarcasm is good for my soul, I would not have finished this project.

Michael Korcuska is the Executive Director of the Sakai foundation and has nearly 20 years of experience in technology-enabled education and training. Prior to joining Sakai, Michael served as Chief Operating Officer for ELT, Inc., a leading compliance-training provider. He has also held leadership positions at DigitalThink (now Convergys Learning Solutions) and Cognitive Arts, an award winning custom e-learning developer. Michael got his start in technology-based learning at Stanford University's Courseware Authoring Tools Lab and Apple Computer's Multimedia Lab in the late 1980s. He holds an M.S. in Computer Science from Northwestern University (where he studied and worked at the Institute for the Learning Sciences) and B.S. in Symbolic Systems from Stanford University. He usually lives in Berkeley, California, with his wife and two children although his writing for this book was done during a year living in Paris, France.

My primary thanks for this book goes to Alan Berg whose consistent writing and diligent project management made this project possible. Not to mention the fact that it was his idea in the first place and I can now fondly remember the lunch we had at the Jardin de Pâtes in Paris to discuss the project.

As the deadline for the book approached it was also clear that we needed additional editing help and Margaret Warner of the University of Michigan stepped in. Margaret has edited the Sakai Newsletter since I've been involved with Sakai and since I submit an item for nearly every issue, I've had ample demonstration of her ability to help my words say what I actually meant.
Thank you, Margaret.

And, of course, thanks to my wife and partner Shannon Jackson. She's been incredibly supportive for over 20 years and it is gratifying to finally have a place to publicly acknowledge how much the success and happiness I've had depends on her.

About the reviewers

Aaron Zeckoski is a Senior Research Engineer in CARET (Centre for Applied Research in Educational Technologies) at Cambridge University. He has been involved in many aspects of system development over the past six years including analysis, design, implementation, QA, deployment, and support. His current responsibilities include project analysis, system design, and system implementation for web application development. Recent work involves Java, Spring, Hibernate, RSF (Reasonable Server Faces), PHP, and Sakai.

He was previously the Manager of Application Development and Lead Developer in the Learning Technologies unit at Virginia Tech for five years.

Ian Boston has extensive experience in the field of highly distributed web applications. He is CTO at CARET at the University of Cambridge and for two other organizations: CBCL Ltd, a Medical Informatics Company, delivering drugs information on a global scale, and Sybermedica Ltd, a Medical Diagnostics company, providing telemedicine solutions on an international scale.

Prior to joining CARET, he was CTO for an early leader in BPM and Activity Based Workflow with customers including Bank of Scotland, New Opportunities Fund, UK Sport, UK Sports Institute, British Olympic Association, Magma Inc., British Telecom, Sema, and PwC.

Ian has been an active investor in 20 or more start-up companies in the Cambridge area over the past 15 years and sits on a number of advisory boards.

He holds a 1st Class Honours degree in Engineering and a PhD in Parallel Computing and he worked on a number of "Grand Challenge" grid problems in the 1990s.

Margaret Wagner is a senior technical writer at the University of Michigan. She has been involved with the Sakai Project since its earliest predecessors, UM.CourseTools, UM.WorkTools, and CHEF, were developed, and she wrote the original help guides for these applications. Margaret is also the editor of the Sakai Newsletter, which is received by members of the Sakai Community around the world every two weeks.

Margaret attended Whitman College, University of Colorado, and the University of Michigan, where she studied linguistics and piano performance.

Tony Atkins is currently a Senior Support Engineer at Atlassian BV in Amsterdam. He currently provides support for administrators at companies, non-profit organizations, and open source projects around the world.

Prior to that, Tony worked for 10 years supporting digital libraries and education technologies in Higher Education. Tony became involved with the Sakai community while working at Virginia Tech, and worked for a number of years developing tools and documentation to help other Sakai administrators before moving on to work in the commercial open source world.

Table of Contents

Preface

This book is the officially endorsed Sakai guide. From setting up and running Sakai for the first time to creatively using its tools, this book delivers everything you need to know.

Sakai represents a Collaboration and Learning Environment that provides the means of managing users, courses, instructors, and facilities, as well as a spectrum of tools including assessment, grading, and messaging.

The book opens with an overview that explains Sakai, its history, and how to set up a demonstration version. The underlying structures within Sakai are described and you can then start working on Sakai and create your first course or project site using the concepts explained in this book. You will then structure online courses for teaching and collaboration between groups of students. Soon after mastering the Administration Workspace section you will realize that there is a vast difference between the knowledge that is required for running a demonstration version of Sakai and that needed for maintaining production systems. You will then strengthen your concepts by going through the ten real-world situations given in this book.

The book also discusses courses that have won awards, displays a rogue's gallery of 30 active members of the community, and describes what motivates management at the University of Amsterdam to buy into Sakai. Finally, the executive director of the Sakai Foundation looks towards the future.

What this book covers

Chapter 1 is an introduction to Sakai.

Chapter 2 explains how to install a demo version of the Sakai CLE. One way to approach understanding the content of this book is to have the demo running while reading the chapters on specific toolsets.

Chapter 3 explains the underpinning technologies and how system integrators have deployed Sakai at large scales in practice.

Chapter 4 describes how to create and manage your first project site.

Chapter 5 involves creation of a course site, and learning more about working with roles and permissions, and sections and groups.

Chapter 6 covers the many different site tools that are available to you and how quality is defended during their development.

Chapter 7 discusses the various types of tools and show how they are used in project, course, and portfolio sites.

Chapter 8 covers tools that have been built by third parties to fulfill specific needs. These tools are not found in the standard Sakai demonstration, but do have a lot of potential for improving a student's online learning experiences.

Chapter 9 discusses how to use tools in combination to create a better online learning experience.

Chapter 10 introduces the administrative features of Sakai.

Chapter 11 discusses the Sakai web services for creating and maintaining users, sites, and groups and list a wide variety of existing services explaining how to discover and connect to them.

Chapter12 is an advanced chapter that explains concepts that you need during first-time Sakai deployments. In this chapter, you will find an overview of third-party frameworks that Sakai is built upon, how to manage and monitor Java, and interviews with various experts.

Chapter 13 is about common error messages in Sakai and how to deal with them.

Chapter 14 presents ten international case studies showing Sakai at its best.

Chapter 15 takes a look at what makes an award winning courses, award winning.

Chapter 16 discusses motivations for deploying open source applications in higher education environments such as at the University of Amsterdam.

Chapter 17 discusses how to successfully interact with the Sakai community.

Chapter 18 outlines the biographies of around 30 members of the Sakai community and is intended to give you a feeling for the strength, wealth, and vibrancy of the community's being.

Chapter 19 is a discussion about the future of Sakai.

Appendix A consists of a rich set of concepts and an overflow of terminology

Appendix B consists of links to diverse sources and helpful information available on the internet

Who this book is for

This book is written for a wide audience that includes teachers, system administrators, and first-time developers. It will also appeal to the Sakai open source community, potential community members, and education's decision makers.

Conventions

In this book, you will find a number of styles of text that distinguish between different kinds of information. Here are some examples of these styles, and an explanation of their meaning.

Code words in text are shown as follows: "We can include other contexts through the use of the `include` directive."

New terms and **important words** are shown in bold. Words that you see on the screen, in menus or dialog boxes for example, appear in our text like this: "clicking the **Next** button moves you to the next screen".

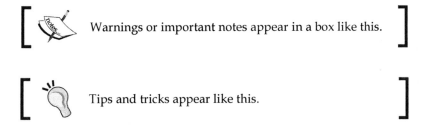

Warnings or important notes appear in a box like this.

Tips and tricks appear like this.

Reader feedback

Feedback from our readers is always welcome. Let us know what you think about this book—what you liked or may have disliked. Reader feedback is important for us to develop titles that you really get the most out of.

To send us general feedback, simply drop an email to `feedback@packtpub.com`, and mention the book title in the subject of your message.

If there is a book that you need and would like to see us publish, please send us a note via the **SUGGEST A TITLE** form on `www.packtpub.com`, or send an email to `suggest@packtpub.com`.

If there is a topic that you have expertise in and you are interested in either writing or contributing to a book on, see our author guide on www.packtpub.com/authors.

Customer support

Now that you are the proud owner of a Packt book, we have a number of things to help you to get the most from your purchase.

Errata

Although we have taken every care to ensure the accuracy of our contents, mistakes do happen. If you find a mistake in one of our books—maybe a mistake in text or code—we would be grateful if you would report this to us. By doing so, you can save other readers from frustration, and help us to improve subsequent versions of this book. If you find any errata, please report them by visiting http://www.packtpub. com/support, selecting your book, clicking on the **let us know** link, and entering the details of your errata. Once your errata are verified, your submission will be accepted and the errata added to any list of existing errata. Any existing errata can be viewed by selecting your title from http://www.packtpub.com/support.

Piracy

Piracy of copyright material on the Internet is an ongoing problem across all media. At Packt, we take the protection of our copyright and licenses very seriously. If you come across any illegal copies of our works in any form on the Internet, please provide us with the location address or website name immediately, so that we can pursue a remedy.

Please contact us at copyright@packtpub.com with a link to the suspected pirated material.

We appreciate your help in protecting our authors, and our ability to bring you valuable content.

Questions

You can contact us at questions@packtpub.com if you are having a problem with any aspect of this book, and we will do our best to address it.

1
What Is Sakai?

Sakai is an open source, web-based, collaboration learning environment (CLE) that is focused primarily on higher education. It supports the activities of students, teachers, researchers, and Sakai administrators. Sakai is flexible and enables users to configure it for their own specialized audiences.

Sakai is mainly a courseware management platform that provides users with learning, portfolio, library, and project tools. Teachers can create course sites and add chat, forums, blogs, wikis, and many other tools. Students can, among other things, upload assignments, use the tools, and interact with instructors and classmates. Finally, researchers and groups of peers can create project sites for sharing materials and ad hoc interactions. Sakai is flexible by design and has a set of frameworks (internal structures) that makes it easier for those who want to build tools.

Sakai scales to even the largest and most demanding environments! For example, Indiana University maintains a deployment for at least 100,000 students and that number keeps rising. The University of Michigan deploys for 70,000 students.

Sakai tools

The basic concept behind the functionality of a CLE is that users control their own sites; for example, they can choose which tools to include in the sites they create. The application treats users as adults and enables flexibility through choice. The tools include chat, forums, wiki, polls, Google-like search capabilities, and others — with more tool options with every new version of Sakai. Numerous tools enhance group formation, allowing for intuitive interaction (hence the word "collaboration" in Collaboration Learning Environment).

The range of tools is rich indeed, especially if you include all those contributed by the energetic and motivated Sakai community. Many local deployments have specialized tools for which they develop their own enhancements. They then contribute these extra tools, software for connections to external systems, and various other new features back to the community. As Sakai grows in strength, the number of extras is increasing explosively. The Sakai Foundation web site mentions at least 20 extras and the Foundation's source code repository has around 120 contributed directories.

Sakai was designed with a framework that significantly simplifies the creation of tools. Developers do not have to reinvent the wheel for fundamental services like finding a user's name, managing a site's look and feel, or internationalization. There are strong, well-established lines of support for developers, including style guides, best practices, a programmer's café, workshops, and central quality assurance (QA), throughout a development project's full life cycle.

To help organizations decide which tools to deploy in their production environments (for example, a college campus), which tools to start looking at for future use, and which to retire, each tool is assigned a status:

- **Core** — Tools with which the community has a great deal of experience and is confident about their robustness, stability, and scalability.
- **Provisional** — Tools with which the community has less experience or which are becoming obsolete. They are disabled by default.
- **Contrib** — Tools with which the community has little experience and which the QA work group does not recommend for broad usage in a production environment. Contrib tools are available, separately from the release, in the Contrib area of Sakai's source repository.

Watching the codebase over time, you see a convection effect where contrib tools move to provisional, are thoroughly tested, and move to core; and then older core tools move down to either provisional or are pensioned off. As time progresses, there is a quality convergence — the software gets thoroughly debugged first by a team of dedicated testers and then by real-life high-scale deployments. In the end, the user has more choices and sophistication in the toolset. The extra choice of tools costs more server effort. Luckily, due to the trend known as Moore's law, servers double in computational power roughly every eighteen months. The end user thus directly benefits from a scalable framework, an increasingly functional-rich toolset, and ever-improving server specifications.

The Sakai Foundation

The Sakai Foundation is a not-for-profit organization that was set up in late 2005 to encourage community building between academic institutions, nonprofits, and commercial organizations. It coordinates the release cycle and stimulates the ongoing health of the Sakai community by organizing and sponsoring conferences and fellowships. It manages the software creation life cycle, from development, through testing and quality assurance, to polishing the user experience.

Recognizing the need for best practices and a methodology for decreasing the learning curve for new tool developers, the Sakai Foundation, with the help of Aaron Zeckoski (`http://aaronz-sakai.blogspot.com`), set up the programmer's café.

The programmer's café is a set of lectures and hands-on programming labs focused on building new Sakai tools. By the end of the café, the programmers have learned enough to create their own masterpieces. The programmer's café is also about best practices and how to use the Eclipse programmers' IDE effectively.

Sakai conference organizers traditionally schedule the café for the day before the main conference presentations, and occasionally, a trainer delivers the café as a separate set of planned events. See `http://bugs.sakaiproject.org/confluence/display/BOOT/home`.

You can find the most up-to-date information on the Foundation's web site (`http://sakaiproject.org`), shown below. Notice the links to documentation and downloads. Foundation members work to ensure that the most current information possible is online.

The motto: collaboration and learning for educators, by educators, free and open source, is not accidental. Much care has gone into creating an educationally supportive infrastructure that is free to download, change, and use as you like, with a clear vision of keeping this true for all time. The all-too common nightmare of IP trolls attacking your organization for licensing dues has no role here.

The development of the Sakai CLE has been date-driven with aggressive milestones and a transparent requirements process. The implication is that by the time you read this chapter, the next version of Sakai will be out. There will be more tools for users to choose from, many minor enhancements and performance improvements, numerous bugs spotted and removed, and much honest discussion at local and international conferences and especially in the mail lists.

There is a positive, intelligent, and constructive business-like atmosphere that surrounds the open, but sometimes difficult, discussions within the community.

Sakai worksite

The next figure shows a generic Sakai worksite for a newly-created user who has logged on for the first time. On the left side are links to the default set of tools. The main area is for expressing the tools' functionality, and the tabs at the top of the screen enable you to move between sites of which you are a member.

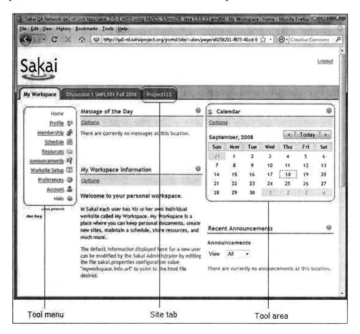

By default, a new user owns a worksite with only a basic set of tools enabled, including a few for self-administration purposes. If the user wants, he or she can request a project, course, or portfolio site:

- **Project** — A project site has two main types of users: the site maintainer and those who can use and share the resources and tools. Typical users of a project site include researchers working on the same study, teachers who wish to compare notes, and ad hoc groups of users who wish to interact together online.

- **Course** — A course site is a virtual online expression of a real course. The target audience are teachers who maintain the site with teaching assistants and students who use the site. Teachers can post exams, send announcements, upload syllabi and grade book results, and choose which tools the students can use to interact. Teaching assistants have less power, but can maintain forums and help maintain processes such as the ebb and flow of marking assignments. Students can chat, take tests, upload files, and send mail to others in the course.

- **Portfolio** — Portfolio sites are places where students store evidence of their work in a structured format. As a student progresses through his or her education or course, that evidence builds up within an online structure set of links and web pages. This can be helpful for finding employment later because potential employers can make judgments based on the evidence presented.

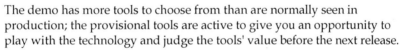

Where have the tools gone?

The demo has more tools to choose from than are normally seen in production; the provisional tools are active to give you an opportunity to play with the technology and judge the tools' value before the next release.

Later chapters cover these three types of sites in more detail, beginning with Chapter 4, *My First Project Site*. For the administrator, a special admin site includes tools for daily business, such as sending "messages of the day" to the entire user base, managing sites and users, scheduling tasks, and generally tweaking the whole environment. Chapter 10, *The Administration Workspace*, provides extensive information about this site.

The community

In a wider sense, Sakai is not only an application, but also an active community of educational institutions working together to solve common problems and share best practices. The professional development and cross-institutional knowledge sharing are benefits that are hard to find elsewhere.

The vibrant, open source community has structured management and strong commercial support. The central pillar is the Sakai Foundation (`http://sakaiproject.org/portal/site/sakai-Foundation`).

Sakai is open sourced under the Educational Community License, currently version 2 (`http://opensource.org/licenses/ecl2.php`). This allows commercial partners to provide hosting, support, and custom modifications, and lets developers work with the full code base. A proprietary license would have slowed down deployment and held back development and wider support.

The benefit of open source for the assessment of quality is profound. You can handle and manipulate the code without having to worry about accidentally violating any commercial license, advanced developers can learn through review, and issues and bugs are more amenable to resolution locally.

The Sakai open source community is confident, open, and not afraid to show the good, the bad, or the ugly. An Amsterdam University-based QA server automatically tests the main parts of the source code for bugs three times a day and publishes at the end of each test a report (`http://qa1-nl.sakaiproject.org/codereview`) that is viewable by the whole universe and a couple of parallel ones as well. Anyone can download the source code and send modifications to a branch manager.

Branches

Different organizations have different timelines for patching and updating their production servers. The source code of Sakai is evolving fast and, once or twice a year, the Foundation releases a new version of Sakai. Some organizations do not have the time or resources to upgrade, but do want to patch their servers for known bugs and security issues. To achieve this, the branch manager copies the source code into another part of the source code repository (this is called branching). The branch manager for the older code is responsible for updating with patches, leaving the newer code in a different branch to evolve.

Being a branch manager is quite a lot of work and it is easy to make mistakes. If you see one of this endangered species at a conference, pat him or her on the back, make encouraging noises, and try not to look at his or her greying hair and the stress lines in his or her face.

Workgroups

Workgroups are factions of similarly interested parties that gather information and requirements on Confluence and share advice and best practices with the community. Visit the main page of the Sakai Confluence (`http://confluence. sakaiproject.org/confluence/dashboard.action`) and you will see a list of workgroups mixed in with other links on the left side. The workgroups meet online and, usually at conferences, in person. Workgroups exist for developers, quality assurance, management of the software life cycle, the user experience, teaching practices, and so on.

The email lists from the various workgroups are also viewable to the world and there are no limits on who can subscribe. A wiki is in place with a large number of contributors changing content without central editorial control. In general, the community responds quickly.

 A full list of workgroups with descriptions is given as part of Chapter 17.

 The official Sakai FAQ

`http://confluence.sakaiproject.org/confluence/pages/ viewpage.action?pageId=27807` is very readable and is a good jumping off point for further study. It contains many useful and up-to-date links as well.

Developers

The architects have not just designed Sakai to be a place for excellent online learning experiences; it is also a platform for easy development, especially of tools. At least 100 developers are actively enhancing Sakai directly or through contributions for local deployments right now. That's a rather large number, so you can expect rapid evolution of the product base.

Tool creation is straightforward; most developers within the Sakai community use the industrial standard Eclipse IDE (`http://www.eclipse.org`) to bash away at their code.

For tool builders, at first development may seem daunting. However, the basic skills needed to create a tool are the same as those for building a standard web application. Thankfully, there is a wide range of supportive material in the wild.

It is beyond the scope of this book to go into the detail of setting up your development environment.

Tool creation

For those of you who are interested in tool creation, the online Development Environment Setup document (`http://bugs.sakaiproject.org/confluence/display/BOOT/Development+Environment+Setup+Walkthrough`) is a necessary read.

Roots

Sakai has deep academic roots and, at the time of writing, is deployed or in pilot in more than two hundred large organizations—mostly universities—around the world. Volunteers have meticulously translated the application into an ever-increasing number of languages. In the worksite profile, the user can choose his or her language preference.

Although its roots are American, Sakai's presence is at the tipping point of rapidly spreading. The following figure shows a Google map of current Sakai deployment locations.

The sites include Australia, South Africa, France, England, Holland, China, Japan, and Egypt and many other countries. Sakai is a world traveler, capable of speaking multiple languages and supporting various learning modalities.

A brief history

Sakai is relatively young, but has multiple strong roots and has grown fast.

In late 2003, four universities — MIT, Michigan, Stanford, and Indiana — saw a common cause to jointly develop an Open Source Virtual Learning Environment. They agreed to contribute labor to the tune of $4.4 million, and slightly later that year the Andrew W. Mellon Foundation (`http://mellon.org`) seeded another $2.2 million.

The project did not need to start from scratch; the University of Michigan already had a significant code base and, just as importantly, a conceptual framework and essential experience from the creation of its own set of tools called CHEF. The Java-based CHEF tools encompassed a subset of the Sakai functionality and were mature, with first deployments as early as 2001. The original Sakai code base also included code from the other universities (including coursework and assessments from Stanford) and OSIDs (a set of standard coding APIs and architecture for educational purposes based on Service Oriented Architecture) from the OKI project (`http://okiproject.org`).

The first phase of Sakai was the so-called "best of refactoring", during which the code was unified and the main framework put into place.

Sakai 1.0

The newly formed team officially announced the Sakai project at Educause (`http://educause.edu`) in November 2003, and in June 2004 the team released Sakai 1.0. Date-driven development cycles resulted in a high evolution rate and both Michigan and Indiana rolled out Sakai to their student and instructor audience at the end of 2004 and during 2005.

For the Sakai project to survive beyond the first two years, it needed to move away from potential grant addiction toward a model in which the community and project were self-sustaining. The vehicle for this transition was the Sakai Foundation, to which, in a fit of good judgment and self-interest, individual organizations transferred copyrights and resources.

A separate project, the **Open Source Portfolio (OSP)** initiative, was later merged into the code base and it improved both the overall value of Sakai and OSP products by enriching functionality and allowing a combined use of resources for quality assurance and tool building.

Sakai membership costs an organization $5,000–$10,000 per year. The members channel the money to fund the Foundation, which then helps manage the evolution of the software and stimulates the health of the community.

Recognizing early the significant role that commercial support can play in helping academic organizations deploy, the Foundation created its Sakai Commercial Affiliates (SCA) program to foster commercial partnerships.

Present day

Currently there is a healthy biosphere with commercial partners providing a variety of support, from hosting to customizations and tool building. Selling Sakai to local management becomes that much easier. For a relatively few bucks, management can buy commercial support of a known quality to support any new deployments or personalizations. There are small start-up companies that specialize in training or turnkey solutions such as Edia (`http://edia.nl`) and Airplane (`http://aeroplanesoftware.com`), and large more established players such as rSmart (`http://www.rsmart.com`) or Unicon (`http://www.unicon.net/`). Management is not stuck to a choice of one and competition has the strong tendency to lower costs.

The goals of the Foundation include measuring and understanding the needs of the user, sponsoring inter-organizational collaboration, supporting the growth of the community, and keeping decision-making processes as transparent and accessible as possible.

 Recently, there has been a push to improve the end-user experience with particular attention to the user interface. We can expect more good things to come.

Advantages for organizations

In the next chapter, you will discover how easy it is to install and use the demonstration version of Sakai on any modern desktop computer, be it Windows, Mac, or Linux. However, why would you deploy Sakai in the larger organizational context in the first place?

No man is an island and no learning system lives outside the context of the organization it supports. Here are some key points for why an organization can be comfortable choosing Sakai:

- Educators and software engineers have designed the application from the bottom up and top down to be an effective and flexible learning environment.

- An active community is adding useful tools to the mix all the time.

- The Sakai Foundation stimulates the growth and good order of the community and is the contact point for project coordination and life-cycle management.

- There is a strong central quality-assurance process with many early adopters of new releases. This makes it much less likely that you will have to wake up a system administrator in the middle of the night to deal for the fourth time with an unexpected crash.

- There is a commercial partnership program, which means you can buy in support or outsource when you need to.

- With standard hardware such as load balancers and Oracle or MySQL databases, Sakai has been deployed for individual organizations past the 170,000-user mark and is relatively simple to set up for even the smallest of pilot programs.

- Sakai is a Java-based application using technologies such as Tomcat (`http://tomcat.apache.org`) as its application server and Spring (`http://springframework.org/about`) for managing the way it interacts with databases and injects services into tools and other well-known and widely understood frameworks. Java plays well when developed in distributed teams, and the use of mainstream technologies makes it easier to find developers or support in the marketplace.

- Sakai supports web services for loosely couple Service Oriented Architectures (SOAs). SOAs are the structure of choice for many organizations' internal administration.

- To create, modify, or delete users, courses, and groups externally, this learning environment has integration points called providers that allow relatively easy incorporation into your own administration systems.

- Sakai is not going away at any time soon. It has easily passed the critical user-base mass for long-term growth.

 Leon Raijmann, an educationalist and top-level manager at the University of Amsterdam, further discusses management buy-in factors in Chapter 16, *A Crib Sheet for Selling Sakai to Traditional Management*.

Long URLs and Confluence

An approximate description of Confluence is that it is an enhanced wiki. The Sakai community uses one (`http://confluence.sakaiproject.org/confluence`) as a place to quickly build up documentation and expand ideas. However, the URLs of content are not always particularly readable, and some of the links may be difficult to copy into your web browser. If you get stuck or content has moved, search adding key terms in the search bar found at the top of any Confluence web page.

Summary

Sakai is a Java-based open source Collaboration Learning Environment that is flexible, easy to use, and highly scalable. It has an active community of educational institutions working together to solve common problems and share best practices.

The Sakai Foundation supports the community and helps form a coherent project management structure around the life cycle.

The Sakai CLE is not only an application but also a framework for easing the burden of tool creation. Sakai is evolving fast and many developers are busy enhancing frameworks and tools.

The next chapter explains how to install a demo version of the Sakai CLE. One way to approach understanding the content of this book is to have the demo running while reading the chapters on specific toolsets.

2
Feet First: Running the Demo

An interactive approach to understanding the behavior of Sakai involves downloading the self-standing demonstration version, and running and using it. For a user — whether administrator, teacher, student, or ad hoc project worker — getting hands-on experience with a live system is helpful in gaining an understanding of the wealth of tools available and how to work with such a range of positive choices.

It is possible to try out all the roles: administer your own local Sakai demonstration version, and act as a teacher and a student. You will gain an appreciation of all the aspects and interactions that affect you in a real-life production environment without the pain of angry villagers knocking at your gate. To be honest, it's just plain fun to be in control of your own learning environment, adding courses with multimedia and chat, creating portfolios, exploring the full potential, and unleashing it through your web browser.

The demonstration is a supportive sandbox in which to learn because it has more tools enabled than normally exist in a production environment. It includes everything you need to run the program and does not require an extensive installation effort. The coders have built the demo with the support of a Tomcat server (`http://tomcat.apache.org`) and an in-memory database, which stores changes into text files.

Sakai is built with the Java programming language. Java is platform agnostic, meaning that in practice it runs from your Macintosh, Windows PC, or Linux box without any problems and probably runs on many untested platforms as well.

Every time the community releases a new version Sakai code, it simultaneously releases the equivalent demo. In general, the community releases three different packages to the wider public:

- **Demonstration** — A self-standing package that is easy to install, use, and, if necessary, discard.

- **Binary** — A pre-built version of Sakai without Apache Tomcat, Java library dependencies, or extra configuration files. The recommendation is that you download the binary release if you want to just drop the Sakai bundle into a pre-existing Tomcat environment. The binary version is handy for system administrators who do not want to change their production servers, but would like to test a drop-in replacement in an older version.

- **Source code** — The code enables developers and quality assurance specialists to get into the innards of Sakai quickly. It is an excellent collection of example code for those of us who want to learn about modern design and the related Java-based frameworks.

This chapter shows you how to install the demonstration version (currently at 2.5.3) and then, for the developer with a keen interest in getting his or her hands dirty, it shows how to compile from source. It also identifies jump-off points for learning more.

After starting up your demonstration server for the first time, you may want to practice creating a project site and a course site. How to do this is detailed in Chapters 4 and 5.

Installing the demo

Because Sakai is a Java-based application that runs within a Tomcat server, the source code is independent of the Operating System (OS). It does, however, require that you have a particular Java version — currently Java 1.5 JDK — installed on your machine.

The demo is self-contained. For initial learning, however, it's a good idea to deploy for more than a few users. For that, you will need to connect to a more substantial database such as MySQL or Oracle. The Foundation-supported quality assurance teams have thoroughly tested both MySQL and Oracle infrastructures under numerous sites and variations and over a whole series of versions.

The change from one database to another requires only eight lines of configuration in the `sakai.properties` text file as you'll see later in the chapter, so there's a clear path from demo to mid-sized production. (The route to large-scale deployments involves multiple servers and hardware such as load balancers. Chapter 3 briefly discusses high-scalability structures. The technologies used are standard, well known, and they work well under high user demand.)

Installation is straightforward, assuming that you have a computer with 1 GB of RAM (preferably more) and Java 1.5 (`http://java.sun.com/javase/downloads/index_jdk5.jsp`) installed.

 As Sakai evolves, so will the Java version it uses. Java 1.5 is reaching the end of its lifespan and Sun Microsystems will no longer support it after October 2009. Therefore, as Sakai moves through version 2.6, expect a transition to Java 1.6 and later to higher Java versions.

At the time of writing, the following simple installation instructions are accurate. To confirm that you have the correct version of Java installed on your system, run the following from the command line:

```
java -version
```

Java version numbering

One point of confusion is Java version numbering (`http://java.sun.com/javase/namechange.html`). Java 1.5 is currently also known as Java 2 Platform, Standard Edition 5.0 (J2SE 5.0). Java 1.6 is known as Java Platform, Standard Edition 6 (Java SE 6). The fuller version with more programming libraries is known as Java 2 SDK. To avoid confusion, most administrators and developers use the version number to keep track of changes rather than the more confusing, harder to remember, names.

Next, download the demo package (`http://www.sakaiproject.org/portal/site/sakai-downloads`) and unpack it in a location of your choice—your home directory, for example. A subdirectory, `sakai-demo-x.x.x` (where `x.x.x` is the current Sakai version number) should appear.

Now, verify that the environment variable JAVA_HOME exists and points to the top-level directory of your Java 1.5 instance. For Unix operating systems, you would typically modify a startup file like `~/.bash_login` to set and export shell variables, while Macintosh users usually set and export environment variables in `.bash_profile`. For Windows, select **Start | Control Panel | System | Advanced | Environment Variables** and set JAVA_HOME via the GUI. The JAVA_HOME value should look similar to the following, with the value of JAVA_HOME specific to your environment:

Linux/Unix: `export JAVA_HOME= usr/lib/jvm/java-1.5.0-sun-1.5.0.15`

Mac: `export JAVA_HOME=/Library/Java/Home`

Windows: `JAVA_HOME=C:\j2sdk1.5.0.15`

The value takes effect after your next login. Later in this chapter, you'll define the MAVEN_OPTS variable in exactly the same way.

To start the demo from the command line, in the root directory of Sakai, type:

Windows: start-sakai.bat

Linux/Unix/Mac: ./start-sakai.sh

A lot of Java-related logging gibberish will start flowing down the screen. Don't worry: it's just debugging information stating that the world is perfect. Be patient and wait a few minutes until you see text similar to:

```
INFO: Server startup in 168687 ms (2008-09-25 10:22:35,175 main_org.
apache.catalina.startup.Catalina)
```

The first time, startup takes about 40% longer than the later startups. This is because the Tomcat server needs to do its magic by expanding the web application parts of the tools from archive files and adding some initial seeding information to the clean database. Because there are many tools that initially load, the average startup time is longer than it would be for a less feature-rich application.

Stopping the server requires running another script:

Windows: stop-sakai.bat

Linux/Unix/Mac: stop-sakai.sh

Congratulations! You are now the proud owner of a sparkling, brand new Sakai instance running locally that is viewable using your own web browser on port 8080. The URL for your web browser is http://localhost:8080 and the main page will look similar to the next figure. The welcome message in the center of the screen mentions the sakai.properties file, which can be found under the home directory of your Sakai instance in the Sakai subdirectory. It is a text file that contains the global property configuration from which you can define database settings, email addresses, and other important personalization. You'll tweak this important file, periodically, throughout this book.

Administrator's account

The default administrator's account is named `admin` with the password `admin`. To change the password, before a potential cracker takes control, requires that you log on as the admin user, select the **Administration Workspace** tab, and then click on the **Users** tool on the left side of the screen. Choose the administrator's account, enter a new password in the **Create New Password** field, and enter it again in the **Verify New Password** field. Click **Update Details** to submit the changes, and use your new password the next time you log in.

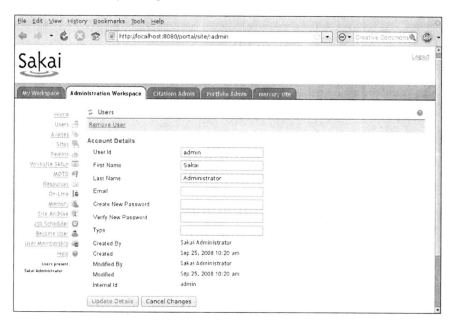

Create some test users on which you can practice your benign and benevolent administration. You can add a user from the **Users** tool, or you can log out and create a default set of accounts from the public-facing first page (the welcome page you saw earlier). For the latter, select the **New Account** tool from the menu on the left side, complete the **New Account** information (the email address is optional), and click **Create Account**.

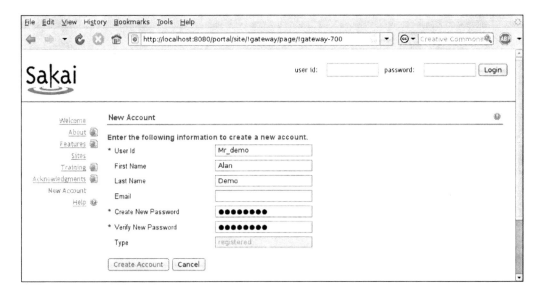

Removing Sakai

Removing Sakai is as simple as removing the installation directory via your favorite OS's GUI or from the command line. For example, under Unix/Linux:

```
rm -rf install_directory
```

And under Windows:

```
RMDIR install_directory /s /q
```

Expanding the demo

After you try out Sakai, you'll probably want to invite a few other users to take a look. Using the in-memory database, other than for demo purposes and for small numbers of users, is not recommended because you're likely to hit bottlenecks in memory usage, and performance will suffer. To alleviate this and to roughly double the number of simultaneous users, you can modify the default memory ceiling via the JAVA_OPTS setting in the startup Sakai script; -Xmx1024m defines that limit and you can modify it via a text editor of choice. For example, to increase the maximum memory setting to 2048 MB, the JAVA_OPTS should look roughly similar to the following:

```
JAVA_OPTS="-server -Xmx2048m -XX:MaxNewSize=256m XX:MaxPermSize=256m
-Dsakai.demo=true"
```

Chapter 10 (section *sakai.properties*) discusses how to attach Sakai to MySQL or to an Oracle database. Both database types scale to high numbers of users, have widespread commercial support, and are industrial standards in the enterprise and web application spheres. The QA team has thoroughly tested both of these databases and has codified recommendations on device driver version numbers and other detailed trickery. Skilled administrators have already searched out these highly specific details so that you don't have to.

In Chapters 4 and 5, you will find out how to run your first project and course site.

Community member
Anthony Whyte is the Sakai Foundation community liaison. He has written volumes of supporting material including the most up-to-date installation instructions, which I used as a basis for this section.

Help is your friend

The Sakai instance administrator has his or her own set of tools for manipulating sites, users, membership resources, and the like; teachers, students, and project members have other sets. As Sakai evolves, new tools come into play and older tools slowly fade to a well-earned retirement.

Universities such as Indiana (`https://oncourse.iu.edu/portal/site/!gateway/page/!gateway-500`) have a large corpus of helpful online material. However, the most immediate and up-to-date source of information is Sakai's context-sensitive help. You'll find a question mark icon in each tool's work area; click it and searchable context-sensitive help appears:

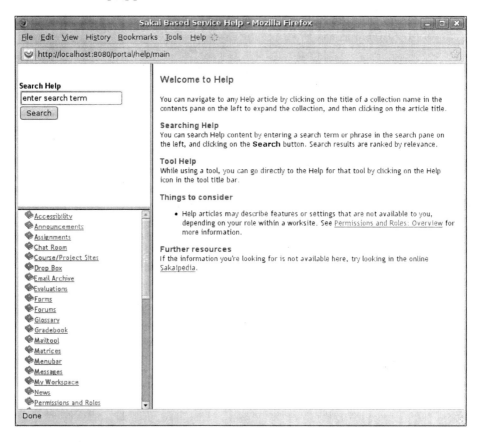

Each tool registers its help file to a central service that is kept in synchronization with the most current changes. If you find the help text wanting and wish to participate, there is always room in the development effort for extra hands and opinions.

 I cannot emphasize this enough: the help tool is the first place to look for current information.

Live demos

After all of your hard work, here is some good news: there are several live Sakai demonstrations scattered across the Internet, where you can get a free account and play around. The advantage is that there is no startup cost in time or effort; the disadvantage, for the adventurous, is that you do not get the opportunity to play around with any of the administration tools. Further, the Sakai instances tend to be slightly older than the currently available demonstration version.

Below is a screen grab of the first page of the RSmart offering. RSmart (http://www.rsmart.com/sakai) provides commercial support and an enhanced Sakai instance with extra tools and some well-thought-out nudges to the GUI.

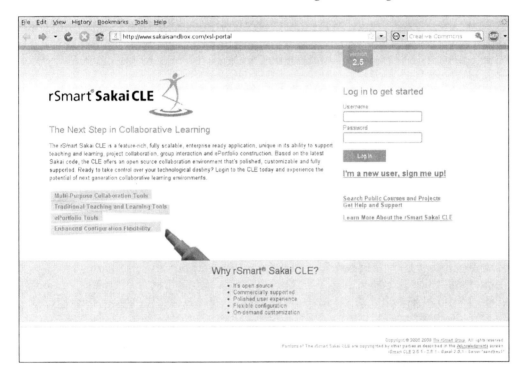

RSmart gives back to the community its enhancement and is an active supporter of the community effort. Currently, the company, in the person of Chris Coppola (http://coppola.rsmart.com), was until recently an active board member of the Sakai Foundation.

Live demos tend to be supported by commercial companies like Serensoft, RSmart, and Unicon. These companies also supply hosted solutions for those wanting to run Sakai services, such as a set of course sites, but not wanting to install Sakai in production for themselves. For example, at the time of writing, Serensoft has an introductory program for piloting single course sites with up to 50 students. This enables small organizations to kick the tires and test the engine without having to take many risks. If you are motivated, it is well worth trying out the default demonstration mentioned in this chapter and comparing it to the commercial offerings (`http://sakaiproject.org/portal/site/sakai-support`).

Building from the source

This is an advanced-use section for those of you who want to build Sakai from source code and perhaps develop tools later. If you are more interested in understanding what Sakai is or how to create great course material, feel free to skip ahead.

Currently, the source code of Sakai and its contributed projects is stored in Subversion. Subversion is a revision control system that stores the source code, the changes, and the comments on those changes. If you are a developer who wants to keep current, or a system integrator who wants to resolve bug fixes efficiently, this is where you want to get your code. The Sakai Subversion repository is available to all. Anyone can browse through it, get the code, and see its quality. The top-level location for viewing is `https://source.sakaiproject.org/svn`.

The project managers have divided the code logically into branches, tags, and trunk. The most up-to-date source code is the trunk (`https://source.sakaiproject.org/svn/sakai/trunk`), which is the central place where developers place their ever-changing code. The trunk mostly builds without any problems, but occasionally, there is a hiccup due to a premature committing and for a few hours, the source may fail to build. Do not worry; this is normal in a development cycle.

Currently, the safest place to obtain the source code is from the 2-5-x maintenance branch (`https://source.sakaiproject.org/svn/sakai/branches`), which has added patches to resolve known issues. This is the code recommended for production deployments. As Sakai ages, expect the 2-6-x and 3-0-x branches to emerge. Currently, there are supported branches for versions 2.4 and 2.5.

Tags (`https://source.sakaiproject.org/svn/sakai/tags`) are snapshots in time that testers and automatic mechanisms have fully quality assured. The major version number (2.4, 2.5, and so on) is incremented as functionality changes, and the branch manager releases point increments in a version number for a set of well-tested patches.

The level of participation from testers and early adopters, who install a tagged version as soon as it is released, has a positive implication: as the community grows and more testers and early adopters are involved, quality improves.

The contributed section (`https://source.sakaiproject.org/contrib`) stores organization-specific modifications and tools that have not yet made it as part of the official release.

There is some discussion in the mail lists about moving towards a GIT (`http://git.or.cz`) repository, which developers use for managing enormous projects such as the Linux kernel. However, at this time, such a change is on the distant horizon.

Building the demonstration from raw source is straightforward and the recipe works for Windows, Unix/Linux, and Macintosh environments.

After building from source, you'll have created two demonstration versions. One runs on Windows, the other runs in Unix/Linux or Macintosh environments.

You first need to install Subversion tools so that you can download the code. You also need Java 1.5, which you installed previously, to run the Sakai demonstration the first time; and Maven, a tool for managing the build cycle. On a Debian Linux box, the following recipe works:

```
sudo apt-get install subversion-tools
sudo apt-get install maven2
```

For Windows and Macintosh computers, you can find the Subversion binaries at `http://subversion.tigris.org` and the Maven 2 binaries at `http://maven.apache.org/download.html`.

Under a work directory of choice, run the Subversion tool to download the code:

```
svn co https://source.sakaiproject.org/svn/sakai/trunk/ sakai
```

The command `co` means checkout and Sakai is the directory to store the source code. Navigate to the source code directory via:

```
cd sakai
```

On my development machine, it takes about 20 minutes to build the binary. The source code contains hundreds of thousands of lines of active code. Therefore, the Maven tool requires a significant amount of memory while running to complete its task. Setting `MAVEN_OPTS` defines the upper limits to the memory allocated. For example, to reserve 256 MB you need to set `MAVEN_OPTS` to `-Xmx 256m` and then run Maven from the command line:

```
mvn -Ppack-demo install
```

A lot of text will flow past with a success message at the end. At the end of a successful build, you will find the Windows and Linux/Mac demos under the `pack-demo` directory.

Summary

The Sakai demonstration is easy to install and run. In this chapter, we covered the straightforward downloading of source code and building Sakai from scratch. Its context-sensitive online help is the most up-to-date location to find information on how to use the tool.

Many organizations have deployed Sakai and much helpful support material exists in various locations around the Internet. Indiana University has great examples of value-added support.

The Sakai project website `http://sakaiproject.org` has a wealth of links to supportive information and tutorials.

Test accounts are freely available on the Internet, and some companies offer commercial support for first-time deployments.

The next chapter, *Sakai Anatomy*, explains the underpinning technologies and how system integrators have deployed Sakai at large scales in practice.

3
Sakai Anatomy

Sakai is not only a collaborative learning environment; it is also a framework for building tools, such as the Wiki and chat tools, as easily as possible. The designers based the whole enchilada on open source industry-standard technologies with well-defined internal structures and a clear division of responsibilities between the logical parts. Sakai is a Java-based web application that uses the most modern frameworks and architectural best practices.

The application was forged in the fire of campus-wide deployments and now, with at least four years of hammering and hardening, Sakai efficiently integrates in a modern enterprise. Various internal hooks allow data integration with external systems, authentication, and single sign-on.

A discussion of core technologies is rife with terminology. All I can do is promise to define the terms immediately after they appear and summarize within the glossary.

If you are a content provider such as an instructor who just wants to use the CLE rather than understand the inner workings, feel free to skip the rest of this chapter or come back to it later.

Physically, Sakai resides in a Tomcat server that responds to application requests from the Internet. The application needs to obtain information from and send information to a database and the file system. For small setups with only hundreds of users, a modern server can host all of the parts. However, as usage scales and the value of the service increases, more redundancy and distribution of load is required. In a scaled-out environment where a number of application servers sit behind a load balancer, it is safe to serve hundreds of thousands of end users, which Sakai deployments do every day at locations around the world.

Sakai is designed to be a stable, scalable infrastructure that uses standard technologies to achieve its goals. This is evidenced not only by the use of standard and well-understood hardware, such as load balancers and Solaris, Linux, Mac, or Windows servers, but also in the range of well-known Java frameworks called within the application such as Spring and Hibernate, Servlets, Java Server Faces, and so on.

The multiple pressures of rapid life cycles, fixed release dates, and the need to deliver flawless Sakai applications to vast numbers of students forces a strong quality assurance cycle. Over the course of its history, Sakai has been tested and the code examined by hundreds of volunteers.

This chapter tackles the fundamentals of Sakai starting from the conceptual top: first, the abstract framework concepts, then the less-abstract definition of core technologies and the motivations for the use of these technologies, and finally, how system integrators have deployed Sakai at large scales in practice.

The Sakai framework

With the ever-increasing velocity of technological change, the wisest among us can only rarely predict the winners and losers in the market place. For instance, the builders and engineers of the so-called Web 2.0 social online explosion based their web-based applications on AJAX technology. This technology was lying dormant for years, hidden in the vague details of JavaScript and ActiveX components. The change was rapid and learning professions have yet to fully explore the implications in terms of interactive and responsive socially aware ecosystems.

An application builder, to save work later as technology changes, needs to decouple the graphical user experience from the underlying services, business model, and data. You want users to archive sites, be they course, project, or resource sites, and reuse the data no matter what the evolutionary pressures and workflow changes are.

Today, most users still interact via a desktop computer. However, mobile phones, portable games consoles, PDAs, and so on are becoming more powerful. They have the CPU cycles of a common desktop of less than ten years ago, their screens are getting larger, and they are more touch and voice aware. With campus-wide wireless connectivity and a few creative thoughts, you can imagine yet another rapid change to come. Perhaps your institution uses portals such as uPortal (`http://uportal.org`) and you want to aggregate a campus-wide view taking data directly from the Sakai underlying services. How does the Sakai framework support change?

The framework needs to be flexible enough to plug and play into a different aggregation of views; it needs to support different development groups working at the same time within the whole. It should to be as simple as possible, using standard technologies that make it easier to find support, administration, and development personnel.

There is a difference between framework and architecture. Here's how Mark J. Norton, Senior Technical Consultant of the Sakai Project, explains it in his "Overview of Sakai Technology" for an audience at the University of British Columbia: The architecture is the abstract design upon which the framework is based. The diagram below explains the architectural division of labor from within Sakai. The framework actualizes the architectural concept.

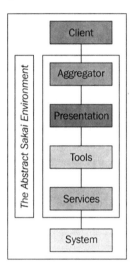

The aggregation layer

Users interact with sites. A site contains pages and tools. To build a view of the whole requires the aggregation of fragments of pages and tools. To change the overall look and workflow of your site, the aggregation layer would be the place to plug in your own custom code.

Sakai has a couple of different aggregators. The default (and the one you interact with the most) is the portal aggregator. The screen grab shown next is the PDA view as found under /portal/pda. On hitting the main page, Sakai determines which browser you are using and then chooses the correct view to render. The main point here is that the architects had not designed the PDA functionality at the start, but because of the flexibility of the architecture ad hoc change is straightforward.

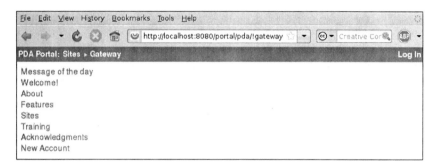

 Currently, there is great effort going into the creation of other aggregators for support of desktop tools and widgets and for PDAs and telephones.

Sakai is an international player with extra functional pressures to reconcile. For example, South Africa's North-West University (http://nwu.ac.za/) and the University of South Africa (http://unisa.ac.za/) have Internet bandwidth issues. The price is high and connectivity is spotty at times. To alleviate these problems, the universities have designed an offline viewer of Sakai content. The viewer and project are named SOLO (http://bugs.sakaiproject.org/confluence/display/SOLO/Learning+offline+with+SOLO). SOLO hooks into the low bandwidth PDA view just mentioned. The tool makes Announcements, Resources, and Lessons supplied by the Melete tool (http://www.etudes.org) available to learners. SOLO replaces the standard web interface with a rich interface similar to those found in Windows and the Macintosh OS, which is more familiar to users, and eliminates browser refreshes, thus lowering bandwidth demand and costs for the learner.

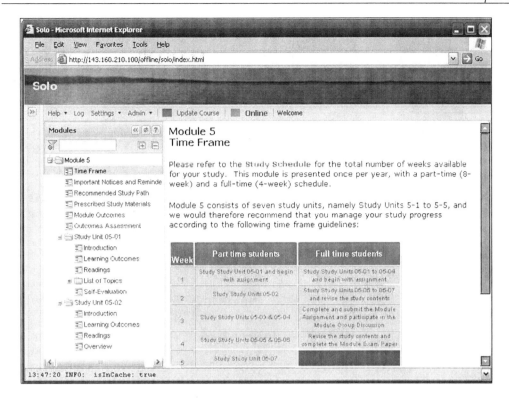

 SOLO is described in more detail in Chapter 14 *Show Cases*

The presentation layer

Underneath the aggregation layer is the presentation layer. Sakai has a number of widget sets that tools can use to generate their final rendered output. The sets help enforce a consistent look and feel, and they play well with accessibility and internationalization. The current technologies used within the presentation layer are JSF, JSP, Velocity, and Struts, with RSF (`http://www2.caret.cam.ac.uk/rsfwiki/Wiki.jsp?page=Main`) being an up-and-coming star.

The use of standard widgets lowers costs, accelerates development life cycles, and makes the creation of good-looking applications that much easier. At the time of writing, the Fluid project (`http://fluidproject.org`) is heavily involved in improving the GUI experience, so expect more choices to come.

The tools layer

Tools are units of discrete functionality — a poll tool, a wiki, or a content search tool, for instance. Each tool helps build the overall usefulness of Sakai for the end user and packages development into doable bits. Developers build large areas of functionality such as the portfolio system on top of a series of smaller tools.

Tools manipulate their information via common services such as getting or modifying users or courses, and so on. Furthermore, the Sakai framework is highly extendable. Kernel functionality enables new services and tools to be registered. While building tools, developers can add their own services, such as adding, modifying, and deleting grade books. Other tools can then make changes to a grade book based on the information gathered from the service. One example is adding the option to print a grade book in different formats in a new print tool.

The services layer

Services simplify development by hiding implementation details. The tool does not need to know which database type the service is using or where or what the file system is doing. As long as the service implementation uses a standard API, you can plug and play with different implementations and versions. The framework includes common services, such as the ability to get and add users or courses, to build compound services that are more complex.

As tools move from provisional to core, the number of services increases and so does the potential richness of development choices. This increasing set of service options is a heavy foot on the accelerator of functional improvement.

Only the programmers see the services layer directly and therefore this layer will not be mentioned further in this book other than briefly in Chapter 11, the web services chapter. The best location to find further information is the programmer's café (`http://confluence.sakaiproject.org/confluence/x/yH8`).

Core technologies

You can roughly define Sakai as a series of web applications running in a s ervlet container with some shared central services. What is a servlet? A servlet (`http://java.sun.com/products/servlet`) is a Java object that gets a request from the servlet container — the Tomcat server in this case — and sends a response. The web browser makes a request; an application receives the request, does some work, and then generates a response (normally a web page) that the end user gets to see. Of course, the exact details are more complex: first, the web browser request goes to an aggregator that dispatches many requests to specific tools, which use services and fire back responses. The aggregator then collects the responses to make one view for the end user.

Luckily, for Java developers, the architects based the Sakai framework on standard technologies. That was smart: it's easy to find employable developers because the technology is well known. At a technical level, just as importantly, the servlet container isolates each tool from the others, and the use of services decouples the underlying data from the presentation layer. The whole framework is malleable and can be changed by groups — you can tear out one piece and replace it with another while others are working elsewhere.

Each tool has its own separate space for Java libraries; Java developers know this by the term **classloader isolation**. For example, if one web application wants to parse XML using a particular version of library X and a second application wants to use library Y, the libraries will not interfere with each other. In practical terms, this implies that development teams can build their code without fear of side effects from or to others. The exception to the enforcement of isolation is the core Sakai framework that lives within a common classloader space and is visible to all.

The database interaction relies heavily on the well-known and much loved Hibernate (`http://hibernate.org`) framework. Hibernate maps objects, such as a course and a user, onto tables in a database; the mappings take place via XML configuration files. Theorists call this method of using mappings the Object Relational Model (ORM). There are advantages to using Hibernate:

- It reduces the amount of code that a developer needs to write to get the work done.
- It performs well and is normally database optimized. However occasionally, administrators notice some strange database queries created that need to be cleaned up.
- It abstracts away database details so that you do not have to worry about the plumbing.
- Developers can think in terms of objects and database specialists in terms of index optimization.

A positive side effect of Hibernate's methodology is that much of the translation from object to database that normally sits hard-coded in the Java application's source, and makes code fragile, now sits in text-based XML files readily editable. Just as good, the Hibernate community is large, which allows a large effort in testing and improving the Hibernate product. Sakai takes advantage of new features as the product rapidly evolves and becomes enriched.

Hibernate itself uses the reliable standard Java Database Connectivity (JDBC) framework (`http://java.sun.com/products/jdbc/overview.html`) to connect to numerous database types. However, Sakai currently is tested and supported only on MySQL, Oracle, and in-memory databases. In theory, an interested third party is welcome to expand the list. However, the amount of work associated with testing a new database type is enormous and makes additions to the list unlikely.

Managing Sakai-related services is achieved via the Spring framework (`http://springframework.org`), another practical industrial standard. The developers configure its details via XML.

Programmer's cafe

As a mature developer myself, I am tempted to talk techno geek here and mention Inversion of Control (IOC) (`http://martinfowler.com/articles/injection.html`) and provide an example of a particular service with source code. However, better still, I will point you towards the programmer's café documentation (`http://bugs.sakaiproject.org/confluence/display/BOOT/Home`) on the community Wiki. It was written mostly by Aaron Zeckoski, one of the original Sakai fellows. For the rest of the non-advanced Java programmer human race, suffice to say that Spring is an excellent choice that, once understood, makes the development process easier.

Chapter 12, *Tips from the Trenches*, mentions a fuller list of third-party frameworks applied within Sakai.

The final technologies I shall speedily mention are associated with servlets. The first is a filter: A filter intercepts all incoming requests and/or the responses from a servlet and takes actions on those requests and responses. Filters can sit in a chain with a request or a response passed from one filter to the next. In Sakai, the plumbing, or generating the view for the end user, is heavily dependent on filters.

The second technology is a listener. It listens for different parts of the life cycle of a servlet. For example, when a servlet initializes or when it shuts down, the listener can do some work such as cleaning up some temporary directories or removing database connections that are no longer required. This is handy for injecting services in each tool at startup and for the clean shutdown of the services at the end. Again, the configuration of listeners and filters is XML-based, enabling plug and play through text-editing.

Basically, the architects have based Sakai on complex interactions and configuration, but they have used standard technologies that Java developers would commonly find in the course of their work.

Now, let's take at look at Sakai's physical infrastructure.

How Sakai is deployed at scale

Sakai relies on keeping persistent information in a database. It stores content in the database or on the file system, and the application itself resides on the local file system. For small deployments, it is possible to have the database, file storage, and application on the same computer. However, the impact of a disk failure and the lack of stability under high-load conditions and long-term scalability make that structure less attractive for middle-sized and especially large-scale deployments. By placing the file system and database on separate servers, you not only gain more capacity, but it becomes easier to diagnose performance bottlenecks. Scaling out, where more than one application server is used, allows load balancers to distribute sessions across the frontend applications. This ensures predictable increases in the number of requests the scaled out infrastructure can take as administrators add new servers. The scaled-out infrastructure also enables a higher overall availability and ensures stability under much higher loads than individual servers can achieve.

Of course, there are many configuration possibilities and realities in the wild, and the examples in this chapter represent only the most generic. Suffice it to say, Sakai scales well and in a number of reliable configurations.

The System Administrators Handbook

Tony Atkins wrote the majority of the System Administrator's Handbook (`http://bugs.sakaiproject.org/confluence/display/DOC/Sys+Admin+Guide`), which is an excellent reference for those of you who are directly involved in large-scale deployments.

Within many organizations, such as the University of Amsterdam (UvA), the online learning environment is core business and therefore decision makers have designated the service mission critical with a related service level agreement. At the hardware level, this implies that power supplies are redundant and large batteries sit charged in case of power failure, hard disks are hot swappable, and extra servers are available for quick replacement. In practice, however, the stability of the system also depends heavily on having highly knowledgeable application administrators. System administrators proactively look in logs and deal with daily problems before the end user notices. In my opinion, one of the classic mistakes that organizations make is dividing application administration tasks over a department where too many individuals are involved in understanding the overall infrastructure. Ideally, you want a couple of application administrators focused on the task. The long-term reliability of your infrastructure may well be dependent on the thorough Sakai-specific training of the administrators. In a successful project, management needs to factor in resources for training during the initial phases of deployment.

Below is a diagram of a generic scalable structure. It is a redundant infrastructure — the gold-plated solution in which the accountants have calculated that the cost of hardware is cheaper than the loss of service or reputation from a failure. Two load balancers sit in front of the application servers. One deals with incoming traffic, while the second passively monitors whether the first balancer is still functioning via a heartbeat. If a frontend application server fails, the active load balancer stops sending requests to the failed server.

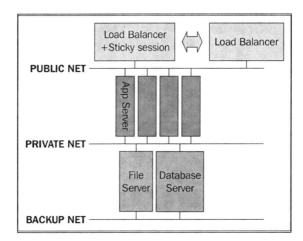

Load balancing

Load balancers are highly reliable and are the least likely part of the whole to fail. However, in the most expensive and sumptuous environments, the infrastructure and data are mirrored to a second geographically dispersed data center. In most situations, the cost-benefit ratio is much too high to consider doing that. If you have the luxury of a shared data service center with other organizations, economies of scale have the potential to push down the per-organization costs to the point of action.

Load balancers know which application server a particular user needs to go to. The cheapest solution, known as IP spraying, is to divide the incoming requests by IP address. However, that makes assumptions about how your users are distributed and in the worst case, you can get more load on one machine than another. The University of Amsterdam has study centers scattered citywide, sitting unevenly distributed in the IP address space. Furthermore, there are proxy servers and firewalls that hide the IP addresses of client web browsers, making the IP space lumpy. This lack of homogenous distribution invalidates IP spraying for Sakai-specific deployments.

A poor man's load balancer is round-robin Domain Name Service (DNS). DNS translates the readable hostname of a server into an IP address and vice versa. If the DNS server returns a different server's IP address for each request, it will divide the web browser traffic evenly. This technique does not work for scaling out, however, because users need to stay on one Sakai instance for each login session and if a server fails, the DNS will still send the failed server's address back to the client.

Load balancers used to be expensive, but their cost has diminished and their capacities rapidly increased (Moore's Law). A modern balancer can also keep track of how quickly a particular frontend server responds and distribute load better. It keeps track by adding its own cookie to the incoming request. Requests with a particular cookie are stuck to a particular frontend. The manufacturers name this aptly a "sticky session".

Frontend servers

The frontend servers normally contain a Sakai instance, one per server, with very standard specifications. The specifications change as hardware becomes cheaper. At the time of writing, our local admin considers a dual core CPU and 8 GB of RAM reasonable.

It is also possible to place an Apache web server in front of a number of Tomcat instances on the same machine. That allows for better use of large amounts of memory and the possible offsetting of SSL, and the responsibility for static files such as web page images to the Apache server. Furthermore, Apache has many modules that extend its functionality — to turn it into a software load balancer or a reverse proxy for caching, for instance. Apache enables you to offset authentication away from the built-in Sakai login and you can compress responses to speed up connections. All this comes at a price: complexity. In the end, the decision to use or not use Apache may simply depend on whether your local administrators have had previous experience with it and are confident with the underlying technologies.

It is also possible — and cost effective — to have your SSL off-loaded onto the load balancer itself via hardware accelerators. This has the advantage of decreasing the level of configuration required to achieve safe logins and securely read email.

Because Java-based Sakai is not OS specific, the University of Amsterdam runs its critical services in acceptance and production environments on Sun Solaris. The development team can choose its own OS and some members develop on Linux, some on Solaris, and one lonely figure on Windows. (I will not discuss the pros and cons of each OS; suffice to say I am comfortable with the current situation and am slightly jealous of the cool Mac notebook and telephones one of the ponytailed webmasters parades around.)

Each frontend has the same specifications and some organizations have a hot spare ready to plug in, in case of emergency. Another approach is to use the same hardware elsewhere. In the UvA's case, we test patches and newly-developed code in an acceptance environment. This is true for all large-scale deployments. The acceptance environment is a cut-down version of production, but uses the same software OS versions and hardware. For example, the acceptance environment for our current Learning Management System has one load balancer instead of two and it has fewer frontend servers. The database hardware and file storage structure is also the same as production's. At first glance, this may look costly, but over the years, it has enabled local administrators to capture problems early before the evil plays out with real users. The secondary advantage is that the infrastructure sits physically within the same data center as production. If a failure occurs, a system admin can switch a machine from acceptance to production via a few typed commands, router rule modifications, and changing a couple of cables.

The private net (which was shown in the last diagram) is reserved for network traffic between the application server and the file and database servers. This increases security and potentially removes a bottleneck under high load. The backup net is for traffic from backups. However, if you are using **Storage Area Networks (SANS)** or other modern storage devices, they can also potentially lie on the backup network.

Database preferences

Different organizations have different database preferences. The demo version of Sakai uses an in-memory database. However, the centrally organized Quality Assurance effort has also thoroughly tested Oracle and MySQL.

Traditionally, web clients unwittingly see MySQL as part of an open source LAMP environment (Linux, Apache, MySQL, and PHP) used for Internet application by a large slice of the service providers. On the other hand, Oracle has a significant reputation as an enterprise, mission-critical database. The Sakai Foundation recommends both MySQL and Oracle for the largest scales. The Performance Work Group, mostly from the University of Michigan, has stress-tested and tweaked the various aspects until you can see your face in the polished surfaces that remain. Sakai has been beaten, X-rayed, and interrogated until the vast majority of any performance glitches have been eroded into history.

The Java Virtual Machine

A Sakai instance runs in a **Java Virtual Machine (JVM)**. Among other things, the virtual machine is responsible for managing memory by removing old unused Java objects. In general, the JVM does a very good job, but needs its environment to tell it how much memory it can use and the best way to clean up old garbage. The system administrator achieves the configuration of the relevant setting by modifying the JAVA_OPTS environment value.

There are two instruction sizes for the JVM: 32 bits and 64 bits. The 32-bit version can allocate up to 4 GB of memory to any given instance. However, the OS may limit the real ceiling to a lower value. By default, the 32-bit version of a Windows server limits the real memory available to less than 3 GB and 32-bit Linux kernels to less than 2 GB (http://goobsoft.homeip.net/Wiki.jsp?page=JavaDebianTuning). It is, therefore, a good idea to run with a 64-bit Linux, Windows, or Solaris kernel and, if you want to use more than 4 GB of memory, then set JAVA_OPTS to the corresponding -d64 option.

To make life somewhat more confusing, you may not want to use more than 4 GB of memory even if you can do so. Java divides its memory up into areas. One or more parts of memory are for short-term objects and another for long-living objects. If the long-living objects fill their allocated space, the JVM does a full collection of garbage, stopping the application until it has traced its ways through all the long-lived objects' relationships. The stop-the-world garbage collection normally runs in milliseconds, but under load, the wait can become noticeable to the end user. The more memory you allocate, the longer that wait may become.

JVM configuration is somewhat of an art. The best tip I can give is to look at the configuration from other production servers and reuse when appropriate. The deployment configuration information from the production servers is stored in the Sakai Foundation's centrally-maintained bug tracking database known as Jira (`http://bugs.sakaiproject.org/jira/browse/PROD`). For example, the current University of Delaware settings are:

```
-server -d64 -Xms8g -Xmx16g -XX:PermSize=512m -XX:MaxPermSize=512m
-XX:NewSize=2000m -XX:MaxNewSize=2000m -XX:+UseConcMarkSweepGC -
XX:+UseParNewGC -XX:+UseMembar -XX:-UseThreadPriorities -XX:+CMSPermGenSw
eepingEnabled -XX:+CMSClassUnloadingEnabled -Djava.awt.headless=true
```

In English, the JVM is set to start using 8 GB of memory and can take up as much as 16 GB. Urban legend has it that the most efficient settings are when `-Xms` equals `-Xmx` so you can argue that `-Xms` should equal 16g.

The `-server` option is interesting. Java is self-tuning; specialists call this ergonomics. JVM ergonomics improve from version to version. The JVM can choose from a number of algorithms and can keep statistics internally. Setting the `-server` option tells the JVM to treat the system it is running on as a server and not a client. The other options mentioned manipulate how the JVM will clean up its memory and tell the JVM not to load certain Java classes at startup because we are not using a GUI. In the Delaware case, the system administrators certainly know what they are doing, but if you do not, I advise you to keep the configuration settings to a minimum unless you have time to experiment via stress testing.

As new tools bubble up to production, tweaking database indexes and configuration values may make the difference between a quiet and a busy day. Luckily, due to the scale of use, early adopters such as the University of Cape Town in South Africa (`https://vula.uct.ac.za/portal`) get to do the potentially tricky early optimizations and are rather good at their work. This implies that a not-so-secret vector to success is to have a system administrator keep contact with the incoming patches from the ever-changing maintenance branch and then patch early in their own acceptance environment.

Enterprise data integration

If you have more than a few students, teachers, and project workers, you could save many person-hours and lower the total cost of ownership (TCO) by integrating Sakai with the data from other enterprise systems. Luckily, the application is flexible and has numerous hooks to get the job done. It tries very hard to avoid forcing you into one methodology and understands the most common approaches. Just as important for management buy-in, mature turnkey solutions are available from commercial companies such as rSmart and Unicon.

Commercial offerings normally include a few extra tools and, much more importantly, help and support for deployment into your own organization. Sakai can at times be complex to integrate into the wider context of your enterprise and it is often cheaper to buy in experience than to pay employees to learn from scratch.

The brute force anti-pattern—not recommended in the majority of situations—is to update and query data directly from the Sakai database. The negatives are that the community does not guarantee the stability of the database schema and your integrations may fail incrementally over time. This approach works only as long as you are prepared to test every patch and update. The advantages are that transactional raw performance may be slightly better and there is no Java or framework understanding required. If you have metadirectory solutions with generic adapters (code that talks to Sakai), you're probably tempted to hit the database directly. I advise you to first look further.

The correct attack vector is to integrate via calling fully-tested framework services. There are numerous ways to achieve this. Sakai has web services built in so you can directly hook into a standard **Service Orientated Architecture (SOA)**. Sakai comes with a basic set of services, which you can enable by adding a small amount of configuration to the now famous `sakai.properties` file. Custom web services are relatively easy to build and deploy. In practice, the developer places his or her code in a text file with the `.jws` extension. The file then needs a sys admin to drop it into a specific directory. The service becomes available to the universe immediately.

Another well-tested approach is to use the Scheduled Task Tool within Sakai to schedule a task through the GUI. The task then runs at definable times and within the Sakai context. This allows custom Java code to pull data out of external systems and to populate locally.

The pumping of text files from Sakai to an external system and in reverse via scheduled tasks may sound old fashioned, but it has proven reliable and straightforward to do.

Sakai has built in three types of providers: user, group, and course. At a logon, the Sakai instance interrogates the providers for what to do next. There are user providers that can go to multiple LDAP servers, user providers for Kerberos, and so on, to ascertain the user's details and to agree that the user is a valid one. When a user logs on for the first time, Sakai asks providers for permission to create a local account. If the provider returns a true value, the Sakai instance applies the provider's user information to create a local account—a prompt and elegant solution.

Sakai is nothing but flexible and forgiving. If you want to build your own hook, you can create a tool and let it listen for your own triggers. You can pump data over HTTP or listen for other protocols and provisioning solutions. (The only thing we ask is that if you develop something useful, make it as generic as possible and upload your code to the community Subversion server with good documentation. Let us all benefit from your efforts and team wisdom.)

Summary

The community has built on stable and standard technologies with architecture that cleanly divides responsibilities into different layers. The core Java frameworks include Spring, Hibernate, and JSF/JSP widgets.

The technologies behind Sakai are terminologically-challenging.

As the number of services in Sakai increases, so do the possibilities for new functionality.

With the use of load balancing, Sakai has proven to scale to a user base of more than 160,000 and counting. Sakai is fully web service enabled, has numerous hooks for data integration, and plays well in a modern enterprise.

Looking ahead, the next chapter describes how to create and manage your first project site.

4
My First Project Site

There are some brilliant, yet ecologically unsound car advertisements where you can almost breathe the fresh air and feel the water splattering across the side of the window as you traverse muddy nature in its full glory. You may get that same feeling of unrestricted freedom and flexibility when you create a project site within Sakai for the first time. The original planners have designed project sites for minimum fuss and lots of ad hoc interaction. Tools such as Wiki, resources, announcements, and podcasting make a lot of sense and enable researchers, teaching professionals, and interest groups to get together and do work online with little Sakai-orientated learning effort.

There are two types of users in the site; the first type is the members who can gain access and interact with each other via the selected tools, and the second type is the maintainers of the site. The maintainers have extra powers to configure the tools and modify membership and other properties of the newly-created site. If you create a site, then you are, by default, the site's maintainer.

This chapter details how to create a project site without publishing it immediately. Avoiding publishing until the last minute enables you to experiment with the toolset balance without others seeing your finer messes. It also enables you to place your content and nudge it until perfection strikes.

A big difference between the demo and production-orientated servers is that, in the demo version of Sakai, any user can create project sites. For project sites in many large enterprise-wide deployments, users need to request their site through a service desk or automated external page. Another significant difference is that by default, the demo does not have its email subsystem configured and you cannot trigger tools such as the email archive and general email notifications by your actions. This is a good thing; I would not like you to be accidentally involved in mass emailing to unsuspecting populations. If you are learning within a production server, please remember to not use accounts with real users behind them for testing. Otherwise, expect some interesting feedback and exercises in running and then limping.

Tool-specific help

The online help tool is your best friend. It will be an extensive source of information throughout the rest of this book. Sakai is evolving rapidly and there will be subtle changes that emerge after publication. Luckily, the developers keep the online help current and focus the text on the actions needed to produce results. Each tool has its own section, called on by using the tool's internal well-known name. For example, the Sakai application knows the announcements tool as `sakai.announcements`. Most of the time, when there are context-sensitive links to help, the relevant well-known name is used as part of the link. To review text for announcements from within the unmodified demonstration, browse the URL `http://localhost:8080 /portal/help/main?help=sakai.announcements`. For other hosts and/or port numbers, simply replace the `localhost:8080`. Throughout the rest of the book, the relevant URLs will be mentioned. For example, without the host or port parts, for announcements, this is `/portal/help/main?help=sakai.announcements`.

If you are having trouble following the link tree structure in the online help, please use its powerful search function. For example, if you want to know which versions of Firefox are currently supported by Sakai, search for the term **supported browser**.

Numerous large-scale deployments brand their own help. If a link is broken during the erosion of time, then you can use the search functionality to find the missing content.

Managing project sites

To run through the workflow mentioned in this chapter, let's assume that you have made two user accounts, one named `project_access` and the other named `project_maintain`. If you want, you can provision your accounts via the **New Account** option on the lefthand side of the front page of Sakai before you have logged on.

Each site has a membership of users. Each user can have one of a number of specific roles. For a project site, you can either be a maintainer or have access rights. Each role gives you specific permissions. The maintainer of the site has many more powers than someone who is just going to use the site. Each tool has its own set of permissions. For example, in announcements, by default, the application allows the maintainer to send out announcements, but the tool does not allow a user in the access role to do this.

Course sites are different from project sites in a number of interesting ways. One of the most significant differences is that course sites have three roles: instructor, teaching assistant, and student. The instructor has almost total power for the site. The teaching assistant has only enough powers to assist in the daily tasks, and the student has the fewest powers, just those necessary to fulfil their learning tasks.

Sakai is ultra-malleable. Administrators can create new site types with different roles. Therefore, if you were using an account on your organization's systems, it would not be surprising if you have an even greater choice of site types.

Browsing the demonstration

If you prefer, you can install two different browsers on your computer. Firefox (`http://www.mozilla.com/en-US/firefox/`), Opera, Google Chrome (`http://www.google.com/chrome`), Safari (`http://www.apple.com/safari/`), etc. are all acceptable. Having two browsers running simultaneously allows you to log in as two different users and interact with your multiple personalities from different roles. You can send announcements to yourself, write in the Wiki, and then stop your alternative personality from changing pages, and so on.

Browser recommendations change over time. However, it is a safe bet that the most modern versions of Firefox, Safari, and Internet Explorer are acceptable. The Wiki tool is badly displayed under the Internet Explorer browser on the Macintosh. This is because Microsoft has not kept the browser up to date. There have been sporadic issues reported for Opera, but Opera is still worth using for testing purposes. At the time of writing, there were no obvious complaints about the Google Chrome browser. However, please search the Sakai online help for certainty.

Logging in as `project_maintain`, you will find yourself within your default **My Workspace** as shown next. Each user has a workspace that is not associated with any specific site. The space has some basic tools.

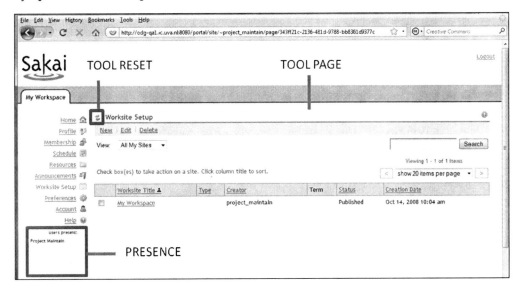

Let us quickly explore the tools and then focus on the worksite setup tool. With the worksite setup tool, you will be able to create project, course, and portfolio sites. When creating a project site, your role by default is that of the maintainer with powers to control the tools and groups in the site.

On the lefthand side of the screen, you will see a default set of tools:

- **Home:** A combined set of handy must-have-always tools, such as your announcements and message of the day, merged onto one page. Home is the first page seen as the user logs in. There is no online help for the overall page, but there is for each tool contained therein.

- **Profile:** This is where you keep and maintain your information that you wish to publish to the rest of the local Sakai population. The profile may include an image. Other users can search for your profile via your ID or last name. The course-based roster tool enables the instructor to view the images next to each other for the roster of any given course.
  Online help: /portal/help/main?help=sakai.profile

- **Membership:** This is the place to maintain your own membership in other sites. You can search for sites that the application allows you to enroll in and then you can join or unjoin a specific site.
  Online help: /portal/help/main?help=sakai.membership

- **Schedule:** This is similar to the calendar that is part of the home page However, this calendar is more comprehensive: it is a combined view from all the calendar events from all the sites that you are involved in. This is handy; the user can separate out the work and schedule of their personal agenda from the more corporate set.
  Online help: /portal/help/main?help=sakai.schedule

- **Resources:** This is where you can store files online. You can upload and download using a form-based web interface, and there is good support for WebDAV, which allows you to drag and drop files from your desktop to the web server with a minimum of fuss. Resources are the Foundation for many other tools. For example, the presentation tool uses resources to store files that the application can later display, site copying allows you to copy resources from one site to another, and the list goes on. The resources tool has its own HTML basic editor, so you can directly create web pages without leaving content on your own machines.
  Online help: /portal/help/main?help=sakai.resources

- **Announcements:** This tool offers a combined summary view of all announcements in all the sites of which you are a member. The home page announcement tool displays specific announcements for the My Workspace.
  Online help: /portal/help/main?help=sakai.announcements

- **Worksite Setup:** This is where you can manage sites. Once you create a site here, the site info tool in the site allows you to manage the details of the site. Online help: `/portal/help/main?help=sakai.sitesetup`

- **Preferences**: This tool sounds like what it does: it allows you to manage preferences for your own workspace and for the tab view, and influence a number of the tools. When an empowered user uploads a new announcement, syllabus, or email to the email archive tool, email notifications are sent to the membership of the site. In preferences, you can manage at which priority level you wish to subscribe to notifications. You can also set the time zone and language values here. Expect more options in the future. Online help: `/portal/help/main?help=sakai.preferences`

- **Account:** This is the place to change the values that you set when you first created your account, such as email address, first and last name, and especially your password. In this acidic time of aggressive Internet attacks, your site is a prime high-value target. Changing your password once every few months lowers the hidden enemy's opportunity to do embarrassing damage.

- **Help**: This is the main jumping off point for context-sensitive help. Remember, help is your friend and it is the first place to look for support.

Learning each tool, one at a time, is not too difficult. However, if you throw yourself in at the deep end and try everything in one go, then headaches may ensue. Underneath the tool list is **presence**. This is where you can see who else is currently logged on and interacting with your site.

The Reset icon

An important note and a point of confusion for first time users is that the browser's back button does not behave as you expect within Sakai. If you want to go back to the beginning of a sequence of events within a given tool, you may need to click the tool reset icon, as shown in the previous figure. Within a couple of log-on sessions, you will find this form navigation, although not always intuitively obvious, second nature. The tool designers have already realized that this is a minor counter-intuitive feature and are actively planning to improve this interaction glitch.

Site creation

Before you create your project site, a couple of significant points need to be mentioned. The first is that once you have created a site, you can maintain the site via the site info tool within the site itself. The second point is that you can also maintain site-specific groups using the site info tool. There are several group-aware tools. Sakai allows you to send announcements or enables you to restrict content to a specific group and thus divide larger projects or courses. Course sites are even more complex than project sites and in the next chapter you will discover that you can subdivide course sites into sections so that you can allocate teaching assistants to the different sections.

To create a project site, click the **Worksite Setup** link on the top lefthand side of the screen, as shown previously.

Creating a new worksite involves first choosing which type of site you want. By default, you can choose from course site, project site, and portfolio site.

 The main differences between site types are the set of roles in the given site type, the tool mix you can choose from, and the initial structure of the site. Project sites have two roles and course sites have three.

As already mentioned, project sites have two roles, that of maintainer and that of a user who can access and use the tools in the site. Chat, blog, Wiki, forums, and resources make a lot of sense in this context and enable flexible and interactive contact within ad hoc groups of similarly interested parties. Compared with other Learning Management Systems, Sakai steps out of the way of the user and does not try to control the composition of your site.

A course site has three roles: instructor, student, and teaching assistant. Each role has different initial permissions per tool. For example, in the forum tool, a student may not be able to delete messages, but a teaching assistant has that power. The teaching assistant has fewer powers than the instructor does—just enough to be supportive, but not enough to gain overall control.

The community has designed the **Open Source Portfolio** (OSP) site to assist in the creation of online portfolios for students. Portfolios allow students to prove that they have done specific work or have had experience in different areas by collecting a history of evidence, in this case, in a matrix format.

The designers have built up the OSP infrastructure within Sakai from a number of tools and a custom navigation that meshes into a consistent whole. Creating portfolios in a well-known format enables reuse and exchange between institutes, helping with the inter-organizational flow of students and an understanding of their knowledge. Students should realize that potential employers gain insight into the student's knowledge level from their online portfolios.

In the demonstration, the developers have written code that populates the worksite setup tool with test data, such as the value for the academic term. If you are practicing on a local deployment, expect to see other more realistic values.

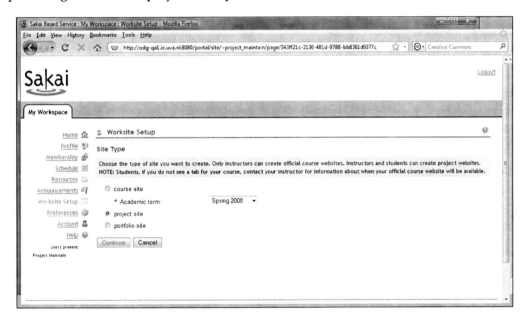

Selecting the **project site** checkbox and pressing **Continue** leads you to a form to fill in for the site properties **title, description, short description, site contact name, site contact email**, and a URL to an icon associated with the site.

Be careful with your site title

The only mandatory attribute is the title. The tool displays the title in the site tab at the top of the screen. The title is constantly visible, so it would not be too ridiculous to consider an in-house style guide for naming conventions or to give guidelines in your institution's FAQ page.

The designers intended that the icon URL point to an online icon, which Sakai then displays above the tool menu in the site and thus enables a simple form of branding. The site maintainer's email address is optional. However, the attribute is necessary if you are a large organization and wish for efficient routing of help desk calls.

An excellent open source Photoshop competitor for image manipulation is Gimp (http://www.gimp.org). Although it has an initially steep learning curve, you have the ability straight out of the box to create fantastic icons.

The icon URL can point out to an external server or, if you have uploaded to the resources tool, you can cut and paste the resources URL. The advantage of consistently using resources rather than scattering the files across the Internet is that you can reuse the resources later for other sites and tools, and you do not need extra servers elsewhere.

After clicking on **next,** you will find yourself looking at a large set of tools that you can enable for your project site. The community intended that a number of the tools be for course site or portfolio-only interaction. It normally does not make sense to use these specific tools. However, with user freedom in mind, you get the choice anyway.

As the Sakai Foundation manages the release of new versions, expect a greater and more varied choice in tools and a richer, warmer experience in a number of the older tools. One approach to course management is to keep sites as clean as possible and slowly add tools as the members of the site become incrementally more active. You will need to ask yourself what you want to achieve with the site. Project sites are excellent and malleable groupware for a wide range of situations, many of which the original designers did not consider. Ask yourself, is the project site going to just be a central place for resources, or is it going to be a communication hub active in keeping road warriors in contact.

Tools of immediate value

A number of tools that have immediate and obvious value include:

- **Announcements:** This is for site-specific announcements. Announcements are group- and section-aware. Within a site, you can define groups and their memberships. This allows for flexible division of information flow, especially for larger sites with more than ten or twenty members. Some tools are group- and section-aware and others are not.

- **Blogger:** This is a tool for publishing your random thought stream to a wider public. Members can keep a naturally evolving text of events, keeping interested parties informed, and sometimes delighted. Blogging is helpful for students who need to turn in written assignments, and if used carefully under fire, blogging can help control writer's block.

- **Chat room:** The chat room is used by many for interactive distributed feedback and group building. It is mostly used for peer-to-peer communication and is a valid tool for building social coherence.
  Online help: `/portal/help/main?help=sakai.chat`

- **News:** This is an excellent way to bring in RSS feeds from various sources, including externally-managed blogs. The tool gives immediacy to the situation and is a frugal person's solution to integrating external information feeds into Sakai.
  Online help: `/portal/help/main?help=sakai.news`

- **Resources:** This is the one-stop shop for managing your project-specific file storage. Depending on how your instance has been set up, expect overall upload quotas and upper limits to be set on file size. The demonstration version has a stated limit of 20 MB, large enough for a Word document, but not large enough for that 20-minute video on why your organization needs to promote you. If you own the resources when creating a site, you are also given the option to copy them from another site you own. This is handy as you move from one project to the next or migrate a course from one academic year to another.

- **Schedule:** The scheduling tool allows you to add events for the given site.

- **Web content:** You can load an external website(s) into the tool page area of the screen or in an extra window. For each URL, you have an extra link in the tool list area on the lefthand side of your screen. This feature can save repetitive effort. For example, perhaps your project workers need periodically to visit your corporate address book or the home page of your institute. This tool allows you to define the area size that your external content displays in and is another cheap integration point for external systems.
  Online help: `/portal/help/main?help=sakai.iframe`

- **Wiki:** This tool is good for building a community document like a knowledge base or group project work. Cambridge University, and in particular their CARET (`http://www.caret.cam.ac.uk/`) organization, has been a bedrock of the Sakai community and this was one of their first gifts.
  Online help: `/portal/help/main?help=sakai.rwiki`

The list of tools is larger in each new release and the mix changes and improves. The online help is the source of the most consistent and up-to-date information. Most of the questions asked by new users can be answered by looking at the help text. For example, next is a screen grab of the FCK editor (`http://www.fckeditor.net/`), which runs within the worksite, and which is used by Sakai in numerous locations. However, pasting content from Firefox is difficult. Over time, the issue became well known and the answer was placed in help. The result is that if enough Sakai users read the online help, the calls to the help desk drop. In the online help, search for the term **firefox** and then click on the link, **Pasting text in Firefox**.

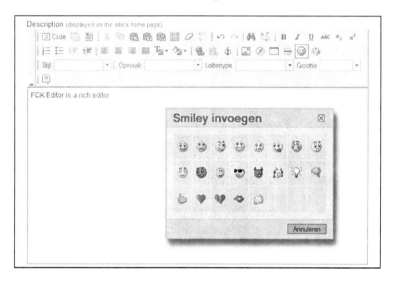

 In the next chapter, which is about course sites, you will discover that some tools play well together. For example, the Tests and Quizzes tool and the grade book share the results of tests. As Sakai matures, expect more integration between tools.

After making your selections from the ever-growing list of tools, you will see the option to copy resources (if you have already created other sites). Ignore this and click **Continue**. You will find yourself on the site access page.

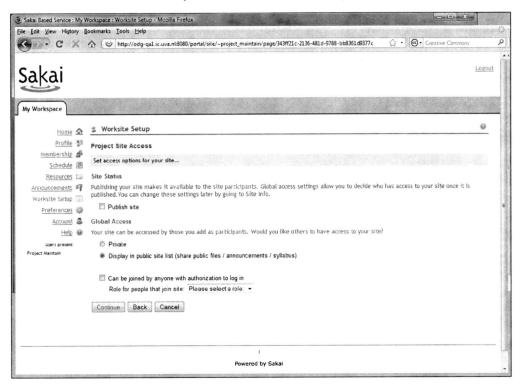

The page enables you to choose whether you want to publish your site immediately, whether anyone can join the site, and if they can, which role they will have. In most real-life situations, you will not want to publish your site until the last minute and only then will it be displayed in the public list. It is better to get the site in good shape and ready to wow your target audience, and then publish. Before that, you may want to play around with various tools, editing the mix from your worksite, and fiddle with little features such as your lefthand side tool order and the initial content set.

If you select **Display in public site list,** your site will be in this list, which is available on the front page of Sakai before you log on. You can search for the site using the sites tool on the lefthand side. To make things even more interesting, in the resources tool, you can set file permission in a way that allows the public to see the file. The application has this also enabled for announcements and syllabus. This means that you can, for example, publish a flyer or syllabus on a site and an anonymous user can use it to help decide whether to join the site or not. Note that the options are not set in concrete. You can change them at any time using the site info tool in the created site.

Maintaining your site details

For any site with more than a few tens of users, it is also beneficial to choose whom you want to invite to your site and what role they will be assigned. (Make sure that you have not checked the option **can be joined by anyone who is authorized**.) Click **continue** and then, on the confirmation page, click the **create site** button.

At the top of the screen, you will see a new tab with the title of your project site. Clicking on the tab leads your browser to the project site's home page. A site maintainer has more options enabled than a user with only access rights. The site info tool is the one-stop shop that controls the options for your site. Selecting the link on the lefthand side of the screen directs you to the main page of the tool. The online help details the mechanics of the site.

Online help: `portal/help/main?help=sakai.siteinfo`

The main page offers you the following options:

- **Edit Site Info**: This is the same as in the worksite—you can decide on a title and description for the site, and so on.
- **Edit Tools**: With this feature, you can select and unselect the set of tools for your site.
- **Page Order**: From here, you can decide the order of pages on the lefthand side of the screen by dragging and dropping, using this option.

- **Add Participants**: This is the most used feature in the site info tool. You can decide who has what role, add participants, and also modify and delete the participants. When you click on **Add Participants**, you are presented with text boxes where you can add usernames. If you are an administrator, you can collect your user list from the user tool in the administration site. Otherwise, you may have to ask your local administration. The official users exist already in Sakai. The non-official users do not. If you add non-official users, Sakai will create an account automatically with the new users' email addresses as the ID with the type guest, which does not have permission to create sites. If your Sakai instance is email-enabled, the non-official users quickly receive an email with their account and password details.

- **Manage Groups:** A number of tools such as resources and announcements are group aware. You can route your announcements to a given group and allow access to files to specific groups as well. In the next chapter, I will discuss sections. You will discover that you can use sections in a manner that is roughly similar to groups. However, there are differences. For example, a teaching assistant is in control of a section of a course. There is even a tool named Section Info that is enabled by default for teachers for each course.

- **Manage Access:** This gives you the same page and therefore the same options as displayed in the previous figure. When you want to publish your site and make public your glorious expression, this is where you change the checkbox value.

If you wish to see instantaneous results of your actions, start up two different browsers and log in with one as the project maintainer. You can visit your newly created project site and manage access via the site info tool. With your second browser, visit the front page of Sakai, i.e., `http://localhost:8080/portal`, and search for your site using the site link on the lefthand side. By changing the public settings, you should be able to hide and unhide the site.

- **Duplicate Site, Import from Site, Import from File**: All are choices for the creation of sites from other sources. Sometimes, an organization or individual wants a standard project structure. Having a template site based on best practices and then duplicating it is an excellent starting point. The tool copies all materials from a project site, but only the instructor's material in the course site. Therefore, when you copy a course from one academic year to the next, you leave behind the student material that no longer applies.

As a site maintainer, you have the power to set permissions for each tool and for each role. For example, as you enter the chat room tool, at the top of the page next to the options link is the permissions link, shown in the following screen grab. Clicking the link brings up the permissions page. As site maintainer, you have permission to delete any chat messages, but the access role does not. Checking within the access column on the **delete.any** permission and then saving, gives access members the same rights. I find the naming of the permissions such as **revise.channel** most of the time understandable; however, it may be nice to have an online help file for this level of detail as well.

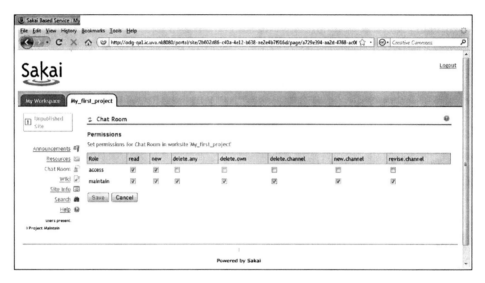

In general, within a project site, the access role sees the same tools as the maintainer role but has a more limited set of choices that are viewable because of permission restrictions. For example, the site info tool will only display some basic information and not allow you to modify a site.

The resources tool is a spider at the center of the web of use by other tools. The resources tool is WebDAV enabled (http://www.webdav.org), which means that once you have set up your computer properly, you can drag and drop many files at the same time to upload and download them from Sakai. To add your first file to Sakai, go to your workspace, select the resources tool, and then click the **Add** drop-down box. Select **Upload File** and then use the browse button to look locally on your machine for a file to upload.

To experiment with WebDAV, click on the **Upload-Download Multiple Resources** link at the top of the page. The web page that Sakai returns explains in gory detail how to get your drag-and-drop workflow going. Follow the instructions for your specific OS.

With the resources tool in the My Workspace context, it is not possible to use groups. You can either enable the public to see your resource or not. In a project site, you can be more specific and create a group with members using the site info tool. For courses, you can do the same or use the course-specific section tool to create a section with a teaching assistant in control and section members. Currently, resources treat sections and groups the same way. I expect that section-aware features will expand in the future.

Congratulations, you have created a project site from your workspace and modified it using the site info tool. You have even updated permissions for the chat room so the access user can delete chat messages. Feel free to explore your site as a maintainer and access user at the same time.

Summary

In Sakai, you can create project, course, and portfolio sites from the worksite setup tool. Within a site, you can manage the site itself via the site info tool. There are two types of role within a project: the access and maintainer roles. The access role has fewer permissions than maintainer. Publishing at the last minute enables you to get your site just right.

Online help is your first stop for current information about a specific tool or point of confusion.

Tools such as resources and announcements are group aware.

Sakai is changing rapidly; expect the tool mix to vary.

Using multiple browsers allows you to play out different roles at the same time.

In the next chapter, we will explore the basic interactions of a course site and contained sections. The course site is somewhat more complex than a project site, so it is well worth a little practice with a project site first.

In the next chapter, *Your First Course Site*, you will create a course site, and learn more about working with roles and permissions, and sections and groups.

5

Your First Course Site

Course sites are the main type of site used for learning in the majority of Sakai deployments. The course site expresses the traditional educational structure found in most universities and higher educational establishments.

Course sites differ from project sites in a number of ways: The first is that by default, there are three roles in a course site, each with different permissions. There are only two roles in project sites. The second difference is that a number of tools, such as Assignments, Test & Quizzes, and Gradebook, interact with each other, and the third is that the administrator can subdivide courses into sections.

The three roles in a course site are instructor, teaching assistant, and student. The student has the fewest powers, but still gets to use most of the tools. The teaching assistant has sufficient permissions to be able to take over some of the regular chores from the instructor, such as having the power to moderate forums or send announcements to the site members. The instructor has the most powers and sets the structure and atmosphere for the whole of the site.

Below is a diagram of a simple course. The course has three sections; two are labs, and one is a lecture. Depending on how you wish to manage your site, each section can have an unlimited number of members or a more limited set.

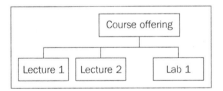

Groups are sets of users. Sections are groups that have extra features and related data, such as the ability to add scheduling information, the name of the section, and if membership is allowed for the whole course. The definition of sections is difficult to understand, but the extra features of sections, compared to groups, give programmers the extra features they need to build a complex course structure that matches the needs of many universities.

Unlike groups, each section, such as a lab or a particular lecture, has a teaching assistant associated with it. Further, the instructor defines the membership of groups, but not always sections. Depending on how you set the course up, you can specify a limit for the number of students included in each section and whether the students can opt in or out of the section. To add to the complexity, site and section information can be transferred automatically from Student Administration Information Systems.

Most organizations use student administration data to pre-populate sites with student rosters, course names, and section divisions. As a result, for some, choices may be narrowed when they create a course site. In a first-time deployment, architects normally hook up Sakai to the local Student Administration System and a direct feed provides course data either on demand or automatically as the academic year progresses. However, the student administration system may not be able to define all the sections and courses that the teachers expect in a year. In these cases, manually adding the information may be necessary.

Sections can be a little daunting at first. This chapter explores how to use them accurately. The complexity is due to the number of different ways that sections are used and also because of the different approaches that may be used in the same organization.

Tools such as Announcements, Resources, and Gradebook recognize groups and sections and currently treat them as equals. You can choose to make an announcement to students in one section that cannot be seen by the students in other sections.

The instructor manipulates the tool selection, groups, and other properties using the Site Info tool in a specific site. Sections, however, are handled using the separate Section Info tool. One of the key properties of Sakai is that it is evolving and improving fast; in the future, we can expect the Site Info tool and the Section Info tool to merge.

The next part of this chapter shows you how to create a course, create its sections, and set up membership in the sections. This is something you can try doing on the demonstration version of Sakai.

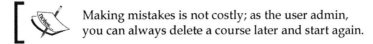

Making mistakes is not costly; as the user admin, you can always delete a course later and start again.

Creating a course site using the Sakai demo

The two main options open to you in the demonstration are either to make a course as an ordinary user from your own **Worksite Setup** tool in your workspace, or create a site as an admin. For practice, you can be an admin and create a number of user accounts. This allows you to experience being different users with different roles in a course, and you can observe how some tools, such as Resources and Announcements, interact with sections. If you follow the recipe mentioned in this section, you will end up with two students, one course instructor, and two course assistants.

The purpose, in this practice exercise, is to divide the course site into example sections and then to practice managing and routing information through announcements. If you are working through this exercise, feel free to add more users and sections. The demo has as many features and tools enabled as possible.

As administrator, you can use either the **Site** tool or the **Worksite Setup** tool to create a course. It is a little confusing, having two tools for essentially the same task. However, there is a clear purpose to this. The **Worksite Setup** tool limits your options. The developers designed the tool for efficient creation of standard site types. If you want to do some of the more advanced application administration tasks like creating a custom site type, adding extra tools to pages, or adding hidden properties in a site for custom tools, the site tool exposes these features. We shall stay focused on creating a standard course and thus use the more constrained and user-friendly **Worksite Setup** tool.

The first steps make a course site with some sections that are suggested by the course creation wizard, which is part of the **Worksite Setup** tool. After creating a course site in this way, the admin is then the only site member. The admin (you) needs to add another user in the instructor role. Then, the instructor needs to log on and add members to the site within student role. Finally, the students, new to the course, need to join specific sections. This top-down approach follows one of the typical methods for creating a course site and is common for small and medium-sized deployments. Larger deployments tend to have full integration with other enterprise-critical systems, such as Student Administration Systems, and instructors have less freedom to manage student populations and structures in their course sites.

You can create the accounts as follows:

1. Log in as admin (default password: admin).
2. Select the **Administration Workplace**.
3. Click on the **Users** tool on the lefthand side of your web browser window.

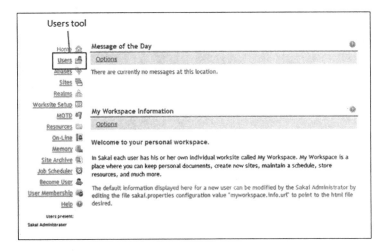

4. Click the **New User** link at the top of the page.
5. Add five new users named: course_instructor, course_assistant1, course_assistant2, and course_student1, course_student2. Simply fill in the IDs and password. You do not have to fill in the email address or the account type.

Online help: /portal/help/main?help=sakai.users

While creating your account, you can define your account type by adding an entry to the **type** input field. Users can have either registered accounts or guest accounts. By default, a new user will have a registered account. Normally, account types define user permissions relating to use of the tools in **My Workspace**, and guests cannot create sites via the **Worksite Setup** tool. In production environments as well, a registered user also has more powers associated with the **Worksite Setup** tool than a guest does. However, this is a matter of local policy and may vary from institution to institution.

Online help: `/portal/help/main?help=sakai.sites`, `/portal/help/main?help=sakai.sitesetup`

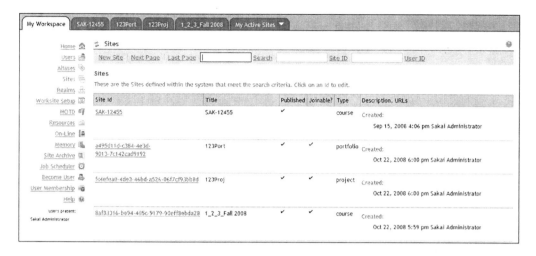

As part of the exercise, you, as administrator, will make a site with some default sections and then manage the site as the course instructor. The course instructor has permission to use the Section Info tool in a site to manipulate the individual section memberships and the global properties of each section.

The Sakai demonstration is set up with example data. This includes a consistent structure for choosing course sections. In a real-world deployment, coupling between a Student Administration System and Sakai would keep these values accurate for your organization's needs. Sakai is a Swiss army knife for data integration and boasts numerous possible routes, including custom web services, a course management API, and course providers (bits of custom Java code that work with a standard interface to the underlying services of the Sakai Framework).

To create a course:

1. In the **Worksite Setup** tool, click **New**.
2. On the Site type page, choose **Course** with any academic year that you wish.
3. Click **Continue**.

4. You are now in the **Course/Section Information** page. Near the bottom of the page is a link, **Add course(s) and/or section(s) not listed above....**

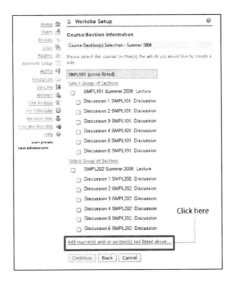

5. Click the link and you will find yourself on the **Course/Section Information** page.
6. Select a department.
7. The other two select boxes, **Course** and **Section**, become active.
8. Choose a course and then choose the first option in the section select box. Two text boxes should now appear.

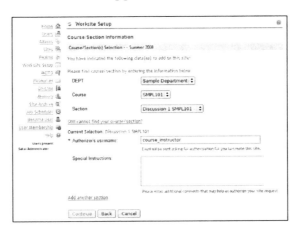

9. Add your name in the **Authorizer's username** box and leave the **instructions** box blank.

The authorizer's username is part of the extra plumbing for feedback to the Student Administration System. You do not get to use it in the demonstration version. Further, the example values in the select box are liable to change, so do not be surprised if the choices you see are different from those described in these instructions.

When you create a course site, no extra section can be created. You need to do that later as an instructor.

You will find yourself on the **Course Site Information** page. This is similar to the page you need to edit when you create a project site. However, in this case, you have less freedom because the application automatically generates the title of the course from your course and section choices. The motivation behind this is to give the students and instructors intuitive course names so they can find the courses easily in the **Sites** tool, which is on the front page of Sakai before you log in.

 The front page of Sakai is also known as the Sakai Gateway page.

Selecting the pre-populated Appearance (icon) will later place an icon above the tool links in your newly created course.

You can leave the **site contact name** and **contact email** address alone. Click **Continue** to advance to the **tool selection** page. For a minimum set of tools, you can put a check in the boxes next to **Announcements**, **Drop Box**, **Email Archive**, **Resources**, **Search**, and **Section Information**. The site instructor can always change the tool selection later.

Normally, with a wide range of tools selected, you would need to configure a number of the tools as part of the course creation process. Do not worry if you make a mistake here because you can make adjustments later using the **Options** menu in the Site Info tool.

In the small set of tools listed above, the only tool you will need to configure is the Email Archive tool. With the Email Archive, each site has a unique email address. Normally, when a member of the course sends an email to the email address of the course, the members, depending on the notification options that they set in their own preferences, may receive the email. Further, the email is stored in a folder in the course site resources. The email archive is an excellent tool for looking at the historical ebb and flow of course communication. You can choose any reasonable email address for your course as long as it is not already in use.

Sakai will direct you to the Course Site Access page. In production, you will not want to publish your course site until the last minute. However, for experimentation purposes, feel free to publish now, so that you can play within all the roles. To publish, press **Continue**, without changing the default options.

Publishing a site simply means that you are allowing other members of the site to view the site. Unpublishing a site has the reverse effect, where site members can no longer see the site in the list of sites to which they belong.

Finally, press the **Request Site** button on the **Confirm Your Course Site Setup** screen. The confirmation summary should look similar to the next screen grab. Notice my bad practice of having an empty description.

 No empty descriptions
If you search for this site later, a description is valuable to help you decide if you want to join or not.

If you do not see a site tab with the title of your course site, you should see it in the **My Active Sites** tab at the top of your web browser area.

To add the course instructor to the newly-created course site you can, as admin, go back to the **Worksite Setup** tool, select the check box for the course, and click the **Edit** link at the top of the page just below the reset tool icon. Then, click the link **Add participants** at the top of the screen and type course_instructor in the **Official Email Address or Username** text box.

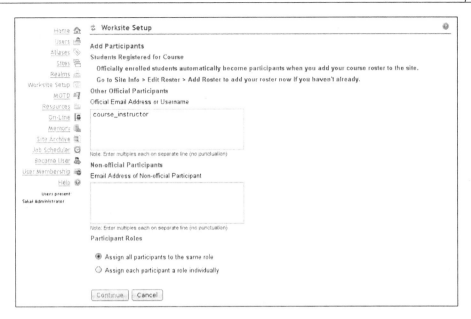

On the **Choose a Role for Participants** page, you can select the role **instructor** and click **Continue**, then **Continue** again for the default notification options on the next screen. Finally, click **Confirm**. You will find yourself back in the main editing screen for the site. You can now log the admin out and then log in as the course instructor you just created.

Alternatively, you can use the Become User tool to perform the same action.

Congratulations, if you have performed the exercise, you are now ready to manipulate the course site.

Starter tips

Here are some tips that are useful the very first time you create a course.

Descriptions are important

Taking time to write a short and succinct description for your site is well worth your energy. When given a choice, students will probably read the description and short description of your site before deciding whether to join. At some university installations, site creation is done automatically and the descriptions have a uniform corporate structure.

Password strength

Best practices for passwords vary slightly from institution to institution. Creating passwords of at least ten characters in length and with at least one number and one special character, such as `adf$awe1`, makes them difficult to guess.

To help you remember all the passwords you need to use in the day, you can consider using a password wallet. A password wallet is a commonly used piece of software that stores multiple passwords safely in an encrypted file. The wallet normally has convenient features such as the ability to cut and paste the passwords to login pages. One such wallet is KeePass (`http://keepass.info/`). It has the potential to save embarrassing calls to the helpdesk.

Becoming another user quickly

A shortcut for a busy administrator is the Become User tool. You can click this tool link (on the lefthand side of the site window) and type an account name to quickly become that user. This tool is particularly useful just after the creation of a site when you want to see how it looks to a student or instructor.

Online help: `/portal/help/main?help=sakai.su`

The motivation for sections

The architects have designed sections to meet real-world demands. Each section of a course site has a title, a description, a section number, possibly a limit on the maximum number of students who can enroll in any given section type, status, a meeting time, and a location. You can imagine lecturers reserving resources such as rooms and light projectors based on the metadata for a given section.

Unlike groups, a student can belong to only one section of a given type at a time. For example, it does not make sense for a student to be in two labs in the same course. The student would be redundantly learning knowledge twice and probably expected to do so at the same time.

Creating sections

After you have created the course site as described above, you can manually add the student and teaching assistant accounts. You can then create two lab sections, each with a teaching assistant. Finally, you will see how to set up the sections to allow the students free will to join and switch between sections.

Adding members (students, teaching assistants, or instructors) to a course site follows the same workflow as adding members to a project site. As the instructor, you can select the site in the Site Info tool and click the link **Add Participants**. Then, add the four account names `course_student1`, `course_student2`, `course_assistant1`, and `course_assistant2` to the textbox **Official Email Address or Username**. Tick the radio box **Assign each participant a role individually**.

On the next page, you can select the roles **Teaching Assistant** and **Student**. Then, click **Continue**. Agree to the default notification value of **not sending mail**, click **Continue**, and finally click **Confirm**.

Online help: `/portal/help/main?help=sakai.siteinfo`

To manage your sections, you will now need to use the Section Info tool. As the instructor, add two sections that are not tied to a roster from an external Student Administration System, with one teaching assistant in each. You can then allow any student to join or unjoin any section. Finally, as the instructor, you can make an announcement to any one section or to all of the sections.

Within the site, select the Section Info tool. Click **Add Sections** at the top of the page. Select two sections that are both labs and click **Continue**.

Read the **Add sections** page to understand the range of configuration possibilities, but accept all the defaults including the unlimited number of students allowed to join any section.

At the bottom of the page, click **Add Sections**. You will now find yourself within the Section Info page. From here, you can add teaching assistants and students by clicking on **Assign students** and **Assign TAs**.

Online help: `/portal/help/main?help=sakai.sections`

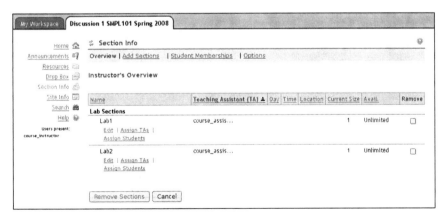

To follow this exercise, add `course_assistant1` to **Lab1** as a `teaching assistant` and `course_student1` as a `student`. Add `course_assistant2` and `course_student2` for **Lab2**.

Next, as the instructor, you can make an announcement directed at **Lab2**.

To do this, open the Announcements tool and add an announcement by clicking the **Add** link near the top of the window. Fill in an announcement title and body. Scroll down to the **Access** option, and select **Display to selected groups** and select section **Lab1**. At the bottom of the page, click **Save Changes**.

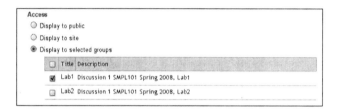

To view a directed announcement, you can log on as `student1`. Go to your Announcements tool and you will see the newly created and sent announcement. To verify that only one student in one section can read the announcement, you can log on as `student2` and you should see no announcements.

If you go to the Section Info tool as `student2`, you will see the option to switch between sections, but not to join a second section.

 Unlike a group, section business logic only allows you to be a member of one section at a time.

Congratulations. If you have followed the exercise, you have now added a course with sections and you have routed information to one of those sections.

Real-world sections

To inject a degree of realism, I include an interview with an educationalist with extensive experience in the use of sections. This interview explains why we need the extra complexity in the demonstration. The complexity reflects organizational demand in the real world and thus I cannot realistically avoid its description.

The interview: One of the Sakai community's most active members is Ray Davis. Ray Davis currently works at the University of California, Berkeley, and has created core APIs and code testing frameworks within Sakai. He has been heavily involved with the integration of sections into Sakai. I caught up with him by email and this is what he had to say:

API stands for Application Programmers Interface. An API is an agreed set of function and method calls that programmers can use to build parts of an application.

How is Ray Davis involved with Sakai?

I led the Gradebook project, helped define section and course management services, worked on many framework issues, and was an early and outspoken proponent of open process, loose coupling, agile practices, UX-driven development, and the Not-Invented-Here.

How is Berkeley involved with Sakai?

The University of California at Berkeley joined the Sakai Foundation in late 2003, with our group (Educational Technology Services) contributing many resources since. We are also founding partners in the open source Fluid and OpenCast projects (http://www.opencastproject.org/). We are currently supporting far more users with our local version of Sakai than we did with Blackboard or WebCT.

What is the course management API and how does Berkley use it?

The Course Management interface resulted from an ambitious cross-institutional effort to model the structural units of higher education flexibly enough to cover known use cases and yet richly enough to be of use in real-world application UI. Since its release, I understand our work has been of assistance to standards bodies such as IMS, and we are proud of that result.

In 2.5.x Sakai, UC Berkeley relies on the CM API to show official instructors what classes and sections are assigned to them and available for course sites, to automatically populate sites and section-groups with student members, and to help with submission of final course grades. Other universities use it to give departmental administrators automatic membership in course sites or to display section-meeting times.

 The course management API is services for creating courses and populating the courses' with data such as the courses descriptions.

Unlike the static data you'll find in the Sakai demo, in real life, a class may be defined (as far as its name, department, and term go) before its subgroups are determined and long before any students enroll in it. In Course Management jargon, that top-level class (like "Chemistry 101 Spring 20xx") is called a "course offering", and subgroups (like "Lab 1", "Lab 2") are called sections.

Here are a couple of typical workflows:

- Administrators create a course site associated with the course offering before there's an instructor assigned to it. When the instructor *is* assigned to it, they are automatically added to the course site and then they can decide whether to go on to add sections.
- An instructor assigned to a class goes to create a course site and sees her class listed as one of the possibilities. She associates that class (and its sections, if she cares about them) with her new site.
- An instructor, administrator, or graduate student creates a course site that student administration has not hooked up to anything but a term. Later, they associate the site with the official class and section data when they are assigned official responsibility, or they ask an admin to do the association.

Summary

In the Sakai demo, you can create a course either as an admin or as a registered user by using the Worksite Setup tool.

As admin, you can also use the Sites tool to manipulate your own custom sites.

You can divide a course into multiple sections, for example, for labs and lectures. Each section can include students and one teaching assistant. Each section has associated metadata such as location and time range when the section is available. For large-scale deployments of Sakai, it is common for organizations to automatically populate sections with rosters. The demonstration shows this common situation with a set of options during course creation.

As an instructor in a course, you can use the Section Info tool to manipulate sections. As a student, you can join or switch sections using the Section Info tool.

Tools such as Announcements, Resources, and Gradebook are "section aware".

Over time, expect more tools to become section aware.

In the next section *Tools, Tool, Tools* you will get to read about the many different site tools that are available to you and how quality is defended during their development.

6
Enterprise Bundle Tools & Quality Assurance

All software projects must keep an eye focused on product quality and determine when features are ready for end users. Multi-user, enterprise software packages like Sakai face additional concerns of scalability and performance. Successful open source software projects, furthermore, tend to attract a wide variety of add-on components provided by a variety of sources. These may or may not be developed according to community development standards. These projects must have a way of informing potential adopters which components are ready for small pilot projects and which for enterprise-wide deployments, where scalability is a significant concern. Sakai has many large-scale deployments, several of which have over 160,000 total users and regularly operate with more than 7,000 simultaneous logged-on users. Any significant flaw translates into frustrated end users, sleepless hours for system administrators, and software developers with crammed email inboxes.

The Sakai community addresses these challenges with a three-tiered classification of tools: Core, Provisional, and Contrib. "Core" tools are those that the Sakai community feels are ready for enterprise deployment in large installations. Contrib tools are tools donated to the community, but have yet to be tested. Provisional tools are in the process of being tested for a few release cycles until they have shown to be of the highest quality and ready for large scale deployment.

Core tools are highly scrutinized and fully tested during the formal Sakai Quality Assurance (QA) process. The Sakai community has confidence that they will be stable under heavy production loads. When you download Sakai, these core tools are enabled by default, and we call this the "Sakai Enterprise Bundle". It is the collection of Sakai functionally that is proven ready for enterprise use.

This chapter outlines which tools are core, explains how Sakai tools are tested for quality and scalability, and describes the criteria the Sakai community uses to determine whether a tool is ready to be part of the Sakai Enterprise Bundle.

Core tools in Sakai 2.6

Not all core Sakai tools are part of every user's experience with Sakai. In addition to the common end user tools that are easily found in most Sakai sites, a number of administrative tools have reached core status. In addition, Sakai's ePortfolio system, the bundle of tools collectively known as OSP (for "open source portfolio"), is also part of the Bundle. Some organizations deploy Sakai without OSP tools and some organizations deploy OSP without using the other tools in Sakai. The table below lists the end user tools for Sakai 2.6.

Tool	Common Name	Purpose
Announcements	sakai.announcements	For the posting of current, time-critical information
Assignments	sakai.assignment. grades	For posting, submitting, and grading assignment(s) online
Calendar Summary	sakai.summary. calendar	For calendar summary information
Chat Room	sakai.chat	For real-time conversations in written form
Drop Box	sakai.dropbox	For private file sharing between instructor and student
Email Archive	sakai.mailbox	For viewing email sent to the site
Forums	sakai.forums	Display forums and topics of a particular site
Gradebook	sakai.gradebook.tool	For storing and computing assessment grades from Tests & Quizzes or that are manually entered
Messages	sakai.messages	Display messages to/from users of a particular site
News	sakai.news	For the viewing of content from online sources
Post 'Em	sakai.postem	For uploading .csv formatted files to display feedback (for example, comments, grades) to site participants

Tool	Common Name	Purpose
Presentation	sakai.presentation	For showing and viewing slideshows of image collections from Resources
Resources	sakai.resources	For posting documents, URLs to other web sites, and so on
Schedule	sakai.schedule	For posting and viewing deadlines, events, and so on
Section Info	sakai.sections	For managing sections within a site
Site Info	sakai.siteinfo	For showing worksite information and site participants
Syllabus	sakai.syllabus	For posting a summary outline and/or requirements for a site
Tests & Quizzes	sakai.samigo	For creating and taking online tests and quizzes
Web Content	sakai.iframe	For accessing an external web site within the site
Wiki	sakai.rwiki	For collaborative editing of pages and content

Contrib to Provisional

Recognizing this need for excellence, the community has plotted a clear, evolutionary path for new tools to enter the Enterprise Bundle. A tool typically starts as a contribution from a specific institution. It may have developed this to meet a local need or, perhaps, an individual developer wanted to see a capability in Sakai and has taken it upon him or herself to do the development work. It may not be clear how many others will be interested in using the tool and it may simply be a proof of concept. There is an area reserved in the Sakai source code repository called **Contrib** (`https://source.sakaiproject.org/contrib/`) for this kind of development work. The Contrib repository is very open—anyone can request a development directory there and does not have to follow Sakai licensing practices to make contributions.

The primary quality assurance for Contrib tools comes from the local institutions and developers themselves. The community QA process does not test tools in Contrib. If an organization wants to use a Contrib tool, it will typically want to test it itself before deploying it to their local installation of Sakai.

Lies and Statistics

The Ohloh web site contains the vital statistics for numerous open source projects. It keeps approximate statistics for Contrib, as well (https://www.ohloh.net/projects/4006). The site mentions around 1844 Person Years of development time, $100,000,000 worth of code bashing, and over 6,108,695 lines of code. The statistics may well be an overestimation due to duplication of code, but they do give you a feel for the motivation and energy the community has for developing new things.

As the tool matures and gains wider use in the community, there may be interest in putting the tool into the Enterprise Bundle. This typically happens when the developer of the tool is interested in having even more organizations use the tool (which could mean additional support work for them!), and others in the community are eager to help test the tool. Both of these are critical for a tool to advance beyond Contrib. The community support for quality assurance is especially critical—the Sakai quality assurance resources are limited and there must be enough additional resources available to create test cases and actually test the new tool. And, of course, the developer must be willing to respond to the probable increase in bug reports and feature requests that will result from increased testing and usage.

To advance from Contrib to Provisional, a tool must also meet a set of community-defined criteria, grouped according to several categories:

- Community Support Criteria
  - There must be an identified group of committers within the Sakai community who take responsibility for the tool.
  - The application source code must reside in Sakai's source control system.
  - At least two Sakai production sites must be using the tool successfully in their production environments. Those sites should be able to report that the tool runs properly, is useful to their users, and does not cause any problems with other parts of the Sakai Enterprise Bundle.
  - The developer(s) must be committed to maintaining the tool across Sakai version changes.
  - The developer(s) of the tool must be willing to answer questions on the Sakai dev list.
  - The developer(s) of the tool must commit to helping to develop test plans and specifications.
  - Bugs and feature requests for the tool must be tracked in Sakai's bug tracking system.

- Technical Criteria
  - ° If the tool persists data to a database, it must support all official Sakai databases (currently HSQL, MySQL, and Oracle).
  - ° The tool must work properly with the Sakai **AutoDDL** approach. `auto.dll` is a property in `sakai/sakai.properties` that once set to true tells tools to create database structures on the next Sakai application start up. Individual tools must properly create database tables when tables do not exist and the tables must be named so as not to conflict with other Sakai tables.
  - ° All database access to tables that the tool does not own will take place via published Sakai APIs provided by the application that manages those tables. The tool should use APIs for access to its own data, but it must use APIs for access to data from others.
  - ° The tool must participate in the system-wide configuration (`sakai.properties`) and not require any local configuration to be hand-edited.
  - ° The tool must properly operate in the Sakai Authorization and tool placement structure. It must either use existing appropriate security functions or introduce new security functions for the application.
  - ° The tool will not require patches to other Sakai tools or to the Sakai framework. If application of the tool requires changes to other areas of Sakai, those changes should be negotiated ahead of time and should be part of the full distribution.
  - ° The tool must fully work in a clustered Sakai application server environment.
  - ° The tool cannot force new JARs into Sakai. Sakai's goal is to keep these JAR footprints as small as possible. Any new JAR requirement in those areas requires significant discussion.
  - ° There are a number of system-wide elements in Sakai, including Spring, Hibernate, and others. The application must work with the versions of these elements that are part of the Sakai release.

- Interaction and Visual Design Criteria
  - The tool UI must look like the rest of the Sakai application and properly inherit skins from Sakai (for example, when the site's color changes, the tool colors change as well).
  - The tool should follow general interaction guidelines outlined in the Sakai **Style Guide** (**SG**) so users have consistent experiences and expectations about how to complete actions such as "paging in a list", "navigating between pages", "taking action on items in a list", and so on, across tools.
  - UI components available in the Sakai library should be used where possible (for example, WYSIWYG editor, calendar, paging widget).
  - The application must support all of the browsers currently supported by Sakai.
  - The tool should provide basic help that integrates seamlessly with the Sakai Help system. The help should have a look and feel and writing style similar to the existing help content.

- Licensing Criteria
  - Developers of the tool must have a contribution agreement on file with the Sakai Foundation. If the developers are working on behalf of an organization, the organization must have a corporate contribution agreement on file. The contribution agreements generally certify that the contribution is the author's original work and that he or she has the right to contribute it to Sakai.
  - The code must be contributed under a compatible open source license.

- Documentation
  - The tool should provide documentation that describes basic use, installation, customization, and administration.
  - The tool should provide help documentation in a form that may be integrated into the Sakai contextual help system.
  - The tool should describe a test plan for testing its capabilities.
  - The tool should have a Wiki space on Sakai Wiki site that provides additional technical documentation such as design documents, discussions, plans and roadmaps, and so on.

- Desirable Elements—These items aren't strictly required for Provisional status but the tool developers must be intending to meet these criteria in an upcoming release.

  ○ The tool is properly internationalized and has been localized into at least one language other than U.S. English.

  ○ The tool should pass a Sakai accessibility review.

  ○ If the tool needs to save information or business rule code, it should be factored into a Sakai Component with a published API that has complete Javadoc.

  ○ The authors should provide a web-service layer, which sits on top of their API.

  ○ The tool should participate in the Sakai cross-site import and export system.

  ○ The tool should be interoperable with other Sakai tools where appropriate.

  ○ The tool should generate event codes that are triggered minimally on new, revise, and delete actions on the basic objects created by the tool.

The developers of a tool complete a worksheet that indicates how well they meet the criteria and members of the community, in a number of open meetings that precede the release, determine whether the tool should be granted Provisional status.

Stealthily to Core

Achieving Provisional status has several effects. It signals to potential adopters that at least two organizations have been using it, that the tool is ready for use in a controlled pilot, and that others in the community are interested in adopting the tool. All of these are important because they encourage additional real-world usage of the tool, which is a crucial step on the way to becoming a core tool.

Provisional tools also become part of the official Sakai release. When system administrators download Sakai, the source code for provisional tools is included. When they deploy Sakai, the provisional tools are included but hidden from end-user access in a process called **stealthing**. A tool that has been "stealthed" is actually running, but hidden from view. An instructor creating a site cannot make this tool available to his or her end users. An administrator, on the other hand, can add it to a particular site.

Stealthing is very important to the Quality Assurance process. It allows adopters to use a tool in controlled, but real, production settings, while minimizing risks that might result from releasing a tool to all users at once. This process encourages additional adoption and testing. We have found that administrators are quite likely to try provisional tools in their production settings, perhaps because there is no additional software to download and configure. Whatever the reason, additional users of a tool equate to additional confidence in the quality of the tool.

The ability to stealth tools, while it plays a crucial role in the Sakai quality process, is not restricted to the official Sakai release. Sakai makes it possible to stealth any tool with a simple change to the `sakai.properties` file that can be found in the `sakai` directory at the top level of your Sakai installation. This is the main file for configuring Sakai and it contains hundreds of configurable properties. The property that allows you to stealth tools is called `hiddenTools`. If you add the following line, you will hide the tools Chat, Wiki, Schedules, and Resources:

```
hiddenTools@org.sakaiproject.tool.api.ActiveToolManager=sakai.chat,sakai.
rwiki,sakai.schedule,sakai.resources
```

The changes apply after the next restart of your server. The next figure shows the before and after effect during site creation, when you have the opportunity to select the tools you want. Notice the magical disappearance of the Wiki tool. By adding the common names, as mentioned in the table, separated by commas, you can selectively choose which tools to hide.

Provisional tools within the demonstration version

The demo version of Sakai has the Provisional tools enabled by default to allow integrators to play with the full functionality. However, this may lead to increased expectations by key players in the final production system. If you are responsible for demonstrating to a wider public, be careful to consider which tools to hide before the first important demonstrations.

Sakai administrators often use this capability when they add Contrib tools to their local installation. Administrators may also hide Core tools if, for example, the local help desk is not ready to support hundreds or thousands of users that might use those tools.

Once a tool has reached Provisional status, it is also on the way to becoming a Core tool and therefore part of the Sakai Enterprise Bundle. In fact, the basic criteria listed for Provisional status remain the same, although more scrutiny may be placed on how well the tool meets the criteria. The only substantive change is that tools are expected to meet most of the criteria listed as "desirable". In addition, since at least two organizations (and generally many more, some of which have large user bases) have been running the tool in production for it to reach Provisional status, there is additional evidence available for the tool's overall quality, reliability, and scalability. When a tool meets these criteria, and assuming enough additional community interest in the tool, it will be advanced to Core status.

Achieving Core status has two additional effects. First, it signals to potential adopters that the tool is being used successfully in production and, if it meets their functional requirements, it is safe to provide to end users. Secondly, it becomes part of the Sakai Enterprise Bundle. This means the official Sakai release includes the tool and it is available by default to site owners. When users create a site, they can add the tool to the site with a single click of the mouse.

Enterprise-level quality

High-quality core tools are not born accidentally. The Sakai community undertakes a variety of deliberate processes to turn its aspirations of quality into reality. The processes that contribute to the quality of the end release include:

- The Quality Assurance process
- Maintenance releases
- Automated testing
- Automatic code analysis

In this section, we describe each of these processes and its role in creating a high-quality Sakai release.

The Quality Assurance process

Because Quality Assurance (QA) is crucial to the success of the community, the Sakai Foundation takes an active role in orchestrating the testing of the Sakai software. The Foundation employs a QA director whose role is to orchestrate a variety of different testing regimes. In November 2008, there was a transition in leadership from Megan May of Indiana University to Pete Peterson of the University of California, Davis. In addition to employing the QA director, the Sakai Foundation also hires contractors to supplement quality assurance efforts and ensure that resources are available exactly when they are needed in the QA cycle. In addition to staff provided by the Sakai Foundation, the Sakai community provides a number of volunteers to help with QA. These efforts are first directed at testing Core and Provisional tools, with an emphasis on ensuring the quality of the Core tools. To date, this testing has primarily consisted of manual testing — individuals logging into Sakai and working through a variety of test scripts.

The functional testing of Sakai proceeds in the following major stages:

- Feature freeze
- Code freeze
- Betas
- Release candidates
- General availability

The process begins with the documentation of the changes planned for the next release, which is then tracked on Sakai's Wiki (`http://confluence.sakaiproject.org/confluence/x/`). This early information enables institutions to feed their own requirements into the release as well as understand, in advance, the potential effects of any changes on their local installation. This documentation also serves as the basis for developing or revising test plans for the upcoming Sakai release. The documentation of expected features culminates in a "feature freeze" — the deadline for communicating your intended functional changes to the Sakai community.

Approximately two months later, "code freeze" arrives. At this point, no new features can be introduced into the software. The only code changes occurring in the release branch should be bug fixes or performance improvements. In reality, there is usually a grace period lasting approximately a week during which developers have a chance to finish important features that did not quite get completed by code freeze. There is often community discussion about whether these deadline extensions are appropriate for particular features and the final decision rests with the Sakai Foundation Quality Assurance director.

After code freeze, we begin to create a series of Quality Assurance "tags" that allow QA servers around the world to deploy identical versions of the software for testing. These QA servers allow functional testing of the Sakai application. As testers find bugs, they document them in the Sakai bug tracking system and developers begin working on fixing them. After a certain number fixes are verified locally and merged with the code base, a new QA tag is created and the QA servers are updated. There are no strict rules about how often QA tags are created, but, generally speaking, a new tag is released every week or two.

As more and more bugs are fixed, typically over a period of approximately six weeks, the software approaches a level of quality that is suitable for at least limited use. At this point, a "beta" tag is created. The beta tag is the first version we recommend putting in front of actual end users. The Sakai community looks for an organization that is willing to use a beta version of Sakai in a production setting. For versions 2.5 and 2.6, the University of Cape Town played this crucial role. While this may seem risky, it is important to note that for tools to reach Core status, they must have been used by multiple institutions in a production environment. These institutions essentially serve as beta testers for individual tools, not only to shake out bugs that weren't encountered during the QA process, but also to provide valuable insight into the scalability of the tool. Still, putting out a beta version of an enterprise software platform is a big responsibility and an important service to the entire community. It is probably no coincidence that two Sakai fellows (see Chapter 18, *Rogues Gallery*), David Howitz and Stephen Marquard, work at University of Cape Town. They've earned the respect of their peers through this and other acts of leadership.

The beta testing process continues indefinitely until all the critical bugs and performance issues are resolved. At that point, the first "release candidate" is created. A release candidate is just what it sounds like—a version of the software that could become the official release if no additional critical bugs are found. Sometimes, despite best efforts, a release candidate may have a previously undetected problem. In this case, the problem will be fixed and a second release candidate will be created and tested. This process can continue indefinitely but, in all likelihood, release candidate 2 or 3 will become the official release. In the case of Sakai 2.5, release candidate 2 became Sakai 2.5.0.

Maintenance releases

Like any software product, Sakai releases contain both known and unknown bugs. It is impossible to find all bugs in the testing process and many are insignificant enough that they should not prevent general use of the software. At the same time, bugs should be fixed and the fixes should be made available to users. In the 2.5 series of releases, Sakai introduced "maintenance releases" for this purpose. Maintenance releases are releases of the Sakai software that include bug fixes, performance improvements, or security enhancements. No new features are introduced. The fact that maintenance releases contain no new features is especially important. This means that organizations can upgrade to the latest maintenance release without much risk or the need to train their users. The software behaves the same way. It is just faster and more reliable.

Sakai's maintenance release strategy is still evolving, but the goal is to deliver a maintenance release every 2 or 3 months and to continue providing them for approximately 2 years after the initial release. Sakai 2.5.0 was released in March of 2008 and Sakai 2.5.4 was released in February of 2009, slightly less frequently than we would ideally like, but still within the general range. To determine which bug fixes are included in the release, the Sakai QA director examines all the bugs that are being fixed in the maintenance branch (which Sakai calls 2.5.x) and determines which tools contain important fixes. Bug fixes for these tools are included in the next maintenance release.

Perhaps counter-intuitively, this means that other tools will continue to have bugs that someone has fixed, but are not being included in the maintenance releases. To be able to make maintenance releases quickly, it is important to focus changes on a small number of tools. This constrains the scope of testing, one of the major expenses in ensuring high-quality maintenance releases. It may be easy to test whether a particular bug fix does what it is supposed to do, but it is also important to verify that the fix does not break something else—a process known as "regression testing." It is the regression testing that is time-consuming and benefits from consolidating the bug fixes into a small number of Sakai tools.

If your organization wants a fix that is not included in the current maintenance release, you have a few choices. You can ask the QA group to include the fix and offer to assist in testing that tool. Because the main constraint on including bug fixes is testing resources, this is often enough to convince the QA group, represented by the QA director, to include the fix. You can also wait for the next maintenance release, which, depending on your circumstances, might be soon enough for your local needs. The last option is to apply the fix to your local installation. You will then be running a version of the software that is slightly different from the official Sakai release. This can be a good strategy if you have the appropriate technical resources to apply the change and do other updates to Sakai that may affect that change.

The Sakai QA group would, of course, like to be able to include more bug fixes in every maintenance release and provide releases more often. This puts a greater burden on testing, which takes time. As the Sakai software release has gotten larger and more complicated, testing bug fixes to make sure that they work and do not break something else has gotten correspondingly complicated. Even with additional resources, it takes significant time and is prone to human error. Because of this, the Sakai community is increasingly incorporating a variety of automated testing procedures. This is the subject of the rest of this chapter.

The automated testing

The first and the most important line of automated defense is for developers to make sure that they do not break code as they add code in Java. Current best practices dictate that unit-testing frameworks are implemented and cover the majority of the code base. Unit testing is the testing of the smallest units of a program (`http://www.stpmag.com/retrieve/stp-0808.htm` pages 15-18). For Java, that means testing at the individual method level. Good unit tests do not change the code. Continuous build infrastructure (for example, the compiling of code on a regular basis or the ad hoc compiling of code on demand) can run the tests outside the main code base, triggering the required methods on the inside. This enables a clean separation between testing and deployment. When developers add code, they generally run the existing using unit tests and, if something breaks, they know they have more work to do before the code is run in production. Continuous Sakai builds, and reports on those builds, exist at `http://nightly2.sakaiproject.org`.

Unit testing saves pain later, even for the most careful and experienced developer. You can think of unit testing as insurance that you are not adding new bugs or breaking things as you change your code. Java is a programming language intended for teams; objects and packages encapsulate areas of responsibilities and allow for well-defined divisions of labor. Teams tend to build faster than individuals do. Java is also a verbose language when compared to procedural languages such as Perl. Without decent unit tests, quality assurance becomes increasingly resource intensive and uneconomic, and you risk an implosion and massive inertia to safe change. People dare not patch, as they do not know which part of the edifice will fall down next. Life cycles become less ambitious and more defensive.

After unit testing, documentation is the most important factor in the chain of quality processes. There are numerous sources of documentation in Sakai: Confluence, Sakaipedia (`http://bugs.sakaiproject.org/confluence/display/ENC`), the mailing lists, Javadoc, release notes, reference articles downloaded with the Sakai source code, and presentations. The most consistent end user information is the actively maintained online help.

Documentation is equally important for developers, and Java allows you to mix code with comments about the code. By following a certain structure and sets of conventions known as Javadoc, programmers enable continuous-build systems to generate reports detailing the evolving source code. In a large, dynamic project like Sakai, developers can use the generated Javadoc reports to zoom in on evolving features of interest. If you have set up a local build environment for Sakai, then in the top-level directory you can run the following Maven command:
`mvn javadoc:javadoc`.

Interested programmers can find the most current Sakai Javadoc at
`http://nightly2.sakaiproject.org/javadoc/sakai-javadoc/`,
and there is a link on the front page of the web site, as shown highlighted in the next screen grab.

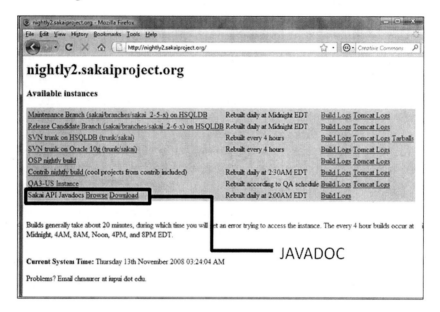

The Quality Assurance Work Group also expects developers to include test plans with any new functional change. The plans describe the set of actions that a user should perform and the expected results. The combination of the testing of functionality by hand and automated unit testing catches a wide and diverse range of potential errors.

It is unlikely that in the near future automated testing will replace human-driven functional testing. However, we may be seeing the beginnings of a discussion on automated functional testing via frameworks such as Selenium-RC emerging on the Sakai developer's mailing list. A Firefox plug-in records a user's action as a test plan and then, later, the testing infrastructure can replay those actions against a number of test machines.

Why is documentation important

Tim Archer is responsible for coordinating all testing activities for CSU `http://csu.edu.au/` with particular focus on the development and implementation of methodologies and processes to improve the quality of our applications and systems. When I asked Tim about the importance of documentation, he stated:

Documentation is a crucial component of testing as it helps to add transparency and accountability to the process. It enables objective viewers to look over completed work to check for holes or suggest additions. It helps to assure the organization that the risk of any new or changed system has been properly identified, managed, and reduced. Documentation reduces the amount of duplicated work and helps to isolate and identify bugs as it will tell you when was the last time test x successfully ran so that focus can be on changes that happened since that time. The final word on documentation comes down to the fact that, in the mind of the business, if it has not been tested and written down in sufficient details, it NEVER HAPPENED.

After all testing, the tools still have to pass through the Performance Workgroup's attention (`http://bugs.sakaiproject.org/confluence/display/PERF`). Stress test tools such as The Grinder and JMeter hit realistic load balanced infrastructure under expected peak loads and beyond. Subtle database issues and synchronization problems emerge and are resolved. Testers push any gross flaws back to the developer and the architects learn lessons for future design and implementation.

In the final analysis, none of the Quality Assurance processes is effective without responsive developers and supportive project managers. If you ask relevant questions on technological issues on the dev distribution list, expect quick responses from multiple sources.

Automatic code analysis

Recognizing the ever-increasing cost in human resources of Quality Assurance as the code base expands, a refactoring of the Sakai code base is currently taking place. Roughly speaking, the project planners have separated the refactoring into two phases, the first phase is consolidation of core functionality, and the second is a significant overhaul of the underlying technologies. During both of these phases, the technical leads have placed emphasis on building in a significant degree of regression testing. If something gets broken during change, then the developers will find it before the Quality Assurance team.

A second line of defense is the automatic scrutiny of the main code base two to three times a day by the University of Amsterdam's QA server. The Amsterdam server automatically downloads the most current source and builds.

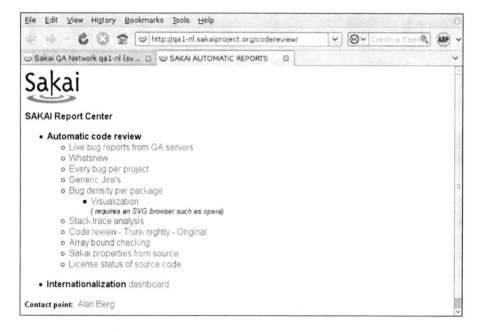

Tools such as Findbugs (`http://findbugs.sourceforge.net/`) and PMD (`http://pmd.sourceforge.net/`) check the source code for bad practices, license violations, and the compiled binary for bad practices. Scripts then scrub and clean the data and create a developer-friendly set of reports.

Open source tools perform a static analysis of the code base. Static analysis is the process of checking source code for patterns that indicate programming faults.

 Findbugs looks for anti-patterns known as bug patterns in compiled Java code. The tool searches for more than 400 common error patterns.

Static analysis comes of age for large code bases, with multiple teams striving to fulfill stringent targets with feature-rich functional requirements. In this extreme and acidic type of environment, the velocity of change and inconsistent code quality across teams makes it costly to do QA by human effort alone. Quality Assurance focuses on the most important features of any given product, normally functionally testing a thin path within the whole code base.

One issue that is not always addressed is the consistency of bad practices by a given team, or the general level of defects. Static analysis works from the bottom up and pays attention evenly throughout the whole code base. The tool can be considered a success if the analysis does not generate too many false positives. Under these conditions, the tool acts as a neutral and objective observer with abundant patience, defanging the potential for very real and human friction. When one subproject is failing relative to the quality generated by another, the statistics will point this out quickly and painlessly—Findbugs does not feel pain.

Further, static analysis captures a large swath of real errors. Not all of them are particularly interesting; sometimes the reports sound more like nags or are difficult to understand. However, the number of real errors, trivial or not, is around the 50 percent correct rate. This efficiency affords coding teams the time to breathe and then fire off reports and act on them, with a potentially significant boost to quality. In the end, this will simplify debugging of the more challenging issues as background noise is diminished.

In the preference tool in **My Workspace**, a user can change his or her language preference and choose from around 17 variants. The messages shown in Sakai by tools such as **confirm password, You have forgotten to fill in your email address,** and so on, change immediately to the corresponding language. These properties reside in text files called property files. Interested programmers can find an excellent document on the subject at `http://confluence.sakaiproject.org/confluence/x/sS4`.

The Internationalization and Localization Work Group (`http://bugs.sakaiproject.org/confluence/display/I18N/Home`) work hard supporting efforts to get Sakai translated and functioning correctly in a multitude of languages. In support of this effort, the Amsterdam server generates a report on a specific language's translation progress. A development team at the Liedse Onderwisinstelligen (`http://www.loi.nl`) has written an open source tool that measures how fully translated into different languages a particular Sakai tool is. Wrapping the tool with some extra reporting code (as shown in the next figure), the University of Amsterdam now writes the state of play for internationalization efforts per Sakai version. The Amsterdam server updates the report three times a day.

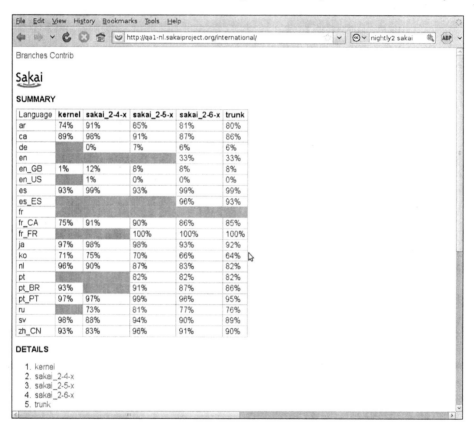

To change the default language of a Sakai instance, the system administrator needs only to change an environment setting. For example, to change the default to French Canadian, the JAVA_OPTS variable needs to be set in the startup script as either (1) for Windows or (2) for Macintosh, Unix, or Linux.

```
(1) set JAVA_OPTS=%JAVA_OPTS% -Duser.language=fr -Duser.region=CA
(2) JAVA_OPTS="$JAVA_OPTS -Duser.language=fr -Duser.region=CA"
```

Notice in the above figure the language column gives you the list of acceptable values. By the time you have read this book, you can expect a few more language choices.

The fun thing about automatic reporting is that there are so many possibilities for future improvements. Take, for example, visualization. The majority of the input to the brain comes through the eye. What is simple for a four-year-old child — to recognize a sweet hidden under 50 toys — still takes quite a lot of programming effort, a lab at NASA, and tens of years in the development. For example, if you can plot defect density or other interesting metrics like the Sakai scorecard vs. location in the Sakai codebase in a visually meaningful context, then planning where to place your QA effort becomes more deeply informed. The figure below is a proof of concept of such a plot. What you are seeing is the defect density found by Findbugs against some arbitrary codebase location.

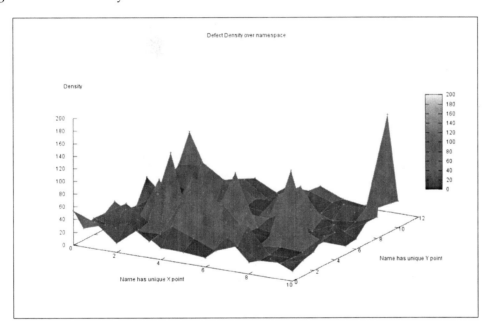

With the refactoring of the code base, increased regression testing, automatic reports, the efforts of various work groups, and the swift response to technical questions by the development community, expect the quality of the core tools in particular and the Sakai code base in general to improve.

Summary

The community takes the quality of the Sakai code base very seriously. Methodologies such as unit testing, static code reviews, and reports of internationalization progress help automate the QA process and lower overall costs. Current refactoring of the Sakai code base will improve the coverage of regression tests and the quality of documentation, specifically Javadoc.

Functional testing is the main tool of use by the QA Work Group. The Performance Work Group primarily performs stress testing. The Internalization and Localization Work Group support the translation of Sakai into a multitude of languages.

The current home of a number of automated daily reports is the Amsterdam server `http://qa1-nl.sakaiproject.org/codereview`. The continuous build server and the home of the most up-to-date Javadoc is `http://nightly2.sakaiproject.org`.

In the future, expect more visualization within the automated reports and a trend towards automated functional testing.

In the next chapter, Worksite Tools, we will discuss the various types of tools and show how they are used in project, course, and portfolio sites.

7
Worksite Tools

This chapter will first discuss the types of tools, briefly highlighting the difference between their core functionality and how they are used in project, course, and portfolio sites. We will, however, defer administration tools and tools that help integrate Sakai with other systems, until Chapter 10.

Sakai is highly configurable, so if you have an account in Sakai, do not be surprised if you see other worksite types or roles. To add to the variation, there are numerous examples of high-quality tools that are not part of the enterprise bundle. Chapter 8, *Contrib Tools*, includes a long list and descriptions of the contributed tools.

The two main types of site that the book has focused on, until now, are course and project sites. These site types differ in the number of roles that are available and the selection of tools you can choose during creation. In the demonstration version of Sakai, project sites are the simpler of the two with fewer tool choices and (by default) two roles, Access and Maintain. Project sites support ad hoc interaction. Course sites can do approximately everything project sites can do plus you can have extra tools to support learning activities, for example, Test & Quizzes and Gradebooks.

The demonstration has more

In the demonstration version of Sakai, the tool list for project sites contains all the tools available in course sites as well. This is normally not the case in production.

The Sakai Foundation is active in keeping the tool summary accurate. The best location to look for the Sakai 2.5 set of tools is: `http://confluence.sakaiproject.org/confluence/display/DOC/Tool+List+(2.5)` The hardworking page maintainers will replace the 2.5 in the URL with the correct version number as the product moves incrementally upwards through major version numbers.

By the time you read this book, Sakai will be in version 2.6 or later. The choice of enterprise core tools changes relatively slowly. This keeps the servers stable, and allows students and instructors to be familiar enough with the system to be able to create complex training material. However, technologies improve, real-world deployments teach development teams lessons, and the tool requirements evolve and become more precise and detailed. The overall user experience thus becomes richer.

There are two processes currently taking place that may lead to radical updates. The first is a team of experts looking at the user experience and the second is developers renovating and refactoring the core services. Studying user experiences will lead to a radically updated interface, with so-called Web 2.0 technologies, that make tools more responsive to user input. This update will be immediately noticeable to teachers and students alike. The core service renovations are just as important, but in terms of the quality of service and flexibility of Sakai, they are hidden.

For the 2.5.3 release, the community considered the following tools as provisional: Blog, Mailtool, Podcasts, Polls, Reset Password, and Roster. Furthermore, there is talk on the developers' distribution list about the retirement of the Presentation tool and the Mailtool.

The Blog tool has competition from the contrib project Blogwow (`http://bugs.sakaiproject.org/confluence/display/BW`) and with little effort; your local deployment team can replace one tool with the other.

The Reset Password tool is useful for guest account users who wish to reset their forgotten passwords.

The Podcast tool allows a site maintainer to upload media and publish the media at a specific time on the Internet. This simple tool allows the sending out of lectures with little effort from the teachers involved. One can imagine an institution giving all its lecturers iPods if they learn how to use them to record their lectures.

The Mailtool has useful functionality including the ability to email everyone who is a member of a given site, or send to a selected set of users who all have a specific role. The Mailsender tool (`http://bugs.sakaiproject.org/confluence/display/MAILTOOL/Mailsender`) will replace this tool. The designers based the Mailsender tool on the experience and extra functional requirements accumulated since the release of the Mailtool, and include the ability to send mail internally without the need for external SMTP infrastructure. In terms of the demo version of Sakai, this is excellent, as the tool will allow practice without extra configuration.

The Roster tool is teacher-friendly; it displays site members' profiles with the associated photographs (if they exist). On the first day of the first term, you can imagine a teacher printing out the main tool page and using the photographs to learn student names. There is also the contrib tool named People from Lancaster University that has similar functionality and is well worth a test run.

For the most up-to-date roadmap and planning, I recommend visiting the following two Confluence pages: the Sakai roadmap (`http://confluence.sakaiproject.org/confluence/display/MGT/Sakai+Roadmap`) and Release management (`http://confluence.sakaiproject.org/confluence/display/REL/Home`).

Sakai has many hooks for interacting with complex enterprise infrastructures, for example, via web services as described in detail in Chapter 11. A number of institutes transfer syllabuses, schedules, and so on from their Student Administration System. The need to integrate well with other systems has led to extra detail, especially in course sites. An example is having course sites be section aware. Tools such as Announcements allow you to choose which sections of a course or which group you can send messages to.

A flashcard activity

Most tools have similar structures and once you have learned a few basics, learning the next tool is easier. The Online Help explains how to perform functions like adding and deleting an item such as a forum or an announcement. The Help also has accurate descriptions of each tool and the benefit of being the most up-to-date source of user support.

Reading the Help is like looking at an old television picture close up: you see the dots, but the overall picture may be harder to discern. However, before you can truly understand the overall picture, you need to have some feeling for what a Sakai tool is. To build an understanding of the relationship between tools, you can create a set of flashcards, one per tool.

An example flashcard editor that runs on the same platforms as Java is JFlash (`http://flashcards.sourceforge.net/`). JFlash is a simple editor and viewer that runs on any machine with Java 1.5. For an example of learning flow, after reviewing flashcards, each with an overview of one specific tool, you can make a second set of cards, one per tool, with a list of actions, such as add announcement, add forum. You can leave for later the harder-to-learn tools such as Portfolios and Test & Quizzes. Portfolios and Test & Quizzes have greater functionality and require more attention and time.

The following screen grab captures JFlash in action. A list of tools to learn is shown on the left side and the full description of the selected tool on the right side, in this case, the Drop Box.

To make the experience more tactile, you can consider exporting the cards to PDF and printing them out, then placing the cards upside down and randomly choosing one.

The following table defines the set of tools you can initially use as part of the flashcard learning process. The Sakai application uses the common name as part of the help URL, for example, for announcements: `http://localhost:8080/portal/help/main?help=sakai.announcements`.

Tool Name	Purpose	Common Name
Announcements	For posting current, time-critical information	sakai.announcements
Blogger	A blogger	blogger
Chat Room	For real-time conversations in written form	sakai.chat
Email Archive	For viewing email sent to the site	sakai.mailbox
Link Tool	For linking to external applications	sakai.rutgers.linktool
Mailtool	Send mail to groups in your course (attachment-enabled)	sakai.mailtool
Messages	Display messages to/from users of a particular site	sakai.messages
News	For viewing content from online sources	sakai.news

Tool Name	Purpose	Common Name
Podcasts	For managing individual podcast and podcast feed information	sakai.podcasts
Polls	For anonymous polls or voting	sakai.poll
Resources	For posting documents, URLs to other web sites, and so on	sakai.resources
Search	For searching content	sakai.search
Site Info	For showing worksite information and site participants	sakai.siteinfo
Web Content	For accessing an external web site within the site	sakai.iframe
Wiki	For collaborative editing of pages and content	sakai.rwiki

 At the time of writing, there was no online help available in the demonstration version for Blogger.

The Search, Site Info, and Resources tools are all core.

Most tools mentioned in the table have search capabilities included. The search functionality not only indexes PDF, Office formats, HTML, and text, it also keeps track of much of the metadata included in the files you upload to Resources. If you have more than a few students, search becomes a vital time saver in finding and navigating the vast range of resources generated during a normal academic year.

Site Info is the tool for site maintenance functions such as adding to or deleting from the tool list.

 Do not destroy
Once you have created a site, try not to delete tools as you may be deleting a site member's content by mistake.

Using flashcards helps overcome initial barriers. In a large organization, expect hands-on training to be available. If you are stuck when using a particular tool, there is a lot of handy documentation scattered throughout the Internet.

The University of Indiana, which uses Sakai for over 100,000 students, has released its support material under a creative commons license. A good starter's link is `https://oncoursehelp.iu.edu/helptool` and more specifically, `https://oncoursehelp.iu.edu/helptool/doc/aube`.

Commonalities between tools

There are many types of relationships and collaborations between users of a Sakai site. An instructor may wish to push information out through announcements, notifications, and messages. They may communicate their knowledge through blogs, forums, Wikis, or via stored files in Resources. The Podcast tool is an easy method for delivering the recorded voice of lecturers. In the future, live interactions will happen with the contrib tool, Agora (`http://agora.lancs.ac.uk/`), which is an online meeting tool with white board functionality.

Sakai is flexible: the owner of a site can choose which tools to include and decide on the permissions for each of the user roles. Perhaps the site owner wants a less instructor-centric view of the universe and chooses to enable the students to be more responsible. The Wiki tool is excellent for ad hoc document generation and the contrib tool Forum can be used for viewing and marking the value of an individual's forum contributions.

The architects have designed Sakai from the bottom up to make tool building straightforward. Contrib tools move to provisional and then to the core. A number of the core tools have competition from contributed code: Forums, the News Feed tool, and Blogs sit under fire. This competition is healthy and can only improve the user experience in the end.

As more tools bubble to the surface and older tools become more polished or get replaced by competitors, the opportunity for creating wonderful learning experiences increases. Tools ease the administrative burden and enable multiple paths of communication and expression, but do not take the responsibility away from the educator. If you use Sakai as a file storage system to preserve your handouts from lessons written four years ago, it is easier on your students because they do not have to be in class to pick up the printed version, but you will hardly be stretching your or the system's possibilities. Understanding and making use of the relationships between tools can make a better learning experience. For example, if you have set up a series of quizzes or forums, why not make them more visible by enabling the Schedules tool and then adding them as events with their times?

Most tools are straightforward to learn. It will probably take you only a few minutes to read and understand the online help for Announcement, News, Polls, or Search. However, larger tools such as Test & Quizzes take more practice and time. As you get to understand the tool set, you will get to see more opportunities to combine them. As developers build tools, they see more functionality worth adding and rough edges worth smoothing. The number of developers working with Sakai is increasing over time.

Tools need to work within the structure of a given site. The site, itself, needs to work within an organization, with the site's look and feel, help files, links to the support desk, perhaps internationalization, and data from the Student Administration System. As you look at the tools mentioned in this chapter, try to think in terms of relationships. Ask yourself what this tool can deliver and how can you make it more useful it by having it interact with another tool. For example, is there a relationship showing an external web page inside Sakai via the Web Content Tool and additional help? External blogs support RSS, so you can push blog updates into your site with the News tool and place the tool link next to the students' own Blog tool.

There are several relationships built into tools. For example, teachers build Portfolio structure out of parts created in a number of tools such as the Matrix and Form tools. A grade book in Sakai can contain information gleaned from spreadsheets, CSV files, and internally from Test & Quizzes, Assignments, or Forums. Project sites tend not to need tools with these inter-relationships as often.

Tools have a lot in common. Tools that create items that students act on, such as Resources, Announcements, Test & Quizzes, Polls, etc., are able to restrict access to the item to a specific target audience: the public, only members in the site, or to a selected group or section. By default, within a course, Sakai sets the default restrictions to site-wide; only members of a site can view and modify a given item. The next figure displays part of the configuration you can set for an announcement, created using the Announcements tool. Each tool may have a slightly different audience or display options with other rendering, but the principle is the same.

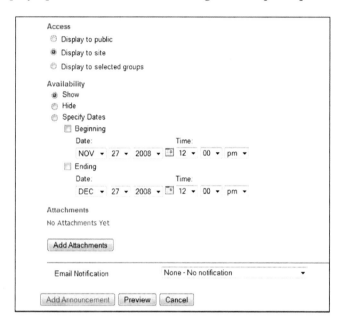

In general, you can also decide when the application displays the item and you can change the settings later to force an item into hiding. If your real-world scheduling is accurate, you can write a set of assignments, announcements, and tests and have them appear at the right time. If a leaky pipe, an unexpected promotion, or other unplanned pleasantries occur, you can always go back and edit the timing.

Mail notification is important as information becomes available outside the learning system. With judicious use of mailbox filters, it is easy to have a secondary history of events within a given course that can be easily browsed. You specify notification options during item creation. You can choose to send no notification, low-level notification, or high-level notification. The system sends the high-level notifications by default. In the user **preferences** tool in their workspace, Sakai users can set their preferences for receiving low-level notifications. Like using bold when writing or capital letters in emails, you should use high-priority notifications for the most crucial information such as announcing end-of-term assignments or exams.

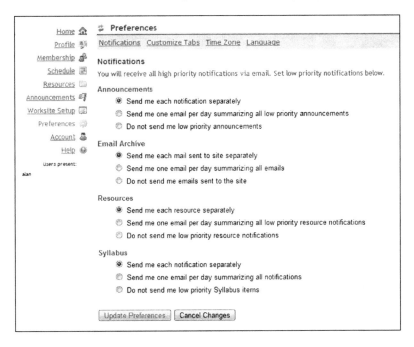

Over time, you can expect more tools to become notification-enabled.

One species of tool we have not explained so far is the helper tool. You do not see these tools separately from other tools and they just help. One such helper tool is the Permission tool.

When you create a site or have one created for you, Sakai copies the roles (student, instructor, and so on) with the site information. Each role has a default set of permissions per tool. For example, Sakai does not allow a user who is in the student role in a given site to create a forum, whereas a user in the teacher role has permission to do so.

The Permission tool displays the role and the set of permissions for a given tool. The next figure shows a real-world example for a CTools site at the University of Michigan (CTools is the name used for the University of Michigan's instance of Sakai). In this example site, a student can only read content, but nothing else, whereas an affiliate, assistant, instructor, or owner can do no official wrong and has the power to change and modify all content. Librarians and observers have fewer powers, but still more than students.

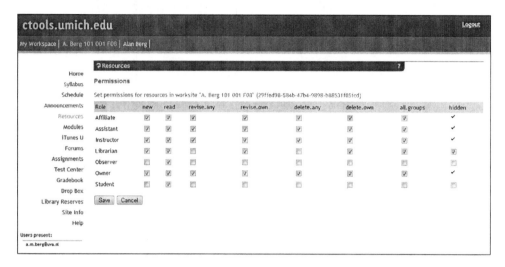

Permissions such as **new** and **read** are obvious, but others such as **all.groups** (allowed to see all resources, even those assigned to specific groups) are less so. The permission **hidden** does not hide all your resources from others, rather it gives you the power to see hidden resources and unhide them.

The more permissions you delegate to the student or another role, the more responsible they will become for their own actions and the more student-centric the learning experience will potentially become. If your class size is not too big and you can maintain an overview of what is happening on the site, it is worth empowering the students. The more a student can do within a particular course site, the more they feel involved.

The Wiki tool is an excellent test case as it maintains a history of modifications. If a student misbehaves and writes nasty words in the Wiki, you can always set the content back to a particular version number. If you can trust your students with Wiki content, then perhaps you should also consider empowering them with tools such as Blogs and Forums.

Expect the tuning of permissions to also play out at different educational levels. A student learning at the K-12 level will probably interact with Sakai with fewer permissions per tool, and perhaps fewer tools, than a more mature and empowered university-level student.

The Resources tool

The Resources tool is the most used tool in Sakai. Think of it as your online storage container—a location where you can safely place your education-related files. You can use the Resources tool as part of My WorkSpace or as a part of any given site you are a member of.

Each resource has its own unique URL, which you can copy by right clicking (control-clicking on a Macintosh) in your web browser. You can use the link in Wiki documents and email messages, and the resource can be made public for others to use by editing its properties from within the Resource tool.

By default, resources in MyWorkSpace are hidden from others and not public. They cannot be configured to restrict access to a given interest group such as a membership of a course. However, you can restrict resources in sites to sections or groups, or you can make them available to the whole site membership.

As long as you remain with the same user account in Sakai, the URL for a given resource in your workspace will remain the same, whereas the lifetime of a resource in a course site tends to be shorter. If you are giving out a specific resource URL for others to use and you later copy content such as Wiki information or HTML documents with hard-coded links from one course to another, I would advise placing the resource in your workspace. Further, if you are running multiple courses with a subset of resources that are the same, keep that subset of resources in your workplace or you risk having different versions scattered across the application.

It is possible to link to external sources from inside Sakai by adding a link as a resource, using the Web Content tool, adding links to blogs, Wiki announcements, or via news feeds, and so on. If the link is very important, such as pointing to a local support desk, then adding it the lefthand side of the screen by using the Web Content tool is best.

Storage is a potential issue for large organizations with learning management systems. The University of Amsterdam is currently seeing a growth of around 50% in storage space demand each year for its system. This translates into longer backup times and costs. Traditionally, the content was Microsoft Office suite-dominated with large PowerPoint presentations with uncompressed bitmaps, which caused occasional problems. However, over the last few years, multimedia content is slowly taking over as the largest consumer of storage space.

Scalability tip

By placing services such as streaming video external to our learning management system and linking to content outside of Sakai (known as linking out), we can avoid a large subset of scalability issues and ensure continued stability.

To protect itself from misuse, Sakai has the potential to enforce quotas on resources. You will have to read your local support documentation to know your Sakai installation's limits.

At the very core of Sakai are the services related to storage and manipulation of resources, such as word documents, HTML pages, podcasts, and so on. Resources are stored either in a database or on the file system of the server. Instructors use syllabuses to communicate the goals of a course, grade books to store scores, HTML files to communicate ideas, and so on. Students store work pieces in drop boxes. Without resources, there is no learning experience. Consequentially, the manipulation of resources, though not as exciting as, say, online meetings, is vital to the overall quality of the Sakai experience.

The Resources tool includes WebDav support. WebDav, also known as web folders in Windows-speak, allows an end user to upload files by dragging and dropping files into a folder on their desktop. A number of institutions have used this as a poor man's migration strategy for pushing content from Legacy systems into Sakai. It is a lot less frustrating to drag and drop multiple files than to use the web-based form of the Resources tool. However, the Resources tool works via a web browser in most environments and WebDav, which has only been thoroughly tested for Windows and Macintosh, has had some nagging issues reported for Windows (for example, asking for the password multiple times).

You can copy content from other sites anytime afterwards using the **Site creation** option in the Sites tool or the **Import from Site** option in the Site Info tool.

Copying content in specific tools requires that you have the tool enabled in your new site. During worksite setup, on the page that lists the tool options, you must first choose the tools you want and then select from a list of sites from which you want to copy content. As is usual for select boxes in web forms, holding down *Ctrl* (*Shift* on a Macintosh) and clicking on the different sites, allows you to select more than one site. The following figure displays a project site with all the tools enabled, copying all that it can from a number of sites. Notice that since the administrator is logged on, the Administration workspace is also included with only the Announcement and Resources tools available, as no other relevant tools were enabled.

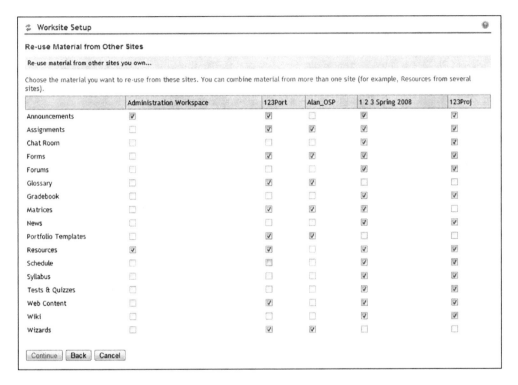

The degree and type of content copying depends on which tool you are discussing. However, the Sakai instance does not copy the student content. In general, this is a nice self-cleaning feature for when you copy from one academic year to the next. The process saves the instructor the time of removing the now-irrelevant history of student efforts.

Course tools

Depending on how your local institute has set up the worksite setup wizard, you will have the choice of extra tools on top of the ones available for project sites. The following table describes some extra core tools not mentioned in the first table that are more specific to course sites.

Tool Name	Purpose	Common Name
Assignments	For posting, submitting, and grading assignment(s) online	sakai.assignment
Drop Box	For private file sharing between instructor and student	sakai.dropbox
Forums	Display forums and topics of a particular site	sakai.forums
Gradebook	For storing and computing assessment grades from Test & Quizzes or that are manually entered	sakai.gradebook.tool
Mailtool	Send mail to groups in your course (attachment-enabled)	sakai.mailtool
Post'Em	For uploading .csv formatted file to display feedback (such as, comments, grades) to site participants	sakai.postem
Presentations	For showing and viewing slideshows of image collections from Resources	sakai.presentation
Roster	For viewing the site participants list	sakai.site.roster
Schedule	For posting and viewing deadlines, events, and so on.	sakai.schedule
Section Info	For managing sections within a site	sakai.sections
Syllabus	For posting a summary outline and/or requirements for a site	sakai.syllabus
Test & Quizzes	For creating and taking online tests and quizzes	sakai.samigo

For proper use of the tools, it is important to consider the inter-relationship between the tool sets. To give you a clear picture, let us examine one workflow. The flow is simplistic and is only for demonstration purposes. The flow is teacher-centric and does not take into account how students can work together with other students, or how to delegate responsibility. However, it does have the advantage of being relatively easy to explain.

Context

Our imaginary course has one teacher (you), no teaching assistant, and a few tens of students. You have divided the course over ten lectures, each with an associated assignment and a test every second lecture to keep your students' attention. The Sakai instance you are using has automatically created your course, published a syllabus, and populated the course with some basic tools and student membership. The application administrator has also populated the email address for the email archive tool with a rather boring name `mycourse_1_7@my_sakai_instance.org`. On your tried-and-tested USB stick, reside your lecture notes and few miscellaneous notes that are not ready for student viewing. The site has a quota on it of 200 MB and a link using the Web Content tool to your local helpdesk. You have your own web site with all kinds of interesting information and resources accumulated over the years and you have made another link to that via the Web Content tool. This means your site has a link to the tools on the lefthand side of the screen with the two links to external content.

Communication plan

Before thinking in terms of content, try thinking in terms of how you are going to communicate online with your students. In the real world, you can communicate plan changes at the beginning of lectures, for example, and mirror this in the Schedule tool. If students know that vital communication is going to occur via the Schedule, Announcements, and perhaps email through the Mailtool, then you have prepared your students to react promptly. You should keep the email notification process, discussed in the last section, to a low notification level unless, for example, a schedule changes, and then you can send a high-priority notification to all members of the site.

Your students also want to be able to communicate with you. They can use the Drop Box, the Mailtool, and perhaps even the Chat tool, where you and the students can agree on times for question and answer sessions to take place. For slower and more thoughtful communication on a particular issue, you can set up a Forum. You may even consider promoting one student to a teaching assistant and making him or her responsible for moderating. Some schools and universities have structures that pay students for these extra responsibilities.

The last line of communication is the Mail Archive tool. Consider using this to keep a history of emails for the entire course membership.

Content

The next layer of this delightful and tasty cake is where and how to place content. Your USB stick is full of documents in a complex structure of directories. Using the Resource tool and WebDav saves you many keystrokes; you can drag the content directly to the course site or, if you think the content will be reused between courses, to My WorkSpace. You should hide any content items that you do not want students to see from within the Resource tool and then either make them visible (unhide) manually or set a specific date to have them automatically unhidden.

Random events have mixed up your notes, so it may be worth adding what you can to the course Wiki and then updating it as you produce more content. You consider adding HTML pages on the fly by creating them using the Resources tool. At the last minute, you remember you already have some valid Wiki content in another of your sites. You go to the Site Info tool and then **Import from other Site:** selecting only the Wiki tool.

Assessing individual students

You fire off one assignment per lecture and print out the returned work. Sakai transfers student grades from assignments directly into the Gradebook, where students can review them, and behind the scenes, the application passes the results to the Student Administration System. The same is true for your tests and quizzes. Throughout the academic year, you play with Forums to see if you want to grade student activity in a forum.

Finally, you can start to experiment by adding other tools and slowly increasing the permissions for the student role. You use the Poll tool and talk in the real world with your students to judge the relevancy of your work and then pass your experiences on to the Sakai community, which will then use your feedback in the next round of collecting ideas for new tool development.

Introducing Portfolios

Due to the relative complexity of its setup, this book has not covered the Open Source Portfolio (OSP) site type yet. An eportfolio is a set of web pages, perhaps containing attachments, which show who you are and what you have accomplished. Institutions use ePortfolios in numerous ways: they may serve as student resumes or be used to assess the education history of instructors, teaching assistants, or students.

The majority of use cases center around the student. Portfolios have the potential to make the flow of students between different institutions and into employment easier by communicating the skill sets and experience in straightforward online structures. For the most up-to-date information about the OSP, please visit: `http://osportfolio.org`.

The application designers have designed the Portfolio site from a series of wizards, forms, and resources. A form is the electronic version of a paper form and allows inputs of type text, date, integer (whole numbers), decimal, or complex entities, such as telephone numbers or email addresses. A portfolio site owner can reuse forms many times as part of wizards.

Currently, there are three types of wizards: sequential, hierarchical or tree like, and matrices. In practice, the matrix is the most often created. The sequential wizard steps you through a series of steps, the hierarchical through a series of categories and subcategories.

Matrices are similar in structure to a spreadsheet with rows and columns. Each column can, for example, represent a level of achievement: level 1, level 2, and so on and each row a particular competency, such as critical thinking, oral communication, and so on. Each cell is able to contain evidence of the student's ability, additional information about the standard the student needs to achieve, and possibly feedback from forms.

Due to web page size constraints, the portfolio designer may need to abbreviate the headings of the rows and columns. The glossary tool allows you to define the meaning of each heading so that when a mouse cursor moves over the matrix, the participant sees the term and the definition.

Within a Portfolio site, the coordinator has tools that support each piece of the puzzle. The forms, matrix, and forms tools are used to create the various parts. The portfolio template enforces a particular structure. For example, when students want to create a new portfolio for themselves, the glossary, layouts, and styles helper tools refine the look and feel.

Students do not have to use a template and can build a portfolio out of parts if they so desire.

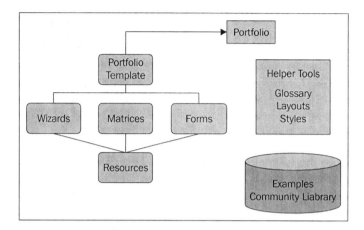

The following table shows the current Portfolio toolset.

Tool Name	Purpose	Common name
Evaluations	View outstanding evaluations from student's eportfolio matrices and wizards	osp.evaluation
Forms	Add XSD forms for collecting structured data (for example, in matrices and wizards)	sakai.metaobj
Glossary	Create a glossary of terms referenced in matrix row and/or column names	osp.glossary
Matrices	Create and use a structured, guided eportfolio matrix	osp.matrix
Portfolio Layouts	Add XHTML page layout templates for free-form ('design your own') portfolios	osp.presLayout
Portfolio Templates	Add XSL design templates for portfolios that incorporate form data (or for 'forms-based portfolios')	osp.presTemplate
Portfolios	Create personal ePortfolios using existing templates, layouts, or free-form design	osp.presentation
Styles	Add Cascading Style Sheets (CSS) for controlling the appearance of wizards, matrices, and portfolios	osp.style
Wizards	Create and use a structured, guided ePortfolios wizard	osp.wizard

The flexibility of and multitude of potential uses for ePortfolios comes at a price. Describing how to create a properly skinned, beautifully rendered, and educationally valid portfolio structure would require at least one thick book in itself. Good teaching practices, on top of the concepts and use of the underlying XML and XSLT (http://www.w3.org/TR/xslt), require a large skill set. However, I do not doubt the value of using ePortfolios within Sakai. It has highly useful functionality. The real issue is the large learning curve for a new-to-deploy organization that may be associated with the high level of flexibility provided by the tools. Luckily, others have been through the process before with support when necessary from commercial partners (http://sakaiproject.org/portal/site/sakai-support).

Once a team has made an eportfolio and its subcomponents, a site administrator can export it to a ZIP file and later import it to another site.

The OpenEd site http://openedpractices.org that shares best educational practices, has a central repository of example ePortfolios with information about their real-life usage. This is an excellent location to showcase what your institute has done. If you want to give back to the community, then please donate your archives here. The more active this site is then the lower the initial learning curve.

On the front page of the OpenEd site is a link to the resource section. If you browse the section, you will find a search form.

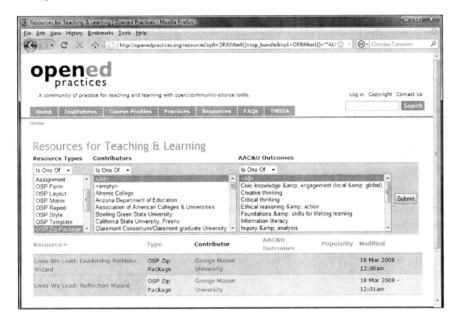

Select an OSP ZIP package and click **Submit** to return a set of example portfolio archives. The downloading and importing of the archive will be described in the administration worksite chapter. Suffice to say this is an excellent shortcut to start making your own portfolios. For the curious, try downloading an archive, importing, and then practicing manipulating various parts with the related OSP tool.

The next section is an interview with a portfolio expert Sean Keesler, who has been busy with OSP since near its origins.

Portfolio expert interviewed

Who is Sean Keesler and how is he related to Portfolio and Sakai?

Sean Keesler is an IT consultant with Three Canoes Consulting (`http://threecanoes.com`). He was the project manager for a Sakai portfolio implementation at the School of Education at Syracuse University. During his eight years as an instructional technologist at Syracuse he was involved in the development and support of several technology integration projects in K12 and higher education. He is available for Sakai consulting through his consulting group, which provides "just in time" services.

Can you explain what the community library is and how this can help a teacher?

Many of the portfolio tools have dual purposes. Students and most faculty members will be presented with a user experience that is actually the product of considerable design and configuration work done by an instructional designer who has already used the tools to create various data structures to support the portfolio experience. The structures include portfolio matrices, wizards, forms, styles, layouts and templates. These data structures may also be exported from one Sakai worksite and imported into another to replicate a part or an entire portfolio experience

The community distribution of the Open Source Portfolio tools in Sakai has never shipped with any default data structures. However, the tools can be (and have been) configured by members of the Sakai community in a number of creative ways to address institutional portfolio requirements. Some schools have decided to document their configuration and use of the portfolio tools and contribute their ideas and data structures for others to use and/or build from.

This "community library" of documented use of and reusable data structures for the Open Source Portfolio tools is available at the OpenEd Practices web site. By browsing the links **Teaching and Learning Practices** and **Resources for Teaching and Learning** related to OSP, newcomers to the portfolio tools can get a sense of the capabilities of the tools, how others have used them, and they can download the data structures necessary to recreate and/or build upon an existing portfolio experience in their own instance of Sakai.

What is your motivation for creating a demo portfolio distribution in contrib?

Although some schools may want to use Sakai as an eLearning platform that includes traditional courseware/collaboration tools and portfolio tools in one instance of Sakai, others have an interest in deploying an ePortfolio solution completely separate from their enterprise choice of courseware platform. For such schools a deployment of Sakai that includes all of the core tools may not be desirable. The "portfolio demo" distribution of Sakai allows you to check out the core portfolio tools (and their dependencies) as well as a select a set of relevant contrib tools that are related to portfolio work. This trimmed, custom distribution is quicker to download, compile and startup than a full Sakai installation and may require less code maintenance than the full set of Sakai tools. Keep in mind that that this project does not have the release management and QA resources dedicated to it that the "official" tags of Sakai have. The current state of the project is to simply include the maintenance branches of the relevant sub-projects.

What improvements to the demo version do you intend to make in the future?

Ideally, a portfolio distribution of Sakai would include a more full-featured out-of-the-box experience for instructional designers. One way to accomplish this would be to include select data structures with the distribution to provide an enhanced, self-documented, out-of-the-box experience for quick evaluation by pilot groups and instructional technology staff. Bundling a set of data structures and content from the community library and additional documentation with the distribution may be a reasonable next step in the evolution of this project.

Summary

Numerous tools have common structures such as permissions, the choice of an email notification (on creation of an entity such as a folder or an assignment), and a link into resources.

Initially learning some of the smaller tools helps when you are trying later to learn tools that are more complex and dependent on other tools. One approach to initial learning is the use of the online help in combination with flashcards.

In general, the more permissions the student role has in a course site, the more responsible the students are for their own activities and the more student-centric the teaching is.

Test & Quizzes in combination with the Gradebook tool encapsulates much functionality and hence is harder to learn than tools such as Polls.

Consider your teaching workflow based on discrete learning activities such as writing an assignment or taking a test. Consider using tools such as Schedule, Announcements, and the notifications functions to communicate events clearly.

The Roster tool is a great help in learning the names of new students, especially when photos are included.

Chat and Forums enable synchronous and asynchronous communication and are indicators of an individual student's online participation in a given course.

Deploying Portfolio functionality in Sakai requires developer(s) with XML, and XSLT skills. Resources on the OpenEd site and a portfolio demonstration distribution can ease the initial learning curve for new deployment teams.

Storing files online in the Resources tool ensures that the system backs them up and they can be readily copied between courses, and gives students direct access to relevant materials.

In Chapter 8, *Contrib Tools*, you will get to meet tools that have been built by third parties to fulfill specific needs. The tools are not found in the standard Sakai demonstration, but do have a lot of potential for improving a student's online learning experiences.

8
Contributed Tools

 If I have seen further it is only by standing on the shoulders of Giants.
Isaac Newton (1643 –1727)

The Contrib section (`https://source.sakaiproject.org/contrib/`) of the Sakai source code repository is the location where organizations and individuals place their code that is not going directly into a Sakai release. Contrib code is diverse in origin. It includes a massive amount of code, from large, well-tested, and supported projects such as Etudes (`http://etudesproject.org/`), through tools created for local needs to personal contributions and proofs of concepts. Contrib bubbles with creativity and source code at various levels of quality and maturity.

The Contrib area is open for everyone to use. This implies that individual organizations can roll their Contrib tools out to their own students without having to be stuck to the Foundation-coordinated release cycle. Local quality assurance takes the place of the centrally coordinated QA. This approach allows for more rapid development and deployment. However, it risks the maturity of the Contrib tool, as there is no central guarantee that QA has taken place during development.

Another hindrance to choosing a tool from Contrib is the sheer volume of choices combined with a lack of documentation for some of the smaller projects. There is so much to choose from that the process can be overwhelming.

Before you consider building new exciting tools or integration with other concern systems, it is well worth performing a background study of what is out in the wild. If you visit Confluence (`http://bugs.sakaiproject.org/confluence`), you will find on the lefthand side of the first page links to well-known projects. The contributed projects in the Wiki are easy to spot as all the relevant link names start with the abbreviation Contrib. These projects include a large subset of the code, but not everything. Even after reading all the entries in Confluence, it still worth browsing the repository.

There are so many offerings and so much information, that it is impossible to mention all that is valuable.

 This chapter has focused the screen grabs and explanations on the smaller project that have less opportunity to self-publicize than the larger and better-resourced projects.

An apology of sorts

Now for my apology to the reader: The amount of code in Contrib is very large—I could spend the whole of this book explaining all the extra features. Therefore, if this chapter fails to mention your favorite tool or supporting utility code, sorry, this is purely accidental.

There are particular organizations such as CARET (`http://www.caret.cam.ac.uk/`) and individuals such as Ian Boston, Charles Severance, Stephen Githens, and Aaron Zeckoski, who achieve much and give back to the rest of us for appropriate reuse. However, then this book would, no doubt, be burnt by hordes of the tribe angrily pointing out the vast contributions from others in the community, such as Nuno Fernandes, David Norton, Stephen Marquard, Beth Kirschner, and so on (visualize a long line of relevant contributors queuing into the vast distance). The community is active, from large organizations downwards and all the activity is difficult to summarize within a few short pages.

The range of contributed tools

Contrib tools range in code size from small personal experiments to detailed and elegantly crafted large-scale team efforts. This section mentions some of the most usable tools in that spectrum.

Sponsoring creativity

Contrib is a place where good ideas from individual efforts can make an impact and where complex projects mature. It is the Wild West, where you can add value to the Sakai offering. In general, the individuals who have given succor to the writing of this book are themselves not confined to a nine-to-five mentality. They have written significant parts of Contrib in personal time or spare hours and based their efforts on a refreshingly unselfish perspective typical for open source pioneers.

The variety of code includes enhanced tools to replace already existing functionality, such as the forum or blog tool, or testing within Sakai, and bridges for tight integration with external systems such as LAMS (`http://bugs.sakaiproject.org/confluence/display/LAMS`). There is example provider and web service code for tight integrations for specific institute's administration and administrative tools such as SakaiAdminX (`http://bugs.sakaiproject.org/confluence/display/ADMX`) that supports more refined delegated administration. Solo is an offline client for solving bandwidth issues and there is a case study included within this book. MySakai provides widgets for the desktop that spice up the end user's experience and make browsing of the online content more efficient (`http://bugs.sakaiproject.org/confluence/display/MYSAK`).

The downside of unfettered activity is that there is no guarantee from the central quality assurance effort that any particular contributed piece of code is mature enough to deploy. If you are actively thinking of including a project from the code repository, you will need to verify its basic stability. It is a sure bet that tools that more than a few organizations have deployed are fit for purpose. For example, BlogWow, which is a straightforward replacement for the provisional blog tool (`http://bugs.sakaiproject.org/confluence/display/BW`), or JForum.

Even if you cannot find a tool for your purpose, the source code has the potential to act as an excellent hint for the best way to attack specific issues. Therefore, this chapter includes a brief section on the most common way to build and run a project in your test environment.

Pros and cons

Sakai's strength stems from the community support. If you have a common problem that others have already partially addressed, then it is worth contacting the original authors and suggesting collaboration. This approach builds up the central value rather than diffusing and repeating effort. However, for a number of the smaller tools, expect little documentation and even less support. This may sound negative, but in part is not. Developers place their prototypes and proofs of concept in Contrib and sometimes these seeds grow into fully-fledged and welcomed functionality or die. The process supports a quick and agile change. The software lifecycle does not strangle innovation—rather it gives space to the community for exploration. That said, there are a number of gotchas with using Contrib:

1. You will need to verify the license of the code.

2. Many of the tools do not have any content viewable via the online help.

3. Another pain point is the range of versions of Sakai supported by any given piece of code. You can build Sakai via the Maven tool calling on the compiler in Java. However, there was a switch from Java 1.4 to Java 1.5 and Maven 1 to Maven 2 as Sakai jumped from version 2.4 to 2.5. Some of the Contrib tools still only support Maven 1 or specific versions of Sakai.

4. Currently, the main maintenance branch of Sakai is 2-5-x and soon it will be 2-6-x. A number of institutions are still running 2-4-x and will upgrade in the course of their own organization's lifecycle. Therefore, expect some of the contributed tools to build properly only on the old tags due to the needs of the local institutes that developed the tools.

5. The Sakai enterprise tools support three database types, including an in-memory database used for demonstration purposes. A number of tools, including Etudes, do not support the in-memory database, which in turn implies that the tools do not function properly with the Sakai demonstration.

6. The quality of documentation and support varies from being able to buy in hosting to dead and forgotten code with no README.

7. The Performance Work Group or the acidic nature of real-life deployment has exposed scalability issues for a couple of the core tools, such as searching for members in sites. The Performance Work Group has then optimized and removed the problems. However, for the least well-known tools, this proof under fire or performance testing has not occurred yet and there may well be hidden bottlenecks waiting to pounce at unexpected moments.

The list of potential pitfalls reinforces the point that for any large-scale deployments make sure that your quality assurance team has tested the code thoroughly.

On a positive note, scanning the contributed section regularly gives you early warning of the tools that are likely to make it to Provisional and then later to Enterprise Core.

A list of tools

The following table lists a variety of tools that are identified in from within Confluence along with their purposes. Confluence has mixed small distinct tools with only a few hundred lines of code with large projects. Notice that the Sakai Library project (`http://dlib.indiana.edu/projects/sakai/`) has already delivered the citation tool and due to the massive pace of development will further develop better integration with generic library systems. Notice also that a number of large-scale deployments have integrated the tools from Etudes. As of December 2008, Mneme, used for assessments, has won a prestigious $50,000 Mellon Award for Technology Collaboration (MATC). This is a good hint about the quality of the Etudes product range.

Base URL: `http://bugs.sakaiproject.org/confluence/display`

Name	Category	Brief Description
Agora	Conferencing	A simple-to-use and powerful online meeting tool
Assignments 2	Tool replacement	A second generation of the assignments tool
BlogWow	Tool replacement	Blogging
Breeze Link	Integration	Connector to a Breeze (Adobe Connect) server
CANS `http://cansaware.com/`	Integration	Integration with an external Context-aware Activity Notification System
Clustering with Terracotta	Integration	This project cluster-enables Sakai to support session failover using Terracotta.
Conditional Release	Enhancement	Adds workflow to control when certain learning artifacts are released.

Name	Category	Brief Description
Config Viewer / Config Editor	Administration	The Config Viewer displays a list of available properties along with a host of value-added data. The editor allows editing of properties.
Edia Tools `http://www.edia.nl`	Tools Enhancements	A number of tools and enhancements donated back to the community, including a live demo on USB, Skin manager, Google map integration, web classes
Elluminate	Integration	Integrates Elluminate Live, a commercial elearning and collaboration suite, with Sakai via a tool
Evaluation System	Enhancement	Enables online Course and Instructor Ratings
Feed Tool	Tool	The feed tool allows users to quickly see an aggregate set of events posted in their Workspace from all the sites of which they are members.
Form Builder	Tool	A graphical user interface for creating XSD files for use in ePortfolios
Goal Management	Tools	The tools enable users to create goal sets within worksites.
I10NSTATS	Command line	A tool for analyzing the status of the Sakai translations in the source repository and generating a report.
LAMS	Integration	Provides a lightweight integration between Sakai and the LAMS environment. The integration supports single sign-on, and the ability to access and start authoring LAMS sequences from a Sakai tool.
Mneme, JForum, Melete `http://etudes.org`	Tool replacements Tools	High quality award winning tools for lesson building, forums and tasks, tests, and surveys
MySakai	Improved user experience widgets	MySakai is a collection of projects that aim to make Sakai more user-centered and improve the user experience.
News Feeds	Tool	A news feed aggregator

Name	Category	Brief Description
OpenSyllabus	Tool	OpenSyllabus is a model-based Syllabus Editor.
Questions and Answers	Tool	Enables students to ask questions anonymously, which can be answered by other students or lecturers or tutors
SakaiAdminX	Administration	A web application that seeks to simplify and ease Sakai administrative tasks
SakaiLibrary `http://dlib.indiana.edu/projects/sakai/`	Integration Tool	A project to integrate Licensed Library Resources
Sakai Groovy Shell	Administration	The Sakai Groovy Shell projects allow you to execute Groovy code within Sakai.
The Sakai Electronic Lab Notebook for Research and Groupwork (SENRG)	Tool	The tool is intended to act as a replacement for traditional notebooks.
Sign-Up	Tool	A tool that allows users to organize office hours, review sessions, study groups, and similar activities
SiteStats	Tool	A tool for showing site usage statistics
Solo	Client side tool Offline	The Solo tool makes Announcements, Resources, and Melete lessons available to learners offline.
Sousa	Tool	The Sousa project is aimed at creating simple, sequenced content for delivery to a student.
Wimba `http://www.wimba.com/`	Integration	Integration code to the commercial Wimba collaborative learning software

The table only captures a large subset of the full range of code that is free and wandering in the wild. A distinct population of code sits in Contrib but the code authors have simply not mentioned it in Confluence. The authors have hidden a subset of the code because it is only used for specific institutes' needs. Examples of this are provider code for log on, course creation, system integrations, and integration with legacy systems. Some code is not placed in the central Subversion, but rather locally, because the developers do not think it is ready for prime-time use and aren't ready to support the code for a wider audience that may expect time and resources that the local organization cannot easily allocate.

This chapter will mention two example institutes and shines a light on their choices. The chapter then briefly describes how to compile a generic tool, followed by an interview with Stephen Githens, a toolmaker and rapid writer of useful code.

Example deployments

Unless your institute is aggressively ambitious, when deploying Sakai for the first time it is sensible to keep the range of additional tools to a minimum. The more code there is, the more code you will need to verify and the more configuration possibilities exist. This minimalistic mentality ensures the greatest opportunity for stability and lowers the risks of random calls at random times for those poor administrators that are so very busy in the engine rooms shovelling coal.

Sometimes the balance is difficult to find. Tools such as Evaluations beg for deployment due to their wealth of enhanced pedagogically supportive functionality and wide-scale deployment by well-known universities around the world. Even under these circumstances, test thoroughly first before deployment. Bringing administrators in early at this point increases their specific tool-related skill levels before the noise of daily battle.

During the course of time, as administrators and key personnel start to understand the deployment's personality; you can then fulfil extra requirements and pent up end-user demand in part by appropriate selection of extra tools and additional integrations.

Luckily, this restrictive mentality is not necessary for your development or demonstration environments. You may well want all the tools from Contrib possibly turned on and allow free range for creativity. A luxurious in-between ground is to look at what others have done with these seductive optional extras, knowing that other institutes have done some preselection and quality assurance. This makes for a significant short cut to discovering a quality solution, standing on the shoulders of giants.

This section briefly outlines two sets of choices. The first is from the University of Michigan and based the list on an email interview with David Haines, a senior developer working hard on Sakai since its very beginning. The University of Michigan originally donated core parts of the initial code base of Sakai and the university has been involved in the project since the start.

The second list is surreptitiously stolen from an email from David Howitz to the developers Work Group distribution list. Not only has David Howitz won a Sakai fellowship, he works daily with Sakai in the field at the University of Cape Town. The Sakai deployment is known as Vula (`https://vula.uct.ac.za/portal/`) and Cape Town is an early and aggressive deployer. For the extra pain of initial coughs and colds, they gain functionality early; have greater moral weight in the community, which translates into quicker responses to bug and, just as importantly, feature requests; and gain a significant standing and voice in the community. At the time of writing, Stephan Marquard, another fellow Cape Towner, was voted onto the Sakai Board in part in recognition of the experience and respect from the community that he has built up under these, at times, testing conditions.

The University of Michigan

The next table lists the extra pieces of functionality deployed at Michigan. The table does not include integrations to legacy systems, and, due to the fast pace of change, is no doubt different from reality at the time of reading. Notice that the administrator only sees SASH and Config-viewer (both tools are explained later in the chapter).

Name	Purpose
Config-Viewer	The Config Viewer displays a list of available properties along with a host of value-added data. The editor allows editing of properties.
Course Evaluation	Enables online course and instructor ratings
iTunesU	Make podcasts available through the iTunes store
Melete	A lesson builder
(`http://www.etudes.org`)	
Mneme — Test Center	Tasks, tests, and surveys
(`http://www.etudes.org`)	

Name	Purpose
SASH	HTML terminal inside Sakai where Groovy scripts can be run ad hoc
Sakai Portlets	Enables deployment of JSR 168 portlets within Sakai
Textbook Tool	A tool to allow students to find and sell textbooks

The Contrib base URL is `https://source.sakaiproject.org/contrib/`.

The Config-Viewer tool `https://source.sakaiproject.org/contrib/config-viewer`, is necessary for any budding administrator to have. It allows viewing a large number, and definitely the majority, of configuration setting and properties and their purposes within Sakai and its various supported versions. The main effort in producing the tool is not the coding of the tool itself, but rather collecting the definitions across a large and malleable code base.

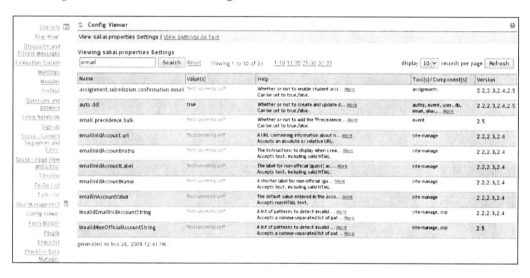

Each time the Foundation releases a new Sakai version, new properties emerge and old properties die, and the mainstream stays the same in purpose. Due to time pressures, some developers forget to pass on these changes. Until recently, Anthony Hopkins has been very active in maintaining definitions. However, he has recently been headhunted and is no longer working directly within the Sakai community. It will be interesting to see if anyone picks up the challenge of keeping this tool up-to-date. Automation of property gathering is difficult, as the definitions lie scattered in many places. For a new administrator, it is well worth browsing values using the tool and reading the underlying meaning. If a particular attribute's purpose is not clear, you can always try to find it by searching Confluence, and as a fallback, a generic search engine such as Google.

A second tool, the Config-Editor tool, also allows direct changes to global settings.

Sakai-Portlets enables the deployment of **JSR 168** standardized portlets within Sakai. A portlet follows conventions that make it interchangeable between portal systems that follow the same standard. The big plus is that this enhancement implies that developers can at times write a Sakai tool as a portlet, and then reuse it in other portals later or vice versa. The downside is that the standard constrains the tool's potential for interaction as it defines a minimum set of events, such as clicking on the close or minimize buttons, whereas most tools would like to respond to a wider range of actions.

Podcasting and the use of MP3 players such as iPod to record lectures live is a low-cost and low learning-barrier way to deliver lecture content, scheduled over the Internet. With RSS support, users can view live bookmarks in most web browsers. As this tool becomes more popular, you can imagine expansive functional growth such as specialized indexing for easily finding a particular moment in a lecture, and the repackaging and synchronization of content with presentational material and handouts.

The form builder is a supporting tool for Open Source Portfolio. It deskills the creation of portfolio-specific forms to a level that most of us can understand, rather than keeping this as a specialised task for the deployment team. Again, the developers have not supplied this tool for the end user.

SASH is a tool close to my heart and I use all the time. It supplies a command line-like terminal through your web browser, which allows you to run scripts. It has value for developers who wish to try out pieces of code live on a test-only server before codifying in a specific application. For administrators, there are built-in commands for adding, modifying, and deleting sites or users. Steven has built the tool with a plug-in architecture that allows interested parties to expand the set of commands SASH recognises.

The Textbook tool fulfils a specific student need of finding and selling textbooks.

The Evaluation tool (`http://bugs.sakaiproject.org/confluence/display/ EVALSYS/`) empowers an institution to measure, evaluate, and rate courses based on student feedback.

Instructors have the ability to create an evaluation and the students fill it out. The ease of use within Sakai enables instructors to manage their own set of questions, which are generally part of a wider combined end-of-term evaluation. This methodology enables organizations to collect targeted information from their students, while preserving a consistent set of questions used throughout the institution.

QNA, the question and answer tool, enables the setting of questions by site owners. The tool uses a student-centered approach to learning, where students can set and answer questions. Who can write the questions and who can answer depends on how the site owner has set it up. One method is to allow teachers and teaching assistants to write questions and students to answer them. Another more student-centered approach is to allow students to write questions that other students who wish to help can answer. The tool is compact, but its functionality is compelling. You can imagine a link into the grading book or expansion as an FAQ generator later.

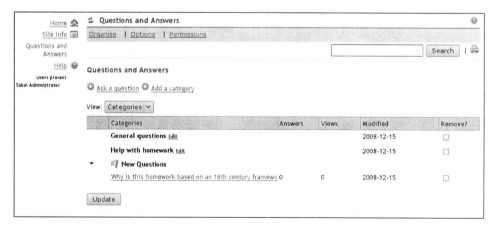

The tools (JForum, Melete, Mneme) from Etudes are all heavily deployed all around the world, well built, and feature rich. They do not work with the in-memory database of the demonstration version of Sakai, but run highly reliably with specific versions of MySQL and Oracle.

Etudes, Inc. is a non-profit organization that leads open source software development of learning, assessment, and collaboration tools. Additionally, Etudes offers centralized hosting, support, site and account management, and professional development opportunities to higher education institutions and other organizations.

The offerings follow their own lifecycle and QA track, but one should consider the tools as valued and as stable as the Enterprise core tools. I would personally advise any new to Sakai organization to try them out as part of the prerequisite market research before making any buy-in decisions.

Etudes offers support and hosting, including a convenient package per course. This may very well be a cost-effective approach for testing the waters when adding additional functionality.

It is hardly surprising that the University of Michigan has selected both Melete and Mneme; not only has Mneme won a prestigious Mellon Award for Technology Collaboration (MATC) (`http://matc.mellon.org`), and through this has had an extra $50,000 dollars injected for further development, but also Michigan was significantly involved in the tool's creation. To quote the press release (`http://etudesproject.org/cgi-bin/news/news.cgi?news=1&num=40`):

> *"Mneme is an open source development effort that was launched by the Etudes team in February of 2007 — collaboration between Foothill College and the University of Michigan to respond to critical assessment needs by the Etudes and Sakai user communities. Joseph Hardin, University of Michigan, Chair of the Sakai Board of Directors at the time, assigned Software Architect, Glenn Golden to work closely with Vivie Sinou, now CEO of Etudes, and lead the architectural design and development of Mneme."*

Interview with David Haines, Senior Developer at Michigan

Who is David Haines and what is his relationship with Sakai?

Initially a developer funded by the original Mellon grant. Currently, I am a senior developer for CTools, the University of Michigan instance of Sakai.

What is CTools?

CTools is the brand name of the Sakai installation at the University of Michigan. While we have a few locally developed tools, the majority of tools available in CTools are standard Sakai tools.

Are any of the tools in CTool in Contrib?

ItunesU is a tool to administer and deliver local podcasts on iTunes. We have others under development.

How does the University of Michigan use the SASH tool?

We use SASH to run a Groovy script we upload to resources. SASH is just used to start it running in a Sakai environment. This has proven very useful for local specific changes that do not justify building a complete tool. In particular, we have used it several times to add new tools to a user's My Workspace.

We are very careful to limit access to SASH. It allows the user to do anything from a script so it makes Sakai very vulnerable if it is installed on a public server. When we need it, we install it on a private server and only leave it installed as long as it takes to do the required task.

The University of Cape Town

As you can expect from an ambitious and consistent early adopter such as Cape Town, the tool extras, mentioned in the following table, have similarities with Michigan and a few more goodies besides. Commonality includes the Evaluation tool, Config-Viewer, Melete, and form builder. In addition, there are skin-manager, sakai-maps from Edia (`www.edia.nl`), and integration to LAMS, and an anti-plagiarism system called Turnitin.

Name & Location	Purpose
Evaluation	Enables online Course and Instructor ratings
Turnitin `http://turnitin.com`	Integrates with an anti-plagiarism system
Sitestats	A tool for showing site usage statistics
skin-manager	Manages different looks and feels

Name & Location	Purpose
sakai-maps	Google Maps overlay to Wiki
Config-Viewer	Configuration view of Sakai global properties
LAMS	LAMS integration
Melete	Etude lesson builder
Formbuilder	A simple-to-use builder for OSP forms
QNA	Question and answer tool
sakai-feeds	Allows users to quickly see an aggregate set of events posted from all of the user's Sakai sites
BlogWow	A blog replacement with extra functionality
test-center	Etudes Muse, tasks, tests, and surveys
Timeline	Tool for generating timelines

The newsfeed tool (`http://bugs.sakaiproject.org/confluence/display/NFS/`) is a dynamic Web 2.0 news aggregator that allows fast rendering of specific views of the news based on how old the content is or by title, details, or fully displayed. It builds using the recipe just mentioned and you can find the source code at `https://source.sakaiproject.org/contrib/ufp/sakai-feed`.

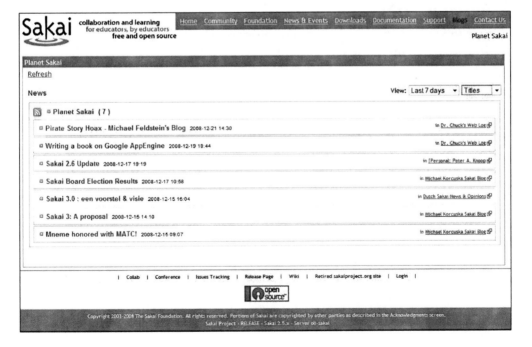

Currently, the Sakai Foundation web site is using the tool to render a view of Planet Sakai, which itself is a choice aggregation of the blogs of key players in the Sakai community. See: `http://sakaiproject.org/portal/site/sakai-blog`.

BlogWow is a competitor and drop-in replacement for the current provisional blogging tool. It has enticing enhancements, including the use of RSF, which makes it visually appealing. Although BlogWow has not gone through a formal QA, it is widely deployed.

The timeline tool makes it easy to generate and deploy timelines (`http://simile.mit.edu/timeline/`) from within a site. This implementation of timelines is online and interactive. The intended audiences are faculty and students at liberal arts campuses with a preference for visual and/or kinesthetic modes of information presentation. However, I expect history students, project managers, and other audiences to benefit from such enabling and visually self-describing functionality.

 The next section describes the most common way to build a contributed tool. After this, there are descriptions of specific tools written through the perspective of the code creators.

Creating tools

This section looks at building tools from source code and later describes an Eclipse plug-in called AppBuilder that can kick-start the creation of your own tools.

Building tools

To give an interested reader with some basic Java knowledge a head start, an approach to downloading and deploying tool source code is described.

Please note: this chapter makes the basic assumption that you have previously installed Maven, Subversion, and Java and have a connection to the Internet.

The majority of tools build in the same way. First, this section describes the build recipe in words and then in actions for the question and answer tool. For a developer, a working recipe is first to retrieve the source code and then to build the demonstration version of the code. After that, you can deploy the demonstration package. The important point to realize is that you need the source code and binary of your server on the same machine.

Next, download the source code of the particular tool in question, placing it inside the root directory of the source code for Sakai, then build the tool, and finally, deploy into the runnable demonstration version.

Version dependence

The majority of the contributed tools are Sakai version dependent. The actively maintained code bases normally run well against a specific maintenance branch such as 2-5-x or 2-6-x.

To download the 2-5x maintenance branch:

```
svn co https://source.sakaiproject.org/svn/sakai/branches/sakai_2-5-x
```

To build a working demonstration in the pack-demo subdirectory:

```
cd sakai_2-5-x
mvn -Ppack-demo install
```

Next, move, unpack, and run the demonstration instance and verify in the log files that you have a working instance. Stop the running instance, go back to the root directory of Sakai, retrieve the newest version of the question and answer tool:

```
svn co https://source.sakaiproject.org/contrib/qna/tags/qna-1.0
cd qna-1.0
```

Please note that by the time you have read this book, there will be a newer version. Feel free to download that one instead and try it out.

Move into the top-level directory of the tool, build, and deploy via one Maven command, for example:

```
cd qna-1.0
mvn clean install sakai:deploy -Dmaven.tomcat.home=/home/alan/Sakai/
instances/sakai-2-5-x
```

Notice that the environment variable `maven.tomcat.home` points to the top-level directory of the demonstration version you have just run. This recipe works for most tools.

If the demonstration was still running when you deployed, then to make sure the tool works properly, you will need to restart your server. If not, you can still select the tool during site creation, but once you click on the tools link within that site you will see an error message similar to:

```
[INFO] ------------------------------------------------------------
------
[INFO] BUILD SUCCESSFUL
[INFO] ------------------------------------------------------------
------
[INFO] Total time: 44 seconds
[INFO] Finished at: Mon Dec 15 15:16:37 GMT+01:00 2008
[INFO] Final Memory: 41M/312M
 [INFO] ------------------------------------------------------------
-------
```

```
org.sakaiproject.portal.api.PortalHandlerException: java.lang.
NullPointerException
    at org.sakaiproject.portal.charon.SkinnableCharonPortal.doGet(Skinnab
leCharonPortal.java:891)
caused by: java.lang.NullPointerException
```

After creating a site with your new tool enabled and clicking on the link to the tool, you should now see a screen similar to the last figure.

Read the README

Before compiling any tool, it is important to read the Readme or its equivalent. For example, for the sitestats tool you can find excellent advice at: `Contrib /ufp/sitestats/branches/ sitestats_2.5.x/README.TXT`.

In the case of sitestats, there is a general permission that needs to be granted by an administrator via the Realms tool. Without that nudge, the tool would appear to have failed, when perfect functioning was only a matter of configuration.

If any particular tool exists without basic documentation, consider this a strong hint about its quality.

Sakai Electronic Lab Notebook for Research and Groupwork (SENRG)

For bonus points, you can compile and deploy the Sakai Electronic Lab Notebook for Research and Groupwork (SENRG) `https://source.sakaiproject.org/contrib/senrg/`.

SENRG enables the user to take notes and store them in a tree structure. This functionality is particularly useful within laboratory and large lecture settings and the contributors intended that the tool be a replacement for the traditional notebook.

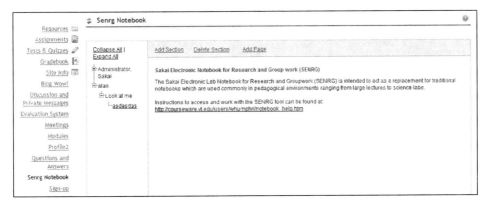

SASH

The SASH tool `https://source.sakaiproject.org/contrib/sakaiscript/sash/trunk` enables administrators and developers to programmatically interact live with the underlying services in Sakai. The tool user is presented with an HTML terminal where commands and scripts can be run. The tool can pick up text file scripts from resources and run them.

The terminal is very useful. As a developer, you can explore services and write code fragments and if the code fragments are good enough, you can run them from a text file. For an administrator, there are several built-in tasks and the list is expanding. For example, you can add, delete, and modify sites or users.

In a real-world situation, SASH is excellent for ad hoc changes such as changing site permissions or running prewritten Groovy scripts. Its flexibility is a significant strength that enables agile administration without the necessity of restarting a server. However, for security reasons, do not deploy it directly into production, but rather on a secure server without end users.

For the SASH tool, there is only one main developer and that is Stephen Githens. Now it is true that within his body there is enough energy to power a couple of teams or nuclear reactors; however, he cannot always focus his attention on a pet project. Therefore, if you wish to use this tool vigorously under fire it would be helpful to volunteer some development person hours back for any new function requirements you expect to have fulfilled.

Interview with Steven Githens, the force behind SASH

Steven can you tell us a little about who you are and what you do?

> I'm an open source software developer and advocate. I grew up in the Upper Peninsula of Michigan and studied Computer Science and Bioinformatics at Michigan Tech. In addition to coding, I am a big fan of distance running, playing mandolin, and various forms of activism.

Why did you build SASH?

> While I love GUIs I went to school with a traditional Unix background (half of the lab machines ran Linux, the other half Solaris), and I generally enjoy using the command line quite a bit—there is a fascinating element of timelessness to it, the same sort of timelessness I find when I play traditional fiddle tunes on the mandolin. There is a depth and understanding to really be appreciated there.

> So that's part of it. Also, since I do view Sakai as more than a web page, and as a Service Oriented Architecture that has many of the same qualities as those of an operating system, I think it needs a terminal.

What is the target audience for the tool?

This falls into three general categories:

System administration: It is very easy to write new SASH commands and it makes doing things such as adding admins, users, and sites, very easy. You can list the contents of folder in the content repository. Almost anything you would use a shell for on a Unix box applies here.

Development and debugging: Using any number of dynamic JVM languages (Jython, JRuby, Lisp, and so on) makes it very easy to test your code, as well as explore the APIs for existing services.

Education and just plain fun: I occasionally envision that this could eventually be used for Computer Science and programming courses, that is, if SASH could be tooled to operate in a safe and secure way for access by students.

There are several very complete implementations of the Scheme language that run on the JVM, for example Jython is a very good Python implementation, and since these are often used in introductory programming courses, it would make sense for students to be able to upload, run, and submit them inside their Course Site. Also, it's incredibly fun for me to work on all the different pieces that are required to implement a terminal shell.

Have you example usages in the wild you wish to share?

I think most usage so far has been for development and debugging purposes, which a number of individuals have found very useful. I think eventually it will be used for more admin tasks on production instances, but it's something that needs to be carefully tested, vetted, and processed to ensure it meets the security, stability, and integrity required for live systems. We are making good progress towards this.

What is the future of SASH?

One of the things that really excited me about a DHTML-based terminal was the ability to put more than text in the responses. Therefore, a finger command might actually include the photo of the person embedded in the output. The return output from a `upload /home/sgithens` command might actually put a browser upload button in the response line that I can use to pick a file to upload, and then would disappear after upload; that sort of thing. Very soon, there will also be support for launching other "things" from the terminal. I envision it will be able to launch installed widgets, gadgets, and whatnot, and that these could be easily embedded in the return output from commands.

In addition, I intend to keep moving closer to Bash-like syntax and functionality. A larger portion of the SASH core is now in Jython, which is speeding this up. For instance, the ability to redirect output to a file in Resources is nearly working and should be available shortly. I would also like to be able to stream output from long-running commands. The number of languages you can write scripts and commands in will expand. Currently, Jython, Groovy, and BeanShell are supported. JRuby and Rhino are low-hanging fruit here. I also would like at least one Lisp-like language, probably one of the Scheme implementations. Support for interactive prompting is also underway.

AppBuilder

Eclipse (`http://www.eclipse.org`) is one of the best-known and loved programmer's IDEs for Java. In general, Sakai programmers use Eclipse to support their tool creation efforts and it is a core assumption for the tutorials associated with the programmer's café. The tutorial writers mentioned setting up Eclipse for the first time as part of the introductory programmer's café (`http://bugs.sakaiproject.org/confluence/display/BOOT/Development+Environment+Setup+Walkthrough`).

A significant and welcome shortcut to the tool development cycle and one that eliminates many repetitive steps is to use an Eclipse plug-in that has the power to build the basic structure of a Sakai tool project. Aaron Zeckoski has written and maintains the AppBuilder. For basic details, please visit `http://bugs.sakaiproject.org/confluence/display/BOOT/Sakai+App+Builder`. The key point to note for motivated Eclipse users is that the location to install the plug-in from is `http://source.sakaiproject.org/appbuilder/update` via the usual update mechanism.

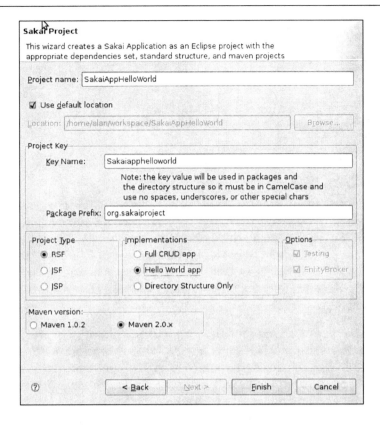

Within a few keystrokes and a click on the **Finish** button, you can generate your first simple working application or fully-fledged Create, Read, Update, and Delete (CRUD) application.

Notice that JSF, JSP, and RSF are all technologies that include components that are used for generating GUI parts of web pages.

As Aaron is an energetic contributor to Sakai and is heavily involved in the creation of the core frameworks, you can expect as Sakai evolves that the AppBuilder will evolve as well.

The following sections are written about tools from the eyes of those involved closely with the specific tool at hand. If anything, by the time you have read the sections and discovered the differences in writing style, you should go away with the feeling that there are a lot of motivated and knowledgeable individuals working towards the betterment of Sakai.

Sousa—Content authoring and delivery for Sakai

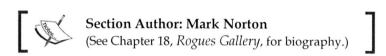

Section Author: Mark Norton
(See Chapter 18, *Rogues Gallery*, for biography.)

What is Sousa?

Sousa is a set of content authoring and delivery tools for Sakai. It pulls together many ideas from online learning, training applications, interactive context exploration, and material that supplements classroom lectures (so called blended learning). In particular, it draws on the concept of Learning Structures (http://www.nolaria.com/archi/LSWhitePaper.htm). Learning Structures define different access and sequencing methods, as well as template-based page descriptions.

Sousa can also be seen as a kind of toolkit or platform where you can experiment with proven and new approaches to pedagogy. It has extensible architecture that allows new kinds of media objects to be added easily. Sousa currently supports structured and unstructured text, many different kinds of image formats, audio, video, Flash, and tabular data based on comma-separated value files. These will be expanded in the future to include Flash, markup languages such as MathML, CML, and MusicML, simulations, virtual labs, and so on.

Currently, two kinds of structures are used to deliver Sousa content: pages and sequences. Pages (described using XML) contain a set of content objects (for example, text, media) organized and laid out for display. Layout uses a 2x2 table of cells that enable basic section and column organization. Sequences describe a linear presentation of Sousa pages, though other kinds of sequences are planned (branching, remediated, random access). In the long term, an additional high-level object called a module will allow sequences to be packaged together for easy installation and use.

From a technical perspective, Sousa consists of two Sakai tools written in Java using Reasonable Server Faces (RSF) for presentation and a set of application services used to model both pages and sequences. RSF has proven to be a powerful and easy-to-use user interface system that enables rapid development of Sousa features including file upload and presentation of media objects. I implemented the Sousa Sequence Service on top of the Sakai Content Hosting service, which is used to persist media objects, Sousa pages, and Sousa sequences.

Sousa is freely available to all Sakai users at `https://source.sakaiproject.org/contrib/mnorton/sousa/`. Developers are invited to participate in the project. User and technical documentation are available at `http://confluence.sakaiproject.org/confluence/display/SOUSA/Home`.

An Interview with Mark Norton

Who are you and how are you involved in Sakai?

I'm an independent software consultant working in higher education on technology-based teaching and learning. Since 2003, I've worked on a number of high-profile projects including the Tuft's VUE project, IMS Global Learning specifications, the Open Knowledge Initiative, and (of course) Sakai. I have been part of the Sakai project since its kickoff in February of 2004. In the early days of Sakai, I helped to lead the Sakai Educational Partnership Program and served as technical liaison to Sakai architecture and user interface design. I have done a lot of technical training of Sakai developers. More recently, I have worked on a number of high-profile Sakai projects for MIT, UC Berkeley, and several major US publishers.

Which tools have you placed in Contrib?

Besides Sousa, I have developed a set of web services for the Content Hosting Service, an installer for OCW (OpenCourseWare) content formatted as IMS Common Cartridges, and a null portal that allows MIT's Stellar course management system to use Sakai tools.

Have you any plans for those tools?

I will be doing more work on the OCW installer in early 2009. I am also hoping to integrate Fluid's Reorder component into Sousa in 2009, as well as continue to add new features.

What is your motivation creating Contrib tools?

I am in a unique position to be able to take action on perceived Sakai needs. Rather than just talk about it, I can (as time allows) design and develop applications. I find that writing code is a good way to learn about new technologies. Sousa and other contributed applications allow me to explore new Java libraries and see how they might be more broadly used for Sakai development. All that aside, I enjoy writing code.

Have you any suggestions for new committers, such as links, best practices, methods of support and so on?

As much as possible, Sakai developers should try to use established best practices. These include database persistence, internationalization, accessibility, and well-formed user interfaces that conform to Sakai standards and styles. Most of these practices are described in `http://confluence.sakaiproject.org/confluence/display/SCP/Criteria+for+Supported+Status`. Beyond that, I'd encourage new developers to be engaged with the community via email lists and Sakai conferences. Present your work!

People want to hear about it.

Edia

Section Author: Jaeques Koeman (1978) has a background in Social Science Informatics and is a business developer and project manager at Edia. Earlier in his career, he gained experience in many educational innovation projects in Dutch higher education during his former function as project manager of ICT at the University of Amsterdam.

He currently co-coordinates the Dutch Sakai Special Interest Group and is a board member of Stichting Educatie Technologie and a board member at Academic Factory.

What is Edia?

Edia focuses largely on the development of custom functionality for Sakai. Edia has created a number of Sakai tools, many of which we contribute to the community as open source software under the ECL or LGPL license. Edia also offers tryout versions of all the tools on the increasingly popular demo-instance `http://sakaitools.edia.nl`.

The following part reviews some of the tools that have been developed by Edia. First, the Skin Manager is a tool to upload and manage Sakai skins using delegated administrators. Second, the Sakai Maps tool integrates Google Maps with Sakai, offering an interface to manage points of interest. Third, the Sakai Fedora Research tool allows researchers to manage collections of data in a community. The last tool that I will discuss is the Web Course tool, which provides an easy way to set up and populate Sakai sites for distance education.

Skin Manager

Initiative: Edia
License: LGPL
Users: Admin/maintain

Edia supported a number of departments in creating community sites in the Sakai instance of the University of Amsterdam. We offered each department a custom look and feel based on a Sakai skin. As the number of skins within the instance grew, and each skin had to be added by accessing the Sakai file system, the whole process of managing skins became rather bothersome. However, the use case for building the skin manager was just as simple as it was necessary: How can skins be added by people without root access? The result became a tool that allows users to upload .zip archives with the style sheets and images. It also has the ability to upload new versions or revert to older (deleted) ones. The figure below shows skin details and information on the sites that use a particular skin.

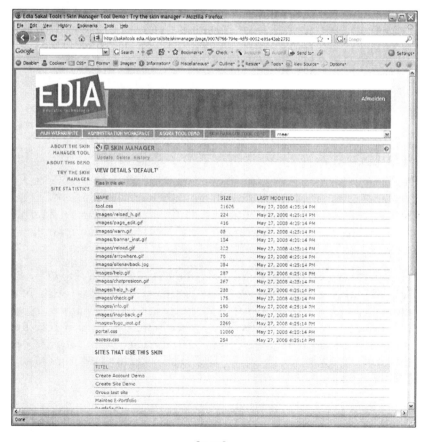

Sakai Maps

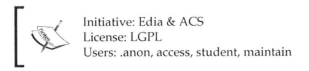

Initiative: Edia & ACS
License: LGPL
Users: .anon, access, student, maintain

The Amsterdam Centre for Conflict Studies (ACS) has been a significant driver of many principles underlying the Sakai Community platform at the University of Amsterdam. As part of a public Sakai Community site with collaboratively-written Wiki texts about various conflicts, the Sakai maps tool was developed. Wiki pages support the collaborative writing of conflict descriptions nicely, but as the database of descriptions grow, a Wiki lacks adequate classification and representation functions to order the descriptions of different conflicts. Since all conflicts have a geographical aspect, the idea was born to use Google Maps as an overlay for the Wiki. The result was an integration of Google Maps with Sakai: Sakai Maps. Instructors can define points of interests (POI) on the map and relate those to wiki pages, URLs, or resources. In addition, the type of markers can be set. The next figure shows the instructor view on POI.

Fedora tool

 Initiative: Library & Department of Psychology UvA
License: ECL
Users: .anon, access, maintain

The development of the Fedora tool for Sakai was partly funded by the Dutch SURF Foundation within the SurfShare program on virtual collaboration to support exchange between researchers. The department of psychology provided the use case with a collection of psychological test data spanning over 40 years. By joining the community site, researchers are allowed to browse metadata and request download of datasets of interest. Datasets consist of multiple data streams, including raw SPSS data. The following figure shows the selection and request of a particular dataset found in the repository. After an authorization by the department, researchers can download data in multiple formats. New or altered datasets may be contributed. The Fedora tool supports browsing and (generic) search. Future plans with this tool include user-defined (meta) data profiles, making it a generic tool to support researchers from other fields.

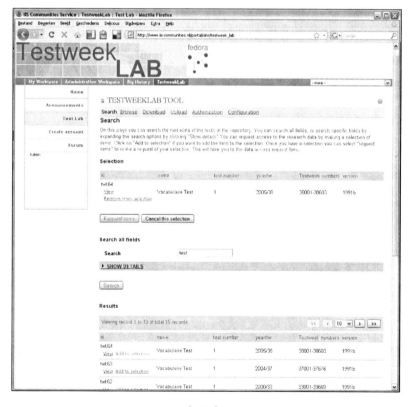

Web course tool

Initiative: Edia & Communication Services UvA
License: LPGL
Users: .anon, access, student, maintain

Edia supports the University of Amsterdam in a unique project where scholars follow short distance courses as part of their orientation in a field of study after high school. Architecture was needed to publish available courses, allow subscriptions to courses, and to automatically populate those courses with subscribed scholars. The instructors of a web class can select a period in which the course is given and what the maximum number of participants will be, and open the course for subscription. Additional options include automatic enrollments and removal of participants. Scholars who want to follow a web course can browse available courses and (un)subscribe to courses that are available. The tool is designed for distance education, but it is generic enough to be used for any Sakai course for any type of education. The following two figures show the Web Course tool for different users. The first screen grab shows how an instructor can select a Sakai site and open it for registration, and the second one shows how a student can search and register for an available course.

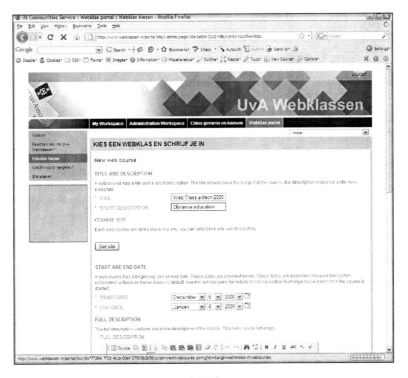

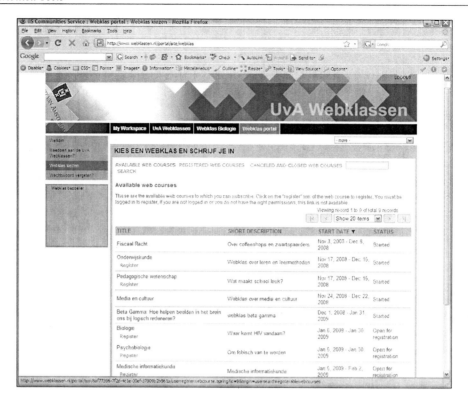

Open Syllabus

Section Author: Jacques Raynauld is a faculty member at HEC Montréal. He holds a Ph.D. in Economics from Queen's University (Kinsgston, Canada). Since 2003, he has held the Chair on Teaching and Learning in Management Education. With his colleague Olivier Gerbé, he was in charge of the Zone Cours initiative and has developed numerous learning environments, both for university and high school students. He is also the director of MATI Montréal, a research center on technology and learning regrouping researchers from the University of Montreal campus.

The members of the Open Syllabus team are Pascale Blanc, Robert Bolduc, Mathieu Cantin, Claude Coulombe, Laurent Danet, Mame Awa Diop, Robert Gérin-Lajoie, Tom Landry, Yvette Lapa Dessap, Sacha Leprête, Remi Saïas, Vincent Siveton, and Emmanuel Vigne.

Syllabi are universal gateways to teaching and learning in universities. In many cases, syllabi take the form of a paper or electronic document (an MS Word doc or PDF), where the key aspects of the course are described: instructor information, course material, assessment and grading, course calendar, and so on. In other cases, syllabi are embedded in a course web site and can include numerous electronic resources (PowerPoint files, videos, URLs, and so on). Open Syllabus (OSyl) is a forthcoming Sakai tool that offers a comprehensive solution to syllabi or course web site authoring.

- OSyl is an XML model-based approach to syllabi in which all the information is organized and kept in a general semantic format that can accommodate most course web sites.

- OSyl organizes all the resources (files, citations, assignments, and so on), activities (quiz, forum, and so on) and other elements (description of the course, goals, assessment, news, and so on) through direct input of the content or links to specialized tools. Simple configuration rules can be set to reflect different university practices.

- OSyl interface is quick since it is based on the new AJAX/Google Web Tool Kit environment.

- OSyl course web sites are very flexible and can be shared, exported, printed, and archived easily.

- OSyl is built to take into account permission rights so any resource imbedded in an OSyl syllabus can be accessed by registered students only, colleagues, or by the general public as in the OpenCourseware initiative.

- OSyl can push any pedagogical information (description, learning goals, assessment, and so on) present in a syllabus to administrative systems for reporting or auditing purposes.

The following diagram shows an example of a possible syllabus structure and illustrates the approach and the flexibility of our tool. The syllabus, represented by the top square, is organized in three parts: an overview of the course content, the exams list, and the lectures list represented by black squares. Lectures have been sub-organized in two parts: Theme 1 and Theme 2. The content of lecture 1 has been itself divided in two parts: Part 1 and Part 2. Overview, exams, or lectures contain resources (white circles). Not all resources are used in the same way, so we created different contexts for particular use of a resource (black circles). Contexts are then grouped in containers (black diamonds). These containers may group resources into reusable modules. A container may reference another reusable module as shown at the bottom right of the diagram.

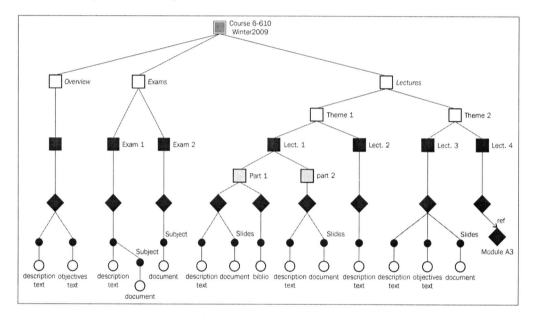

The next figure illustrates the Alpha version interface of OSyl. The menu bar is displayed horizontally on the top of the editing panel. The tree on the lefthand side represents the structure of the syllabus, while the content of Lecture 1, organized in rubrics, is displayed on the panel on the right. **Objectives, Description**, as well as any other resource, can be added by activating the **Add** command on the menu bar. Editing is done by clicking on the **Edit** command activated by passing the mouse cursor over the content to be modified.

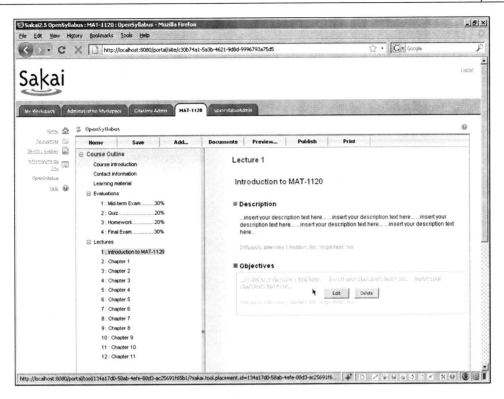

Open Syllabus is an improved version of ZoneCours, a system used at HEC Montréal since 2004. All HEC Montréal syllabi have the same interface and, in the spirit of the OpenCourseWare initiative, can be accessed through a unique portal at `http://zonecours.hec.ca`. ZoneCours was developed using Teximus Expertise, a proprietary environment. When it was decided to rewrite the application in Java, the idea of sharing ZoneCours in an open source community like Sakai was the logical next step.

Open Syllabus is based on the Google Web Toolkit technology. Since it creates JavaScript code and can use widget libraries, it could be integrated as a widget tool in most compliant environments, including the forthcoming Sakai 3.0. Planned functionalities include PDF printing of a summary syllabus, offline use by faculty and students, support for multiple sections, students as syllabus authors, management of Creative Commons licenses, and absolute and relative dates for easy migration across semesters. Updates on the project and releases can be obtained at `http://bugs.sakaiproject.org/confluence/display/OSYL/ OpenSyllabus+Home`. Open Syllabus is currently developed by HEC Montréal with the collaboration of the University of Montréal and Sakai Québec/CRIM.

Summary

Many tools in the wild are not included in the Enterprise code set. The source code of these tools is stored in part in the contributed section of the Sakai Foundation's Subversion repository (`https://source.sakaiproject.org/contrib`).

JForum, Melete, and Mneme from Etudes (`http://etudes.org`) are of the highest quality and deliver significant functionality.

Unlike the core tools in Sakai, Contrib tools vary in quality. Checking out what others have deployed and performing your own vigorous testing lowers production risks. I included in this chapter toolsets currently in place at the Universities of Michigan and Cape Town as a strong hint.

The SASH and Config-Viewer tools are for administers.

The AppBuilder plug-in for Eclipse lowers the initial cost and learning curve for creating your first Sakai tool.

If neither I nor others have mentioned any tool that you like in this book or in the Sakai confluence Wiki, I would advise that you update Confluence with pertinent information.

Individuals or small groups of individuals have written many of the tools; therefore, if you like a specific tool and wish to enhance its functionality, volunteering time and resources will help progress.

Chapter 9 discusses how to use tools in combination to create a better online learning experience.

9

Putting Sakai to Work

The fundamental determinants of course quality have always been, and remain, the course content, the instructor(s), the learning activities in which the students are engaged, and the students themselves.

We do not make any exaggerated promises about the transformative nature of technology in education. Technology like Sakai can be used to improve your course by allowing you and your students to do things that might have been impractical without the technology or by reducing the amount of time spent on administrative issues. But the tools Sakai provides are just that—tools—and unless they are used purposefully they will not make much of a difference. So it is most important for you to consider what you want to accomplish with your students and how the capabilities Sakai provides can support the course activities.

There is not a single "best" way of teaching. What works in a small graduate seminar in philosophy may not work in a large introductory computer science class, and what works for one instructor may not work for another. The good news is that Sakai is designed with this variety in mind.

The tools and structure of a Sakai site

You can think of Sakai as a framework that allows you to create the kind of online experience you want for your students. There is not a single way that a Sakai course site needs to function—it is ultimately up to you, with assistance from your Sakai user support team, to determine how the course is presented to the students online.

Still, there are common ways courses are structured as well as common activities (such as explaining a homework assignment) that take place in most classrooms. This chapter addresses how to best use Sakai to support these structures and activities.

Not all Sakai sites are used for courses. In many institutions, it is common to find Sakai used for research work groups and administrative collaboration. In fact, at many institutions, there are more "collaboration sites", as they are called in the Sakai community, than there are course sites. So, these types of sites are included in the overview.

Many institutions integrate Sakai with other enterprise systems—automatically creating a Sakai site for each course being taught, for example, and adding students who are registered for the course to the site. Other organizations require instructors to create a site online but, once that's created, students are added and removed based on data from the registrar's office.

Regardless of the type of course (or collaboration site) you might be teaching, there is a basic structure to Sakai that is useful to understand. This section describes that basic structure and common tools. It also gives you a quick and easy way to customize a Sakai site, so we recommend having a browser window handy with access to an instance of Sakai.

If you have not yet created a Sakai site or if you don't have access to an instance of Sakai at your organization, several Sakai Commercial Affiliates host trial versions of Sakai that you can access free of charge. Check www.sakaiproject.org for the current listing. At the time of writing, hosted trials were available from rSmart (http://sakaisandbox.com), Serensoft (http://sakaisthelimit.com), and Unicon (http://testdrivesakai.com). When you create your account, a site is automatically created for you.

Sakai's site structure

As explained earlier in this book, once you've logged into Sakai the top of the screen consists of a Sakai banner that contains your organization's branding and a logout button. Just below that banner is a series of tabs, one for each Sakai site that you are a member of. Every course or project consists of a Sakai site and is accessed by clicking a tab labeled with the name of the site. If you are a member of more than one site, you have more than one tab across the top of your screen.

If you have too many sites to fit, a More Sites menu (often renamed My Sites or My Active Sites) is present; it enables you to access the appropriate site. Always be sure you're in the correct site when you're doing your work.

My Workspace

There is also a tab called My Workspace, a special site that only you have access to. You use it to manage your preferences, store personal files, manage site memberships, and even provide a calendar that pulls information from all the Sakai sites to which you belong. Contact your local Sakai support team for more information about uses of My Workspace.

> You can modify which sites appear across the top of the page so that your most frequently accessed sites are a single click away. To do that, go to your My Workspace site and choose the Preferences tool. The Customize Tabs function enables you to change which sites are visible.

A basic Sakai site is a collection of tools that users have access to, typically presented to users in a sidebar on the left of the screen. In most Sakai installations, each link in the left sidebar corresponds to a single tool. To access the Assignments tool, for example, a user clicks the Assignments link in the sidebar. The Assignments tool then appears in the main content area of Sakai. In most cases, it is as simple as that.

The major exception to this rule is the site Home page. It is a significant exception because it is the first page you see when you access a site.

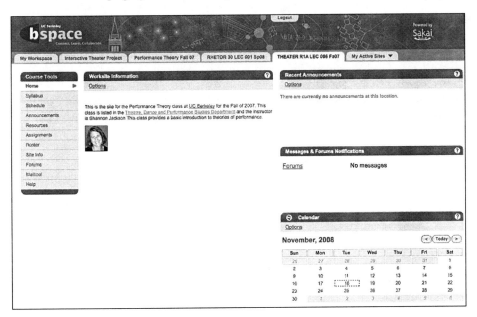

The Home tool contents

Unlike most tools, the Home tool is not a tool at all. It is really a summary page. It generally includes information pulled from several different tools. Sakai tries to be helpful by providing the most commonly useful information and, therefore, a typical course site Home page includes areas (called *panels*) that present the following information:

- A site description (a description of the course or project)
- Recent course announcements
- Recent discussion forum posts
- Recent chat messages
- A course calendar

Most of the panels on the Home page can be configured directly from the Home page. The Calendar panel, for example, allows you to specify whether the calendar is presented by week or by month. To add events to the Calendar, however, you need to use the Calendar tool itself. The Announcements panel lets you to determine how many recent announcements are shown (you can specify either a certain number of announcements or have the panel display announcements that have been created since a specific number of days in the past). Some panels enable you to edit the content itself. The Site Description panel, for example, provides an Options link that allows you to edit the content directly, obviating the need to access the tool directly.

Of course, if you are not planning to use a tool in your site you do not want its information panel to appear on the course Home page. If you are not going to make a chat room available in your course, for instance, you do not want your course Home page to include a summary of recent chat messages because that would make your site look unfinished.

Thankfully, Sakai is generally very smart about this—if you turn off the Chat tool in your site, the recent chat messages summary panel on the Home page simply disappears. Except for editing the Course Description content, you can mostly ignore the Home page and let Sakai take care of it for you.

To edit the Site Description, simply click on the **Options** button. There are four things you can do:

- Specify the title for the panel. A good title reflects the type of site you have (for example changing the default Site Description to Course Description or, better yet, Welcome to Theater 101).

- Create the content that appears in the body of the panel. An easy-to-use HTML editor enables you to enter whatever content you want. If you don't know HTML, the default WYSIWYG mode can be used like a simple word processor. Just type away using the built-in text styling buttons to add bold, italics, bulleted lists, and so on. You can also add images, hyperlinks, and tables quite easily. If you know HTML, you can use the source code mode to view and edit the HTML directly.

- Specify the height for the panel. You want to make the panel large enough so there is no scroll bar within the panel itself. This is easy if there is not another panel just below it. If there is, make the panel just large enough to hold your content but not so large that there is excessive white space between the panels. This may take a bit of trial and error.

- Enter a URL instead of writing content. If you already have an HTML page that describes the site published elsewhere, you can simply enter that web address. Sakai will display that page in the Site Description panel.

Then simply click **Update Options** to save the changes you've made. If you have access to Sakai, this would be a good time to try it out. Remember to ensure you are working in the correct site.

There are, certainly, many instructors who want their course Home page to appear in a very specific manner. There are risks to that level of customization—remember that your students are likely taking several courses at one time and they may benefit from a consistent Home page experience. Nonetheless, it is often quite appropriate to create a custom Home page. Later, you'll see a number of ways to significantly customize the appearance of your site, including the Home page. First, though, let's review tools to make available and just let the Sakai Home page do most of the work.

The basic collaboration tools

There are four basic tools that almost every Sakai site uses, regardless of whether it is a course or a collaboration site:

- Resources. The tool for storing files that can be accessed by other members of the site. You can create folders to organize these files, and even make certain files publicly viewable (such as a web page you want to show to those who aren't part of your site).

- Announcements. Use it to send announcements to members of the site. These announcements appear on the site Home page and can be sent to all site members via email.

- Email Archive. This tool provides a dedicated email address for your site (`mysitename@sakai.myschool.edu`, for instance). While permissions can be configured to make Sakai behave differently, typically members of your site can send email to this address and everyone belonging to the site will get the email. All emails are archived and accessible using the Email Archive tool.

- Calendar. Sometimes called Schedule, the Calendar tool allows you to put important events on a calendar. The Sakai Calendar supports recurring events and has different icons for different types of events such as class meetings, exams, and special events.

With these four easy-to-use tools, you can have a simple, effective online presence for your class or project.

Site administration

As a site owner, there are certain tasks that you may want to undertake to modify the site and/or the members of the site. The Site Info tool allows you to:

- Modify the tools available in your site, including modifying the order in which those tools appear in the toolbar and changing the names of the tools.

- Manage access to the site, including specifying whether individuals can join your site without your approval.

- Manage the membership of your site. What you can and cannot do with membership depends on your local Sakai installation and often varies based on organizational policies, but typically includes the capability to add and remove members and change the role of individual members.

- Manage groups of users in your site. Many Sakai tools have special features that allow you to work with a particular set of users inside your site. Groups and class sections are good examples of predefined groups that may be automatically created by your Sakai administrators. You can also create ad hoc groups for particular purposes. If you have project teams in your course, for example, it might be useful to create a group for each team.

- Import content from an existing site or export content from the current site to a new one.

As a site owner, you always have access to the Site Info tool. Depending on how you use Sakai and how Sakai is integrated with other systems on your campus, you may never use Site Info. Still, you should take a quick look to familiarize yourself with what is available to you.

 Every Sakai installation is different from every other. Your organization may not make the same Sakai tools available as another organization. This book mainly restricts itself to those tools that will be commonly available in installations of Sakai version 2.6.x, but there may be instances where we mention a tool that is not available in your instance of Sakai. In many cases, you can request these tools from your Sakai administrator. We also try to mention alternatives to the recommended tool where they exist.

The basic teaching and learning tools

In addition to the basic collaboration and administration tools, there are three tools that are commonly used in Sakai Course sites: Syllabus, Assignments, and Gradebook.

- Syllabus. Use this tool to put your syllabus (clear guidelines and expectations for your course) online. You can upload a document (such as a Microsoft Word document or a PDF), build a structured syllabus in Sakai, or even point to an existing syllabus you have posted online in another location. Regardless of how you use the tool, you can have Sakai automatically email students when you've made a change to the syllabus.

- Assignments. This tool allows you to create and post assignments that students can submit electronically. Using the tool can help eliminate paper assignments and reduce class time spent collecting and returning student work. It allows students to send questions about assignments and enables you to post online comments, grade assignments, and transfer grades to the Gradebook automatically. The tool lets you set opening and closing times for each assignment, supports resubmissions, and marks each student submission with a date and time stamp.

- Gradebook. The Gradebook tool allows instructors to record and compute cumulative student grades. Students can refer to the Gradebook to check their progress in a course. The Gradebook tool is often used hand-in-hand with the Assignments tool although they can be used separately.

With these three tools and the four basic collaboration tools reviewed earlier, you can create a solid online presence for your class. Students will get course announcements and can send and receive emails via the class email address and can check past messages online. You can post reading material and other resources for students online and build a course calendar to remind students of important events and deadlines. Your syllabus is available online and students are automatically updated with any modifications to it. You've provided a facility for students to submit their assignments electronically, and they can receive feedback on those assignments via Sakai as well. Their grades are computed online and they can check to see how they are doing at any time.

Now that you have your course's online infrastructure set up, we can begin to add some more sophisticated uses of online tools. We'll do this by turning our attention to the several common types of courses and discuss how a Sakai site can be structured to support each type of course.

Types of Sakai sites

There are more than four thousand universities and colleges in the United States alone. Each of these teaches hundreds or even thousands of classes every year. Trying to create some structure from such a diverse world would be an exercise in oversimplification. The categories discussed here along with the associated recommendations about how to support them in Sakai are not meant to be rules or even best practices but rather a place to start when thinking about structuring your Sakai site. Do read through all of the site types because it is likely that your course mixes the structures and activities in two or more site types. And your own personal comfort with technology will also determine how many (and which) tools you might want to use.

The site types you'll be working with are as follows:

- Problem-based courses
- Small discussion courses
- Large, introductory courses
- Project-based courses
- Collaboration sites

The following sections highlight a small number of tools that are especially useful in a site used for that purpose. Other tools are often useful as well, but because you're just starting out, you'll have more success using a few tools well. Still, we encourage you to read through all the class types and mix and match the tools you feel will work best for your situation.

Problem-based courses

A problem-based course presents learners with one or more problems to solve on a regular basis (weekly, for instance). The problems are presented by the instructor and generally have either correct answers (such as a Calculus problem set) or at least a fairly clear way to distinguish better solutions (such as an analysis of a poem in an English literature class). Problem-based courses are often targeted at developing skills related to the topic at hand and students are therefore asked to apply what they've learned by solving problems. Math courses might include weekly problem sets, computer science courses might include small programming assignments, creative writing classes may have weekly writing exercises, an acting class may have a series of small scene studies—the general approach is to increase the level of student skill through repeated practice with frequent feedback.

The tools introduced so far serve this type of course very well, with a special emphasis on the Assignments and Resources tools, and with the addition of just a few extra tools, you can make the online aspect of your problem-based class very effective:

- Assignments. Use this tool to enter all or most of the term's assignments at the beginning of the term. That provides students with an excellent guide to the weeks ahead and helps them plan their time accordingly.

- Resources. For problems with correct answers, use this tool to share sample problems and solutions to past problem sets. For classes where high-quality answers are less well defined (such as a performing arts or product design class), share samples of previous classes' best work. You can even upload video or audio recordings. By providing examples of excellent solutions to open-ended problems, you help your students understand what you're looking for.

- Forums. This tool, introduced in Chapter 6, provides online discussion that allows students to help each other with difficult problems. You can set up a forum for each problem set. (Be sure to monitor the forum to ensure that students are giving each other good advice and aren't crossing the boundaries by helping too much.)

- Chat. Use this tool, described in Chapter 7, to provide online problem-set help two nights before an assignment is due (don't encourage procrastination by scheduling it the night before the assignment is due). From the comfort of your home, you can take student questions about the assignment and suggest resources they might refer to while working on it.

Small discussion courses

A small discussion course has a relatively small number of students and small group discussion is a primary activity. Depending on the instructor, the students, and the subject matter, the size of this course can be as small at 10 or up to approximately 50 students. At first glance, it might seem that a class with a small number of students that meets in person on a regular basis has the least to gain from use of Sakai, and the benefits of automation are relatively small compared to a large multi-section course. The real benefit, therefore, is enhancing the student learning experience. That comes in two primary ways: Maximizing the use of the face-to-face time in class and continuing the discussion between class sessions.

Because much of the value in a discussion class is derived from the interaction with other students and the instructor, it is critical that the face-to-face time is spent productively. You want to ensure that students are prepared (they have done the reading or research required before coming to class) and that the maximum amount of time is spent discussing class topics rather than administrative issues. The relationship between the students and with the instructor is also important—students are asked to provide ideas and opinions in front of others they may not know well. For many students, this comes naturally; for others, this is difficult even when the instructor does an excellent job in creating a challenging but safe space for learning.

Small discussion classes tend to meet less frequently in favor of longer class sessions that allow discussions to progress and reach a depth that might not otherwise be possible in a 50-minute class session. It is common for a class of this type to meet twice a week for ninety minutes or even once a week for 3 hours. Even with the extended class meeting time, there are often discussions that do not come to a satisfying close, yet the next class session needs to be devoted to a different set of ideas and readings. Encouraging the discussion to continue between class sessions is important for students to get the most out of the experience.

The basic Sakai tools come in handy here. Start by using the Announcements and Email Archive tools to handle administrative issues. This ensures that all students have the latest information about changes to any assignments. Use the Resources tool to upload any electronic reading materials, and then send emails to the class when readings become available, ensuring that everyone has access to the readings and that there are no excuses (such as, I didn't get your email). The Calendar tool is probably not necessary but it can be useful for highlighting events outside of class such as an important speaker on campus that you want the class to think about hearing.

There are a few additional Sakai tools particularly recommended for small discussion classes:

- Blogs. Have students use a Sakai Blog tool to post their reactions to weekly readings and research assignments. This ensures that they complete the assignments and gives you a chance to see where certain misunderstandings or conflicts in interpretation might be lurking. If you assign some portion of their grade to completing this each week, you will see excellent participation levels. You don't need to grade the blog entries—the fact that they are visible to all members of the class generally is enough incentive for students to take them seriously.

- Forums: Here are a few ways to use forums in this type of class:
  - Use Forums at the beginning of the term to have students introduce themselves to each other by posting statements about why they are taking the class, what they hope to get out of it, and what previous exposure they have to the topics. Kick off the conversation with an introductory post of your own. Not only will that encourage others to jump in, but it also gives you a chance to provide a good example for students to follow.

  - Ask students to post to Forums their reaction to that week's readings or research. You can also continue unfinished discussions in a Forum. As class is ending, ask those who seem to have unanswered questions or unfinished comments to initiate a discussion in the class Forum. (One common discovery among instructors who use a discussion forum for the first time is that students who are reticent in class can be quite eloquent online. Giving them a chance to have their voice heard there can help them in class as well.) Forums may sounds like a lot of extra work, but they do not need to be. You will probably find that students respond to each other's posts in helpful ways and you, as instructor, can clarify key points or quickly steer a discussion that is going off track. While this may take some time it can reduce the number of individual emails you'll get from students. Because all the students can see your responses, you can answer a question once rather than several times.

- Drop Box. This tool allows instructors and students to share documents within a private folder for each student. It works like Resources, enabling you to upload many types of files and many files at a time. Because Blogs and Forums are public spaces, the Drop Box is a good way to allow for private communication between you and each student. This might be useful, for example, if a student wants your feedback on an early draft of an essay or research project. Drop Box works best when there are a relatively small number of items that you are working on iteratively with students. If you have a larger number of formal assignments that will be graded, use the Assignments tool instead.

Large introductory courses

A large introductory course often has a hundred or more students, usually divided into sections, each led by a teaching assistant. Anyone who has taught a large course, regardless of whether it is divided into sections with teaching assistants, knows the administrative and organizational challenges that they involve. The large number of students creates a great deal of administrative overhead in communicating with students about the practicalities of the course—when assignments are due, what the grading criteria are, when office hours are for section leaders, when special help sessions are before important exams, and so on. Sakai can really help the course instructors stay organized and facilitate communication.

You'll definitely want to be taking advantage of the Announcements, Email Archive, Resources, Syllabus, Assignments, and Gradebook tools. But Sakai recognizes that in a large class these tools need to behave differently than they do for a small class and Sakai provides a set of group and section management features. Taking advantage of these features is critical to a successful online experience for a large class:

- Section Info. This tool allows you to manage groups of students in your course and is fundamental to success in a large course that includes teaching assistants. If your educational institution integrates Sakai with the registration system (called a Student Information System), it may have already created groups of students inside your site based on the class sections to which students are assigned. If not, you can use this tool to create sections manually. Once the section information is configured, many of Sakai's other tools exhibit new capabilities to let them work with sections. You can also assign a teaching assistant to each section, giving them permissions to do a variety of things with the students in their section. The following tools are "section-aware":

    ◦ Announcements. A teaching assistant can send announcements to his or her section but, by default, cannot send announcements to the entire class.

- Assignments. Teaching assistants can send assignments to their sections or the lead instructor can send assignments to the entire class.

- Forums. Set up forums for the whole class or for each section of the class. (You can allow students to reach the forums for other sections without giving them permission to post there.) This is a particularly powerful tool for a large class. Think about basing part of the course grade on participation in the class forums and definitely post a weekly discussion question to get things started.

- Resources. A great way to use Resources in a large class is to store lecture notes. It's inevitable that some students will miss an occasional lecture. Even for those who attend every session, lecture notes make great review material and posting the notes allows students to focus more on what you are saying rather than worrying about taking detailed notes.

- Gradebook. Instructors can filter the Gradebook to view grades for students in particular sections. Teaching assistants are limited to viewing and grading assignments for students in their own section.

- Mailtool. While the Email Archive tool is, in many cases, more than sufficient for class communication, a large class may need more sophisticated features and functions. Mailtool provides HTML email authoring with a WYSIWYG editor, supports attachments, and, most importantly, is aware of the sections in your course. Emails sent through the Mailtool also appear in the Email Archive, if you like.

- Tests & Quizzes. This tool enables instructors to set up assessment activities for students. It can also be used to gather survey information or informal course feedback. There is a fair amount to learn about online tests, so you may want to contact your local support team for assistance with this tool, but straightforward, low-stakes weekly quizzes are quite easy to set up and are a great device to use in large classes. They ensure that students are keeping up with the material and can serve as early warning signs to you about students who are struggling. Because many question types (such as multiple choice) can be graded automatically by Sakai, you can give quizzes on a regular basis without increasing the grading burden for yourself or the teaching assistant.

- Modules. Instructors can use this tool (also called Melete) to publish learning sequences by using a rich text editor, uploading learning objects, or pointing to existing URL resources. You can also use it to present instructional content that you may not have enough time to cover in class or that is not adequately covered in a textbook you may be using.

- Polls. Quick and easy polls can be useful in classes of any size, but are especially useful in large classes. You might ask students if they have heard about a relevant news event, to what degree they agreed with the point-of-view of a guest presenter, or if they found the readings for a current topic difficult to understand.

- Chat. There are many possible uses for this tool in a large class. One excellent use is to have teaching assistants hold online office hours where they are available to answer student questions. Even students who are just "lurking" (reading what others are typing but not typing any messages themselves) can derive benefit from participating in a chat session with an instructor or teaching assistant.

- Podcasts. If you are teaching in a classroom that is equipped to record your lectures, the resulting audio files can be provided to students via the Podcasts tool. Some universities even automatically add recorded lectures to your Sakai site thereby providing a valuable tool to your students without you having to do anything extra. Even if your university doesn't have such a service, adding recordings to the site using the Podcasts tool is very easy.

 Sakai provides two ways to manage groups of students, the Section Info tool and the Manage Groups functionality inside the Site Info tool. This chapter assumes the presence of the Section Info tool. If your organization doesn't provide this tool, you can do many of the things described within by using the Site Info tool.

Set up a separate collaboration site for teaching assistants. You can keep everyone on the same page, discuss matters of student performance and grading privately and begin to create a set of materials that will be useful to future instructors and teaching assistants.

Project-based courses

A Project-based course centers on one or two single large projects. While the end product is important, the process of discovery and the problem solving that the students go through are equally important, if not more so. The question becomes how you can use Sakai to encourage and make visible the decision-making process students use as they work on their project. This is especially important in classes that include group projects where the contributions of each individual can be difficult to discern. Here are a few Sakai tools that are useful in a project-based course:

- Wiki. This tool is a cornerstone for project-based courses. A Wiki is a living document that students can revise as the term progresses. It represents the current state of their project but also documents the decisions that were made along the way.

- Blog. Use this tool as a student's personal journal for the class. While the Wiki serves as the student's "official" record of the project, the blog can be used to document personal reflections. This is especially important when the students are working on projects in groups. While it is often difficult to assess each individual student's contribution to the end result or even the Wiki, their blog entries provide evidence of their personal contributions. Blogs also encourage reflection about the project and its relationship to the ideas and theories the project is intended to reinforce.

- Guest Access. Project-based courses often benefit from outside expertise — a consultant or advisor or judge who can interact with the students in some way. Give your outside experts access to the class site and give them appropriate privileges so they can see and even comment on student work.

Collaboration sites

There are a variety of uses for collaboration sites, common ones being for a research group, a student club, or an administrative committee. They are similar enough in their use of Sakai tools to group them together. A successful collaboration site can be built from the basic Sakai tools, especially Email Archive and Resources. Sending email and sharing documents are key activities for any collaborative group and for some they may be just enough.

A collaboration site that will exist for a relatively brief period of time — one dedicated to hiring someone to fill a job vacancy, for example — will work quite well using just the basic tools. For collaborative groups that either have a longer life expectancy or are more focused on creating content (rather than distributing and discussing it), enhancing the site with a few additional tools can make a big difference. Here are a few ideas for these types of collaborative group sites:

- Wiki. This a great tool for collaborative document creation. It preserves a history of document changes and serves as a record of how the thinking of the group has progressed over time.

- Web Content. In collaborative projects there are often other web sites — perhaps a public-facing web site for a research group or academic department that is hosted on another server — that are used by the group. This tool allows you to add those web pages to your Sakai site. They appear as links in the Sakai toolbar as if they were just another Sakai tool, and when you click on a link, the corresponding web page appears in the main content area of the site. You can also use the Site Info tool to add web content to your site.

- Forums. A discussion forum is a valuable addition to a group that regularly debates certain questions and tries to come to a decision or shared perspective. While the Email Archive can be, and often is, used for these purposes, a discussion form can keep important conversations organized. By creating a discussion thread for each question or decision, a collaboration site has an organized record of the debate that can easily be found and referenced. Reading through the history of discussions surrounding important decisions is valuable for both current members and new members alike.

- Search. Search is not so much a tool as a capability, enabling members of the site to search its contents. If a collaboration site contains a large amount of content or email, search is a valuable addition.

- News. Use this tool to add RSS feeds to your site, making it easy for your site members to follow news important to the group directly from the Sakai site.

Building your Home page

To keep your site as simple as possible for users, remove, or at least hide, the tools you do not expect to use in your site. While Sakai speaks of "adding" and "removing", it is perhaps better to think about this as "activating" and "deactivating". Your actions aren't permanent—you can always add (activate) a tool later if you decide it will be useful. You can remove a tool using the Add/Remove Tools link in Site Info. To hide a tool, use the Page Order link in Site Info.

The Page Order functionality also allows you to rename tools or to change the order in which they appear. This can be very useful in certain circumstances but use these features cautiously. Changing the name of a tool can confuse users, especially students who may be taking other courses at the same time. Changing the order of the tools is less disruptive to users but can still contribute to a sense of unfamiliarity.

Check out the new look

Now revisit your site Home page to see how it looks. The panels associated with tools you've removed should no longer appear on the home page and, depending on how your Sakai site is configured, panels may have appeared for some of the tools you've added. At this point, you have a few possibilities for modifying the appearance and functionality of your Home page. You can edit the standard Home page, replace the site description with a different Sakai tool, or even create a custom Home page.

Edit your page

Editing the standard Home page is the easiest option. Earlier in this chapter, you saw how to edit the site description content using the built-in WYSIWYG editor. If you haven't done this yet, you should do so now. Each tool summary panel also has some configuration options. Explore these to see which options produce the view that you think your users will find most useful when they log in to your site. Try a few options and see what you like best.

You'll also notice that the Announcements summary panel is empty at this point because you haven't sent an announcement yet. Compose an initial announcement about the class so that there is useful content in that summary panel. You can, for example, create an announcement that welcomes students to your class, reminds them of the initial class meeting time and location, and informs them of what to expect in the first class session. If you're using Forums, you'll see that there are no recent posts. Again, consider getting things started. One simple thing to do is create a discussion thread called "Introductions" and post an initial message introducing yourself.

Replace the site description

After creating the initial content and configuring the panels, your Home page is hopefully now both attractive and useful. If you want something different, though, one option is to replace the site description panel with something else. Notice that the site description options include a field for a URL. Enter a URL there, and the page associated with that URL will be displayed instead of the site description content.

You can use this capability to display an external site if you want, similar to how you would use the Web Content tool. But you can also use it to display another tool inside Sakai that may not provide a summary panel for the Home page. For a collaboration site, you might want to display the contents of a Wiki page that contains the minutes from past meetings, for example. You'll need, of course, to grab the URL of the tool you want to display. Simply right-click (*Ctrl*-click on a Macintosh) on the link for that tool and select Copy Location to send the URL to the clipboard. Then paste it into the appropriate field in the site description editing screen. Save your changes and take a look at the result. Depending on the tool you've selected and the configuration of your Sakai instance, you may be seeing exactly what you hoped for.

On the other hand, because of the way space is allocated on the Home page, the resulting view may not appear as you expect. There is little you can do at this point with the standard Sakai Home page, although your user support team may be able to help change the spacing of panels on the Home page for you.

Customize the Home page

If, however, you know exactly how you want your home page to look and you can't make the default Sakai Home page appear that way, you can replace the Home page with one of your own construction. The following figure shows an example of just such a site in Sakai.

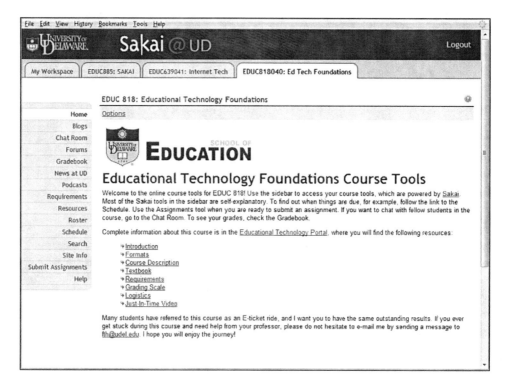

You can do the same using the Web Content tool and the Page Order functionality in Site Info. Follow these steps:

1. Build a web page or series of web pages using a tool of your choice. Put those pages on a web server somewhere—you can probably even put them on the Sakai server using the Resources tool. (If you do this and you're building multiple pages, be careful to use relative links so when you move them to Sakai the links will still work. Also remember that your web pages will appear in the content area of Sakai and therefore won't have the full page width available to them. Be sure to design them accordingly.)

2. Add the web page you created to your Sakai site using the Web Content tool. The Web Content creation process asks you to provide a name for your page. Call it Home.

3.   You now have two Home pages in your list of tools. Use the Page Order function in Site Info to move your custom-built Home page to the top of the list.

4.   You have two choices about what to do with the default Sakai Home page. You can hide it using the Page Order tool or you can rename it, taking into account the tool summary panels that are available. If, for example, you have the Calendar, Announcements, and Forums summary panels, a name like Dashboard or Recent Activity might make sense.

5.   Once you are happy with them, save your changes.

Now your custom web page displays as if it were your Sakai site's Home page. And Sakai's Home page is either hidden or has a different name. That's all there is to it.

Ready to roll

Whichever method of constructing a home page you choose, your site should now be ready to go. Once you're satisfied with the appearance and functionality, send a message to your users to let them know that the site is open for business. The easiest way to do this is to send an email to the site email address inviting participants to log in, take a look around, and, ideally, complete some relevant task (downloading the course syllabus, for example, or introducing themselves on the discussion forum). You can also share the site email address so that everyone knows where messages should be sent.

Of course, all of the preceding suggestions are just that. Experience with Sakai and your style of teaching (or your group's collaboration style) will ultimately determine which tools are most useful to you. There are also new tools and capabilities being introduced on a regular basis so it is likely that you can do much more than is outlined in this chapter. If you have any doubts, tell your Sakai support team what you'd like to be able to do and they can steer you in the right direction. Or join the Sakai community's Teaching and Learning collaboration group and share your questions and experiences with others.

 The Community section of the Sakai web site (http://sakaiproject.org) has instructions for joining the Teaching and Learning group and other groups in the Sakai community.

Summary

Sakai is a powerful tool for teaching and collaboration but, like any tool, it can be used more or less effectively. You can find creative ways of using Sakai by thinking about the type of class you are teaching and the kinds of learning activities you would like students to undertake. The suggestions provided in this chapter are an excellent starting point but you should feel free to adapt them to your own needs—you know your content and students best.

The next chapter, *The Administration Workspace*, introduces the administrative features of Sakai. You can find more information about teaching with Sakai in Chapter 15: *Innovating Teaching and Learning with Sakai*. This chapter describes two courses that won awards for innovative uses of Sakai.

10
The Administration Workspace

From resetting a forgetful user's password to creating custom sites and sending out messages of the day, the administration workspace is the main location for daily chores. The workspace has existed as the primary means of doing the administrative work since the beginning of the Sakai project, and we shall devote the majority of this chapter to it. This chapter also discusses Portfolio administration. Portfolios allow students to show, in a structured way, the work they have done. For the sake of realism, this chapter also includes a walkthrough on installing a portfolio archive.

Deploying portfolios into an organization requires significant effort. The application designers have made portfolios from parts such as forms and wizards into a whole using a portfolio template. XML and XSLT-experienced developers need to create this set of reusable parts with an understanding of the learning context. However, once the development team has done the heavy lifting and released a new portfolio in its entirety to the administrator, it is the administrator's job to add or delete parts.

What is a Sakai administrator?

Application administration requires more specific knowledge than system administration. Not only is the Sakai administrator responsible for understanding the flow of interactions between the end-user tools and the administrator's workspace, he or she is also responsible for tweaking the global configuration files and finding any low-level error messages in the logs. Before day one of administration, it is useful to play as an instructor in a course with all the tools turned on and at the same time, in a second browser, play the student or teaching assistant role. Once a new administrator has a clear understanding of the basics, he or she can start to build a solid picture of any potential pain points. For example, when should you use web folders and not the web interface through the resource tool? Where can the student or teaching assistant make mistakes? Starting to look proactively through the minds of others in different Sakai roles reduces the chances of surprise.

One of the significant issues an administrator occasionally encounters is the inability of the end user to express his or her online problems in specific terms. It would not be surprising for administrators to get emails with such titles as: "The system is 10 times slower than last week", "The Web folders do not work", "I added a folder to resources and no one can see it". The Sakai administrator's role is not just to tweak the names in user accounts, but also to change these nebulous issues into problems that can be defined and solved.

The Become User tool allows you to see through the eyes of a specific user. Noting client environments and seeing wider patterns makes debugging easier.

Sakai is built on modern Java frameworks, and developers on a mission have driven its fast pace of change. You will feel the influence of the developer viewpoint the most in the Sites and Realm tools, which are both very flexible and get their specific jobs done, but are particularly user-unfriendly. To create custom sites or user types with these tools, you will need to learn some terminologically rich background information, which is included later in this chapter. If you are an instructor, this background information is arguably not necessary and you are welcome to fast-forward past the section.

It is important to see the administration workplace in the wider context of enterprise deployment. You can get 80% of your work done here, but at times you need to leave the GUI and go down into the file system to edit configurations. To support you in your learning process, in Chapter 12, *Tips from the Trenches*, a number of community members describe their hard-earned experiences. This chapter also includes an interview with Anthony Atkins, who has been heavily involved in Sakai administration issues and has written large chunks of the Sakai administrators guide (`http://bugs.sakaiproject.org/confluence/display/DOC/Sys+Admin+Guide`).

Organizations have deployed Sakai above the 100,000-user mark and it scales much further; it is a proven rock-solid platform. However, any application has its weak spots and the administrator has to deal with them. Rather than avoid looking at the rough edges, the honest interview with Anthony Atkins at the end of this chapter reveals a number of pain points.

The Administration tool set

In the demonstration version of Sakai, when you log in as an administrator, you have a workspace and an administration workspace, a citation administration tab, and portfolio administration tab. The workspace and administration workspace are the same for the default admin account and are redundant copies. However, for new administrators other than the default admin account, the workspace is the standard My Workspace that all new users get the first time they log in. As admin, you also have the potential to visit directly any site created through site tabs, because the admin user is a member of all sites that are created.

The following table lists the tools and their uses. Notice that the common names of tools, such as Resources, are the same as those of the tools that the end users see. This is because some of the administrative worksite tools are the same as they are for users, but they have a different view due to the extra permissions. The table entries marked in bold are the more advanced and difficult-to-understand tools. First, you will need to read the basic concept section of this chapter before attacking them. If you are comfortable with the use of the flash card exercise mentioned in Chapter 7, *Worksite Tools*, then you can make a set for the simpler tools first and then later for the Aliases, Resources, Scheduler, Memory, and Sites tools.

Tools for the Administration Workspace

Tool Name	Purpose	Common Name
Users	Manipulate user information	sakai.users
Aliases		sakai.aliases
Sites	Create new worksites and modify and remove existing ones	sakai.sites
Realms		sakai.realms
Worksite Setup	Worksite Setup displays a list of worksites on which you can take some action, such as Edit or Delete.	sakai.sitesetup
MOTD (Message of the day)	Manage Messages of the day for all users	sakai.announcements

Tool Name	Purpose	Common Name
Resources	Manipulate all resources, even form tools and users workspaces	sakai.resources
On-Line	Display who is online	sakai.online
Memory	Manage Java object caches and reset the caches if necessary	sakai.memory
Site Archive	Import and export site archives	sakai.archive
Scheduler	Run Java-based scheduled tasks	sakai.scheduler
Become User	Become a user to see what the user sees	sakai.su
User Membership	View user memberships	sakai.usermembership

At the University of Amsterdam, due to the functional administrator's interpretation of Dutch privacy laws, the Sakai administrators are prohibited from using the Become User tool—they are not allowed to accidently look at the private content of the real user. However, the Amsterdam programmers apply the tool vigorously in development for debugging purposes, where there are no real student sites, only random test data sets.

You can see the history of change in Sakai through two administrative workspace tools, the Sites tool and Worksite Setup tool. The Sites tool is older and more flexible for site customization, but far less friendly. This tool allows you, as an administrator, to create sites of any type, including custom types that are not included in the Worksite Setup tool. The Sites tool understands groups, but not sections. It can combine more than one tool into a page, similar to the Home link in a user's workspace.

The Worksite Setup tool is user friendly. By default, you can create project, course, and portfolio sites, and with a little reconfiguration in the XML files, a system integrator can add his or her own custom site types. You can even get this tool to deliver a survey and ask end users questions during site creation. As Sakai improves further, it would be logical to merge both tools together.

The Realms tool is initially difficult to understand. Its main purpose is to allow an admin to tweak the default permissions of sites and the groups and users in the sites when the sites are created. Here, you can make your own custom site and user types, and many institutions personalize Sakai to do so. This is where the administrator meets Sakai-specific terminology. The tool is an ugly beast, but it gets a difficult job done without resorting to programming. I hope over time that developers add wizards to improve the tool's workflow.

At the time of writing, the citation administration tab is a work in progress. If you have enabled the citation type in the resources tool via the options link then students can create a list of citations for books either by searching automatically, using Google, adding by hand, or by importing from a connected library system or directly from a file. The citation administration workspace currently lets you view all the resources created and import and export a list. Developers are actively working on this project, so expect more functionality over time. For the most accurate information, the home for this project is `http://dlib.indiana.edu/projects/sakai/` and its documentation location in Confluence is `http://bugs.sakaiproject.org/confluence/display/RES/Citations+Helper`.

There is a simple administration model: you are either an administrator or you are not. Creating extra administrators requires that the relevant user is also a member of the administration workspace site. To do this, as admin, you can add the user via the worksite tool. It is important to use naming conventions for admin users so they are easily searchable. For example, a good user name is `admin_amberg`. Searching allows you to create lists of administrators easily and delivers an understanding of the purpose of the user in any given site's Presence tool.

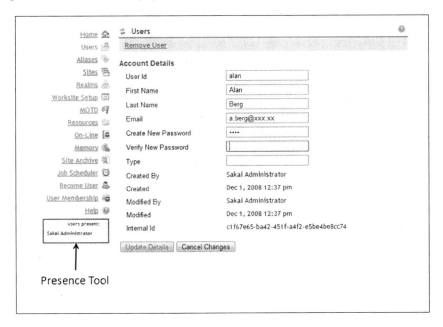

If you are an administrator, you have all of the powers such as the ability to alter course and user details. With power comes responsibility—not only must you administrate efficiently and diplomatically, but you also need to consider how you use the tools, especially the Message of the Day tool. The Message of the Day is a clear communication channel for schedules and for warnings of system downtime and other global events. The tool itself is straightforward: all you have to do is write a title and the body of a message in a text area. Once submitted, it is displayed on the front page of the site, as shown in the next figure. There is no WYSIWIG editor and you need to write any HTML manually.

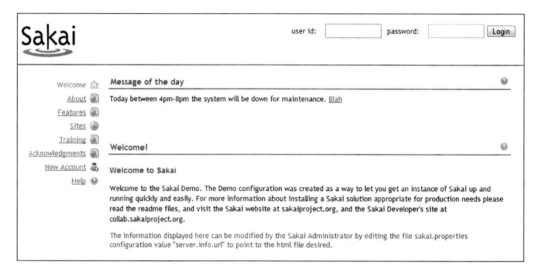

The front page is prime real estate, especially if you have a large number of visits in a day. Constructing consistent messages on time, with the corporate logo, and with links to the help desk and further information, does not just involve the administrator; it may require that others write the text using an in-house style, a communication policy, and knowledge of important events. In other words, workflow needs to bind the use of the tool to its wider context within your organization.

Delegated administration

Large organizations have help desks for their end users. Therefore, it is nice to have a more refined delegation of administration. The contribution tool SakaiAdminX (`http://bugs.sakaiproject.org/confluence/display/ADMX/Home`) uses a client-side interface through web services to fulfill this need.

Most daily administrative tasks are straightforward. Next is a screen grab of the workspace with the default tools listed on the lefthand side.

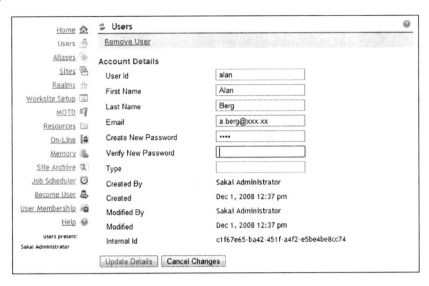

The Resources tool allows the admin user to see a global overview of all the resource content, from the directories generated by tools such as podcasts and from user workspaces, to an individual course. A common problem is when an instructor accidentally hides a resource directory, then students cannot get at their work; an administrator can correct any such errors with minimum trouble.

The Worksite Setup tool is a well-presented wizard where you can make ad hoc sites.

The Become User tool is excellent for seeing through the eyes of the end user and it allows you to decide how serious an issue is. You can use the On-Line tool to gain insight into the activity on your server and to decide when to bring a server down for patching.

The User tool allows an administrator to modify account details. Even in the most well-organized and automated environments, this action is often required.

The User Membership tool enables you to search and find a user's site and group membership information.

The Site Archive is for importing and exporting sites, excluding student-generated content. A lot of work has gone into the development of this tool, but it nevertheless does not take all the content from all the tools. If you use this tool under fire, I would strongly advise you to test a site with all tools turned on and a wide range of content. This will allow you to see the tool's current capabilities.

It is important to consider the academic year, and if and when you want to generate archives. Does the institution want all teachers to have an archive at the end of the academic year? Should each department have a shared storage space and all archives available throughout the whole of history? Law or local custom also play a role; your organization may need to keep courses around for more than four years, in which case the cheapest storage space is not on spinning disks, but rather on a tape backup. None of these possibilities can occur without wider discussion and planning.

The more complex tools to conceptually understand and then to use accurately are the Memory, Aliases, Sites, Realms, and Job Scheduler tools. This chapter contains some relatively difficult concepts, such as helper realms, that a casual reader can skip.

Unfortunately, for those of you who are lucky enough to take on the administrator task, the underlying need for keeping track of who has the right to do what in Sakai requires an understanding of some counterintuitive concepts. Sakai lives in a wide range of organizations with an inherent need for a range of different roles and different site structures, some of which the architects did not think of during the original planning of Sakai. The developers have written the Site and Realm tools for administrators, putting a priority on flexibility rather than ease of use. This makes the tools' user experience a little raw. However, the advanced configurability of the tools ensures that an administrator can do site customization without resorting to difficult programming hacks.

Within a realistic environment, the ability to personalize and plug into enterprise administration is crucial for the organization. With flexibility comes complexity and with complexity, terminology. The next section explores some Sakai-specific basic concepts and terminology.

Basic concepts

To communicate fully with the community requires an understanding of a number of basic concepts and the associated terminology. These are based on the specific technologies used and the Sakai way of doing things. The concepts and terminology are explained in this section.

Internal ID

The first concept is the difference between a user's name, the user's account, and an internal ID. You will come across the internal ID often if you manage users and sites. In the previous screen grab of the User tool, the tool the administrator uses for resetting passwords or changing email addresses, the tool displays the user's internal ID at the bottom.

The internal ID is a randomly generated string that is very unlikely to be repeated (perhaps once in twenty thousand lifetimes of the universe). The internal ID points to a unique object within Sakai and is extremely user-unfriendly. The data architect calls the user ID the **Enterprise ID**, abbreviated to EID. The EID is unique throughout the enterprise and consistent for different applications. At the University of Amsterdam, a campus-wide username looks similar to initials and last name with a number at the end to ensure uniqueness. For example, for the second Fred Blogs that signed up with the University, his username is fblog2, and his ID can be used to log on to Webmail, Portal, the Learning Management Systems, file system, home pages, and a couple of other systems. Other organizations may use a user's email address as their EID, or yet another unique and memorable naming practice.

Objects other than user names may have unreadable internal IDs. For example, when you create a site, it has its internal ID as a unique way to locate itself in the URL space. The URL for a site with ugly internal ID of `57e336af-7a2d-4306-9db7-2119afcd84b2` is reachable via the URL `/portal/site/57e336af-7a2d-4306-9db7-2119afcd84b2`. Most of the time, the inner workings of Sakai are hidden from the end user. However, one place where you will want to alias the internal ID with something a human does not mind reading is the email address for a site via the email archive. The following figure is a screen grab of the Alias tool. When a site creator sets the email address for the email archive of that site, for example `test_here@myhost.org`, then the application automatically generates an alias to the underlying mail channel used for routing mail to the right location. A part of the channel is the internal ID for the site. The Alias tool lets you to modify an alias or add new aliases. This allows you to create a second, third, or more email address for a site and gives you power to remove unreadable addresses.

The end user can see the internal ID of sites in URLs that point into those sites. However, currently, the underlying services are not yet alias-aware. In the future, I expect that the range of things that can be aliased will expand and will include friendly URL generation.

Java

Java is the underpinning language of Sakai. If a rare issue occurs, the user gets to see an error report in the web browser. At this point, the application gives the end user a choice of ignoring the error or emailing a report.

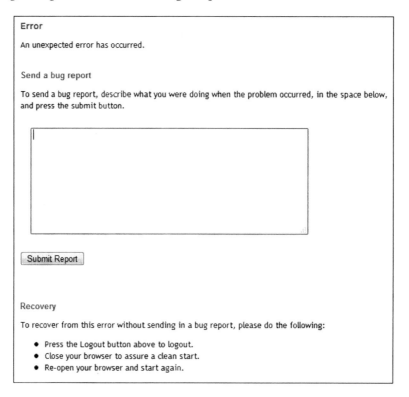

The error's reports are very unreadable to anyone but a developer or someone who has had the error explained to them by a developer. For example, the following error message indicates that a specific tool is not compliant with the in-memory database of the demonstration version. Luckily, the well-written installation instructions clearly warn the administrator of this specific issue. Expect an increase in this type of report if a deployment has a badly configured tool or there is a performance bottleneck.

```
org.sakaiproject.portal.api.PortalHandlerException: org.sakaiproject.
tool.api.ToolException: Servlet.init() for servlet jforum threw exception

    at org.sakaiproject.portal.charon.SkinnableCharonPortal.doGet(Skinnab
leCharonPortal.java:891)

caused by: org.sakaiproject.tool.api.ToolException: Servlet.init() for
servlet jforum threw exception

    at org.sakaiproject.portal.charon.SkinnableCharonPortal.forwardTool(S
kinnableCharonPortal.java:1343)

caused by: javax.servlet.ServletException: Servlet.init() for servlet
jforum threw exception

    at org.apache.catalina.core.StandardWrapper.allocate(StandardWrapper.
java:791)

caused by: net.jforum.exceptions.ForumStartupException: Error while
starting jforum - java.io.FileNotFoundException: /home/aberg/sakai/
instances/sakai-demo-M2/webapps/sakai-jforum-tool/WEB-INF/config/
database/hsqldb/hsqldb.sql (No such file or directory)

    at java.io.FileInputStream.open(Native Method)

    at java.io.FileInputStream.<init>(FileInputStream.java:106)

    at java.io.FileInputStream.<init>(FileInputStream.java:66)

    at net.jforum.util.preferences.SystemGlobals.loadQueries(SystemGlobal
s.java:342)

    at net.jforum.JForumBaseServlet.init(JForumBaseServlet.java:114)
```

> Sakai error handling is sophisticated and is addressed in detail in Chapter 13, *Common Error Messages*.

Sakai plays well in large organizations. It has hooks to pump data in and out of the application by web services. The framework also has detachable pieces of code that provide specific services. For example, one organization may use LDAP to log on, another Kerberos. The user provider does the authentication, which the Sakai kernel then calls during logon. Other providers include one type called during site creation and another for permission population in Realms.

To select between different providers requires changing the XML configuration deep down in the file system and placing a Java library known as a JAR file in the correct location. It is not the administrator's function to write the code, rather it is to read the developer's install instructions and enact them. The developers have written the providers in Java with a standard structure known as an Interface, but as you will see in the discussion of realms next, the ID of the provider code, which sits in the XML configuration, makes its appearance in the Realms tool itself.

Another location where custom Java is applied is in the Scheduler tool. The Scheduler tool allows the administrator to set predefined tasks at given times using the same trigger notation as a administrator would use with Cron, the standard Unix schedule server (http://en.wikipedia.org/wiki/Cron). The Scheduler runs tasks written in Java. As an Administrator, you have a choice between running tasks inside Sakai where the tasks get to query the application directly, or externally where it is more difficult to get to the information. To write your own internal tasks is a chore, but there are already a number of standard tasks included.

Sakai predominately uses the log4j framework (http://logging.apache.org/log4j) for routing and formatting logging information. The framework is highly flexible; with only a few lines of reconfiguration your logging subsystem can send to a database, create a series of files, send to another Unix system, etc. Logging is a vital tool in delivering vital information that is needed to quickly pinpoint issues to the administrator.

 Configuring logging is covered in Chapter 13, *Common Error Messages*.

You can control Java memory usage by tweaking the JAVA_OPTS environment variable. Java manages its own memory and has many algorithms to clean up memory. Further, different deployments use different hardware and software configurations. The Deployment Workgroup (http://bugs.sakaiproject.org/confluence/display/PROD) keeps a large dataset of deployment descriptions with the purpose of giving you insight into these permutations. Rather than making a best guess, it is wise to see what values others use in the fire of real-life use.

The administrator has the Memory tool at his or her disposal. This allows you to look at the caches in Sakai. Java is object-orientated (`http://en.wikipedia.org/wiki/Object-oriented_programming`). Caches keep objects alive longer in memory, so that if the application requests an object again, time and effort is not lost in database queries to create a new object—it is better to use the previously-created object. The downside is that cached objects may be out-of-date and cost memory. If a cache for a particular object type is being hit a lot and there are some objects that are being missed, you would probably want to add more memory allocation to that cache, and if a cache is not being hit at all, then you may consider lowering the allocation. The Memory tool, shown next, displays the details required to make such decisions.

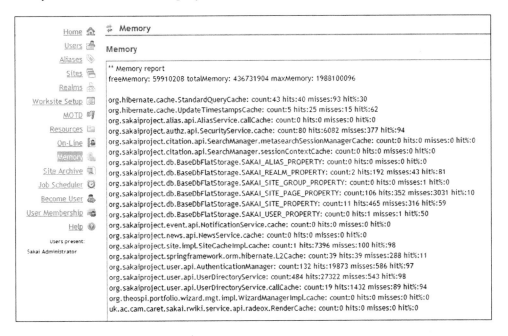

As a last resort, if your application is slowing down, the memory tool also allows you to reset caches. However, I would not advise you, the administrator, to do this at peak times of the day as end users may see a significant performance hit, such as slow web page loading, until the caches fill up again.

Realms

Sakai's adaptability in defining roles and site types in the enterprise is due to clever architecture. However, this makes for complexity. The application builders have mostly hidden the complexity from the user, but not in the case of the Site and Realm tool. To understand these tools, you will need to understand how Sakai applies permissions to a user. The best way to do this is to discuss how the user interacts with the application. There are two stories to tell. The first is about how the user interacts with a site and the second is about how the application creates a site.

Users do not have permissions; rather roles do and users gain powers through their roles. If you are a user in the `student` role in a site, you have different permissions for each tool than a user in the `instructor` role. It is a bit like being in the Army: if you are a private then you do not have permission to enter the Officer's mess and that is true for all privates. The individual does not count, just the role. In one project site, you may have the powerful maintain role. In another site, you may have the access role where you have fewer write permissions, but can read information from most tools.

Two implicit roles that exist are `.anon` for anonymous users who have not logged on and conversely `.auth` for logged on users. If you add these roles to your site then these two groups gain the powers you have specifically set for them. This is handy, for example, if you want a public-facing site where anyone in the Universe can download resources. Under the water, the public face of Sakai `http://sakaiporject.org` uses a couple of `.anon` sites to deliver content to everyone, including users that have not logged in.

A realm contains the permissions that a specific role has for each tool. There are three main types of realm: site, user, and group. I will cover the user and the group realms later. Every time you create a site, the application copies the roles and permissions from a template. A course site has a template that is different from a project site's template. The Realms tool enables you to add, delete, or modify these templates.

After creating the site, you can modify the permissions for this instance of the realm without affecting the originating template.

By default, the site owner has also the power to change permissions per role for each tool in the site.

The next figure shows that each tool has its own set of permissions. For example, if you are the site creator of a course site with the Announcement tool enabled, when you click on the tool link, you will see an option for permissions. Clicking on the permissions link opens a page showing the roles as rows and the associated permissions as columns. Clicking on a checkbox enables that specific permission for that role.

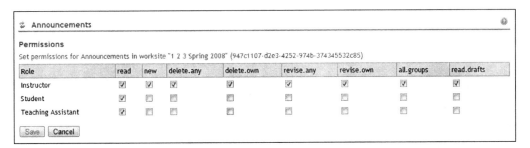

The following table describes the permissions for announcements. The permissions have consistent terms across tools, such as, add, delete, revise. Mistakes in permission settings can lead to problems for the end user. It is common for an administrator to visit custom sites and reset the site owner's modifications.

Permission	Description
new	Allows users to create new announcements.
read	Allows users to read announcements. This permission is needed to view the list of announcements.
revise.any	Allows users to edit any announcement, created by anyone.
revise.own	Allows user to edit only announcements they created.
delete.any	User can delete any announcement regardless of who created it.
delete.own	User can delete only announcements they created.
read.drafts	Ability to read draft announcements made by others. Users can always view draft announcements they create.
all.groups	Maintain-type role members of the site (Instructors and the like) might expect to have permissions to see and manipulate the announcements in the site as well as all the site groups, without having explicit membership in each group. If the user's membership in the site includes annc.all.groups, then the user has access to all the groups in the site without needing explicit group membership.

To recap, realms consist of roles with permissions. The application creates sites from templates and then the site owner or the administrator is free to modify the permissions of a specific site without affecting the template.

To ensure that the Sakai instance can find the right template for a given type of site, for example a course or a project site type, the realm templates follow a naming convention. From within the Realms tool, you can see that the course site template is called `!site.template.course`. However, you will not see an equivalent name for a project site. The reason for this is that if the site type is not named then by default the `!site.template` is used and that is exactly what happens for the project site.

As Sakai changes and the community introduces new tools, the local organization will need to update permissions in a realm. This is straightforward for the templates themselves, but not for the already-instanced sites. For instanced sites, there are two methods of modification. The first is to fire off a developer-supplied SQL script that directly changes information contained in the database. The second approach is to use the `!site.helper` template, which has permissions that are taken into account every time site permissions are needed for authorization purposes. For more details, read `https://source.sakaiproject.org/svn/reference/trunk/docs/architecture/sakai_helper_realm.doc`.

Current documentation

As the community creates new tools and adds extra functionality to the old tools, the range of possible permissions in Sakai increases. Keeping documentation up-to-date is difficult. The Subversion revision control system for Sakai has a directory reserved for the most current documentation on a wide range of technical subjects:

`https://source.sakaiproject.org/svn/reference/trunk/docs/architecture`

The Sakai source code contains the most up-to-date technical documentation under the reference directory.

`sakai_permissions.doc` details permissions per tool. The Sakai Foundation publishes this document under the Creative Commons Attribution 2.5 license. Credit where credit is due: You will see that much of the original reference documentation was written by Glenn R. Golden, who was one of the original Sakai architects. He is currently chief architect on the Etudes project (`http://etudesproject.org/team.htm`).

When creating a site, the admin user is either an instructor or maintainer by default in the new site. In Sakai terminology, in the course realm, the admin user has been "granted the ability" to be a course instructor. The Realms tool allows you to grant ability to any user for any site type.

The application applies the user realm to generate MyWorkspace permissions to each new user of a given type. By default, a user of type "guest" does not have permission to use the Worksite Setup tool to create new sites from within their workspace, whereas a user of type `maintain` does.

Sakai uses the group template to stamp permissions on a new group. The architecture tightly couples the group templates with their equivalent site types.

The Realms tool gives you easy access to the realm templates. The following is a screen grab of an edited realm. Notice that you can change the default realm provider (as discussed in the last section), but leaving the field blank implies using the standard built-in one. You can grant abilities to users in a particular site type and you can add roles with permissions.

Many organizations customize Sakai sites and permissions to their own specific needs. They start with the standard project and course realms and then add and delete roles within the sites and tweak permissions. This has the benefit of avoiding the need to modify the Worksite Setup tool to see the new type, and just as importantly, it avoids having to test from scratch. The hidden risks are role permissions; sometimes the permissions have a subtle effect on how a tool interacts with a user. Therefore, best practice dictates that you thoroughly test any permission changes you make before deploying to a wider and more vicious public.

sakai.properties

`sakai/sakai.properties` is the main text file that configures how Sakai works. Anthony Atkins' Config Viewer tool (`http://bugs.sakaiproject.org/confluence/display/CNFV/`) lists over 300 properties that you can use within this file. These properties have an impact on numerous aspects of how a particular Sakai instance works, and they lead to a wide range of potential customizations. From the URLs of welcome messages to mail routing, locations of DNS servers, and file content, this global configuration file is central to the smooth running of your local infrastructure. The Sakai Administrator's Guide (`http://confluence.sakaiproject.org/confluence/x/PoHj`) delivers an excellent overview of the mainstream properties and the effects of changes of those properties. It is necessary read for any budding administrator.

The key features of the `sakai/sakai.properties` file are: 1. Changes are not seen live. You will have to restart any servers that you have updated. 2. The file structure follows the Java property file conventions, that is, the name of the property followed by an equal sign, for example:

```
property=value
property=some value with spaces in it
```

Sakai adds its own convention for multiple values by adding a `.count`. For example, you can have two values of a specific property. The configuration will look like:

```
property.count=2
property.1=Hello
property.2=World
```

The example `sakai.properties` file in the demonstration version is accurately commented and also has some examples commented out, so that you can quickly remove the comments and activate popular features such as the ability for Sakai to connect to the MySQL or Oracle databases.

To give you a practical example of customizations that you can achieve, you can modify the welcome page that a user sees just before logging on. First, as admin, you will need to add an HTML page via the Resources tool, making sure that it is publicly available. Once you have created the page, note its URL by right-clicking (option-click on a Macintosh) on the file's link. In the `sakai.properties` file, you will need to add the property `server.info.url` and make it equal to the resource link you have just copied, for example:

```
server.info.url=http://localhost:8080/access/content/user/alan/
welcome.html
```

On the front page, you should then see HTML similar to:

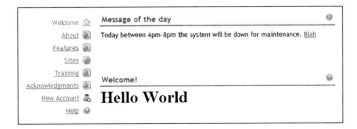

An interview with Anthony Atkins

What is your relationship to Sakai?

I currently work at the UHI (`http://www.uhi.ac.uk`), and among other things, I support collab.sakaiproject.org as a resource for the Sakai community. Prior to working at UHI, I supported both collab and the Sakai and OSP pilots at Virginia Tech (`http://www.vt.edu/`). I have edited and written content for the Sakai Admin Guide for the past two years. I also have written two contrib tools, the Config Viewer and Config Editor (`http://confluence.sakaiproject.org/confluence/x/roQ`), which are intended to be a resource for Sakai administrators.

 Editor's Note: Anthony has now moved on from UHI and is now working in the commercial sphere.

Which extra contrib tools are helpful for an administrator?

I would like to think the Config Viewer and Editor are helpful, I use them myself often. I have also used SASH periodically; it makes it easy to script bulk operations.

Can you think of any common errors or error messages?

Most of the errors that occur when an institute moves beyond the demo install and is setting up Sakai from source, have to do with a missing a step or two along the way. The developer's walkthrough (`http://confluence.sakaiproject.org/confluence/x/zzs`) is really the best cheat sheet for the initial setup, followed by the sections of the admin guide (`http://bugs.sakaiproject.org/confluence/display/DOC/Sys+Admin+Guide`) that are relevant to your particular database, mail server, etc. The types of errors that come up in production are ever-changing, as the software is constantly evolving. The best way to arm is to try the next version of the software well ahead of time and take an active role in exercising the software and reporting bugs.

What are the top five administrator headaches?

The mail configuration is one that still frustrates. The administrator initially deploys the James portion of the mailarchive tool from a WAR file with configuration settings based on the state of the `sakai.properties` file. Subsequent changes to the `sakai.properties` file, such as setting a relay host for outgoing mail, Sakai does not pick up unless you remove the deployed copy of James. Worse, there are key settings, the number of incoming connections allowed, and any aliases for the primary hostname, which the administrator has to add to the James configuration manually.

If you think about the history of Sakai, the performance of the Mailarchive tool was one of the sore spots. A single user searching a large list could degrade performance on an entire site. We had to hide the mail archive tool from end users until Chuck Severance finally came up with a series of performance fixes that allow us to use Sakai itself to search mail archives rather than relying on Gmane (`http://gmane.org/`) or Nabble. If you use the mail archive tool in any significant way, this is one of the key reasons to upgrade to 2.5 or higher.

Adding provisional tools or customized page setups (multi-column pages, etc.) is harder than it should be. Rather than a visual tool, you have to find the worksite in which you are interested in using the Sites tool and edit the list of pages to include the tools that interest you.

Permissions management is still even more of a black art than editing sites. You have to find the site based on the worksite, and the realm based on the site ID. Worse, Sakai displays the permissions as keys (site.upd) instead of human-readable explanations ("Can the user update a site?"). Worse still, if you really want to know what each permission does, you need to either read the source code or go through a lot of trial and error.

I guess the biggest administrative headache in general is how complex site and site template setup is. I cannot imagine delegating this kind of work to most helpdesk staff, where we happily delegate similar functions in Blackboard to the same staff.

Why did you make the Config Viewer and Editor?

The sakai.properties file controls an awful lot of the key behaviors of a working Sakai installation. When I started with Sakai, I read the sakai_properties.doc prepared by John Leasia and others to gain an understanding of what we can and should configure. This required patience to write as each configuration change I made had to be followed by a full restart and careful testing. As each new version of Sakai came out, the list of properties grew, and an increasing number were undocumented. The Config Viewer was born out of a desire to document as many options as I could find based on my own testing, to minimize the number of restarts administrators would require to get their settings the way they needed to be. The goal with the Config Editor was to take that one step further and eliminate Sakai restarts altogether for properties that are now read in real time.

Adding a Portfolio template

This section explains what can be achieved from the Portfolio Administration site and how to obtain example portfolios ready for your own experimentation.

The Portfolio administration site

The Portfolio admin site includes the basic tools: Resources, Email Archive, and Site Info, plus tools to manage portfolios and compose new portfolio types. The administrators mostly use the Resources tool for storing archives of portfolio parts or the generic administration files that a local admin may wish to share. The Email Archive is an excellent way to keep the portfolio administrators in contact with students.

As a member of a Portfolio site, a student can use the Portfolio tool to create a custom portfolio or make a new portfolio based on a template. Templates ensure a consistent portfolio that allows an evaluator to measure and compare a group of students more accurately. Templates enforce a uniform corporate look and feel and ensure a way for students to prove their experience history.

A Portfolio template points to already existing parts, such as matrices and the forms that each matrix references. The Portfolio admin workspace has tools for dealing with each part, plus a reporting tool.

To import a template given to you by your friendly local portfolio creation team or a commercial partner, you not only need to import the template, but also the other parts that the template needs. An example workflow is this: an administrator receives an email with a portfolio attached. The admin uploads the ZIP file into the resources section of the portfolio admin site and then uses the template tool to import the archive from resources. Editing the template allows you to see which parts are required. Counter-intuitively, the administrator then has to import the same ZIP archive a second time using, for example, the Matrix tool. At the last minute, the admin has to go back to the Template tool and publish the fully-formed template to the world.

Again, we see that the original architects have made design decisions for OSP based on the need to be flexible rather than on administrative ease of use. This is because organizations scattered across the whole of the world have different learning approaches and thus require different and sometimes difficult structures.

From the OpenEd site, described in the next section, you can download an OSP template and its related resources and then install it. You can then click on the various tools to see how the components fit together.

OpenEd

To ease the initial creation burden and recognizing the need to share best practices and, more trivially, portfolio components, the OpenEd practices web site has an easy-to-use search feature `http://openedpractices.org/resources` for components.

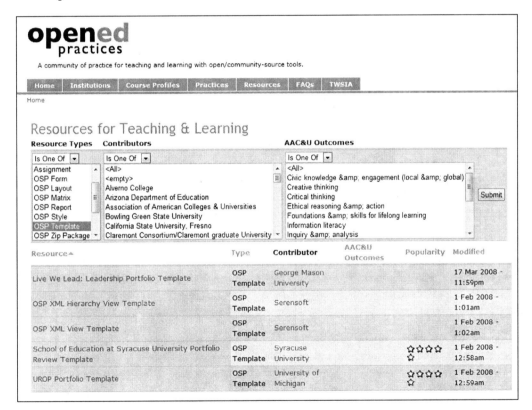

The Reports tool takes a bit of effort to configure and is not necessary for the daily running of a portfolio site. The tool allows you to add a report definition. A report definition includes raw database statements to gain information, for example, about the usage of a particular portfolio, but it can also have wider scope and query beyond OSP boundaries to include any data available. The following figure is an example of a report for the number of unique users that logged on to my test server. Notice that the tool sees that the email specific non-user account called postmaster never logged on. In a learning environment, you can create custom reports to track online attendance.

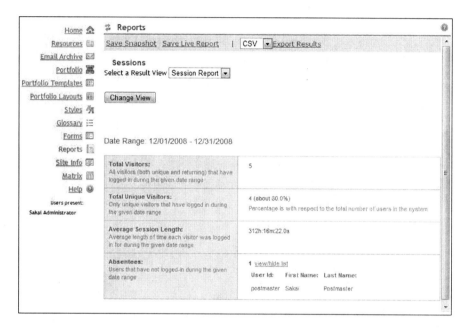

The database schema in Sakai is complex and is liable to change. Therefore, writing a report definition is one of the more unwelcome tasks and is in the province of development rather than daily administration. If your organization wishes for detailed site statics, then you should probably test out the Contributed Sitestats tool first `http://bugs.sakaiproject.org/confluence/display/STAT`.

To generate reports requires placing the Scheduler tool in a specific site and then running the predefined data warehouse job to collect data and generate an instance of the report that is viewable within the resources. Other than the online help, you can find the most current OSP-related documentation at `http://bugs.sakaiproject.org/confluence/display/OSPDOC`.

Summary

The administrator workspace is the online location for the majority of the daily administration choirs. Here, you can manipulate resources, create and modify sites and user populations, and even see through the eyes of those users.

Sakai is a Java-based application and therefore it is a distinct advantage for an administrator to have basic Java programming experience.

The Message of the Day tool is simple to use, but should be seen in the wider context of organizational policy. The messages sent from this tool have high impact, as they appear on the front page of your application.

A realm is a set of roles with permissions. When an administrator creates a site, a user, or group, the running application uses a specific realm template to copy default values for each.

The most difficult-to-use tools are Realms and Sites. This is due to their flexibility and the complexity of the underlying concepts. The Realms tool enables modification or creation of new realm templates. The Sites tool is for the creation of custom sites with pages with multiples tools.

Creating a tailored portfolio experience is outside the responsibility of an administrator; however, deploying the created results later is not. The portfolio administration space has all the tools necessary to do this.

In the next chapter, we discuss the Sakai web services for creating and maintaining users, sites, and groups and list a wide variety of existing services explaining how to discover and connect to them.

11
Web Services: Connecting to the Enterprise

From the very beginning, it was clear that Sakai needed to exist in universities at enormous scales, supporting hundreds of thousands of students. With requirements changing and evolving, and ever-increasing user expectations, Sakai had to be able to connect with a multitude of external systems. When Sakai was designed, the specifics of the majority of the connected systems were not knowable. To adapt to these tough circumstances, Sakai supplies web services that are easy to hook into or to write. Sakai exposes services for creating and maintaining users, sites, and groups. These services are easily extensible to include any part of the Sakai framework.

This is an advanced chapter that explains the two main types of web service, **SOAP (Simple Object Access Protocol)** and **Representational State Transfer (REST)** (`http://microformats.org/wiki/rest`). It also covers already-existing web services and describes how to hook into them. If you follow the examples, you will be able to write and deploy your first service. Lastly, this chapter includes a few simple client-side Perl scripts that create new users using both the SOAP and RESTful approaches.

Connecting to Sakai is straightforward, and simple tasks, such as automatic course creation, take only a few tens of lines of programming effort.

There are significant advantages to having web services in the enterprise. If a developer writes an application that calls a number of web services, then the application does not need to know the hidden details behind the services. It just needs to agree on what data to send. This **loosely couples** the application to the services. Later, you can replace one web service with another. Programmers do not need to change the code on the application side. SOAP works well with most organizations' firewalls (http://en.wikipedia.org/wiki/Firewall), as SOAP uses the same protocol as web browsers. System administrators have a tendency to protect an organization's network by closing unused ports to the outside world. This means that most of the time there is no extra network configuration effort required to enable web services.

Another simplifying factor is that a programmer does not need to know the details of SOAP or REST, as there are libraries and frameworks that hide the underlying magic. For the Sakai implementation of SOAP, to add a new service is as simple as writing a small amount of Java code within a text file, which then is automatically compiled and run the first time the service is called. This is great for rapid application development and deployment, as the system administrator does not need to restart Sakai for each change. Just as importantly, the Sakai services use the well-known libraries from the Apache Axis project (http://ws.apache.org/axis/).

SOAP is an XML message passing protocol that, in the case of Sakai sites, sits on top of the Hyper Text Transfer Protocol (HTTP). HTTP is the protocol used by web browsers to obtain web pages from a server. The client sends messages in XML format to a service, including the information that the service needs, and then the service returns a message with the results or an error message. A readable reference to this interchange is the book *Pro Apache XML* by Poornachandra Sarang, PhD (http://www.freesoftwaremagazine.com/articles/book_review_pro_apache_xml).

The full definition of HTTP is given at http://www.w3.org/TR/soap12-part1.

The architects introduced SOAP-based web services first to Sakai and later RESTful services. Unlike SOAP, instead of sending XML via HTTP posts to one URL that points to a service, REST sends to a URL that includes information about the entity, such as a user, with which the client wishes to interact. For example, a REST URL for viewing an address book item could look similar to http://host/direct/ addressbook_item/15. Applying URLs in this way makes understandable address spaces that are easier for a human to read. This more intuitive approach simplifies coding. Further, SOAP XML passing requires that the client and server parse the XML and at times, the parsing effort is expensive in CPU cycles and response times.

The Entity Broker is an internal service that makes life easier for programmers and helps them manipulate entities. Entities in Sakai are managed pieces of data such as representations of courses, users, grade books, and so on. In the newer versions of Sakai, the Entity Broker has the power to expose entities as RESTful services. In contrast, for SOAP services, if you wanted a new service, you would need to write it yourself. Over time, the Entity Broker exposes more and more entities RESTfully, delivering more hooks free to integrate with other enterprise systems.

 Both SOAP and REST services sit on top of the HTTP protocol, which is explained in the next section of this chapter.

Protocols

This section explains how web browsers talk to servers in order to gather web pages. It explains how to use the `telnet` command and a visual tool called TCPMON (`http://ws.apache.org/commons/tcpmon/tcpmontutorial.html`) to gain insight into how web services and Web 2.0 technologies work.

Playing with Telnet

It turns out that message passing occurs via text commands between the browser and the server. Web browsers use HTTP (`http://www.w3.org/Protocols/rfc2616/rfc2616.html`) to get web pages and the embedded content from the server and to send form information to the server. HTTP talks between the client and server via text (7 bit ASCII) commands. When humans talk with each other, they have a wide vocabulary. However, HTTP uses fewer than twenty words.

You can experiment directly with HTTP using a Telnet client to send your commands to a web server. For example, if your demonstration Sakai instance is running on port 8080, the following command will get you the login page:

```
telnet localhost 8080
```
```
GET /portal/login
```

The GET command does what it sounds like and gets a web page. Forms can use the GET verb to send data at the end of the URL. For example, GET /portal/login?name=alan&age=15 is sending the variables name=alan and age=15 to the server.

Installing TCPMON

You can use the TCPMON tool to view requests and responses from a web browser such as Firefox. One of TCPMON's abilities is that it can act as an invisible man in the middle, recording the messages between the web browser and the server. Once set up, the requests sent from the browser go to TCPMON and TCPMON passes the request on to the server. The server passes back a response and then TCPMON, a transparent proxy (`http://en.wikipedia.org/wiki/Proxy_server`), returns the response to the web browser. This allows us to look at all requests and responses graphically.

First, you can set TCPMON up to listen on a given port number — by convention, normally, port 8888 — and then you can configure your web browser to send its requests through the proxy. Then, you can type the address of a given page into the web browser, but instead of going directly to the relevant server, the browser sends the request to the proxy, which then passes it on and passes the response back. TCPMON displays both the request and responses in a window.

You can download TCPMON from
`http://ws.apache.org/commons/tcpmon/download.cgi`.

After downloading and unpacking, you can, from within the build directory, run either `tcpmon.bat` for the Windows environment or `tcpmon.sh` for Unix/Linux environments. To configure a proxy, you can click the **Admin** tab and then set the **Listen Port** to **8888** and select the **Proxy** radio button. After that, clicking **Add** will create a new tab, where the requests and responses will later be displayed.

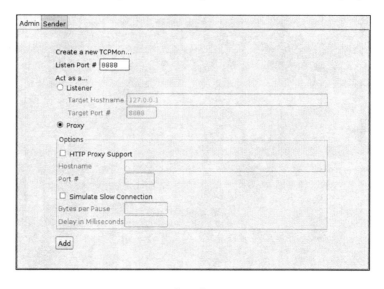

Your favorite web browser now has to recognize the newly set up proxy. For Firefox 3, you can do this by selecting the menu option **Edit/Preferences** and then choosing the **advanced** tab and the **network** tab, as shown next. You will need to set the proxy options HTTP proxy to 127.0.0.1 and the port number to 8888. If you do this, you will need to ensure that the No proxies text input is blank. Clicking the **OK** button enables the new settings.

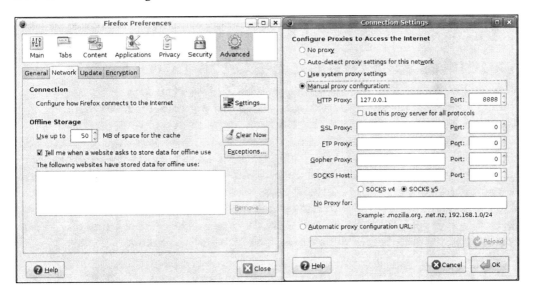

To use the Proxy from within Internet Explorer 7 for a Local Area Network (LAN), you can edit the dialog box found under **Tools | Internet Options | Connections | LAN** settings.

Once the proxy is working, typing `http://localhost:8080/portal/login` in the address bar will seamlessly return the login page of your local Sakai instance. Otherwise, you will see an error message similar to **Proxy Server Refused Connection** for Firefox or **Internet Explorer cannot display the webpage**.

To turn the proxy settings off, simply select the **No Proxies** radio box and click **OK** for Firefox 3, or unselect the **Use the proxy server for the LAN** tick box in Internet Explorer 7 and click **OK**.

Requests and returned status codes

When TCPMON is running a proxy on port 8888, it allows you to view the requests from the browser and the response in an extra tab, as shown in the following screen grab. Notice the extra information that the browser sends as part of the request. `HTTP/1.1` defines the protocol and version level and the lines below the `GET` are header variables. The `User-Agent` defines which client sent the request. The `Accept` headers tell the server what the capabilities of the browser are, and the `Cookie` header defines the value stored in a cookie. HTTP is stateless, that is, in principle; each response is based only on the current request. However, to get around this, persistent information can be stored in cookies. Web browsers normally store their representation of a cookie as a little text file or in a small database on the end users' computers.

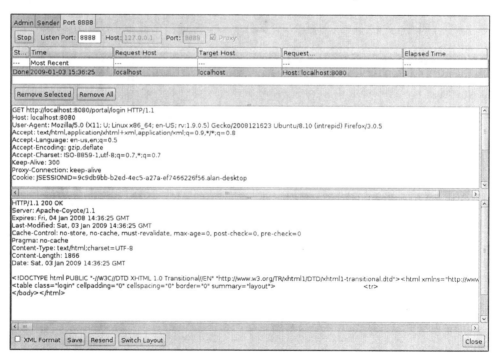

Sakai uses the supporting features of a servlet container, such as Tomcat, to maintain state in cookies. A cookie stores a session ID, and when the server sees the session ID, it can look up the request's server-side state. Server-side state contains information such as whether the user is logged in or what he or she has ordered. The web browser deletes the local representation of the cookie each time the browser closes.

 A cookie that is deleted when a web browser closes is known as a session cookie.

The server response starts with the protocol followed by a status number. HTTP/1.1 200 OK tells the web browser that the server is using HTTP version 1.1 and it was able to return the requested web page successfully. 2xx status codes imply success. 3xx status codes imply some form of redirection and tell the web browser where to try to pick up the requested resource. 4xx status codes are for client errors, such as malformed requests or lack of permission to obtain the resource. 4xx states are fertile grounds for security managers to look in log files for attempted hacking. 5xx status codes mostly have to do with a failure of the server itself and are mostly of interest to system administrators and programmers during the debugging cycle. In most cases, 5xx status numbers are about either high server load or a broken piece of code. Sakai is changing rapidly and even with the most vigorous testing, there are bound to be the occasional hiccups. You will find accurate details of the full range of status codes at: http://www.w3.org/Protocols/rfc2616/rfc2616-sec10.html.

Another important part of the response is the Content-Type, which tells the web browser which type of material the response is returning so the browser knows how to handle it. For example, the web browser may want to run a plug-in for video types and display text natively. The Content-Length in characters is normally also given. After the header information is finished, there is a newline followed by the content.

Web browsers interpret any redirects that are returned by sending extra requests. Web browsers also interpret any HTML pages and make multiple requests for resources such as JavaScript files and images. Modern browsers do not wait until the server returns all the requests, but render the HTML page live as the server returns the parts.

The GET verb is not very efficient for posting a large amount of data, as the URL has a length limit of around 2000 characters. Further, the end user can see the form data, and the browser may encode entities such as spaces to make the URL unreadable. There is also a security aspect: if you are typing in passwords in forms using GET, others may see your password or other details. This is not a good idea, especially at Internet Cafés where the next user who logs on can see the password in the browsing history. The POST verb is a better choice. Let us take as an example the Sakai demonstration login page `http://localhost:8080/portal/login`. The login page itself contains a form tag that points with the POST method to the relogin page.

```
<form method="post" action="http://localhost:8080/portal/relogin"
enctype="application/x-www-form-urlencoded">
```

Notice the HTML tag also defines the content type. Key features of the Post request compared to the GET are: the form values are stored as content after the header values, there is a newline between the end of the header and the data, and the request mentions data and the amount of data by the use of the `Content-Length` header value.

The essential POST values for a login form with user admin (`eid=admin`) and password admin (`pw=admin`) will look like:

```
POST http://localhost:8080/portal/relogin HTTP/1.1

Content-Type: application/x-www-form-urlencoded

Content-Length: 31


eid=admin&pw=admin&submit=Login
```

POSTs can contain much more information than GETs, and the request hides the values from the Address bar of the web browser. This is not secure. The header is just as visible as the URL, so POST values are also neither hidden nor secure. The only viable solution is for your web browser to encrypt your transactions using SSL/TLS (`http://www.ietf.org/rfc/rfc2246.txt`) for security, and this occurs every time you connect to a server using an HTTPS URL.

SOAP

Sakai uses the Apache Axis framework, which the developers have configured to accept SOAP calls via POST. SOAP sends messages in a specific XML format with the `Content-Type`, otherwise known as MIME type, `application/soap+xml`. A programmer does not need to know much more than that, as client libraries take care of the majority of the excruciating low-level details. An example SOAP message generated by the Perl module SOAP::Lite (`http://www.soaplite.com/`) for creating a login session in Sakai will look like the following Post data:

```
<?xml version="1.0" encoding="UTF-8"?>

<soap:Envelope xmlns:xsi="http://www.w3.org/2001/XMLSchema-instance"
xmlns:soapenc="http://schemas.xmlsoap.org/soap/encoding/" xmlns:
xsd="http://www.w3.org/2001/XMLSchema" soap:encodingStyle="http://
schemas.xmlsoap.org/soap/encoding/" xmlns:soap="http://schemas.xmlsoap.
org/soap/envelope/">

<soap:Body>

<login xmlns="http://localhost:8081/sakai-axis/SakaiLogin.jws">

   <c-gensym3 xsi:type="xsd:string">admin</c-gensym3>

   <c-gensym5 xsi:type="xsd:string">admin</c-gensym5>

</login>

</soap:Body>

</soap:Envelope>
```

There is an envelope with a body containing data for the service to consume. The important point to remember is that both the client and the server have to be able to parse the specific XML schema. SOAP messages can include extra security features, but Sakai does not require these. The architects expect organizations to encrypt web services using SSL/TSL.

The last extra SOAP-related complexity is the Web Service Description Language (http://www.w3.org/TR/wsdl). Web services may change location or exist in multiple locations for redundancy. The service writer can define the location of the services and the data types involved with those services in another file, in XML format.

JSON

Also worth mentioning is **JavaScript Object Notation (JSON)** (http://tools. ietf.org/html/rfc4627), which is another popular format passed using HTTP. A significant improvement in the quality of the end user experience during web browsing occurred when web developers realized that they could force browsers to load parts of a web page in at a time. This asynchronous loading enables all kinds of whiz-bang features, such as when you type in a search term and can choose from a set of search term completions before pressing submit. Asynchronous loading delivers more responsive and richer web pages that feel more like traditional applications than a plain old web page. JSON is one of the formats of choice for passing asynchronous requests and responses.

The asynchronous communication normally occurs through HTTP GET or POST, but with a specific content structure that is designed to be human readable and script language parser-friendly. JSON calls have the file extension .json as part of the URL. As mentioned in RFC 4627, an example image object communicated in JSON looks like:

```
{
    "Image": {
        "Width":  800,
        "Height": 600,
        "Title":  "View from 15th Floor",
        "Thumbnail": {
            "Url":     "http://www.example.com/image/481989943",
            "Height": 125,
            "Width":  "100"
        },
        "IDs": [116, 943, 234, 38793]
    }
}
```

To confuse the boundaries between client and server, a lot of the presentation and business logic is locked on the client side in scripting languages such as JavaScript. The scripting language orchestrates the loading of parts of pages and the generation of widget sets. Frameworks such as jQuery (http://jquery.com/) and MyFaces (http://myfaces.apache.org/) significantly ease the client-side programming burden.

REST

To understand REST, you need to understand the other verbs in HTTP (http://www.w3.org/Protocols/rfc2616/rfc2616-sec9.html). The full HTTP set is OPTIONS, GET, HEAD, POST, PUT, DELETE, and TRACE.

The HEAD verb returns from the server only the headers of the response without the content, and is useful for clients that want to see if the content has changed since the last request. PUT requests that the content in the request be stored at the particular location mentioned in the request. DELETE is for deleting the entity.

REST uses the URL of the request to route to the resource, and the HTTP verb GET is used to get a resource, PUT to update, DELETE to delete, and POST to add a new resource. In general, POST=create an item, PUT=update an item, DELETE=delete an item, and GET=return information on the item.

In SOAP, you are pointing directly towards the service the client calls or indirectly via the web service description. However, in REST, part of the URL describes the resource or resources you wish to work with. For example, a hypothetical address book application that lists all email addresses in HTML format would look similar to the following:

```
GET /email
```

To list the addresses in XML format or JSON format:

```
GET /email.xml
GET /email.json
```

To get the first email address in the list:

```
GET /email/1
```

To create a new email address, of course remembering to add the rest of email details to the end of the GET:

```
POST /email
```

And to delete address 5 in the list:

```
DELETE /email/5
```

To obtain address 5 in other formats such as JSON or XML, then use file extensions at the end of the URL, for example:

```
GET /email/5.json
GET /email/5.xml
```

RESTful services are more intuitively descriptive than SOAP services and they enable easy switching of the format from HTML to JSON to fuel dynamic, asynchronously-loaded web sites. Due to the direct use of HTTP verbs by REST, this methodology also fits well with the most common application type: CRUD (Create, Read, Update, Delete) applications, such as the site or user tools within Sakai.

Now that we have discussed the theory, in the next section, we shall discuss which Sakai-related SOAP services already exist.

Existing web services

Sakai has built in, by default, the most community-requested web services, and there are also a few more services in the contributed section of the source code repository. This section describes the currently available services and the next section explains an example use, creating a new user.

Recapping terminology

In general, developers write web services for other developer's code to connect to (consume). Therefore, terminology can be confusing. Recapping from the last chapter: in Sakai, a realm is a set of roles and their associated permissions. When you create a site, a copy is made from a specific realm template for that particular site type. The permissions can then be modified for the roles in the site, and members added to the site with one or other of the specific roles. Internally, Sakai uses AuthzGroups to keep track of groups of users. An AuthzGroup is an authorization group (a group of users, each with a role and a set of permissions of functions assigned to each role). A site contains pages; when you click on the tool menu for a given tool, normally, you will see one tool displayed in a page. However, for the home page tool, you will see more tools contained within a page.

Default web services

The following table defines the default web services and the methods included. Notice that the SakaiScript service is the most comprehensive.

 To enable the web services, you will need to add the property webservices.allowlogin=true in sakai/sakai.properties.

Service	Methods	Description
SakaiLogin	login, logout	Web services need to log in before they can call other services that do work
SakaiPortalLogin	login, loginAndCreate, UsageSessionService_loginDirect	Web services to help connections from Portal software such as uPortal

Service	Methods	Description
SakaiScript	checkSession, addNewUser, removeUser, changeUserInfo, changeUserName, changeUserEmail, changeUserType, changeUserPassword, getUserEmail, getUserDisplayName, addNewAuthzGroup, removeAuthzGroup, addNewRoleToAuthzGroup, removeAllRolesFromAuthzGroup, removeRoleFromAuthzGroup, allowFunctionForRole, disallowAllFunctionsForRole, setRoleDescription, addMemberToAuthzGroupWithRole, removeMemberFromAuthzGroup, removeAllMembersFromAuthzGroup, setRoleForAuthzGroupMaintenance, addMemberToSiteWithRole,add NewSite, removeSite, copySite, addNewPageToSite, removePageFromSite, addNewToolToPage, addConfigPropertyToTool, checkForUser, checkForSite, checkForMemberInAuthzGroupWithRole, getSitesUserCanAccess	Function-rich service that includes the main services you would expect for manipulating users, sites, memberships, and permissions in sites
SakaiSession	checkSession, getSessionUser	Service that returns the session information of the string sent to it
SakaiSigning	establishSession, testsign, verifysign, getsession, touchsession	Enables external application to verify a user and is normally used in conjunction with the Rutgers Link tool
SakaiSite	establishSession, getUserSite, getSiteList, joinAllSites, getSitesDom, getToolsDom	Site manipulation services. The methods with the word DOM return strings in a specific XML format

A number of the services have the same `establishSession` method. This saves the client code calling a second service (`SakaiLogin`).

A consumer of web services is the Rutgers Link tool (`https://source.sakaiproject.org/svn//linktool/`). The link tool is a tool within Sakai that points outward to an external application of choice and makes the end user believe the external tool is actually part of Sakai. The end user clicks the tool link. On clicking, the link directs the user's browser to the external application. As part of the request, the browser passes on a cookie containing an encrypted session ID. The external application then sends the encrypted session back to the `testSign` method contained within the `SakaiSigning` web service, which will return true if the link tool generated the session. Through this approach, **Single Sign-On (SSO)** between Sakai and an external application is achieved and the external tool now looks like part of the Sakai site.

There are extra web services available in the contributed source repository (`https://source.sakaiproject.org/contrib`), including:

- `/rutgers/webservices/` for grade book manipulation
- `/sakaiadminx/trunk/ws/` to support delegated administration
- `/uct/webservices/` for manipulating assignments, users, content, and the message center, presence, and profile
- `/qa/trunk/provisioning/version_2/` — an offering from the University of Michigan and Amsterdam University to support the generation of large numbers of populated sites, ready for use as part of realistic stress testing environment

Sakai and SOAP

Sakai SOAP web services piggyback on top of the Apache Axis project. Creating basic Sakai web services is programmer-friendly because Apache Axis removes many of the hard chores. All you have to do is create a Java class in a text file under the `/web-apps/sakai-axis` directory and any public method is automatically compiled into a service with a WSDL file automatically generated for it, ready for discovery by the client program. The compilation of the web service occurs after creation or modification and is triggered by the next incoming request. What is helpful is that when you make a typo or other mistake, the server displays the compilation error as a web page at the URL of the broken service, as shown in the next screen grab. Notice that the line number and type of error are included. The combination of text processing with a rich set of services to call on, plus the fact that it is not necessary to restart the server every time you compile, makes for rapid development cycles.

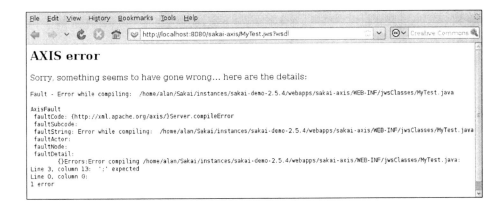

My first web service

To create your first web service, you can add the file `/web-apps/sakai-axis/MyTest.jws` with the following contents to a running demonstration instance of Sakai:

```java
public class MyTest{
    public String YouSaid(String message){
        return "You said: "+message;
    }
}
```

Then, typing in `http://localhost:8080/sakai-axis/MyTest.jws?wsdl` will return a corresponding WSDL file similar to the figure below. Notice that it would take a human perhaps 30 minutes to generate the file and the computer took milliseconds.

My first client

For the programmers among you, the following piece of Perl code consumes the service:

```
#!/usr/bin/perl
use SOAP::Lite;
my $host='http://localhost:8080';
my $soap = SOAP::Lite -> proxy("$host/sakai-axis/MyTest.jws?wsdl");
my $result =$soap->YouSaid("WHAT!");
print $result->result()."\n\n";
```

The returned result is:

```
You said: WHAT!
```

The SOAP Lite module interprets the WSDL file and after that, you can name the web service method directly in the code with the correct number of parameters. This feature results in code that is much more readable and thus maintainable. Changing the variable `$host` changes the server location. Changing the service and method requires the little nudge of modifying lines 4 and 5.

A more realistic client example

Sakai web services will not let you perform any action without fulfilling two prerequisites: the first is you need to set the property `webservices.allowlogin=true` in `sakai/sakai.properties`, and the second is that the client code needs to obtain a session in the form of a returned random string from a login service, and then use this string as part of any calls you make to other services. If the client code tries to perform any action without logging in, the server returns an error message.

The login service requires a username and password and it is very important to note that in production, you are expected to run the client code over an SSL/TLS connection.

The following piece of Perl code gets a session ID and then uses it as part of a second web service call to the `addNewUser` method, which, as you would expect from the name, then creates a new user in Sakai.

```perl
#!/usr/bin/perl
use SOAP::Lite;
my $host='http://localhost:8080';
my $soap = SOAP::Lite

      -> proxy("$host/sakai-axis/SakaiLogin.jws?wsdl");
   my $result =$soap->login("admin","admin");
my $sessionid=$result->result();
$soap = SOAP::Lite

   -> proxy("$host/sakai-axis/SakaiScript.jws?wsdl");
$soap->addNewUser( $sessionid, 'alanberg', 'Alan', 'Berg', 'berg@xx.nl',
'', 'useruser');
if ($result->fault) {
  print "Error";
} else {
  print "Success\n";
}
```

Even if you find the Perl code unreadable, the point of the example is to show how only few lines of coding are required for an enterprise to hook into Sakai.

Entity Broker

Over time, more and more tools and services are included with Sakai. Therefore, there is an ever-expanding set of data, such as courses, users, polls, forums, grade books, assessments, and new data structures, available for integration.

It would be handy indeed if instead of needing to write custom web services per new entity, a tool programmer could call a service, write, and register his or her data for exposure. The kernel would then become responsible for the end delivery and the RESTful web services. Because the programmer does not have to deal as much with the details as before the services existed, the structure reduces the duplication of code and effort and increases maintainability, quality, and scalability, and generally eases the programmer's burden. Further, if by default, the entities are exposed as MIME types HTML, .JSON, .XML, you can write rich web-based applications and widget sets that consume the .JSON and .XML formats from the data within Sakai.

The Entity Broker is one such service that allows code to find and get at important data in Sakai and easily manipulate that data from within Java objects. To accommodate the ever-changing set of requirements, the data needs to have some uniform parts to it, such as an ID and an associated URL, and it needs to have the ability to register its existence to a central service. If the data has this kind of a structure, it is called an entity, the original technical details of which you can find in the source code under `/reference/docs/architecture/sakai_entity.doc`.

You can find the Java-specific details of the Entity Broker on Confluence (`http://confluence.sakaiproject.org/confluence/display/SAKDEV/Entity+Provider+and+Broker`).

Unless you are a hardcore Sakai kernel programmer, it really is not important to understand the hidden and subtle details. You just need to know how to find out which services exist and how to do business with those services.

Finding descriptions of services

For the demonstration instance, the Entity Broker services exist under the `/direct` URL space. To view a human-readable description of all the services, visit `http://localhost:8080/direct/desc`. The following figure is the description of services available on one of the Sakai QA servers.

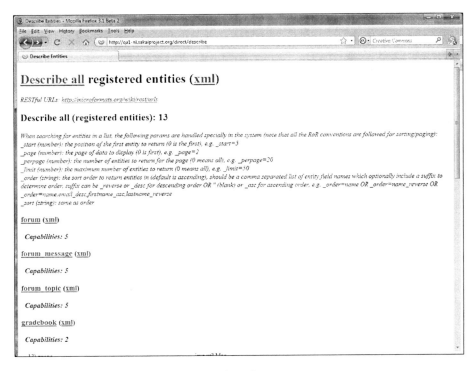

To zoom into the description of the user service, use the following demonstration URL: `http://localhost:8080/direct/user/describe`.

On different tag versions of Sakai, different services exist. However, every available entity is described by the same URL structure: `http://hostname:port/direct/entity_prefix/describe`.

It is helpful to read the specific description page for each entity, as Entity Broker empowers the programmer to add custom actions. The `describe` page next is for the `user` entity.

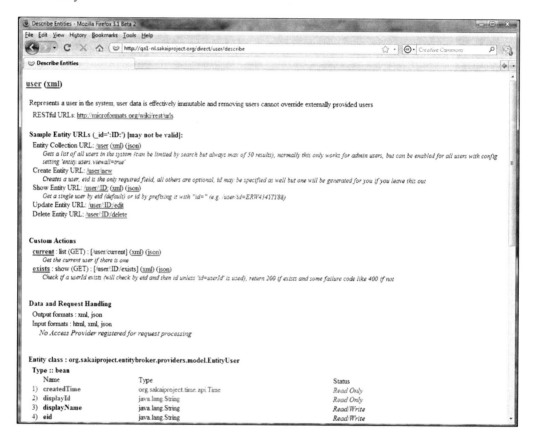

Notice that custom actions currently exist and the server returns data in either XML or in the JSON format.

Before logging on to the demonstration instance of Sakai, first visit the URL `http://localhost:8080/direct/user/current`. Notice that the returned HTML page tells you in a 400 HTTP status error message that there is no current user to get user information about. This makes sense, as you have not logged in. After you log in and revisit the page, the server still does not return the user information. Instead, an error occurs, as HTML is not one of the supported return formats for this entity. The JSON format is, and to obtain your current information in JSON format, simply visit: `http://localhost:8080/direct/user/current.json`

Authenticating

At this point in the section, if you have everything set up properly to run TCPMON and watch the request and responses generated, then running the example code mentioned next will allow you to see how REST works in practice.

For a client-side application to create a new user, it must first obtain a session via a post to the URL `http://localhost:8080/direct/session/new` with the variables `_username` and `_password` set, as described in `http://localhost:8080/direct/session/describe`. The server returns the session ID in the form of one of the header values, `EntityId`, which the script then passes on in any sent requests. You can also pass the `sessionId` as `sakai.session=sessionId` as a header or in the URL. You can also use a cookie with the same values included.

To create a user, the client application will need to post to the user service with at minimum the `eid` (Enterprise ID) variable set. Note that the `user/describe` URL explains which name and value pairs are valid.

A client-side coding example

For the programming-inclined, I include the following listing that creates a session as user `admin`, with the password `admin`, and then creates a user in Sakai with `eid=its_alive`, `firstName=The` and `lastName=Monster`. For the sake of brevity, there is no programmatic error checking.

```
#!/usr/bin/perl -w
use strict;
use LWP::UserAgent;
use HTTP::Request::Common;

my $host='http://localhost:8080';
my $credential = "_username=admin&_password=admin";
my $user='eid=its_alive&firstName=The&lastName=Monster';
```

```perl
my $userAgent = LWP::UserAgent->new();

my $response = $userAgent->request(POST "$host/direct/session/new",

Content_Type => 'application/x-www-form-urlencoded',

Content => $credential);

my $entityid= $response->header('EntityId');

print "Session:  $host/direct/session/$entityid\n";

$response = $userAgent->request(POST "$host/direct/user/new",

Content_Type => 'application/x-www-form-urlencoded',

Content => $user);

$entityid= $response->header('EntityId');

print "User [json format]: $host/direct/user/$entityid.json\n";

print "User [XML format]: $host/direct/user/$entityid.xml\n";
```

On running, the output of the script should look similar to the following:

```
Session:  http://localhost:8080/direct/session/770588c7-9a58-46f6-8d47-
7c92cab93759

User [json format]: http://localhost:8080/direct/user/c9ab941f-3fac-4827-
ad00-c4f98cf9ad5e.json

User [XML format]: http://localhost:8080/direct/user/c9ab941f-3fac-4827-
ad00-c4f98cf9ad5e.xml
```

Once you have written one client script, any new scripts are going to be quite similar. Expect an ever-expanding set of client scripts to be included in the contrib section, waiting for new organizations to pick them up.

Interview with Entity Broker author Aaron Zeckoski

Who is Aaron Zeckoski and what is his relationship with Sakai?

I am a developer and Senior Research Engineer for CARET (Centre for Applied Research in Educational Technologies), University of Cambridge. I am responsible for webapp and service development. I have worked in academic computing for about seven years, maintaining development documentation for Sakai and running training for Sakai developers. I am an inaugural Sakai Fellow and test-driven development advocate, DSpace and Sakai committer.

Can you tell us a little bit about the functionality you have been involved in coding into Sakai in general?

Many bug fixes and patches for various boring things, Integration works at various universities. Development tools like the Sakai App Builder, ReflectUtils, and GenericDAO. Tools like Evaluation and BlogWow. Data feeds for the UX project.

What was your motivation for writing Entity Broker?

I needed a way to generate clean URLs into Sakai tools and wanted to make Sakai development and integration with core services easier for the average developer. Further, I wanted a more standard way to handle REST and data input and output in Sakai. I wanted to make external (non-Java) Sakai development easier.

Why did you choose to use RESTful services over SOAP services?

REST is easier for the average developer to understand and it integrates and works with anything without much effort. It is also much easier to use with things like Javascript/AJAX.

Have you any future plans for Entity Broker

Add more support for standards (OpenSearch 1.1 URL support was just added) and output formats (RSS, ATOM are on the radar), integration with GWT, make it more modular so it can be used in projects like K2 and DSpace 2.

WSRP

Portals such as uPortal (`http://www.uportal.org`) aggregate information from various systems into channels that are part of one view for the user. A typical university may include an accumulation of the newest emails, RSS feeds for up and coming events, and links into important systems such as Sakai and the library systems. An institute can enforce a single corporate look and feel through a portal and empower the end user to transverse efficiently through their most current personalized information.

In the Java world, programmers can package channels into little applications that interact in a standard way with the portal system. These standard packages are called portlets and the interactions are standardized via JSR-168 (`http://jcp.org/aboutJava/communityprocess/review/jsr168/`). This standardization allows the portlets to be shared between different commercial and non-commercial portals and enables organizations to avoid locking in to a particular vendor's solution.

The issue with JSR-168 portlets is that the standardization constrains the range of events the portlet can react to and consequently makes the user experience less rich.

Portlets reside on the portal and, traditionally, get their own external data from RSS feeds or under the water via web services.

Sakai is thoroughly RSS enabled. For example, visit the main page of your demonstration server with the URL `http://localhost:8080/portal/rss` and you will see an RSS-rendered version of the main page. After logging in and visiting the page again, you will get to see more details. For a PDA-compliant page, visit `http://localhost:8080/portal/pda`.

Having all the portlet code on the portal system makes for a lot of code in one place and this is a serious risk for later trouble in terms of performance, code duplication, maintainability, and connecting to external data sources consistently. The web services for Remote Portlets WSRP (`http://oasis-open.org/committee/wsrp`) service allows a Portal to call WSRP-enabled portlets remotely directly from the portal via web services. On the portal side, all you would need now is a connector that an administrator can then configure to target a specific service.

Building a viable Portal system has knock-on effects on the background systems. If users hit the Portal heavily, and potentially the whole of an organizations population, then also expect a considerable increase in usage on the secondary systems. The deploying organization needs to preemptively strengthen legacy systems. Further, end users naturally expect to safely follow links from the various feeds directly into the associated background application. End users do not expect to have to log in more than once and only through the portal. If enacted, Single Sign On through mechanisms such as CAS (`http://www.ja-sig.org/products/cas/`) or Shibboleth (`http://shibboleth.internet2.edu/`) is viable. Uniform provisioning of user accounts across the full spectrum of linked-to applications is also a concern.

For Sakai, it makes sense to expose to a portal user a list of what is new in the user's courses, schedules, the Message of the Day, and other facets of the daily interaction between learners and Sakai. Whenever possible, it is a good idea for system integrators to use current standards to do so.

Activating the services within Sakai requires downloading and installing an extra web application (Servlet) that runs within a specific Sakai instance and delivers the WSRP producer services. The location of the most up-to-date README is `https://source.sakaiproject.org/svn/wsrp/trunk/producer/README.txt`. The code is based on the WSRP4J framework `http://portals.apache.org/wsrp4j`.

As the code is not included as part of the enterprise core tool set, your organization will have to fully test any significant deployments.

In summary to this section, there is code available to connect a Portal to Sakai via WSRP-based web services. However, you need to test the code before you deploy it in production.

Summary

Web services are one of the standard approaches to enterprise integration. The services allow for lazy coupling with consuming applications. Lazy coupling implies that you can replace one service with another without the code in a client application needing to change.

Sakai has a basic set of SOAP-based web services available, which an administrator can turn on by setting `webservices.allowlogin=true` in the `sakai/sakai.properties` file. There are more services that you can deploy stored in the contrib section of Sakai.

By placing a text file with a few lines of Java in the right location in Sakai, a programmer can create new web services rapidly. Many client-side libraries remove the need to understand the underlying complexities of the protocols involved.

The Entity Broker exposes managed data (entities) within Sakai, such as the representation of users and sites by RESTful web services. You can discover currently available services by visiting `http://host/direct`.

It is possible to connect Sakai to Portal systems via the WSRP standard.

The next chapter, *Tips from the Trenches*, is an advanced chapter that explains concepts that you need during first-time Sakai deployments. In it, you will find an overview of the third-party frameworks that Sakai is built upon, how to manage and monitor Java, and interviews with various experts.

12
Tips from the Trenches

This advanced chapter explains concepts that you may need during first-time Sakai deployments. In it, there is an overview of the third-party frameworks that Sakai is built on and information about how to manage and monitor Java.

To inject realism, also included are three interviews with experts: The first interview is with Megan May of Indiana University who was until recently the Director of Quality Assurance working closely with a large number of testers. The second interview is with Seth Theriault, a long-standing and well known member of the community. He is a system integrator at Columbia University. The final interview is with David Howitz, who is a learning environment developer at the University of Cape Town.

Further, two experts have written specific sections: Zach Thomas, Sakai fellow and for-hire consultancy gun, discusses content migration. Zach has previously designed and coded some of the important structures that enable migration of course content within Sakai. David Jan Donner is the senior Functional Administrator at the University of Amsterdam and writes about organizational structures with the call centre as gateway.

The benefits of knowing that frameworks exist

Sakai is built on top of numerous third-party open source libraries and frameworks. Why write code for converting from XML text files to Java objects or connecting and managing databases, when others have specialized, and thought out the technical problems and found appropriate and consistent solutions? This reuse of code saves effort and decreases the complexity of creating new functionality. Using third-party frameworks has other benefits as well; you can choose the best from a series of external libraries, increasing the quality of your own product. The external frameworks have their own communities who actively test them. Outsourcing generic requirements, such as the rudiments of generating indexes for searching, allows the Sakai community to concentrate on higher-level goals such as building new tools.

For developers, also for course instructors and system administrators, it is useful background to know, roughly, what the underlying frameworks do.

- For a developer, it makes sense to look at reuse first. Why invent the wheel? Why write with external framework X for manipulating XML files when other developers have already extensively tried and tested and are running framework Y? Knowing, what others have done saves you time. This knowledge is especially handy for the new-to-Sakai developer who could be tempted to write from scratch.

- For the system administrator, each framework has its own strengths, weaknesses, and terminology. Understanding the terminology and technologies gives you a head start in debugging glitches and communicating with the developers. For a manager, knowing that Sakai has chosen solid and well-respected open source libraries should help influence buying decisions in favor of this platform.

 Chapter 16 explores the Sakai buy-in theme further.

- For the course instructor, knowing which frameworks exist and what their potential is helps inform the debate about adding interesting new features. Knowing what Sakai uses and what is possible sharpens the instructors' focus and ability to define realistic requirements.

- For the software engineering student, Sakai represents a collection of best practices and frameworks that will make the student more saleable in the labor market.

Third-party frameworks

This section details frameworks that Sakai is heavily dependent on: Spring (http://www.springsource.org/), Hibernate (http://www.hibernate.org/), and numerous Apache projects (http://www.apache.org/).

Generally, Java application builders understand these frameworks. This makes it relatively easy to hire programmers with experience.

All projects are open source and the individual use does not clash with Sakai's open source license (http://www.opensource.org/licenses/ecl2.php).

Spring

Spring is tightly architected set of frameworks designed to support the main goals of building modern business applications. Spring has a broad set of abilities, from connecting to databases, to transaction, managing business logic, validation, security, and remote access. It fully supports the most modern architectural design patterns.

The framework takes away a lot of drudgery for a programmer and enables pieces of code to be plugged in or removed by editing XML configuration files rather than refactoring the raw codebase itself. You can see this best for the user provider within Sakai. When you log in, you may want to validate the user credentials using a piece of code that connects to a directory service such as LDAP, or replace the code with another piece of code that gets credentials from an external database or even reads from a text file. Thanks to Sakai services that rely on Spring, you can give (called injecting) the wanted code to a Service manager, which then calls the code when needed.

 In Sakai terminology, within a running application a service manager manages services for a particular type of data. For example, a course service manager allows programmers to add, modify, or delete courses. A user service manager does the same for users.

Spring is responsible for deciding which pieces of code it injects into which service managers, and developers do not need to program the heavy lifting, only the configuration. The advantage is that later, as part of adapting Sakai to a specific organization, system administrators can also reconfigure authentication or many other services to tailor to local preferences without recompilation.

Spring abstracts away underlying differences between different databases. This allows you to program once for MySQL, Oracle, and so on, without having to take into account the databases' differences. Spring can sit on top of Hibernate and more limited frameworks such as JDBC (yet another standard for connecting to databases). This adaptability gives architects more freedom to change and refactor (the process of changing the structure of the code to improve it) without affecting other parts of the code. As Sakai grows in code size, Spring and good architectural design patterns diminish the chance breaking older code.

In summary, the Spring framework makes programming more efficient. It is the main framework on which Sakai relies. Many tasks that programmers would have previously hard coded are now delegated to XML configuration files.

Hibernate

Hibernate is all about coupling databases to the code. Hibernate is a powerful, high performance object/relational persistence and query service. That is to say, a designer describes Java objects in a specific structure within XML files. After reading these files, Hibernate gains the ability to save or load instances of the object from the database. Hibernate supports complex data structures such as Java collections and arrays of objects. Again, it is a choice of an external framework that does the programmer's dog work, mostly via XML configuration.

Apache frameworks

Sakai is rightfully biased toward projects associated with the Apache Software Foundation (ASF) (http://www.apache.org/). Sakai instances run within a Tomcat server and many institutes place an Apache web server in front of the Tomcat server to deal with dishing out static content (content that does not change, such as an ordinary web page), SSL/TLS, ease of configuration, and log parsing. Further, individual internal and external frameworks make use of the Apache commons frameworks, (http://commons.apache.org/) which have reusable libraries for all kinds of specific needs, such as validation, encoding, emailing, uploading files, and so on. Even if a developer does not use the common libraries directly, they are often called by other frameworks and have significant impact on the wellbeing, for example, security, of a Sakai instance.

To ensure look and feel consistency, designers used common technologies such as Apache Velocity, Apache MyFaces (an implementation of Java Server Faces), Reasonable Server Faces (RSF), and plain old Java Server Pages (JSP).

Apache Velocity places much of the look and feel in text templates that non-programmers can then manipulate with text editors. The use of Velocity is mostly superseded by JSF. However, as Sakai moves forward, technologies such as RSF and Wicket (`http://wicket.apache.org/`) are playing a predominate role.

The following paragraph is written for Java programmers new to Sakai—feel free to skip.

Sakai uses XML as the format of choice to support much of its functionality, from configuration files, to the backing up of sites and the storage of internal data representations, RSS feeds, and so on. There is a lot of runtime effort in converting to and from XML and translating XML into other formats. Here are the gory technical details: There are two main methods for parsing XML. You can parse (another word for process) XML into a Document Object Model (DOM) in memory that you can later transverse and manipulate programmatically. XML can also be parsed via an event-driven mechanism where Java methods are called, for example when an XML tag begins or ends or there is a body to the tag. Programmatically Simple API for XML (SAX) libraries supports the second approach in Java. Generally, it is easier to program with DOM than SAX, but as you need a model of the XML in memory, DOM, by its nature, is more memory intensive. Why would that matter? In large-scale deployments, the amount of memory tends to limit a Sakai instance's performance rather than Sakai being limited by the computational power of the servers. Therefore, as Sakai heavily uses XML, whenever possible, a developer should consider using SAX and avoid keeping the whole model of the XML document in memory.

Dependencies

As Sakai adapts and expands its feature set, expect the range of external libraries to expand.

The table mentions libraries used, their link to the relevant home page, and a very brief description of their functionality.

Name	Homepage	Description
Apache-Axis	`http://ws.apache.org/axis/`	SOAP Web services
Apache-Axis2	`http://ws.apache.org/axis2`	SOAP, REST web services. A total rewrite of Apache-axis. However, not currently used within Entity Broker, a Sakai specific component, explained in the *Web Services* chapter.
Apache Commons	`http://commons.apache.org`	Lower-level utilities
Batik	`http://xmlgraphics.apache.org/batik/`	Batik is a Java-based toolkit for applications or applets that want to use images in the Scalable Vector Graphics (SVG) format.
Commons-beanutils	`http://commons.apache.org/beanutils/`	Methods for Java bean manipulation
Commons-codec	`http://commons.apache.org/codec`	Commons Codec provides implementations of common encoders and decoders, such as Base64, Hex, Phonetic, and URLs.
Commons-digester	`http://commons.apache.org/digester`	Common methods for initializing objects from XML configuration
Commons-httpclient	`http://hc.apache.org/httpcomponents-client`	Supports HTTP-based standards with the client side in mind
Commons-logging	`http://commons.apache.org/logging/`	Logging support
Commons-validator	`http://commons.apache.org/validator`	Support for verifying the integrity of received data

Name	Homepage	Description
Excalibur	`http://excalibur.apache.org`	Utilities
FOP	`http://xmlgraphics.apache.org/fop`	Print formatting ready for conversions to PDF and a number of other formats
Hibernate	`http://www.hibernate.org`	ORM database framework
Log4j	`http://logging.apache.org/log4j`	For logging
Jackrabbit	`http://jackrabbit.apache.org` `http://jcp.org/en/jsr/detail?id=170`	Content repository. A content repository is a hierarchical content store with support for structured and unstructured content, full text search, versioning, transactions, observation, and more.
James	`http://james.apache.org`	A mail server
Java Server Faces	`http://java.sun.com/javaee/javaserverfaces`	Simplifies building user interfaces for JavaServer applications
Lucene	`http://lucene.apache.org`	Indexing
MyFaces	`http://myfaces.apache.org`	JSF implementation with implementation-specific widgets
Pluto	`http://portals.apache.org/pluto`	The Reference Implementation of the Java Portlet Specfication
Quartz	`http://www.opensymphony.com/quartz`	Scheduling
Reasonable Server Faces (RSF)	`http://www2.caret.cam.ac.uk/rsfwiki`	RSF is built on the Spring framework, and simplifies the building of views via XHTML.
ROME	`https://rome.dev.java.net`	ROME is a set of open source Java tools for parsing, generating, and publishing RSS and Atom feeds.
SAX	`http://www.saxproject.org`	Event-based XML parser
STRUTS	`http://struts.apache.org/`	Heavy-weight MVC framework, not used in the core of Sakai, but rather some components used as part of the occasional tool

Name	Homepage	Description
Spring	http://www.springsource.org	Used extensively within the code base of Sakai. It is a broad framework that is designed to make building business applications simpler.
Tomcat	http://tomcat.apache.org	Servlet container
Velocity	http://velocity.apache.org	Templating
Wicket	http://wicket.apache.org	Web app development framework
Xalan	http://xml.apache.org/xalan-j/	An XSLT (Extensible Stylesheet Language Transformation) processor for transforming XML documents into HTML, text, or other XML document types
xerces	http://xerces.apache.org/xerces-j	XML parser

For the reader who has downloaded and built Sakai from source code, you can automatically generate a list of current external dependencies via Maven. First, you will need to build the binary version and then print out the dependency report. To achieve this from within the top-level directory of the source code, you can run the following commands:

```
mvn -Ppack-demo install
```

```
mvn dependency:list
```

The table is based on an abbreviated version of the dependency list, generated from the most current source code from March 2009.

For those of you wishing to dive into the depths of Sakai, you can search the homepages mentioned in the table.

In summary, Spring is the most important underlying third-party framework and Sakai spends a lot of its time manipulating XML.

Expanded tour of Java

Sakai is a Java-based application. Not only are its parts written in Java, but the Tomcat server that it is running on is Java-based well. This section explores how to monitor and tune Java/Sakai.

Introduction

Java runs on many operating systems and types of hardware. To achieve this high degree of consistent compatibility, tools compile the Java source into runnable code (known as pseudo byte code) and run the code in a virtual machine that sits between the running code and the operating system. The Java Virtual Machine (JVM) hides the underlying complexity by abstracting details away in the language itself, so that programmers call the same methods, such as for opening files, no matter which hardware or operating system the code is running on.

The JVM also manages the Java application's memory via a Garbage Collector (GC), which cleans up the objects that are no longer used. The JVM manages memory by splitting it up into parts. When objects are first created, they are placed in a young object space. Later, as objects get older, they are copied to other spaces, and for old objects, to a memory location known as tenured space. During the process of copying objects, the GC removes the objects that a running program does not reference. When tenured space fills up, then the JVM stops running the code and the GC does a thorough clean up. Under high student usage, this stops the world process; a process that stops an application from running while running itself, has significant potential to hurt your favorite mission-critical application.

You can configure the JVM via the `JAVA_OPTS` environment variable. You can tell it to reserve a certain amount of memory and which method to use to clean memory up and turn on/off, or generally tweak numerous features. An excellent paper on GC-related options is located here: `http://java.sun.com/j2se/reference/whitepapers/memorymanagement_whitepaper.pdf`.

The JVM has more than one method for garbage collection. On starting, the JVM checks the system it is running on and partially configures the garbage collector to match the systems capabilities. To tell the JVM that it is running as a server application you should set the `-server` option in `JAVA_OPTS`. For Sakai, these options are set in `start-sakai.sh` for Unix/Linux or `start-sakai.bat` for Windows machines.

The minimum and maximum memory that the JVM can use is set by `-Xms` (minimum) and `-Xmx` (maximum). To save computational effort during garbage collection, you should consider setting the two values equal. Further, the JVM can run in 32 bit or 64-bit mode on 64-bit hardware. Theoretically, on a 32-bit JVM, you should be able to address 4GB of memory. However, due to the way the underlying OS manages memory, you may in practice be limited to around 2 GB or 3 GB.

64-bit mode allows for more memory reservation, but using 64 bits results in slightly larger object sizes and potentially longer stop-the-world garbage collections as the JVM has more space to tidy up. The JAVA_OPTS setting for this is `-d64`.

The JVM reserves a space in memory for loading in the definitions of objects and other data. Java specialists know this space as permanent space, or permspace for short. Currently, most production servers set this at around 512 MB; to do so requires the option `-XX:PermSize=512m`.

The JVM loads in by default a number of Java libraries, including ones for graphical display. However, the Sakai instance does not need these libraries, as it runs over the network and not through a local GUI. To tell the JVM of the situation requires setting the value `java.awt.headless` to true.

Finally, the JVM can run the garbage collection in parallel using more than one CPU or serially. Modern hardware has multiple core CPUs, so triggering parallel garbage collection improves behavior. The relevant JAVA_OPT for this is `-XX:+UseParallelGC`.

Below, I give a full JAVA_OPTS example. The options force the JVM to run on the server in 64-bit mode with parallel garbage collection, reserving 8 GB of memory, of which 512 MB is reserved for permspace. The JAVA_OPTS are also telling the JVM it is headless, that is the server runs without monitor or keyboard attached, and you can manage it over the network.

```
-server -d64 -Xms8g -Xmx8g -XX:PermSize=512m -XX:MaxPermSize=512m -Djava.
awt.headless=true -XX:+UseParallelGC
```

Numerous organizations have already deployed Sakai with great success. The Sakai Foundation collects the deployment data, see: `http://bugs.sakaiproject.org/jira/secure/IssueNavigator.jspa?pager/start=100`. Most of the deployments in the list include their servers' JVM options as a reference.

Three recommendations for anyone wishing to optimize are:

- Read the examples given in the link and try to understand what all the options do.
- Use the best-suited values for your hardware as the start point for testing.

- Simplify. The JVM is very good at its memory clean up tasks for most applications, most of the time. Do not use options for influencing garbage collection unless there are good measurable reasons or instinctive suspicions to do so.

Setting your memory size settings to optimum and debugging potential performance issues requires monitoring software.

You can monitor Sakai on multiple levels. If you are looking from the bottom up, the monitoring tools can question numerous network devices, such as routers or load balancers, through the Simple Network Management Protocol SNMP standard and deliver different real-time metrics depending on the devices' capabilities. The SNMP information from load balancers is particularly interesting as load balancers collect all kinds of statistics, so that they can judge how best to distribute load between individual servers. The Windows Operating System also comes with a free SNMP service. Popular open source monitoring tools such as the Multi Router Traffic Grapher, MRTG (`http://oss.oetiker.ch/mrtg/`), and Nagios (`http://www.nagios.org/`) are fluent speakers of SNMP.

Placing a web server in front of the Tomcat server allows the web server to generate log files in a standard format with information pertaining to the requests and responses from Sakai. An abundance of log file parsers exists: AWStats (`http://awstats.sourceforge.net/`) and WebDruid (`http://www.projet-webdruid.org/`) are examples. The generated reports can tell you about busiest times, error locations, and help you predict usage trends into the future. However, neither SNMP communication with network devices nor log analysis will let you see what is going on within the Java JVM and any potential disruptions caused by memory utilization or garbage collection. One possible solution is to tell the JVM to send debug information to a log file. To enable GC logging, set the JAVA_OPTS to:

```
-Xloggc:/var/logs/my_application/gc.log -verbose:gc
```

Please change the location `/var/logs/my_application/gc.log` to one that best suits your environment. Remember to rotate this log or it will reach its maximum size, stop logging, or use up a lot of disk space.

The outputted log file is not particularly readable, but there are a few good log parsers in the wild, such as GCViewer (`http://www.tagtraum.com/gcviewer.html`), that return summarized results graphically.

JMX monitoring

Java Management Extensions (JMX) `http://java.sun.com/javase/technologies/core/mntr-mgmt/javamanagement` is a standard part of Java 1.5 onwards (and you can backwardly apply it to Java 1.4 by adding extra libraries; Sakai currently runs on Java version 1.5). The various aspects of JMX have been mentioned in JSR Java standards (3, 70, 71, 77, 146, 160, and 174). The important point to note is that JMX standard allows for a uniform method of monitoring and controlling distributed systems. Tomcat and JBoss (`http://jboss.org`) are among the many applications that are JMX-enabled with internal features exposed to monitoring.

At a practical level, JMX allows you to observe in real time how the Java Virtual Machine manages memory, and whether you are running short of memory in any particular place, such as permspace or the heap. You can also find out if pieces of code are deadlocked, waiting on other pieces of code and never moving forward to the completion of their work. This happens very rarely, if at all, in Sakai and is an indicator of difficult-to-test defects in the code. This problem is very difficult to debug, as errors will happen. Therefore, the ability to find a deadlock live is an advantageous feature.

For a local test server, to view live, you can enable an open JMX-related port on 1099 locally via the following extra `JAVA_OPTS` options:

`-Dcom.sun.management.jmxremote.port=1099`

`-Dcom.sun.management.jmxremote.authenticate=false`

`-Dcom.sun.management.jmxremote.ssl=false`

See: `http://java.sun.com/j2se/1.5.0/docs/guide/management/faq.html` for common problems and solutions when configuring remote management.

You can monitor the JVM via JConsole, a standard tool included free with the Sun Java JDK.

You can activate JConsole typing `{$JAVA_HOME}/bin/Jconsole` where `{$JAVA_HOME}` is the location of the JDK.

Although Sakai runs on Java 1.5, you can connect to it from a JConsole running within a Java 1.6 JVM. JConsole improves with version. When compared to the Java 1.5 version, the 1.6 version can detect threads deadlocking and has a pluggable structure that allows you to extend the GUI with your own bits of JMX-related code.

If you are running JConsole from a 1.6 JDK locally, then you can log in either through selecting the process ID or via remote localhost port 1099. After doing so, you are presented with a summary page that is updated roughly every ten seconds. The summary includes the main memory for objects, called heap, the number of parallel processes (threads), and CPU usage.

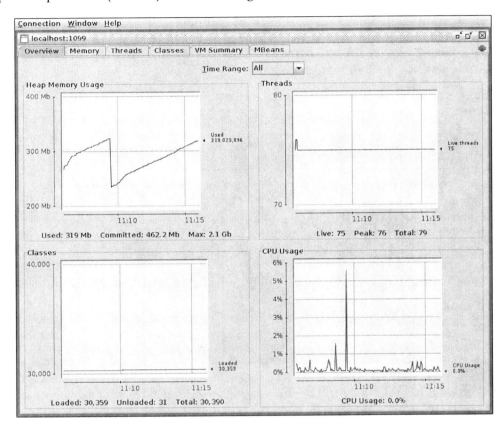

Clicking on the **Memory** tab allows you to zoom into the various parts of memory. The GC occasionally cleans up as new objects are created and older ones stop being used. You can check for deadlocking from the **Threads** tab. The **VM Summary** displays a written report of the main vital statistics of the Virtual Machine.

The **MBeans** tab requires a little bit more explanation. M is an abbreviation for Managed. An MBean is a piece of Java code that represents a resource, such as a cache, memory, or search engine. For example, the writers of a cache may expose how much memory the cache reserves inside an MBean.

Clicking on the **MBean** tab shows all the available MBeans, mostly associated with the Tomcat server or the underlying JVM. Currently, Search and Hibernate have some Mbeans in the list. Expect more features to be exposed later.

JConsole can also load in custom code that is run as an extra tab within JConsole's GUI. An example JConsole plug-in is provided with the Java SE 6 platform. The JTop application shows the CPU usage of all threads running in the application. This is useful for identifying threads that have high CPU consumption. JTop is bundled with the Java SE 6 platform, as a demo application. You can run JConsole with the JTop plug-in using the following command:

```
% JDK_HOME/bin/jconsole -pluginpath JDK_HOME/demo/management/JTop/
JTop.jar
```

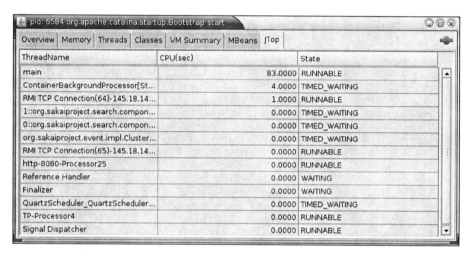

An alternative open source product that has enhanced functionality when compared to JConsole is MC4J (http://sourceforge.net/projects/mc4j).

The Apache web server

The Apache web server is the most popular web server used on the Internet. This indicates that a large proportion of all Internet-related system administrators have encountered and configured Apache before. According to netcraft (http://news. netcraft.com/archives/web_server_survey.html), Apache dominates the market place with over 50% of overall market share. The server is stable, secure, highly configurable, and proven to scale to even the most demanding and acidic environments imaginable. Urban folklore mentions reliable services forgotten and running on very antique computers only to be found wanting when major earthquakes hit.

Sakai is highly scalable, especially behind load balancers with or without Apache server(s) in front of the Tomcat server. Therefore, the need to deploy the web server as part of your infrastructure is a matter of taste. The advantages of deploying Apache normally outweigh the extra complexities of configuration and any extra learning demands placed on system administrators.

Apache uses less system resources for delivering static files than Tomcat. One use of Apache is associated with the default gateway within Sakai. A fresh Sakai instance includes a number of premade sites. With the Sites tool, you can see that the !admin site, which is the administration workspace; !user, the template for the workspace for a new user; !error, the site-unavailable page; and the !gateway site for the front page of Sakai just before logging on. The sites are composed of content that resides mostly in static HTML files. As the administrator, you can change the location of the content by visiting the gateway site and selecting the relevant tool. By default, you will find the static content underneath the `webapps/library/content/gateway` directory. To change the content, you will need to change the `about.html`, `features.html`, `training.html`, and `acknowledgments.html` files. The global configurations file, `sakai.properties`, points to the gateway's welcome page via the value set in `server.info.url`. Therefore, with a combination of changing the property file and the online administrator, you can move most of the static pages outside of the Sakai application and configure Apache to go directly to those files.

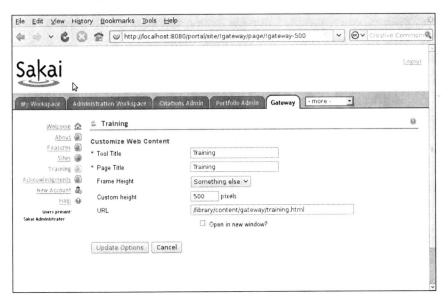

You can configure SSL connections (the secure connections you get in your web browser when, for example, you need to type in a password) so that the encryption takes place within the Tomcat server, the Apache server, or through hardware such as a Load Balancer. Whenever possible, use hardware encryption on the Load Balancer. Hardware encryption is the process of using hardware, such as a Load Balancer, to encrypt plain text, such as web pages. Using encryption on the Load Balancer removes demand on the CPU of the server itself. A big advantage of this approach is that in most computing trends, prices are decreasing rapidly and performance is increasing. For a detailed account of separating static and dynamic content in Apache, you can read `http://www.linuxjournal.com/article/9041`.

Apache is written in the C language and has a plug-in structure in which custom code units (known as modules) are loaded at start up. This allows dropping in extra functionality such as WebDAV support and adding different types of authentication. You can find a full list of modules for Apache 2 at `http://httpd.apache.org/docs/2.0/mod`.

Two examples of handy modules are `mod_jk` and `mod_deflate`. `Mod_jk` helps Apache talk with the Tomcat server. `Mod_deflate` returns resources in a compressed format saving network traffic. Compression increases the server's CPU utilization, but decreases the time to return the resource to the web browser.

Migration

Section Author: Zach Thomas is a software engineer who has contributed to Sakai since its first public release in June of 2004. He is a Sakai Fellow, speaks at conferences on topics relating to Sakai adoption, and runs a Sakai consulting business called Aeroplane Software. In a previous life, he co-founded a modestly famous folk punk rock band called Okkervil River. He lives in San Marcos, Texas, with his wife and two little boys.

Migrating course content

If you wish to migrate site content from an LMS such as Blackboard to Sakai or vice versa, then you should be aware of the current strengths and limitations of Sakai. In this section Zach Thomas, who built most of the migration software, discusses the process.

A bit of history

Sakai has a checkered past when it comes to content migration. In the very early days, the core development team established a mechanism for exporting the content of a worksite's tools. This feature is available in the Administration Workspace and is called **Site Archive**. Each tool developer had to provide code to ensure that the tool's data would be written out to an XML file when requested by Site Archive.

This approach has a few drawbacks:

1. The archive is saved on the server, and is only accessible to system administrators and not site maintainers.
2. The archive format is Sakai-specific, so it is only usable by Sakai.
3. Not all tool developers opted to support the Sakai export mechanism.

As of this writing, these are the tools that participate in the Sakai export:

- Announcements
- Assignments
- Calendar
- Chat
- Forums
- Mail Archive
- News
- Polls
- Resources
- Syllabus
- Wiki

Notably absent are Gradebook and Tests & Quizzes, which have no export and use their own built-in mechanisms for import.

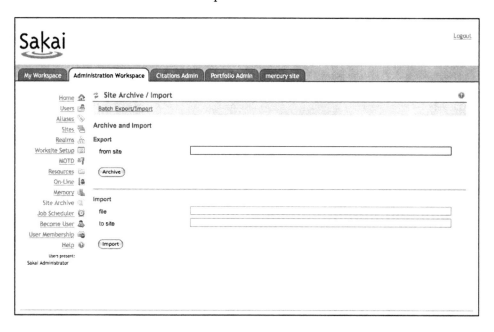

There was one option for site maintainers to move content into their sites: among the features in the "Site Info" tool is "Import from File". Prior to August of 2005, the only way to get a file suitable for importing was to feed a Sakai archive into an Indiana University tool that was not publicly available.

A small team at Texas State extended the "Import from File" capability to work with export files from Blackboard 5.5. We can see from the Subversion repository log exactly when it became public:

```
--------------------------------------------------------------
r13 | zach.thomas@txstate.edu | 2005-08-09 12:31:49 -0500 (Tue, 09 Aug
2005) | 1 line

initial add of the imsimport code. hi from Zach.
--------------------------------------------------------------
```

Since the Blackboard export format was based on the IMS content package standard, it was possible to adapt the same import facility to work with newer versions of Blackboard, as well as WebCT and the IMS Common Cartridge standard.

Enabling LMS content import

As of Sakai version 2.3 and later, the ability to import legacy Sakai archives and limited support for IMS Common Cartridge is built-in. In order to support the import of content from Blackboard or WebCT export files, a sysadmin needs to compile some additional code and modify a couple of configuration files.

The code for the LMS importers is in Sakai's contrib repository at `https://source.sakaiproject.org/contrib/migration/trunk`.

These instructions assume at least Sakai 2.5:

1. From a terminal window, change to `archive/import-parsers` within the Sakai source directory.

2. Get the parser code with:

    ```
    svn co https://source.sakaiproject.org/contrib/migration/trunk/
    import-parsers/blackboard_6
    ```

3. If necessary, modify any `pom.xml` files in the parser so that the version given for the parent tag agrees with what is in `archive/pom.xml`.

4. Modify `archive/pom.xml`, and add the new parser directory to the `<modules>` tag where you see `<module>import-parsers/common-cartridge</module>`.

5. Modify `archive/import-pack/src/webapp/WEB-INF/components.xml`:

6. Add a bean definition for the new parser.

7. Uncomment the bean definitions for the Announcements handler and Samigo handler if you wish to import their content.

8. Add references to the new parser and new handlers (if you uncommented those) to the properties for the `ImportService` bean.

9. Build and deploy the archive module as usual, and the new import capability will be available. Note that Tomcat must be restarted for the changes to take effect.

More detail, as well as a screencast demonstration of this procedure, is available in Sakai's Confluence Wiki at `http://confluence.sakaiproject.org/confluence/x/Mnc`.

A note about IMS Common Cartridge

As of Sakai version 2.6, support for Common Cartridge import is in alpha. Since the IMS specification became final, the code has yet to be updated to the specification. We plan to support proper Common Cartridge 1.0 import in Sakai 2.7.

Using "Import from File"

Once the new code is installed, any instructor or other site maintainer will be able to use their LMS export files with Site Info's "Import from File" feature. It works like a Windows wizard, with several options available while importing new content.

First, you browse to the export file you want to import. The file upload will be subject to Sakai's configured file upload limit.

The tool parses the archive and shows you a summary of its content. You may select the categories you wish to bring in.

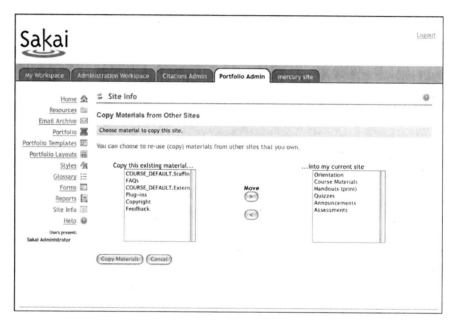

You will then see a summary of your selections and the destinations within Sakai where the content will go.

If the archive is large (more than a handful of megabytes), the import can take several minutes. When it's done, you will see a confirmation message.

Interviews at the deep end

A hints and tips chapter without the hard-earned voice of experts would be a brittle lie. This section displays interviews with three key players who have serious and unquestionable real-life experience. Megan May is the ex-QA director for the Sakai Foundation, Seth Theriault is a system integrator with much Sakai installation face time, and David Howitz is a learning environments developer at the University of Cape Town.

Megan May

Who is Megan May and what has her relationship been, past and present, with Sakai?

I first got involved with Sakai in January 2005. At the time, I was Online Services Analyst at Indiana University. My responsibilities included technical support, managing and distributing information as a liaison between the Oncourse development team and other units in UITS, as well as serving as the university-wide point person of the Oncourse distributed support model. While my primary focus was support related, I spent a great deal of time testing. I spent countless hours testing Samigo (test and quizzes tool), analyzing bugs, and determining which ones would benefit our user base the most. It was such a daunting task—Samigo is an application itself and being new to testing, I had a lot to learn.

Roughly a year later Carol Dippel resigned as the Quality Assurance Director and I was asked to serve in this role for the community. I was in this role a little less than three years (January 2006 until November 2008). I was charged with leading a global quality assurance effort comprised of volunteer resources for an open/community source software Java project for online learning and collaboration.

As the QA Director, I led volunteer workgroup staff in testing three major releases and numerous maintenance releases (2.2.1, 2.2.2, 2.2.3, 2.3.0, 2.3.1, 2.3.2, 2.4.0, 2.4.1, 2.5.0, 2.5.2, and 2.5.3). Through this effort, I determined testing strategies, developed test plans, ensured there was proper documentation of processes/procedures, planned, organized, and scheduled project coordination and management of the overall QA process and eventually the release process.

Another aspect that I often forget about was the formation of the QA Network. When I began with the Foundation, all the QA servers were hosted at MIT. This did not even touch on the various configurations that existed within the community. At the Austin conference, Seth Theriault proposed a network of QA servers. Throughout my time with the Foundation, I worked with him to establish and grow the QA Network.

As I touched on earlier, I advocated and implemented software release management process changes to facilitate higher quality. When I came on board, we had yet to define what constitutes a maintenance release and at the time, it was common to see new feature sets in these maintenance releases. We had similar challenges with merges of bug fixes into the maintenance branches, but I am happy to say that a fairly stringent process that requires testing prior to merge has been adopted.

I should mention that only 50% of my time was dedicated to this role. The other half of my time was dedicated to local issues at Indiana University.

Have you any tips or tricks for the smooth deployment of Sakai into a new organization?

Participate in the Sakai Community—The community is what drives the software and what many people do not realize is that you do not have to be a developer to contribute. Your input on a particular use case, thoughts about governance, time spent testing, or design skills can really make a difference. It is your chance to help drive the direction of the community and/or ensure quality in the product that you are ultimately delivering to your users. This is an opportunity unique in community source software. Not only are there direct benefits, but there is the opportunity to develop really meaningful relationships with colleagues all over the world. You can learn so much from others in higher education.

Manage Scope and Expectations—Be sure to be explicit about the enhancements that you will be providing users. It is really easy for folks to assume one issue will be resolved by some work when it won't. Projects can easily spiral out of control. This can be mitigated by providing documentation, info shares, etc., that makes it clear what users can expect. In addition, be sure to be upfront about issues or limitations (bugs, design) that your users may find troublesome.

Customize carefully — The more local customizations you make, the harder it becomes to upgrade from version to version. When there are 50+ customizations, it is not only hard to keep track of them but very time consuming. It also complicates determining if a problem your users are experiencing is a result of your code changes or if it is a general community problem. My suggestion is that you minimize customizations and when appropriate, work towards getting that customization back into the general codebase.

"Production Pilots" provide a lower stakes real-world deployment. In this phase, be sure to select a range of users and subjects. They teach differently and have different needs.

Finalize tool selection before transition — There is a lot going on when an institution is transitioning from one system to another. Not only are there all the aspects you planned for but there will also be a couple of unplanned aspects that you will need to account for. Having the tools you will offer already selected means there is one less thing to worry about. In addition, documentation can be prepared and available when people start using the system.

Let the users market whenever possible — You can market Sakai as much as possible but when it comes down to it, faculty are more likely to take the advice of other faculty since they are peers. They can also share best practices and provide mentoring — something an IT-focused group can't.

Develop a faculty/student communications plan and ensure there is transparency — Often there are different communication channels to reach the different constituencies of your system. Identify those; developing a tone to convey the message, and the types of information you will share with each is extremely important. Informed users tend to be happy users!

Why is it important to have the developers write test cases as they remove bugs?

Bugs are entered in by so many different members of the community and contain varying information. When a developer reads a bug report, he or she may have a different interpretation of what the problem is. When the person that fixes the bug explicitly spells out the test for the fix, the ambiguity that often occurs disappears.

What is a Sakaiger and how does one get to earn it?

The Sakaiger is a happy dancing creature. It is the logo of the hip, cool, underground, karaoke singing, silly elements of the Sakai Community (that is pretty much everyone). Andrew Thornton, formally of CARET, Cambridge, designed the original Sakaiger image. It came into plush being at an integration week meeting where I threw the idea out as a marketing gimmick. Chuck Severance (http://www.dr-chuck.com/) loved the idea and the Sakaiger came into being. The original plush Sakaiger sports blue stripes and Sakaigers of this type are in very limited supply. They are bestowed by the Sakai QA Director to those with significant contribution/ leadership in Sakai QA activity. Pictures and information are also available at the web site: http://sakaiger.com/.

What is the QA network and what is its purpose?

The QA network is a network of thirteen servers dedicated to testing activity. These servers are located on five continents and provide the community with a variety of operating systems and database configurations. The time and hardware is donated to the community. The server admins are provided build scripts and a stock properties file (sakai.properties) to keep a comparable base between them.

What are conference calls and how do they help bind the QA effort?

The conference calls are held weekly during the official QA cycle prior to a release. The calls serve two purposes: they create a forum for the QA Working Group to interact with the developers, as well as serve to coordinate the many activities that must occur prior to release. During the call, folks can ask questions about the functionality they are testing so there is clarity, lists of outstanding bugs are reviewed, and important issues pertaining to the release are discussed.

How can the QA of kernel 1 & 2 be managed, especially as Sakai evolves?

I think that testing needs to be included from the get go. I'm not talking just about just functional testing, but unit tests, integration tests, user testing, performance testing, etc. The community has a habit of focusing on these activities as an afterthought and thus, suffers from it. I believe that when a project team is being formed, a testing lead and members slated to specifically do testing should be included.

Which QA material on Confluence do you think worth reading?

All of it ☺. Actually, as time has passed, it has sprawled out and needs a bit of housekeeping so that it is organized better. The FAQ is always a good place to start (`http://bugs.sakaiproject.org/confluence/display/QA/FAQ+QA`).

Seth Theriault

Who is Seth Theriault?

I work on research, teaching, and learning systems at Columbia University. Most of my work involves integrating these systems with the larger university-wide infrastructure and taking care of various systems-related (as opposed to applications-related) things like server setup and performance, data feeds, database tinkering, authentication mechanisms, etc. I was the primary implementer of Columbia's Sakai pilot, which began in 2005 and continues to the present.

My experience with Sakai has been largely focused in the same areas because I firmly believe that simplified implementation is crucial to Sakai's success. I maintain the Kerberos UserDirectoryProvider, run one of the community QA servers, and contribute patches and ideas from time to time. I was named a Sakai Fellow in 2006.

But enough about me.

Have you any common error messages and some details that you can share with me?

One of the most common sysadmin errors to make is to not change the database settings in `sakai.properties`. It is highly embarrassing to try to talk to an Oracle database with the HSQL dialect.

Do you have any particular Contrib tools you can recommend?

I can highly recommend BlogWOW, Mailtool (now replaced by Mailsender), and NewsFeeds (now Sakai Feeds). Each fills a need that was either sorely lacking in Sakai or that improved it by simplifying an existing capability.

For example, Mailtool/Mailsender fulfilled a local Columbia need that was lacking in Sakai. We were part of the initial test group and worked with the primary developers as they fine-tuned the original Mailtool. This continues now with Mailsender.

Both BlogWOW and News Feeds are smart replacements for existing capability. The former is, in my opinion and that of local colleagues, a superior blogging tool compared with the main Sakai offering, while the latter is a brilliant idea. And again, using these Contrib tools fills a local need and allows us to shape their development with early adoption.

Have you any best practices for a system admin that you would like to share?

First, always store your binary content outside of the database. This is the recommended practice, is well-tested, and gives you the flexibility that you will eventually need. The corollary to that is to make sure that you can get the best NFS (or other storage protocol) performance you can get, especially if you expect heavy use and multiple app servers. In the traditional "app server + database server + NFS-mounted content" model, you will need fast NFS performance. Some local studies showed that Linux had some excellent numbers compared to Solaris (on identical mounts), but your mileage may vary. No matter what, it needs to be fast since the delivery of the content is done via multiple hops. Oh, and yes, you might need more actual storage than you think.

Second, I highly recommend fronting Sakai on your application server with Apache 2.2+ and some sort of connector (I have a personal preference for `mod_proxy_ajp` for its simplicity, but `mod_jk` works just as well). Apache gives you a lot of flexibility that connecting straight to Tomcat does not: SSL certificate management; `mod_deflate` capability for compressing/decompressing static text content on the fly; and the ability to serve static content in the `/library` module directly.

Also, give your JVM and Tomcat as much memory as you can spare. Install a 64-bit OS and the 64-bit Sun Java package so you can address more than 2GB at once. Most, if not all, hardware being sold these days is 64-bit clean, so there is no reason not to do. I would suggest that each app server have a minimum of 8 GB RAM with half of that dedicated to the Sakai JVM (`-Xms4096m -Xmx4096m`).

Finally, try to automate your Sakai builds as much as possible. Read up on Subversion's "externals" capability (`http://svnbook.red-bean.com/en/1.1/ch07s04.html`) to see how to bring disparate versions of Sakai modules together into a build. You may have to do some patching, but that is straightforward as well. A simple shell script can work wonders for your sanity if you are called on to do builds in any way. You may want to explore using a "continuous integration" system (CruiseControl, Hudson, and Apache Continuum are a few open source ones) to do automatic builds from time to time.

Have you any bad practices for a system admin that you would like to share?

Running a .0 release. In general, this is a bad idea, but Sakai has taken this to a new level. I recommend following the maintenance branch (.x) instead.

Are there any particular features you would like to be added to Sakai?

Sakai needs better ways to export "systems" information (for monitoring, etc.). At one point, Mike Osterman (Whitman College) and I had the idea of implementing an SNMP service in Sakai to ease some of the pain, but it went nowhere.

The existing Search tool capability could be improved. For example, it does not recover gracefully from the shutdown of a single node in the cluster, requiring a total restart and rebuild of the search index. This is just plain bad.

David Howitz

Who is David Howitz and what is his relationship with Sakai?

I work as a learning environments developer in the Centre for Educational Technology at the University of Cape Town. My responsibilities include production maintenance, integration with existing systems, and developing new functionality needed by UCT. As part of the latter goal, we have contributed two tools to the Sakai release: Polls and Reset Password.

Can you briefly describe your University?

The University of Cape Town is a medium sized residential University with around 22,000 students. UCT is consistently rated as the top research university in Africa (179 in the Times rankings). We have been involved with Sakai since 2005 and have replaced a home grown LMS (Connect) and a WebCT installation. Currently our Sakai installation (called Vula locally) is widely used to support courses, research, social outreach, and other activities.

Have you any tips for the smooth running of infrastructure?

One is to script as much of your build and production deployment process as possible, this ensures that each build and deployment happens the same way. The second is to monitor your production environment so that you are aware of unusual behavior. It is particularly important to be aware of factors that affect end users, such as response time, so that action can be taken. We also try to keep measures of quality of service to our end users, so, for instance, measure users who received a bug report per thousand users.

Can you describe any gotchas that are avoidable?

Do not make assumptions — if you have an unusual use case and you are unsure whether it will have an effect of your installation, don't assume that anyone will have encountered this case. Ask on the lists first for any gotchas.

Which monitoring software do you use?

We use Cacti to monitor basic hardware metrics (load, disk usage, network traffic) and MRTG to monitor specific Sakai-related metrics. We like MRTG for the ability to quickly set up monitoring of indicators that concern us. Our MRTG dashboard can be seen at `https://vula.uct.ac.za/web/dev//Dashboard/index.html`. What we monitor is partly based on experience — at one time or another these were measures that alerted us to specific problems or were areas where we tried to introduce more efficiency.

Can you explain why you have a public Subversion repository and how it may help new organizations explore Sakai's capabilities?

> The nature of community work—the better the community understands what we are trying to achieve with Sakai, the more likely they are to take our use cases into account in their own design processes. Also, anyone who uses our code potentially could contribute an important bug fix or improvement.

Functional administration

 Section author: David Jan Donner, born 1960, Universteit van Amsterdam, doctorate Philosophy, worked as administrator of ICT educational applications for 15 years, lives in Amsterdam and is currently senior functional administrator (operational service level manager).

This section explains how Sakai is managed within the Central Computing Services (CCS) at the University of Amsterdam. The experience gained is important. A functional administrator's role is vital for the well-being of the CCS. The functional administrator specifies user needs as a list of requirements and then negotiates the creation of real services with the rest of the IT department. This is helps the organization balance students' needs against the cost of maintaining real servers with real applications on them.

The Central Computer Services at the University of Amsterdam uses the IT Infrastructure Library (ITIL) to organize itself. ITIL is a set of practices and concepts used to set up IT departments. The call center serves as gateway for the community to IT support, and a central management database (CMDB) serves as a tool to organize workflows between the operational, tactical, and strategic managements. The CMDB acts as an inventory of all events, calls, changes, and their work orders, problems, projects, and with those all persons of the company, contacts, and the configuration details. It is great to manage the line support of IT for an institute. It exists less to support software development.

The ITIL principles were introduced in stages so that CCS had time to adapt to the new way of working. As a consequence, the older job of functional administrator remains. At the CCS, the functional administrator controls the application together with operational or technical management (as far as the Sakai application is concerned). Operational management controls the running of servers. A team known as technical support executes the application software updates. However, since the development team (known locally as the webteam) participates in the Sakai community, it is customary that the developers perform the server updates themselves. That custom shows the tension between developing the software and managing everyday use. Line management is not part of the Sakai community and developers are not supposed to work outside the open source project. The webteam has also to work together with technical support to transfer knowledge.

The main task for functional administration is to provide good guidance on how to manage the use of the application. The guidance is only useful when it represents the requirements of the institute and the users. The functional administrator has to work with the operations team to install the software.

In this life-cycle management process, automated testing has proven to be indispensable to find the settings for maximum use and efficient load balancing of servers in an application cluster. The functional administrator indicates which pages and what tools should be included in the automated tests. This indication can change with every update or period because use patterns change over time. Use monitoring is part of functional management, just as monitoring the server and the services is part of technical and application management.

In the case of Sakai, the functional administrator has to specify the requirements to develop: what does operations need to know to install the software, where are the application settings to regulate the load, what are the administrative tools, and how are they to be used? The Sakai project sites provide a lot of information, but some of the things specific to our institute have to be clarified by the development team. Once the application of Sakai is brought from the development environment into production, the maintenance of user requirements is brought to functional management: between the functional administrator and development, the user cases are checked off: skin changes, realms adjustments, rearranging the course sites. In addition, another responsibility arises: the user or the institute changes the requirements, the functional administrator tracks this, and development follows.

The service-level management team will be the first to be confronted by institutional change. The functional administrator is the first to formulate the user change. Depending upon the measure of the change—is it a bug, a feature request, does it require a general update or even a program switch?—the software update follows the test-acceptance-production cycle: the test is done by the webteam, and the acceptance process is organized by the functional administrator who brings the outcome to the go/no go decision whether to bring the update to production or throw it back to development for further tweaking of the code.

The cooperation of functional administration with the development team is a new activity for an institute that is accustomed to working with software providers. Now, we are not able to complain to the supplier, but instead have to manage bug fixes and improvements ourselves. The IT organization needs to have the right people and tools for that.

Students and teachers have to be supported. This involves providing manuals about the navigation and functionality of all the tools and pages. The open source product shortens the distance between the product developers and the product users, but medium- and large-size institutions have to prevent this proximity from becoming a speedy engine of whirling changing applications. The company invests in ITIL implementation to secure stability and reliability of IT infrastructure. Sakai has to grow a development cycle that is in synch with a company's life-cycle management of their applications.

A functional administrator may not be a member of the developer community. However, a workgroup about pedagogy in Sakai is a place to expect such contributions.

Summary

Planet Sakai is an excellent blog aggregator to keep in contact with the Sakai buzz.

Sakai is built up on top of third-party frameworks such as Spring and Hibernate. For the inquisitive, it is worth reading up on which frameworks are used and what capabilities exist. For developers, this may help avoid reinventing the wheel. For administrators, it may provide the background knowledge to support pinpointing issues.

Sakai was written in Java. You can tune the Java Virtual Machine enable Java Management Extensions via the JAVA_OPTS environment variable. The Sakai Foundation has listed the settings for production servers in JIRA. These settings act as excellent initial values for any new deployment.

The Apache web server is useful for delivering static content, rewriting URLs, and for a standard source of logs for log parsing. It has many modules that can extend its functionality, such as mod_deflate, which compresses network traffic.

Course migration is possible, but with some limitations.

The next chapter is about common error messages in Sakai and how to deal with them.

13
Common Error Messages

The smooth running of a Sakai deployment and users' perception of its quality depends on how fast problems are dealt with. The sooner you deal with an issue the quicker it is resolved, and the less the disturbance to an end user. Being honest and admitting that occasionally there are errors does not imply that Sakai is buggy, just that it is designed from the bottom up to help system administrators to act fast.

Things can go wrong, a piston blown in a car engine, lack of petrol to get you to your destination, or without warning, a hanging office application. I have not interacted with software yet that is perfect. There is no strategy to provably remove every single defect from a given software product. The primitive computer used for the first lunar landings had as few as 10,000 lines of machine code to control it. The complexity of the task was high, but the number of lines that errors could hide in was low. A modern operating system contains tens of millions of lines of code. Sakai sits between these two extremes, with around half a million lines of active running code. To aggravate the potential for errors, each line of Java has the power to do a lot more work than one line of machine code. The use of a feature-rich language improves the programmer's productivity and enables the creation of more functionality in a shorter amount of time. However, even in a perfect universe with the most perfect quality assurance, there will always be some residual defects left. Under the pressure of high numbers of users, very occasionally an error will be triggered. Reducing pain and negative user perception depends on the administrator's ability to remove specific error types quickly, and for developers to find and patch the bug in the code base.

Even if perfect, the software still resides on a server that can go wrong. Servers have moving parts, such as the hard disk, that wear out; memory that solar radiations can hit; electrical supplies and CPUs that generate heat, fans that rotate. For small-scale deployments, you can limit risks with regular backups of the most important files, redundant hardware, and uninterruptible power supplies (UPS). A UPS supplies electricity when the power grid is disrupted for a long enough time to safely turn off the servers. For medium- to large-scale deployments, load balancers ensure a lack of dependency on any application server. If one application server fails, the load balancer spots this and then stops passing on requests to the failed server (this is known as failover). However, often the database is still a single point of failure and a cause of concern.

Another type of real-time exception is the consumption of all the available resources. On the busiest day of the year, as much as 10% of your registered Sakai membership is actively online. For example, if your organization has 160,000 students with accounts in Sakai, as many as 16,000 users may be logged on simultaneously. With peak user demand an order of magnitude higher than on a more normal quiet day, the server may consume all the available memory, hard disks may fill up, or network bottlenecks may emerge.

Luckily, Java comes to the rescue. Java is helpful in dealing with real-time problems, allowing the programmer in most situations to decide what to do next. The language uses exception handling. When an issue occurs, the running code passes control to another piece of code, which then deals with the exceptional situation or ignores it. Thus, unless the JVM has no choice, for example because there is no more memory, an application can deal with the problems signaled and keep on running.

This advanced chapter will explain how to configure the logging and error reporting to provide focused early signals. The chapter will also mention how analyzing error reporting helps debugging and long-term trend watching. A number of common error messages are also defined.

 Sakai is heavily dependent on Java, therefore, to understand the most common errors requires a basic understanding of this programming language.

A policy of containment of errors

Sakai is a complex application built out of hundreds of thousands lines of code. It is inevitable that even with the most vigerous testing a few residual bugs will occasionally cause problems for a small minority of end users. This section describes how these issues are found, contained, and reported back.

Reporting

Sakai has a policy of containment and signaling of issues. When all else has failed and there is no way that the application can usefully fulfill the end user's request, then a error form is returned to the end user.

Error

An unexpected error has occurred.

Send a bug report

To send a bug report, describe what you were doing when the problem occurred, in the space below, and press the submit button.

[Submit Report]

Recovery

To recover from this error without sending in a bug report, please do the following:

- Press the Logout button above to logout.
- Close your browser to assure a clean start.
- Re-open your browser and start again.

Technical Details

This information will automatically be included in your bug report.

```
org.sakaiproject.portal.api.PortalHandlerException: org.sakaiproject.tool.api.ToolException: Servlet.init() for servlet jforum threw exception
    at org.sakaiproject.portal.charon.SkinnableCharonPortal.doGet(SkinnableCharonPortal.java:891)
caused by: org.sakaiproject.tool.api.ToolException: Servlet.init() for servlet jforum threw exception
    at org.sakaiproject.portal.charon.SkinnableCharonPortal.forwardTool(SkinnableCharonPortal.java:1343)
caused by: javax.servlet.ServletException: Servlet.init() for servlet jforum threw exception
    at org.apache.catalina.core.StandardWrapper.allocate(StandardWrapper.java:791)
```

At the top of the form is a space for user comments and at the bottom is the rather ugly and unreadable stack trace that the underlying code passes on. When an exception is thrown, it starts in a particular method as part of a Java class. The method might have been called by another method, which in its own turn may also have been called from within yet another method. Note that the depth of the stack trace, especially when you take into account the server interactions, makes for a very long list.

To the average human, stack traces are unreadable and give the feeling that they have trodden in something rather smelly. Even if the stack trace is stating an innocent fact, unless the user understands Java, he or she is going to feel that the system is shouting out very loudly that there are problems. Luckily, most stack trace types are dealt with early by the developer or during the Quality Assurance cycle before the offending code goes into production.

Once the user submits the report, Sakai sends the report via email to a specific address for collection and later analysis. You can set the target email address, like most other global configuration, in `sakai/sakai.properties` via defining the `portal.error.email` property.

The email that is sent out has a fixed structure that makes it possible to process the text relatively easily via scripts; see the following example listing:

```
from   Sakai QA Network qa1-nl (svn tags/sakai_2-5-3_rc03) using MySQL 5/
InnoDB, Java 1.5.0_13 amd64 <no-reply@qa1-nl.sakaiproject.org>
to     xxxx@xxx.xx
date   13 October 2008 13:32
subject       Bug Report: F101671D49BBA3E4A1A59338257B074CA307FB52 / null
user: null (null)
email: null
usage-session: null
stack-trace-digest: F101671D49BBA3E4A1A59338257B074CA307FB52
sakai-version: 2-5-3
service-version:
app-server: qa1-nl
request-path: /portal/tool/!gateway-410
time: Oct 13, 2008 14:32:01

stack trace:
--Long stack trace removed for readability
```

The email's `from` field includes a brief summary of the server and its capabilities. There are extra email fields containing the user name, time, email address of the user, and the request-path. The request-path is the web address that triggered the offending piece of code's error. In the listings case, the `!gateway-410` part is the name that Sakai recognizes for a specific tool. The request-path not only indicates the rough location of the error in the code base, but also is enough for the code maintainers to work out who needs to write a patch to solve the specific issue. The error handling supplies the stack trace for later analysis. The associated stack trace digest is a unique hexadecimal number that is the same for two duplicate stack traces. This number allows you to keep track of the number of unique error types and to count the specific bug's relative importance.

Quality Assurance analysis

There are over ten servers scattered across the world, on which volunteers test functionality. As new organizations become involved with Sakai and they begin to invest time and resources into the community effort, occasionally they add and then maintain a new QA server to the list. For example, in late 2008 the community welcomed a server in Japan and another in Australia. This has the advantage of giving the specific donor organization insight into the current issues running with the newest versions of Sakai and a playground to train system administrators and generally build real-world operational experience.

When an error is generated on one of these QA servers, mail is sent to a specific mailbox. A script running on the Amsterdam QA server checks the mailbox every five minutes and, if a new email arrives, then report generation is immediately triggered and a related web page is updated with a detailed summary of ongoing errors.

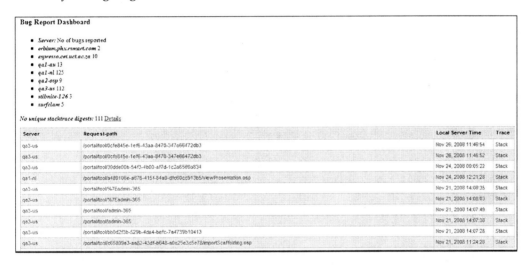

The report includes a summary of all error forms sent and details of the stack traces.

To aid the debugging process, as part of the report, another script checks the source code for known bug patterns (`http://qa1-nl.sakaiproject.org/codereview/bug_dashboard/detail_stack.html`) and a link to those issues is made within the detailed report for each part of the stack trace, as shown in the following screen grab.

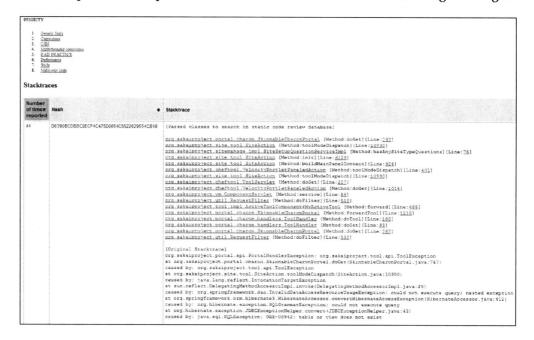

By clicking on the class name in the stack trace column, such as `org.sakaiproject.site.tool.SiteAction`, a detailed report of potential bugs automatically found for the class appears in your web browser. Clicking on the line number next to the class name returns an HTML version of the source code, with the focus on the correct line number.

This automatic analysis of bugs found during the QA process can speed up code cleaning during development.

Production systems

The University of Cape Town (`https://vula.uct.ac.za`) is an early adopter of the most up-to-date version of Sakai. The administrators keep track of the sent error forms and the impact of particular errors on the end user experience based on the purpose of the tool. For example, the negative impact of losing your place in a test is higher than your disruption during a search for documents. Intermittent issues due to server load have the potential to generate many low-level user irritations. Reading error reports gives you an understanding of the scale of irritation levels.

Vula Bug Summary

Updated 2009-01-26 17:00:01

Last 24 hours

Tool	Bugs	Distinct Bugs	Affected Users	Impact	Weighted Impact
sakai.forums	18	2	6	12.0	6.5
sakai.chat	7	1	1	8.0	0.7
sakai.preferences	5	3	1	2.0	0.2
sakai.samigo	5	1	1	6.0	0.5
sakai.resources	2	1	1	3.0	0.3
sakai.rsf.evaluation	1	0	1		

Total affected users: 11 / 1496 (0.74%)
Total distinct bugs: 8
User comments: 1

Last 7 days

Tool	Bugs	Distinct Bugs	Affected Users	Impact	Weighted Impact
sakai.rsf.evaluation	70	0	39		
sakai.forums	35	4	14	12.3	2.2
sakai.samigo	21	2	17	19.0	4.1
sakai.chat	16	1	1	17.0	0.2
sakai.preferences	8	3	2	3.3	0.1
sakai.site.roster	5	1	2	7.0	0.2
sakai.search	3	1	1	4.0	0.1
sakai.syllabus	2	2	1	1.5	0.0
sakai.melete	2	2	2	2.0	0.1
sakai.resources	2	1	1	3.0	0.0
sakai.poll	1	0	1		
sakai.sitesetup	1	1	1	2.0	0.0

Total affected users: 79
Total distinct bugs: 18
User comments: 2

The report makes it very clear where any long-term issues reside and provides an indication for system administrators of where they should focus their efforts first. By comparing reports from different Sakai versions, you can see where you have successfully cleaned up issues and where new issues are emerging. Early adopters work closely with the community to iron out the residual defects so the rest of us do not have to.

Configuring logging

When you start up the demonstration, logging goes to your command console and a lot of text flashes past your eyes. The motivation for this start up verbosity is that if you have any misconfiguration, you will see their warnings early.

Within Sakai, the two most commonly used logging frameworks are Apache common logging (`http://commons.apache.org/logging/`) and Log4j (`http://logging.apache.org/log4j`). Despite the use of more than one framework, a Log4j configuration file manages all the logging within Sakai and allows for central control of all aspects of the logging. You can find code the relevant Log4j property file within the source at `/kernel/log-configure/src/conf/log4j.properties`. Any changes made to this file are only seen the next time Sakai starts up.

Log4j is a popular Java framework for logging application events. It has a reputation for efficiency. The framework separates the formatting and the destination of logging from the programming of the logging code. There is also a facility for sending log messages to the console, files, database, over the network through email or Telnet, and so on. The framework is so successful that it has been translated to work with Perl, PHP, C, and other programming languages.

Logging allows you to write messages at different levels of priority. The least significant message is `trace` followed by `debug`, `info`, `warn`, `error`, and for the worst conditions possibly `fatal`. It is therefore important for administrators that the application log consistently and to the right level of priority, and and that it use logging throughout the code base.

Log4j performs, so the developers can risk verbose logging, as long as it is fired off at the right level, and leave the configuration file to decide when to print the message or not. Log4j can filter messages based on log level and can have different log levels for different parts of the code. For example, it may be more important to have extra logging for potential database issues rather than for a particular tool.

Simply adding the following line to the global Log4j properties file will achieve this goal:

```
log4j.logger.org.sakaiproject.component.framework.sql.
BasicSqlService=DEBUG
```

However, when you start your demonstration instance again, you will end up seeing a vast amount of extra logging similar to this:

```
DEBUG:  Delete 0: delete from SAM_PUBLISHEDITEM_T where ITEMID=?
(2009-01-26 12:37:22,130 main_org.hibernate.persister.entity.
AbstractEntityPersister)
```

The line part `log4j.logger` tells the logger that this is a filter. The rest of the line is the name of the part of Java (known as a package) you want to filter against followed by an equal sign and then the logging level.

Examining the default `log4j.properties` file, the default logging level is warn. However, a number of packages have their level set to INFO. The MyFaces framework is too verbose and has had its logging level set higher to error.

You can also configure the filtering from within `sakai/sakai.properties` in a slightly different format. To set `BasicSqlService` to DEBUG you will need to add the following two lines:

```
log.config.count=1
log.config.1=DEBUG.org.sakaiproject.component.framework.sql.
BasicSqlService
```

If you want to configure more than one filter, the count number will have to increase, for example:

```
log.config.count=2
log.config.1=DEBUG.org.sakaiproject.component.framework.sql.
BasicSqlService
log.config.2=ERROR.org.sakaiproject.portal
```

The demonstration logging uses an appender to stdout, which is the console. This can be seen by the line:

```
log4j.appender.Sakai=org.apache.log4j.ConsoleAppender
```

The appender decides the structure of the sent message using a conversion pattern defined via:

```
log4j.appender.Sakai.layout.ConversionPattern=%p: %m (%d %t_%c)%n
```

The rules for the conversion patterns are fully described at http://logging.apache.org/log4j/1.2/apidocs/org/apache/log4j/PatternLayout.html.

I prefer the timestamp at the beginning of the log entry and with as much detail as possible. The following line reconfigures Sakai to do this:

```
log4j.appender.Sakai.layout.ConversionPattern=%d{ABSOLUTE} %5p %c{1}:%L
- %m%n
```

And a typical log entry will now look similar to:

```
12:46:07,767  INFO ContextLoader:197 - Root WebApplicationContext:
initialization completed in 9 ms
```

To change from sending to stdout to a log file that is rotated once a day is as simple as adding the four following lines:

```
log4j.appender.Sakai=org.apache.log4j.DailyRollingFileAppender
log4j.appender.Sakai.DatePattern='.'yyyy-MM-dd
log4j.appender.Sakai.File=/usr/local/tomcat/logs/tomcat.log
log4j.appender.Sakai.layout=org.apache.log4j.PatternLayout
log4j.appender.Sakai.layout.ConversionPattern=%p %d %t_%c%n%m%n
```

Notice the location of the log files is under `/usr/local/tomcat/logs` and the files start with `tomcat.log` followed by the daily time stamp.

Another useful place to append to is a Syslog daemon. Syslog (`http://www.faqs.org/rfcs/rfc3164.html`) is the logging protocol standard on most Unix/Linux boxes. A log server listens for log messages and the server can be configured to print the messages out to the local file system and/or send the messages on to other Syslog daemons for backing up or centralization. To append to the Syslog daemon, add the following five lines of extra configuration:

```
log4j.appender.SYSLOG=org.apache.log4j.net.SyslogAppender
log4j.appender.SYSLOG.syslogHost=xxxx.xxxx.xxxx.xxxx
log4j.appender.SYSLOG.layout=org.apache.log4j.PatternLayout
log4j.appender.SYSLOG.layout.ConversionPattern=%p: %c - %m
log4j.appender.SYSLOG.Facility=USER
```

Where `xxxx.xxxx.xxxx.xxxx` is the IP address of the Syslog daemon.

In summary, using one central configuration file, it is possible to modify the logging location, what is logged or ignored for logging, and the structure of the log messages.

Common error messages

There are numerous ways that Sakai, as a web-based application, can fail, mostly leaving log file evidence that is ready for interpretation behind.

This section's purpose is to give you a glimpse of which types of issue can exist. It explores a small set of messages. The methodology that was used for discovery purposes was to simulate issues by deliberately breaking the demonstration in a number of interesting ways.

During the experiments, failures forced the consumption of CPU time causing the test computer to heat up, generated many gigabytes of log file within a few seconds, and generally harried and stressed the server.

Java version

Maven compiles Sakai 2.5 or above with version 1.5 of Java. If you run the application with an old version of Java such as version 1.4, the JVM will generate the following error message:

```
Unsupported major.minor version 49.0
```

49 is the version number Sun uses to represent Java 1.5!

Java is backwardly compatible. Therefore, if your system has a higher version of Java deployed, such as version 1.6, then no problems will ensue.

Production servers sometimes have more than one version of Java installed. To ensure that the startup script can see the correct version, verify that JAVA_HOME is pointing to the top level of the Java installation, and that the PATH variable includes a link to the bin directory underneath.

Port issues

To allow more than one application to communicate at any one time on a given server, a specific application can assign itself a port for an associated IP address. There are around 65,000 ports with common port numbers below 1024 reserved for well-known protocols such as POP, SMTP, and HTTP.

When you start up Sakai, you may see the following error:

```
java.net.BindException: Address already in use
```

This is stating that the port number that Sakai tried to reserve is already being used. This can happen if you have another Java-based application like uPortal that uses the same port numbers for demonstrations. It can also happen when you have a proxy server on the same machine, which also uses this port by default.

To change the port number that Sakai wants, simply edit the Tomcat configuration found under conf/server.properties and modify port=8080 to the relevant number:

```
    <Connector port="8080" maxHttpHeaderSize="8192" URIEncoding="UTF-8"
maxThreads="150" minSpareThreads="25" maxSpareThreads="75"
enableLookups="false" redirectPort="8443" acceptCount="100"

        connectionTimeout="20000" disableUploadTimeout="true" />
```

Tomcat consumes other ports as well. It listens via the Telnet protocol for a shutdown command, configured via the `server.xml` stanza:

```
<Server port="8005" shutdown="SHUTDOWN">
```

Tomcat talks with the Apache server via a custom protocol. Within `server.xml`, you can change the port number by modifying the line:

```
<Connector port="8009"

        enableLookups="false" redirectPort="8443" protocol="AJP/1.3" />
```

If you are trying to run two different demonstration versions of Sakai instances on the same machine, you will also need to edit the AJP shutdown port locations. Sakai itself may also hold open the default email port 25, that is if the service is enabled in `sakai/sakai.properties`.

Another point to note is that if Sakai wishes to run on a port below 1024 on a Unix/Linux system, then it needs to be run under a root user's account. Otherwise, you will see an error message similar to:

```
java.net.BindException: Permission denied:80

        at org.apache.tomcat.util.net.PoolTcpEndpoint.initEndpoint(PoolTcp
Endpoint.java:298)
```

Notice that the number 80 is the port number, which is default for a web server.

Out of memory

Modifying the startup script `start-sakai.sh` (or `.bat`) to starve the demonstration of memory is straightforward. Let us do this for the main heap space, where Java objects are kept during their life, and another memory area known as permspace.

The main task of permspace is to store information, a kind of design plan, about Java classes so that that the JVM can create objects later from the plan. Sakai uses numerous frameworks and third-party libraries and each web application has its own space. The more libraries, the larger the range of Java classes used. This reuse naturally translates into a large use of permspace. Permspace also stores string constants from the running application as well.

One of Java's advanced features is that of reflection. A Java program can look at a live object and work out its structure, such as which methods exist. Frameworks can also use reflection to construct and instance an object programmatically. For example, this is useful for when information about a Java class is stored in XML and then a framework wants to create a real instance of that object for use in a running application. Spring and Hibernate are good examples of this genre. The JVM also keeps the housework for reflection in permspace. For Sakai, it can be a crowded space, simply due to the sheer volume of functionality and compiled code, made even more crowded by reflection-driven frameworks.

To limit permspace to 16 MB, instead of the default setting of 256 MB requires changing the JAVA_OPTS and CATALINA_OPTS value -XX:MaxPermSize from 256m to 16m, for example, -XX:MaxPermSize=16m

Starting up Sakai generates the following error message:

```
15:36:15,481  INFO XmlBeanDefinitionReader:293 - Loading XML bean
definitions from file [/home/alan/Sakai/instances/sakai-2-5-x/components/
sakai-chat-pack/WEB-INF/components.xml]

java.lang.reflect.InvocationTargetException

Exception in thread "main" java.lang.OutOfMemoryError: PermGen space

Exception in thread "Thread-0" java.lang.OutOfMemoryError: PermGen space
```

The message is clear: we have run out PermGen memory. The exact cause has to do with reflection. The end result is that the server stops and there are a few lines in a log file explaining clearly what went wrong. However, in the heat of battle the log file may well be full of messages and the one you need to understand be hidden in the forest of words. The simplest solution for a system administrator, if on a Unix/Linux box, is to search the log file for OutOfMemoryError with a command line tool such as grep.

To provoke the same reaction for the main heap space where live objects are kept, change the setting -Xmx1024m down to 64m. On restarting, the outputted error message includes:

```
Exception in thread "Thread-0"  java.lang.OutOfMemoryError: Java heap
space
```

On my local test machine, decreasing heap space down 16 MB instead of 1024 MB provoked a second well known type of response from my Sakai instance: it slowed to a stop and became unresponsive. This is worse than a failure, and without either the use of JMX or setting JVM logging settings is difficult to diagnose. The JVM is spending all its time garbage collecting and has no time to run the application. It is thrashing the CPU. To make matters worse, trying to stop the application via `stop-sakai.sh` (or `.bat`) turns out to be impossible and returns an error message similar to:

```
Using CATALINA_BASE:   /home/alan/Sakai/instances/sakai-2-5-x
Using CATALINA_HOME:   /home/alan/Sakai/instances/sakai-2-5-x
Using CATALINA_TMPDIR: /home/alan/Sakai/instances/sakai-2-5-x/temp
Using JRE_HOME:        /usr/lib/jvm/java-1.5.0-sun-1.5.0.16
14:38:54,199 ERROR Catalina:404 - Catalina.stop:
java.net.ConnectException: Connection refused
    at java.net.PlainSocketImpl.socketConnect(Native Method)
    at java.net.PlainSocketImpl.doConnect(PlainSocketImpl.java:333)
```

You are left with only more radical ways to stop the process. In Unix/Linux, you can find the process ID of the runaway JVM via:

```
ps -ef
alan     17232      1 23 14:52 pts/0    00:00:45 /usr/lib/jvm/java-
1.5.0-sun-1.5.0.16/bin/java -server -Xmx1024m -XX:MaxNewSize=256m -XX:
MaxPermSize=256m -Dsakai.demo=true
```

And when killing the process, the -9 signal tells the process to stop immediately. The 17232 is the process ID.

```
kill -9 17232
```

If you are running on a Windows box, the tried and tested approach is to destroy the process from the task manager via the *Ctrl-Alt-Delete* key combination.

If you consider periodic demand, then under high load, Java web applications have the potential to become unresponsive due to the memory limits involved. Load balancing and trend prediction diminish the risks.

The portal

The majority of error messages seen by the end user via the error form start with:

```
org.sakaiproject.portal.api.PortalHandlerException: org.sakaiproject.
tool.api.ToolException
```

The Sakai application captures exceptions that bubble up and wraps them in a top-level exception called `PortalHandlerException`. The exception that it catches is a Tool exception, a tool being Chat, Blog, and so on. The tool has caught an exception within its own responsibility, hence the `ToolException`. This is stating that there is a problem with a specific tool. Underneath these two lines of stack trace lie the details of the exact problem.

A full example is:

```
org.sakaiproject.portal.api.PortalHandlerException: org.sakaiproject.
tool.api.ToolException

at org.sakaiproject.portal.charon.SkinnableCharonPortal.doGet(SkinnableCh
aronPortal.java:767)

caused by: org.sakaiproject.tool.api.ToolException

at org.sakaiproject.site.tool.SiteAction.toolModeDispatch(SiteAction.
java:10990)

caused by: java.lang.reflect.InvocationTargetException

at sun.reflect.DelegatingMethodAccessorImpl.invoke(DelegatingMethodAccess
orImpl.java:25)

caused by: org.springframework.dao.
InvalidDataAccessResourceUsageException: could not execute query; nested
exception is org.hibernate.exception.SQLGrammarException: could not
execute query

at org.springframework.orm.hibernate3.HibernateAccessor.convertHibernateA
ccessException(HibernateAccessor.java:412)

caused by: org.hibernate.exception.SQLGrammarException: could not execute
query

at org.hibernate.exception.JDBCExceptionHelper.convert(JDBCExceptionHelpe
r.java:43)

caused by: java.sql.SQLException: ORA-00942: table or view does not exist
```

Reading the stack trace from the top tells you where in Sakai the issue is manifesting itself, in this case the Portal, and from the bottom upwards explains the exact cause. An error is returned by Oracle databases. JDBC is a low-level Java framework for database connectivity, and is being used by the Hibernate framework.

The database

Three database types are tested for common configuration settings during each QA cycle. The three types are the open source product MySQL; the mature commercial offering and industrial standard for many enterprises Oracle; and the in-memory database HSQL (`http://hsqldb.org`).

For performance reasons, the release notes recommend that you do not use HSQL for anything apart from demonstrations.

The database is core to Sakai. Any issues here are immediately felt by the end user. Much time and effort has gone into optimization. Absolutely not recommended, if you want to destroy your demonstration instance and generate gigabytes of log files within seconds then modify the database connection from the setting `url@javax.sql.BaseDataSource=jdbc:hsqldb:file:${sakai.home}db/sakai.db`, to the setting `url@javax.sql.BaseDataSource=jdbc:xhsqldb:file:${sakai.home}db/sakai.db`. What is happening is that the Spring and Hibernate frameworks, on which Sakai relies heavily, themselves call database connections via the Java JDBC framework (`http://java.sun.com/docs/books/tutorial/jdbc/overview/architecture.html`). JDBC allows plugging in of drivers for different databases and you can switch between drivers using the URL setting. That is exactly what has just been done: changing from the `hsqldb` driver to a nonexistent `xhsqldb` driver. If you forget to place the database-specific driver's `.jar` file under the `common/lib` directory, you will find the same issue for the MySQL or Oracle drivers.

Any errors mentioned in the logs that have the word JDBC should not be taken lightly, as they pertain to the health of the database.

Both Spring and Hibernate abstract the underlying database details, so that developers have a uniform way of programming over a wide range of database types. However, sometimes subtle differences have the potential to cause problems. For example (`http://confluence.sakaiproject.org/confluence/x/26c`), by default, table names in MySQL are case insensitive on Windows and case sensitive on Unix systems. Portions of Sakai that attempt to access tables directly may specify table names in all uppercase or lowercase. The solution to this problem is to configure MySQL to think of table names as being case insensitive. This can be accomplished by editing `/etc/my.cnf` and adding the following:

```
lower_case_table_names=1
```

Search

Sometimes there are logged warnings that are purely cosmetic. However, stack traces give the impression that the system is shouting loudly for help. At the time of writing for Sakai 2.5.x and specifically for the in-memory database, the following error message is always generated at start up:

```
WARN BasicSqlService:1934 - Sql.ddl: missing resource: hsqldb/sakai_
search_parallel.sql

14:27:40,601 ERROR TransactionSequenceImpl:106 - Failed to check
transaction table
```

```
java.sql.SQLException: Table not found in statement [select txid  from
search_transaction]
    at org.hsqldb.jdbc.Util.sqlException(Unknown Source)
    at org.hsqldb.jdbc.jdbcStatement.fetchResult(Unknown Source)
@org.sakaiproject.content.api.ContentHostingService = vol1
```

What the error is stating is that a database table is missing. Next the error message **java.sql.SQLException: Table not found in statement** is generated by the application because the database table does not exist. Therefore, for the HSQL demonstration database transactions are broken for searching.

To turn search functionality off, set the following in `sakai/sakai.properties`:

```
search.enable=false
```

After restarting Sakai and trying search, you will see the following message returned by the application:

```
The search tool is not enabled, please ask your administrator to set
search.enable = true in sakai.properties
```

sakai.properties

There are hundreds of properties that you can add to the global configuration file `sakai/sakai.properties`. The property names remain mostly stable between versions of Sakai. Occasionally, an unexpected change in a property name or function causes issues. The change is flagged early either through the testing cycle on the QA server network or later by the early adopters. In reaction, the community officer updates the release notes or developers modify the property name to fit its older purpose. Keeping track of the property list is a chore of great importance. However, new properties do emerge and supersede others. With over 500 configuration properties mentioned at `http://bugs.sakaiproject.org/confluence/display/DOC/Sakai+Properties+Reference` there is much detail in which you can make mistakes.

Never underestimate the capacity to make typing errors. (Shush—do not let the editor hear that.) It is sometimes difficult to see the difference between 0 and o, and extra spaces hidden in a bunch of text are easy to miss at the best of times.

An historic example of the vulnerability of `sakai.properties` to potential typos is an issue that thankfully no longer exists (`http://bugs.sakaiproject.org/jira/browse/SAK-9752`).

Sakai can store resources such as videos, pictures, and documents either within the database itself or within the file system. If the system administrators have defined these two properties correctly: bodyPath@org.sakaiproject.content.api. ContentHostingService and bodyVolumes@org.sakaiproject.content.api. ContentHostingService then the binary files are stored on disk, otherwise they are stored in the database. The bodyPath defines the top-level directory where content is stored and the bodyVolumes is a comma-delimitated list of subdirectories. For example:

```
bodyPath@org.sakaiproject.content.api.ContentHostingService = ${sakai.
home}db/bodyContent/
```

```
bodyVolumes@org.sakaiproject.content.api.ContentHostingService=vol1,vol2,
vol3
```

The settings define three directories for storing content:

sakai/db/bodyContent/vol1

sakai/db/bodyContent/vol2

sakai/db/bodyContent/vol3

The bodyVolumes property allows content to be shared across disks or even across file servers mounted by NFS. However, historically, if spaces were accidently included in the list such as:

```
bodyVolumes@org.sakaiproject.content.api.ContentHostingService= vol1,
vol2,vol3
```

then Sakai expects corresponding directories with spaces included.

Another issue for property configuration is that you need to think in terms of groups of properties rather than individual properties. One group of properties configures the database settings, another, the look and feel of Sakai, and yet another authentication. Looking at bodyPath and bodyVolumes, if you configure bodyPath alone then there are no subdirectories for binary content. All the content resides under the top-level directory. However, later, due to increased demand as users upload more and more files, you cannot add extra subdirectories. In other words, from the very beginning both properties need to be defined, or later on, as your system becomes more and more popular, you may have a storage scalability issue.

File permissions

It should not happen, but it does. Permissions on file systems can accidently be changed by errant processes such as tired system administrators working too hard, too fast on too many issues at once, or a poorly written shell script that has worked well for years, but breaks due to new circumstances in production.

If Sakai cannot write to specific parts of the file system, then content cannot be saved (if stored on the file system and not in the database). To make the situation more complex, metadata such as file name and location are stored in the database, so even if you fail to upload a file, then when the particular file is asked for again, the user will see a confusing file not found error `java.io.FileNotFoundException`. Therefore, if in the logs you see consistent `java.io` errors, then start checking file system permissions.

Class not found

If in the logs you see the error `java.lang.ClassNotFoundException` then that normally implies that a Java library is missing. For example if you configure your demonstration version of Sakai to use a MySQL database rather than the default in-memory database then you will see this error message:

`java.lang.ClassNotFoundException: com.mysql.jdbc.Driver`

Each tool has its own space for loading in libraries. The file location is under the `webapps/Toolname/WEB-INF/lib` directory for JAR files and `webapps/Toolname/WEB-INF/classes` directory for compiled class files. These should be the first locations a system administrator checks for missing files. The directory `common/lib` is the location for Java libraries that need to be seen by all parts of the Sakai code base and where the database drivers need to be placed.

You can also generate a `classNotFoundException` when there are two copies of the same JAR file, but they are in different class loader locations in the same hierarchy within the same application. For example if you place your MySQL driver in `common/lib` and in a tools `WEB_INF/lib` directory.

Information sources

A handy source of information is the distribution lists, which are explained in detail in Chapter 17. The lists contain a lot of questions and answers, many of which are relevant for issues associated with live deployments. There is a highly useable searchable index at `http://www.nabble.com`. On the front page of Nabble, there is a search form; if you type in the word **Sakai**, the returned results mention the various distribution lists followed by the most recent postings. Searching in this way, you will find more than 30,000 matching posts. The development list is the highest volume list; it has embedded within its contents a lot of hard-earned experience. Clicking on the link **Sakai** should take you to a page similar to the one shown in the figure below:

By selecting a forum and then searching, you can see if anyone has asked the community directly for help for any given problem.

For system administrators, the bug database (`http://bugs.sakaiproject.org/jira`) mentions more than 9,000 fixed issues or feature requests, with comments and a history of what was done to resolve the specific bug. The bug database is a central point for collecting and maintaining descriptions and status. Any individual is welcome to create an account and then report or comment on bugs.

The web site has an account creation link just underneath the login form.

Each issue is linked to a given part of Sakai, such as the Chat or Blog tools, and the Sakai version number. If the issue, known as a "Jira" (after the name of the software the bug database runs on) has merit, then the Foundation's project coordinator assigns the task of cleaning up the code to a specific developer.

Not only are bugs reported and tracked within the bug database, but so too are feature requests. The community can vote on feature requests. If there is enough interest, then volunteers are assigned.

If you have an error message that you want to gather more information about, searching JIRA using the the quick search input on the top righthand side of the web site (next figure) will list the links to possibly related issues. Clicking on the most relevant link in the key column of the results table will direct you to the bug details page.

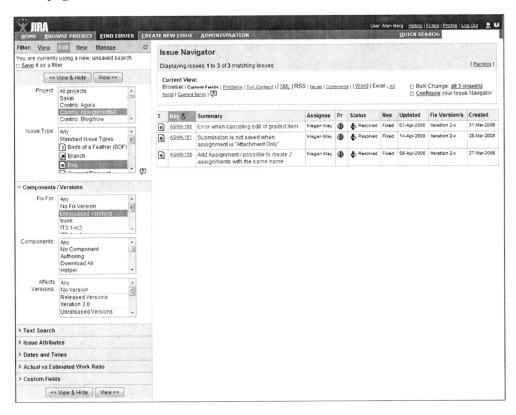

Searching for the term **mysql** mentions around 1000 fixed issues and for Oracle, 1200. This clearly shows that the QA process is active and developers are working hard at improving the code base.

Summary

Sakai has a policy of containment and signaling of issues. The application signals via logging and an error report form in which the user can add comments and give relevant feedback.

Automatic scripts can analyze emailed errors and generate meaningful bug reports. This chapter mentions two examples of scripting. The first was on a server in Amsterdam as part of the QA process, and the second was by the University of Cape Town as part of its monitoring of production systems.

Early adopters work closely with the community to iron out the residual defects.

Log4j is a Java framework for consistent logging. You can modify the structure of the log file and where the log file is sent through one configuration file.

This chapter mentions a number of common error messages.

Nabble and its search engine over the Sakai distribution lists is a viable source of reference for immediate issues. The Sakai bug database is also a good source for researching problems.

Coming in the next chapter are ten international case studies showing Sakai at its best.

14
Show Cases

Sakai shapes the online learning experience of many millions of students internationally. It has been proven to scale from small pilots to deployments greater than 160,000 students, such as at the University of South Africa (`https://my.unisa.ac.za/portal`). Sakai works well within many higher education cultures and with different student learning practices. It has been deployed in single departments, in the entire student population at large universities, and in consortiums and commercial third-party hosting services.

This chapter includes ten case studies that explore real-life situations from a range of individuals' viewpoints. Experts have written the studies. They have written each case study in their own style to emphasize the range of cultures involved in the community. Consider this a low-resolution snapshot of ever changing, diverse cultures.

The ten case studies included in this chapter are:

1. Cambridge University—Patrick Carmichael and Katy Jordan discuss Camtools, the Sakai learning environment at Cambridge, specifically the evidence-informed approach to teaching for Plant Sciences using this environment.
    See: `https://camtools.cam.ac.uk/`

2. Amsterdam University—Frank Benneker details specific examples of e-learning and explains how small project sites are a big thing in Amsterdam. Frank concludes that, "It is expected that Sakai and other open source software solutions will be at the heart of the e-learning services at the University of Amsterdam."
    See: `http://www.iis-communities.nl`

3. The University of Michigan—This study is an overview of Sakai at Michigan and how it transformed the university's educational experience.
    See: `https://ctools.umich.edu`

4. University Fernando Pessoa (UFP) — Nuno Fernandes, Luis Gouveia, and Feliz Gouveia explain how Sakai at UFP has grown in use over the years and how they contributed back to the community by developing a number of tools, including the Site Stats reporting tool.
    See: `https://elearning.ufp.pt`

5. Marist College — This study describes how migrating to Sakai requires effective communication and educational strategies.
    See: `https://ilearn.marist.edu`

6. Sakai Commercial Affiliate (SCA) — There are numerous success stories associated with Sakai where commercial support from companies such as Serensoft and Unicon has helped organizations overcome barriers to deployment. This case study mentions rSmart.
    See: `http://www.rsmart.com/`

7. Students' Engagement with a Virtual Research Environment in Scotland — Dr. Claire Cassidy and Sanna Rimpiläinen explain how using Sakai as a Virtual Research Environment supports new models of collaborative and participative research in Scottish education.

8. SOLO, Taking e-learning Offline — Louis Botha describes how using SOLO, students do not have to be constantly connected to Sakai while studying.
    See: `http://bugs.sakaiproject.org/confluence/display/SOLO/Learning+offline+with+SOLO`

9. The LAMP Consortium — The success factors involved in creating the award-winning Learning Asset Management Project (LAMP) are discussed by Martin Ramsay.
    See: `http://lamp.acaweb.org`

10. Mondo at the University of Stockholm — Johan Kardell, Lotta Pettersson, and Magnus Tagesson look at a distance learning course given at the Department of Criminology at Stockholm University.
    See: `http://mondo.su.se`

Acknowledgements

I would like to acknowledge the hard work of the authors of the case studies. Thank you for showing Sakai at its best.

rSmart kindly compiled three of the case studies — the University of Michigan and Maris College, along with rSmart as an example of third-party commercial support.

CamTools: Using Sakai to support teaching and learning in a research-intensive university

CamTools has contributed not only to enhanced provision, but to a sense of "ownership" of the online environment and improved levels of engagement by both teachers and students.

About the authors

Patrick Carmichael is Head of Evaluation at the Centre for Applied Research in Educational Technologies (CARET) at the University of Cambridge, where he leads a team of education researchers involved in a range of teaching and learning initiatives within the university. He also directs externally funded research projects, including "Ensemble: Semantic Technologies for the Enhancement of Case Based Learning", a three-year project to explore the potential of semantic technologies to support and enhance teaching and learning in areas where complex subject matter makes case-based learning the pedagogy of choice. He has a PhD in Science Education and has written on issues as diverse as pre-school learning, assistive technology, digital archives, and media development in developing economies.

Katy Jordan is a Researcher at the Centre for Applied Research in Educational Technologies (CARET) at the University of Cambridge. With a Master's degree in Plant Pathology from Imperial College, she worked from 2005-2008 on the University of Cambridge Plant Science Pedagogy Project and on its successor, the Teaching for Learning Network. She is currently a researcher on the "Ensemble: Semantic Technologies for the Enhancement of Case Based Learning" project and is particularly involved in developing technologies to support research collaboration across multi-institutional and interdisciplinary research communities.

CamTools: Sakai at the University of Cambridge

The University of Cambridge is an internationally renowned, research-intensive university that is home to a large community of research-active staff, research groups and centres, and a learner community with a high proportion of postgraduate students — nearly 5000 compared with about 10000 undergraduates. Members of the teaching staff frequently integrate their own research activities and experience into their teaching, and advanced undergraduate courses involve students in research activities in which they may work alongside postgraduates or academic staff. As such there is often a blurring of the distinction between formal learning and the development of academic research practices.

At the same time, many of the common drivers for the adoption of e-learning and "distance learning" models are not present at Cambridge. Lectures, practical classes, and seminars are complemented and extended by a system of "supervisions": small-group teaching in which a small number of students (usually between one and three) work intensively with a member of staff. The university is comparatively small and the vast majority of students live within the University environs as members of one of the thirty-one colleges. With the exception of a small number of students involved in part-time postgraduate study and those on initial teacher training courses, students are full-time, study in their colleges or departments, and are used to regular face-to-face contact with teachers and peers. These features mean that the learning technologies employed across the university have to be carefully matched to existing practices and to the pedagogical commitments of teachers and students alike.

In 2005, the Centre for the Applied Research into Educational Technologies (CARET) at the University of Cambridge began a process of replacing its existing virtual learning environment and groupware environments with a single online collaboration environment. Experience of supporting teaching, learning, and research across the university using the Coursework and DotLearn environments had revealed that many of the technical user requirements and the models of collaboration that underpinned them would be better served by a single online platform. This would support transitions: from teaching to research collaboration; from resource management to knowledge construction; and from private small-group working to broader community engagement. The Sakai Virtual Collaboration Environment was selected as it addressed these needs and CARET is now a significant member of the extended Sakai Community, and a centre for research into how virtual research environments can support and enhance teaching, learning, and research across institutional and disciplinary settings.

The Cambridge University instance of Sakai is known locally as "CamTools" and extends the standard Sakai distribution in a number of key respects, including integration of CamTools with "Raven", the university's campus-wide login system and, more recently, the development of a custom "iGoogle"-style dashboard, which acts as a user home page within Sakai.

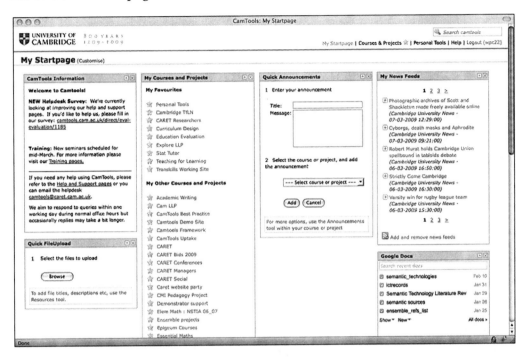

CamTools "Dashboard" with widgets offering access to system information; Sakai worksites and tools; and external sources of information such as RSS feeds and the user's Google Documents. Shortcuts offer quick access to favorite sites and personal tools.

The CamTools environment is used by over 3000 unique users each day, with 14000 unique users over the course of a term. In addition to personal home spaces, over 1800 project and course sites have now been created. The majority of the course sites developed within CamTools provide support for lecture courses and seminar series, characteristically by presenting students with syllabi, readings to accompany and extend lecture content, presentations and other support materials, data sets and collections of images. Discussion, email, and chat tools are also used to support and prepare students for small-group teaching in supervisions, and to maintain communication with those students who do spend time away from the university campus — initial teacher education students on school placements are an example.

At the same time, CamTools has also provided a platform for more advanced and often discipline-specific applications in which technological tools "add value" to established teaching and learning activities. An example is Molstruc, an implementation of the Java-based JMol 3-D Molecular Modeling environment that can be used in lectures, small-group teaching, and self-study activities to enhance learner understanding of the structure, properties, and reactions of complex molecules, the data files for which are available from open-access resources such as the Protein Data Base. CamTools provides a common platform within which these models can be integrated with other resources such as lecture notes, discussion spaces, or links to related online literature.

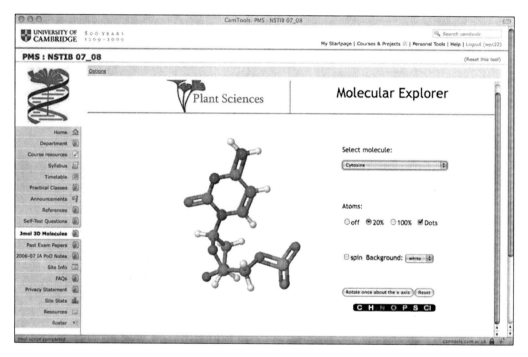

MolStruc embedded in a course worksite, along with syllabus, resources, Wiki, schedule, and other tools and service

Another example of an advanced teaching and learning application is Exegesis, a tool developed to support students as they "gloss" key literary texts. This is a key activity in small-group teaching and learning, and students benefit from the discussions in which they consider the meaning and significance of words and phrases used by authors. Exegesis presents undergraduate students of English with key texts by Shakespeare, in which key words and phrases are highlighted. A "chat"-like interface allows them to enter their interpretations and, once they have contributed, they are able to review other students' ideas about the same texts and engage in discussions with them. Originally designed to support and enhance small-group discussions, students also reported finding this an invaluable revision tool as examinations, which included a compulsory glossing activity, drew near.

This development of specific applications, and the customization of course and project worksites within CamTools, takes place within a broader programme of "evidence-informed" development—both of teaching and learning practices and of the learning technologies that support them. The involvement of teachers, students, and researchers in the design and development of CamTools has contributed not only to enhanced provision, but also to a sense of "ownership" of the online environment and improved levels of engagement by both teachers and students.

Evidence-informed approaches to virtual learning environment development: the case of Plant Sciences

One example of this evidence-informed approach took place within the "Plant Sciences Pedagogy Project," an initiative funded by the Cambridge-MIT Institute. The project team included subject specialists from the Department of Plant Sciences, educational researchers, and software developers. As the project began, CamTools was at an early stage of development and while some research groups were using it for collaborative working, there had been few instances of a complete course being supported online. As a result, there were no pre-existing models of its use within the Cambridge context for the project to draw upon. Given the great potential offered by the flexibility of the Sakai system, the project adopted an evidence-informed approach to determine how CamTools could best be implemented to support undergraduate students in a second-year Plant and Microbial Science course.

A multi-method approach was taken to building an evidence base, intended to inform not just the development of electronic resources but the project as a whole, which also developed new classes for students and support for postgraduate students with a role in teaching and supervision undergraduates. Research activities contributing data to the evidence base included:

- A "value-practice" questionnaire designed to collect students' accounts of teaching and learning practices, together with their attitudes towards those practices and their assessment of their value in supporting learning.

- A "self-efficacy" questionnaire designed to document students' assessments of their self-efficacy in applying skills as well as those specifically developed in the course of the Plant and Microbial Sciences course.

- Focus groups in which students discussed learning, teaching, and assessment.

- Interviews with teaching staff about the teaching practices they reported using, their perceptions of students as learners, and the factors that support and constrain effective small-group teaching.

- Documentary analysis of course materials: course outlines, lecture notes, practical documentation, essay titles, and past examination materials.

Analysis of these data led the project team to structure the course site around the newly released Sakai Wiki tool, which allowed a network of hyperlinked pages to be created reflecting the structure of the taught course. This was then used as an area to collate course documentation, lecture notes, and support materials, whilst emphasizing their context in the course as a whole. Evidence from the research activities was then used to inform the creation of specific learning objects, content, and tools, which were then embedded into, or linked from the Wiki. These specific interventions and their relationship to the research evidence is shown below.

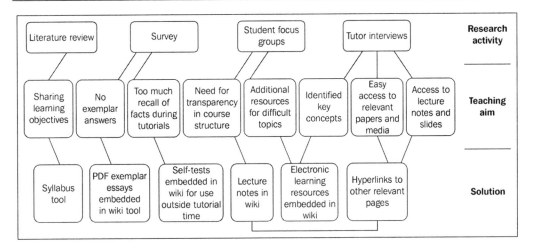

The research activities of the Plant Sciences Pedagogy Project; the desirable pedagogic aims that emerged from them; and how these were addressed using features of CamTools

In October 2006, the course worksite and learning objects within it were introduced to the second-year undergraduate students. Data were collected throughout the course of the 2006-2007 academic year using the Sakai "site stats" tool. These showed that there was a good deal of variation in how students used the site; all had done so, but the extent, frequency, and nature of use differed. It also highlighted the importance of the VLE as a resource when studying for examinations, when frequency of visits peaked during the year.

These data led to questions about why there were these variations in practice, so at the end of the academic year students were given an online questionnaire to gauge their assessment of CamTools, the course site, and the different types of content within it. This highlighted the value they attached to materials of high quality content: materials which aided their learning, particularly in relation to challenging concepts were highly rated, with this outweighing the "production quality" of the content.

To further illuminate the data collected from the site and the questionnaire, the project organized focus groups with students after they had completed the second-year course. It was conducted as a "co-interpretation" exercise; a set of PowerPoint slides were used, each illustrating a different type of learning object, or representations of real data collected from the site, and participants described their use of different learning tools in response to the slide being viewed. This yielded rich insights into the student perspectives and ways to further enhance the course site specifically and the CamTools environment more generally.

New directions

Development of Sakai at Cambridge continues, with increasing synergies between groups of users and the developer team at CARET, and research into use of Sakai taking place as part of a broader programme of innovation in teaching and learning. Additionally, an increase in awareness of the potential of CamTools has meant that previously disparate projects to develop learning technologies now involve integration of new features and services into CamTools.

Currently, evidence-informed approaches are contributing to a new phase of Sakai development including:

- The integration of CamTools with Institutional Repositories: Research teams at Cambridge are concerned to maximize the impact of their work by publishing findings, "pre-prints", and conference papers, and by offering data for open access and secondary analysis.

- Closer integration with "Cloud" Computing: The "iGoogle"-style dashboard described earlier and illustrated in the first figure represents a recognition that monolithic managed learning environments may not be the most appropriate long-term solution to the needs of teachers, learners, and researchers, and that existing institutional environments may need to be coupled to distributed data and application servers.

- Support for Scholarly Networking: With increasing interest in scholarly networking and collaborative working enabled by "Web 2.0" applications, approaches, and frameworks, several projects at Cambridge are exploring the potential to develop CamTools as the basis of academic networking, with contact management, fluid group formation, and "affiliation network" features.

Summary

Sakai and CamTools have become embedded into research, teaching, and learning practice at Cambridge through iterative development processes that pay great attention to user engagement, research, and evaluation. Recognizing and respecting disciplinary approaches, exploring existing practices, and enabling emergent ones has located CamTools, Sakai, and Learning Technologies more generally at the heart of innovation within the University.

Sakai @ the University of Amsterdam

It is expected that Sakai and other open source software solutions will be at the heart of the e-learning services at the University of Amsterdam.

About the author

Frank Benneker works at the Informatiseringscentrum of the University of Amsterdam, center of information technology, within the education and research services development group. He is one of the architects of the e-learning infrastructure and is the Sakai representative of the University of Amsterdam. In 2007, he was the local organizer of the 7th Sakai Conference in Amsterdam.

Introduction of new technologies and ideas for e-learning at the University of Amsterdam are at the core of Frank's work. He is a member the Dutch standards organization working group on e-learning standards.

Frank studied Philosophy and Industrial Robotics at Utrecht University.

About the University

The predecessor of the University of Amsterdam, the Athenaeum Illustre, was founded in Amsterdam in 1632 to educate students in Trade and Philosophy. The Athenaeum remained a small institution until the nineteenth century, with no more than 250 students and eight teachers at any one time. The situation changed in 1877 when the Athenaeum Illustre became the University of Amsterdam and was permitted to confer the highest educational degrees.

The University of Amsterdam has a broad academic curriculum. UvA staff publish around 7,500 academic articles each year. In many respects the university's fundamental academic research is top of the international league, and the applied research programs are often of an interdisciplinary nature and frequently concerned with social issues.

Today, the university aims to offer an inspiring, broadly oriented international academic environment where both staff and students can develop their capacities to optimum effect. The university is characterized by a critical, creative, open-minded, international atmosphere, and is strongly engaged with society. Because the university is located in both historic and modern buildings spread throughout the city, the university forms an integral part of the daily life of the city.

Currently, there are around 28,000 students and 5,500 staff at the University of Amsterdam. The university has seven faculties, covering the humanities, the social and behavioral sciences, economics and business, law, the natural sciences, medicine, and dentistry.

E-learning

Informatiseringscentrum (IC), the central IT department, has a strong track record in providing services for all staff and students. This shared service center provides the entire core IT infrastructure, such as high-quality broadband network facilities to each desk within the university, a broad range of reliable computer desktop services and all the necessary back-office activities including a support desk.

In the mid nineties, a new kind of service evolved based on the World Wide Web revolution. Until that moment, the Internet focus was on email. In 1999, the IT in Education expert group was established to stimulate, support, and coordinate the use of IT in education. Over the years since then this group has developed many innovative Internet services for teachers and students. Currently, the most visible services are: an online course catalogue, a campus-wide implementation of Blackboard, a streaming media server, a student portal based on Uportal (`http://www.uportal.org`), and a personal home page system for students and academic staff. The latest additions are a digital portfolio system based on OSP tools in a Sakai environment and UvA communities, and a collaboration environment based on Sakai.

The SURF Foundation

We spotted the Sakai project back in 2004 as a potential future platform. In a joint project with the SURF Foundation (`http://www.surfFoundation.nl`), which also took an interest in the Sakai project, the university became a member of the Sakai community. The aim of the joint project was to participate in Sakai's activities and to research its potential as an alternative e-learning platform for the whole of the Dutch higher education sector. This project resulted in two conferences (in 2005 and 2006) with the theme, "beyond the borders of the virtual learning environment", and in 2007, the 7th Sakai conference was held in Amsterdam.

The start of the Dutch Sakai Special interest group, Sakai NL (`http://www.sakai.nl`) heightened cooperation between the University of Amsterdam and SURF.

Sakai NL strives to disseminate knowledge to the entire Dutch language region.

UvA communities, a Sakai collaboration environment

Modern universities are developing in the direction of loose conglomerates of (inter)discipline expertise that have a high degree of connectedness with society in the broader sense. Twenty-first century universities may also be regarded as "knowledge servers" in which a number of communities create, share, publish, and apply knowledge. Learning and research, in other words, are becoming a community-wide activity. The use of information technology has obviously been a tremendous catalyst for this development. Like broader Web 2.0 developments, aspects such as openness, accessibility, or sharing are starting to play an increasingly important role. In order to support the formation and development of academic communities, the University of Amsterdam has tailored the open source collaboration and learning platform Sakai and created an integrated community system that meets the requirements for community support.

Unlike most information systems in educational organizations, UvA communities (http://www.communities.uva.nl) are open to the public and are free to use. Their very purpose is to allow people from outside the university organization to connect within the realm of the university and to give insiders means to easily connect outside the university. Every user has access to the same selectable set of tools and services, which are extensible with tailor-made functionality. People from many different cultural and scientific backgrounds collaborate on a variety of topics and take on multiple roles in multiple communities. Supporting a broad audience also means that it is necessary to use common and innovative low-threshold technologies that most computer users know how to use intuitively.

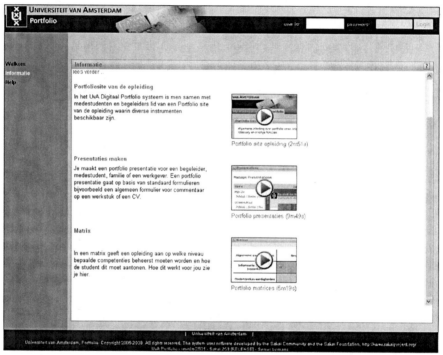

UvA Communities homepage

According to Etienne Wenger, "Communities (of practice) are everywhere and people generally participate in a number of them", (http://www.ewenger.com). The UvA Communities project aims to place this important observation in the context of the 21st century university by creating a ubiquitous community platform that is able to stage a number of different communities and users, including individuals from outside the university. Within one system, users can become a member of one or more communities, and communities may be formed around a number of topics, ranging from a general field of studies to an ad hoc problem area.

UvA Communities started as a pilot project in the autumn of 2006 at the institute of interdisciplinary studies. Together with Edia (`http://www.edia.nl`), UvA's Sakai developing partner, the IC is hosting and developing the community environment. Today (March 2009), the system has grown into a collaboration environment for a broad range of groups within the university. Several thousand users log on to over 300 sites within UvA Communities.

UvA Communities hosts some very interesting use cases. A few of them are listed next:

Webklassen

`http:/www.webklassen.nl` — Web Klassen are short digital orientation courses for prospective students. Anyone with access to the Internet can enroll in these classes and participate in a free distance education course, interacting with university teachers and other participants.

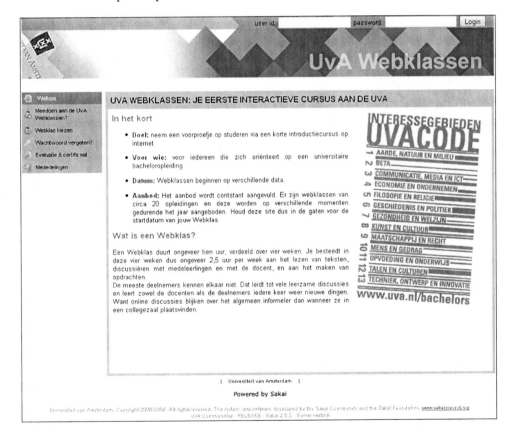

Conflict Studies

`http://www.conflictstudies.nl` — Conflict Studies serves as a platform for knowledge management around conflicts and conflict transformation. Participants range from scholars, professionals, to journalists. The platform currently integrates with Google maps to disseminate information on conflict cases and geographic locations.

 You can find the source code for the Google maps tool at: `http://bugs.sakaiproject.org/confluence/display/MAPS`.

IIS Communities

`http://www.iis-communities.nl` — The community environment of the Institute of Interdisciplinary Studies (IIS). This is the original UvA Sakai pilot project. Most of the courses offered by this institute are now using the Sakai environment in a blended fashion, with face-to-face lessons that are effectively combined with the Sakai toolset. It provides an online community extension to the regular lectures and seminars.

The Hague Forum for Judicial Expertise

`http://cle.hfje.nl` — The collaborative and learning environment implementation developed for this institute provides courses and collaboration tools for an international audience of national judges, magistrates, and other professionals working in the justice sector, offering them the opportunity to upgrade their knowledge and expertise in international law.

Project sites

`http://www.communities.uva.nl` — A project site is a collaboration environment for ad hoc project groups that are using the Sakai environment to share information, work together and to communicate between the project site members.

Testweeklab

`http://www.communities.uva.nl` — A research project whose goal is to offer services to a community of researchers in the field of psychology testing (for example, IQ tests, gender tests). The project was a joint effort between the University Library, the department of psychology, the IC, and Edia. A special tool was developed to integrate a Fedora repository with the Sakai environment to store, manage, and make searchable the research datasets of the psychology department.

Digital Portfolio, a different use case

In 2005 a project was started to look for a successor to a homegrown portfolio system. After comparing several open source and closed source products, we decided to go ahead with the Open Source Portfolio initiative (OSP). In those days, it was an open source project of its own. Just a few months after we made the "go" decision, the OSP community joined the Sakai community. With the strong ties between Uportal and Sakai it seemed that we were betting on the right horse.

2006 was a difficult year. The integration of the OSP tools in the Sakai environment was more complex than expected and the software was not mature. However, by January of 2007 the Digital Portfolio system (`http://portfolio.uva.nl`), based on Sakai and OSP, went into production. The rapid success would not have been possible without the feedback and encouragement of the Sakai community.

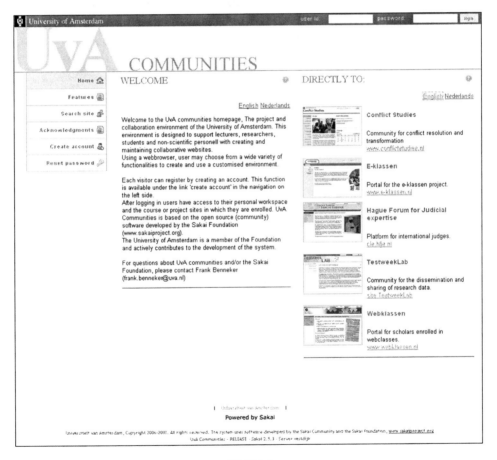

OSP@UvA

Why Sakai?

To be a part of the community and working together on similar projects, and taking control of our ICT solution for education, are the motivations for our efforts with Sakai.

It is not just the software but also the concept of more than a hundred universities working together, exchanging knowledge. This provides a helping hand when you really need it, and is crucial to our core business to provide state-of-the-art ICT solutions for our researchers, teachers, and students.

The experiences with Uportal, OSP, and Sakai showed us that open source, community-based software is a very serious alternative for closed source solutions. Although vendor-driven solutions are still a major part of the university infrastructure, in the coming years, it is expected that Sakai and other open source software solutions will be at the heart of the e-learning services at the University of Amsterdam.

University of Michigan

Sakai does not dictate one way to design or teach a class. This flexibility in the platform, coupled with the best-in-class tools developed by educators, enabled us to have an exceptionally collaborative and engaged learning experience.

Sakai success story

The University of Michigan (`http://vpcomm.umich.edu/aboutum/`) was one of the founding institutions of the Sakai Collaboration and Learning Environment (CLE) and the largest initial contributor of code. "There was nothing accidental in the creation of Sakai", explains Dr. John King, vice provost for academic information and professor in the School of Information. "It grew out of a research project to build online infrastructure for support of globally distributed communities of scientists. We realized that the future required online support for distributed communities of learners in all aspects of the learning process—teaching, research, and administration. We needed an environment we could control, so we built it. Other institutions shared our ambition, and joined us. That was the beginning of the Sakai movement."

Today, in addition to pervasive adoption of the Sakai architecture for the university's collaborative learning environment, the University of Michigan's leadership and administrators are leveraging the Sakai environment to streamline the administrative needs of students, faculty, and staff.

UMICH Statistics

U-M faculty create more than 7,000 course sites each year.

99%+ of Ann Arbor campus students, and 85%+ faculty use Sakai (CTools) for course support.

23,200 course sites and 18,000 projects sites have been created since fall 2005.

Average peak use each week exceeds 5,600 simultaneous users.

Maximum peak use in a semester exceeds 7,500 simultaneous users.

More than 110,000 U-M users have created CTools accounts.

In a typical month, more than 45,000 unique users access CTools.

Transforming the education experience

Dr. Aileen Huang-Saad won both the 2008 University of Michigan Outstanding Professor of the Year Award and the 2008 Teaching with Sakai Innovation Award for her innovative teaching in her two-semester course, Biomedical Engineering Graduate Innovative Design Team. In the course, graduate students explore their own solutions to biomedical challenges, from concept inception to prototype design. "Students spend the first semester exploring biomedical challenges. I post research articles on specific clinical challenges prior to each class. A physician then lectures about the challenge, answering students' questions and participating with them in brainstorming solutions. The idea generation process continues outside the class in Sakai's wiki tool, where students generate class concept design documents, challenge each other's ideas, and self-organize into design teams around a particular challenge or concept by the end of the semester. The second semester is dedicated to prototype development. In this portion of the course, each design team has its own collaboration site, enabling each team to establish the roles, structure and resources that best suit its needs."

The 2007-2008 year was Dr. Huang-Saad's first year teaching the course and her first experience teaching with Sakai. "This course must be adaptive, self-organizing, and highly collaborative for innovation to occur most effectively. Sakai was critical to this process. Students self-assembled, collectively selecting and designing the tools that best met their needs. In particular, the students' ability to design the wiki to meet the needs of class-based concept design documents was crucial to their success."

Dr. Huang-Saad continues, "Sakai does not dictate one way to design or teach a class. This flexibility in the platform, coupled with the best-in-class tools developed by educators, enabled us to have an exceptionally collaborative and engaged learning experience."

Supporting the dissertation process

In 2001, a study was conducted by the university's Horace H. Rackham School of Graduate Studies and the Collaboration Technologies Lab (in the Digital Media Commons) to understand how to better support doctoral students in the dissertation process. The resulting action was the development of Grad Tools, a web-based tool in Sakai that reduces the administrative burden doctoral student's face.

Mr. Rex Patterson, director of information and technology services at Rackham, explains, "There is significant administrative burden during the dissertation process, particularly towards the end. This is often the most taxing time for the student with the dissertation itself, as well. Grad Tools reduces the administrative burden, allowing the student to focus more wholly on the content of the dissertation."

Today, Grad Tools' personalized, secure environment has over 1500 graduate student sites at the university. Each student has access to chronological, department-specific dissertation checklists that can be tailored to any student's particular requirements, a centrally located repository for all dissertation-related links and resources, secure document sharing capabilities, and an online collaboration environment for the student and dissertation committee members. In addition, it provides 1GB of reliable back-up space for the student's dissertation and all the tools to which students have become accustomed with Sakai. Ms. Donna Huprich, director of academic records and dissertations, notes, "The feedback we hear from both the departments and the students is that it is helpful and easy to use. Having one place to find everything is very powerful."

Streamlining academic administration

One of the recent academic administration projects to utilize Sakai is the university's annual promotion and tenure process. The University of Michigan typically reviews between 160-200 faculty promotion and tenure casebooks each year, each more than 100 pages long. Prior to streamlining the process on Sakai, four hard copies were required of each casebook.

Over the past four years, the university has gradually introduced the electronic process. This year, the university did away with all paper casebooks, and every school and college submitted its casebooks in Sakai. Significant efficiency gains were seen with this process change. "Both the units and those coordinating the process have realized significant time savings", states Ms. Lesley Bull, administrative specialist for faculty affairs. "In addition, we are utilizing significantly less paper, we eliminated ergonomic challenges in the workplace, and we reduced the amount of secure physical space required for these highly confidential documents."

The need for a highly secure environment was one of the reasons Sakai was selected as the platform of choice for this process. "Confidentiality is of the greatest concern in the faculty promotion and tenure process", explains Ms. Kati Bauer, assistant vice provost for academic information. "Sakai provides us with the security we require in a fully online process. We can easily establish unique permissions for each casebook based on the reviewers assigned to that particular review, facilitating committee member's access to a shared, secure work space."

Future directions

Scalable, reliable, interoperable, and extensible, Sakai is designed to meet the needs of institutions today and tomorrow. Dr. King explains, "Our goal is nothing less than the transformation of learning. We foresee dramatic improvements in the quality of learning, but we also see great gains in productivity and access. This is a global vision, but of course, we are starting here at home."

UFP-UV: UFP in the Sakai project

Early adoption pays for the teaching staff as the platform allows them to manage their time and helps to organize their student relationships.

About the authors

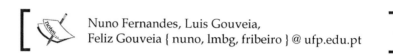

Nuno Fernandes, Luis Gouveia,
Feliz Gouveia { nuno, lmbg, fribeiro } @ ufp.edu.pt

Abstract

This paper briefly introduces the University Fernando Pessoa (UFP) (http://www.ufp.pt) experience with Sakai. UFP is a 20-year-old university with 5000 students and around 600 teaching staff. It is organized under three faculties; Health, Human Studies, and Science and Technology. Since 1994 it has had an excellent record of introducing innovative uses of technology for supporting its learning, such as the 1995 project requiring that each first-year student have a laptop computer. As a result, in early 2004, the university board decided to support the e-learning group efforts to select, develop, and implement an e-learning platform as the institutional response for both face-to-face and distance learning offers. From October 2004 until August 2008, the use of UFP-UV the local Sakai flavor (http://elearning.ufp.pt) saw a growing demand from its users.

The UFP-UV was able to contribute to both the UFP and the Sakai community with a number of tools designed and developed locally; the Site Stats tool is the best example.

Keywords: Sakai, elearning, higher education, technology adoption, Site Stats

Introduction

University Fernando Pessoa (UFP) decided in 2004 to start building an infrastructure for distance education. After an initial survey of the available learning environments, UFP decided to adopt Sakai, a then new project resulting from the merger of the software of several U.S. universities. Sakai was open source, young, and there was an opportunity to work on and influence a product that had, under different flavors, been used at large scale by large US institutions.

The e-learning project at UFP was defined by the following characteristics:

- A large majority of courses taught at UFP are in the Social Sciences and Health Sciences area, and only four courses in the Science and Technology area. This means the vast majority of users (learners and instructors) are not technology-oriented, so you can expect a wide range of adoption questions.

- The platform should support regular university courses, graduate courses, and several formats of training courses; the platform should not constrain instructors to follow a rigid pedagogical model; it should on the contrary also be a tool for research, by allowing several configurations and functions to be tested and included as needed.

- The platform should be open in the sense of being able to integrate with the existing student and course rosters. New features and requirements, not known beforehand, should also be easily included in the system. This was a major requirement, as UFP did not want to rely solely on commercial vendors to integrate the system with legacy software and to add functions.

- Features such as localization and internationalization were secondary in the first stage of the project, although the system later needed to support a multi-language interface.

The e-learning project had a time frame of 2004-05 for requirements identification, tests, and candidate selection; 2005-06 for a medium-scale production; and 2006-07 for a full implementation. The first stage consisted of a literature review, technical literature review, and gathering of experiences from commercial e-learning systems — including visits and interviews at other Portuguese and Spanish institutions that had already deployed such systems.

UFP started a pilot with Sakai 1.0 in October 2004. This placed UFP among the initial group of universities worldwide to deploy Sakai into production. The first use was with an Information Management class for the Master's level with 18 students enrolled.

The initial pilot was open to all instructors and students, totaling 5000 users. A year later, at the end of the pilot, around 782 users had logged in at least 5 times, and 150 sites were active, having visits, resources to download, and having used chat or other communication tools. With such activity, we were able to get early indictors that the project was going to be a success from teaching staff who were "spreading the word" about the benefits of the system.

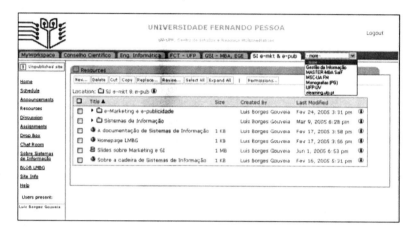

Sakai 1.0 running at UFP

Tools for delivering Assignments and Resources were driving the adoption of the platform. Project (non-course) sites were also a major argument for adoption, as instructors soon realized how easy they were to set up and use. UFP users were consistently working on the platform, even on weekends. Sakai has an email notification system whereby an instructor can inform students when new resources are available, so that users do not have to log in just to see if there is something new. Thus, early adoption pays for the teaching staff as the platform allows them to manage their time and helps to organize their student relationships, mainly by receiving the students work and keeping control of deadlines. Early adoption pays for the students who then get a one-stop shop for their class materials and for keeping in touch with their class, easing the information management burden.

Sakai usage, full adoption

UFP deployed Sakai 2.1 in February 2006, fully integrating it with the Student Information System and the Course Roster, granting access to 5,457 users (instructors, students, and staff), and to 2,088 sites. The sites were created automatically, but the roster had to be manually updated. Instructors had to decide if they wanted to keep information about students that were no longer in their classes.

We dropped full integration in favor of periodic synchronization to control which information was to be deleted. We also moved to a clustered Sakai 2.3 where the Sakai application was distributed across a number of servers.

UFP developed a tool that allows instructors to select the courses and sections they want to create in a site. Upon creation, sections are updated on a regular basis. This tool has fully automated the process of site creation (and naming), allowing us to decrease the support burden. The tool was one the main reasons we could maintain the UFP-UV supporting staff with the same team numbers, even with a strong demand rise.

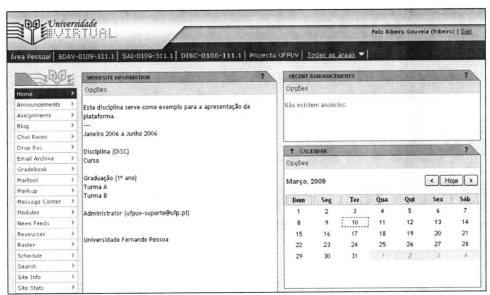

The current Sakai skin at UFP

Ninety percent of work sites are used as a complement to the classroom, and ten percent for blended and distance learning. Acceptance, by students and instructors alike, has been great.

The top requirements of instructors include having more ways to deliver content and follow student progress and to be able to "see" the site as student. Versions 2.4 and later of Sakai brought some improvements in these areas. In an internal University Quality Survey, UFP-UV is ranked among the top services used, and 67% of the teaching staff reported using it on a regular basis. In the same survey, 87% of students reported use.

The UFP tools

We addressed two top requirements of the Sakai community by developing a Site Statistics (Site Stats) tools and a User Membership tool. The former was listed in most of the requests we got for new functionality. The latter was essential to help desk and support activities. Site Stats is built on top of Sakai events, such as logging on, that are recorded in the database. We also developed a summary calendar, placed in the user workspace, showing events from all sites the users belong to. We also added a Portuguese translation of the interface as it was considered one of the top requirements by UFP-UV users.

Site Stats aggregates events generated by other Sakai tools to present site-specific statistics regarding user visits, tool activity, and resource activity. A summary of this information is presented on the tool's start page and further detailed data can be obtained using the tool's reporting abilities.

The newest version of Site Stats goes even further. With several performance improvements and a redesigned user interface, it offers a wide range of data aggregation and presentation options. We expect an official 2.0 version to be released by the time you read this case study. The following figures show several Site Stats screen grabs.

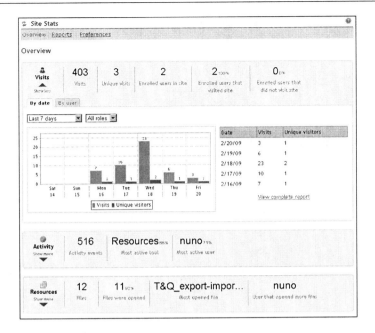

The Site Stats main page

The main page of Site Stats gives general indicators, such as the number of visitors to the site and the number of distinct visitors. The instructor can choose between weekly, monthly, and yearly views. Also shown are **Activity** indicators indicating which tools are being used the most.

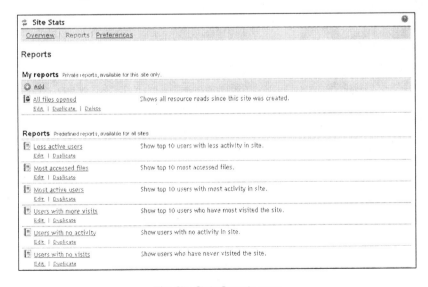

The Site Stats Reports page

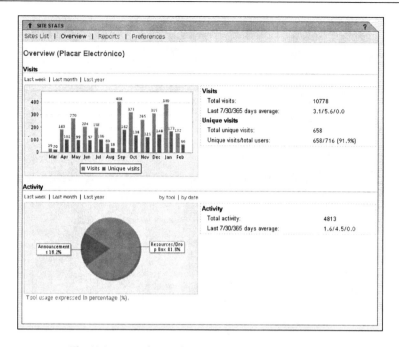

The Main page of a production site running SiteStats 1.x

Site Stats has been used by instructors and support staff to identify actions performed by site participants. In some situations, it can be used to prove compliance with regulations associated with computer-mediated learning, and it provides information for informing student evaluation.

Sakai usage at UFP

Usage of Sakai at UFP is consistent with other institutions deploying Sakai for face-to-face learning. The following figure shows the number of concurrent users during the year 2006. Note that summer holidays take place during August, with classes starting during the first half of September.

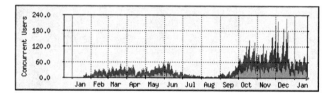

Concurrent users during January 2006 – January 2007

We reached 226 concurrent users in December 2006 during online tests. The monthly concurrent users average was 26, which was 1% of our "active" population (2,600 users). This result is consistent with the experience of our partners using Sakai. The following figure shows the period September 2006 to September 2007:

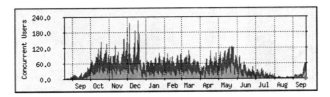

Concurrent users during September 2006 – September 2007

As of March 2007, 4,623 users had logged in at least once. There were 6,500 registered users, staff, and students. There were 1,860 distinct users logging in per week, and 2,600 logging in per month. We believe this figure, 2,600 users, represents roughly the active Sakai population, meaning the instructors that use the platform to deliver content, grade, deliver assignments, and communicate with their students.

Up to September 2007 there were roughly 27,000 logins per month, which means a user logged in on average 10 times a month. There were 19,500 stored digital resources. 200 online tests were published and taken, and we registered 3,800 student online assignment submissions.

There are 2,838 distinct user logins/week. Considering that 5,500 distinct users were active (having at least five logins since August 2008), this means that more than half of the users visited the platform at least once a week.

Our help desk registered frequent requests for help with the online testing. We have had, to date, no complaints about service quality, availability, or lack of support. Monitoring shows 99% availability.

Since September 2008, 900 course sites have been registering activity. Some are blended, meaning students are required to perform some of their work on the platform.

 You can see technical information about hardware and software infrastructure on the UFP-UV Wiki (http://elearning.ufp.pt/wiki) and blog (http://ufpuv.blogspot.com) pages.

Marist College and Sakai

Commercial partners offering assistance for Sakai implementations are heavily involved in the larger Sakai community and have a strong interest in the success of their partner institutions.

Background

Marist College (`http://www.marist.edu/`), located in Poughkeepsie, New York, is known as one of the most technologically advanced comprehensive liberal arts colleges in the United States. Marist, with its 4,300 students and 1000 staff, is a proud recipient of the Campus Technology Innovators Award and recognized by The Princeton Review and Forbes as one of the 25 "Most Connected Campuses" in America.

In early 2006, Marist College embarked upon a rigorous two-year assessment of Sakai. When Marist began this assessment, many considered Sakai suited only to large research institutions. Nonetheless, Marist College was interested in understanding how Sakai might both meet technology needs and allow for substantive innovation in teaching and learning in a smaller institution.

Josh Baron, Director of Academic Technology and e-learning at Marist College, led the learning management system decision-making process at Marist College. "We looked at five decision criteria when we evaluated Sakai: functionality requirements, available support, the health of the Sakai community, innovation factors, and reliability and stability." After a thorough analysis of Sakai, Marist College concluded that Sakai met their requirements under these criteria, and that no other system compared with Sakai's ability to enable teaching and learning innovation. Having reached this conclusion, Marist College began working towards implementation.

To assist with implementation and to provide ongoing support for Sakai, Marist College sought out a partner.

The commercial partner implementation model

There are different models being used for implementation by members of the Sakai community. One model involves enlisting the services of a commercial partner.

Marist has partnered with rSmart, one of several companies providing commercial support to institutions implementing Sakai. William Thirsk, Vice President and Chief Information Officer at Marist College, explains Marist's perspective for the value of obtaining commercial support: "As both an IT leader and a small liberal arts college, we approach technology development differently than a large, research university. Strong partners that support our vision are critical to our success; we cannot achieve what we do alone. rSmart brings a strong, fully verified, and supported Sakai instance and excellent support and maintenance services. As our partner, rSmart focuses on our institution's needs and interests, they invest with us in the development efforts most critical to our college, and they maintain an ongoing dialogue about how to optimize our relationship for the greatest mutual benefit."

A significant example of this optimization is the support rSmart provided for Marist's Sakai-SIS (Student Information System) integration. Working with rSmart's development team, Marist's IT offices were able to leverage Sakai's course management API to tightly integrate their legacy SIS system with Sakai course sites. This work automated the enrollment and "drop/add" process for courses, saving Marist 72 people hours per year, resulting in an overall productivity gain of 4%. rSmart's services significantly reduced the development resources needed to implement the integration. In addition, once the integration was completed, rSmart provided "just-in-time" support to make sure technical issues were addressed quickly, ensuring an extremely positive user experience as the integration was rolled out.

Institutions obtaining commercial support also gain the advantage of being able to redirect and focus institutional resources. Mr. Baron explains further, "The product, support, and services rSmart provides enable us to focus our two internal academic technology resources on working with faculty to innovate their teaching practices. It is this support that truly enables us to innovate."

Commercial partners offering assistance for Sakai implementations are heavily involved in the larger Sakai community and have a strong interest in the success of their partner institutions. Mr. Baron explains, "rSmart is fully invested in supporting our success. In addition, they provide an invaluable bridge for their customers to the broader Sakai community. The commitment and investment rSmart has made in Sakai provides us with great assurance of both Marist College's success and Sakai's success."

Migrating a campus to Sakai

There are always substantive questions to be addressed when anticipating such a significant transition as the implementation of a new learning management system. Of primary importance to Marist College were the questions of how to educate faculty about the opportunities of the new system, how to engage their interest, and how to optimize their ability to translate their knowledge into improved teaching strategies with favorable, tangible outcomes.

Marist implemented effective communication and educational strategies to address these issues. In the initial stages, the approach was mainly grassroots, but as the roadmap to implementation was developed, the communication and educational strategies were formalized. One of these strategies included a summer educational program, initially geared specifically to faculty in charge of fully online courses. This evolved into the "Academic Technology Institute", a program that was adapted to meet specific faculty needs, with flexible offerings such as weekend availability for adjunct faculty or a fully online version of the workshop, run in Sakai itself.

The results of efforts like these have been positive and significant. Setting goals for faculty conversion, Marist College, whose login page is shown in the following screen grab, consistently surpassed benchmarks. The fall 2008 goal was to have 15% of faculty opt to move to Sakai. Actual faculty conversion was 65%. Spring 2009's conversion goal was 75%, with actual conversion being 85%. Marist's ultimate goal is that by fall 2009, all faculties will have transitioned to Sakai. Given the expedited rate of conversion experienced thus far, Mr. Baron feels comfortable that this goal will be met.

The Marist login page

Tangible outcomes

Dr. Mark Van Dyke, an associate professor in Marist College's School of Communication and the Arts, was intrigued by the possibilities of Sakai's collaborative learning environment, and early in the implementation process, he integrated Sakai into his teaching strategies. The impetus, he explains, is that previously he had struggled to establish collaboration between different groups of students taking the same course at different times or on different days. Compounding the complexity was Dr. Van Dyke's desire to afford not only collaboration but also incremental achievements built upon learning gained by students in separate courses, taken in previous semesters.

For the spring semester of 2008, Dr. Van Dyke created separate work sites, using Sakai, for two sections of a public-relations case studies course that would be the beginning of a year-long project. These sites promoted active learning among students within each section. However, Dr. Van Dyke wanted to take the course collaboration to the next level, to allow collaboration among students in different course sections. Building upon the success he was experiencing with Sakai, Dr. Van Dyke moved the project forward to a fall 2008 communication capstone course. He created two more Sakai worksites for each section of the course and he added a project collaboration site. Course materials were then migrated from the spring and fall courses into the project site. The collaboration site connected all students from both sections of the fall course and created a bridge to the experience and knowledge gained by students in his spring course.

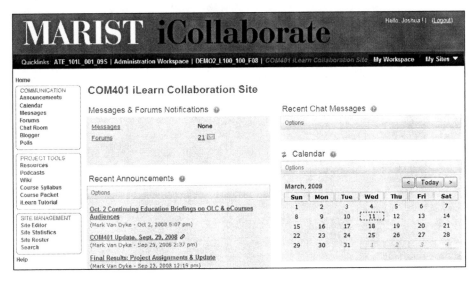

The Marist iCollaborate site

As he explains, "The collaboration site was like the hub of a wheel, with the spokes being the connection between the collaboration site and unique course sections." The students were largely responsible for populating the collaboration site, which they did, adding forum discussions, chats, blogs, podcasts, Wikis, resource folders, contact lists, and more. This initial venture into Sakai collaboration drew together 32 students working in seven teams from two different spring course sections. Through the collaboration site, 38 students in eight teams in his fall capstone class sections were able to apply conceptual and cultural knowledge from coursework completed in the previous semester. Ultimately, the project site facilitated collaboration among 70 students working in 15 teams from four different course sections, over two semesters.

As remarkable as his success with Sakai has been, so is the fact that neither Dr. Van Dyke nor his students had ever used Sakai before or had received any specialized training other than what was offered to all faculty and students. In fact, he explains, "We completed a couple of tutorials, and the students took to it right away."

rSmart

With rSmart's goal of making Sakai easy to "consume" for all types of intuitions, the first order of business is to make it easy to try.

Overview

rSmart (www.rsmart.com) is an open source software company serving the global education market by providing software support and services for the Sakai and Kuali (http://www.kuali.org/) community source projects. rSmart has been involved with the Sakai project from its early beginnings, both as a founding member of the Sakai Commercial Affiliates program and as a founder of the Open Source Portfolio project (OSP), which was later merged with Sakai. As an active participant in open source projects like Sakai and Kuali, rSmart is able to provide its customers with software applications specifically designed to meet the unique needs of educational institutions. The company's collaborative approach allows it to offer open source applications that break the dependence of educational institutions on traditional proprietary software vendors and at more attractive prices than closed source alternatives.

rSmart was established to help open source enterprise applications thrive in education. Lack of support is a significant barrier to the adoption of open source software; rSmart helps remove this barrier. The company has a unique model of community source engagement that includes community activism and participation, market outreach, and commercial services and support. rSmart's goal is to make the innovations of the Sakai community easy to "consume", whether by small schools like California Northstate College of Pharmacy (http://www.californiacollegeofpharmacy.org), with fewer than 500 users, or by large research universities like Virginia Tech (http://www.vt.edu).

The rSmart Sakai CLE is the company's fully packaged, tested, and supported distribution of the Sakai software. Similar to the way Red Hat distributes and supports the Linux operating system, rSmart distributes and supports Sakai. The company also provides professional services, including Sakai evaluation and assessment, configuration planning, training, installation, customization, integration and data migration, and application hosting to complement its support offerings. With nearly 50 educational institutions, including Marist College, Radford University, Cerritos Community College, and the University of Limerick, using rSmart Sakai CLE as the basis of their e-learning, ePortfolio, and online collaboration activities, rSmart is helping grow the number of Sakai users worldwide.

History

rSmart, based in Phoenix, Arizona, is the second venture by the company's three founders: John Robinson, Chris Coppola, and Anthony Potts. Their first venture developed a learning management system in the late 1990s that was eventually sold to SCT (now SunGard Higher Education). After several years at SCT they set out a second time to start a different kind of company – a company more aligned with the values of education.

John Robinson observed, "We wanted to start a company better aligned with higher education's values of collaboration, community, transparency and value. We felt it was time for a new kind of vendor; one more similar to my first company than to the companies that have emerged since those early days. What better way to do this than to align ourselves with the emerging open source communities in higher education." John is often regarded as the "father" of the packaged enterprise software business for higher education. He started Information Associates in 1968 when software was mostly home grown at colleges and universities.

Intrigued by the open source software development model and inspired by the early success of uPortal and other community-driven projects in education, they started rSmart and quickly became involved in OSP in both development and leadership capacities. Their work with OSP soon led to a deeper involvement in Sakai, which has since led rSmart to become a founder in the Kuali project. The Sakai community has acknowledged the depth of rSmart's commitment to the project by electing Chris Coppola to the Sakai board of directors and selecting John Ellis, an early rSmart software developer, as a Sakai Fellow. Chris remains the first and only non-academic representative elected to the Sakai board of directors where he served 3 years, 1 year as vice-chairperson.

Easy to adopt

rSmart has always viewed its role in the community ecosystem as one of adoption enabler. Like many of today's commercial affiliates, early on, rSmart's business was driven mainly by consulting projects. The maturity of the OSP and Sakai products (and the company) at the time necessitated this business model. As Sakai matured the company recognized that Sakai adoption would benefit from making it more "consumable" in a way that would scale. Inspired by the success that Red Hat and other open source companies were having with "productizing" their support and maintenance services, rSmart set out to invest in and develop a scalable Sakai support model that would provide a predictable level of support that customers could depend on.

Achieving economies of scale could not be achieved with the standard consulting model. Rather than operate and be capitalized as a consulting organization, rSmart needed to operate and be capitalized as a product company. The former requires little investment, as long as every hour of work is billed for. The latter requires significant upfront investment. The company raised the capital necessary and invested in building out its productized Sakai support offerings. Investments in dedicated Sakai support engineers, full-time documentation writers, Java developers, release engineers, quality assurance personnel, and other resources allow institutions to use and consume Sakai as a product—just as they are accustomed to using any traditional proprietary software product. By permitting institutions to consume Sakai in a familiar way, rSmart enables greater adoption of Sakai in a scalable manner.

These "product" investments have led to the creation of a unique support offering that includes:

- The rSmart Sakai CLE. The CLE is the company's fully packaged, tested, and supported distribution of the Sakai software. With Sakai's ultimate configurability and broad collection of tools at various stages of maturity and development, it takes engineering resources to configure, test, produce, and maintain a distribution of the code. rSmart also includes additional tools in its distribution to make installation and configuration of Sakai much easier to manage. The rSmart Sakai CLE enables rSmart to provide consistent support across all customers while scaling its services to many more.

- Bi-monthly service pack updates. Sakai evolves at a very fast pace. Regular service packs keep customers' code up-to-date.

- Fully staffed, multi-tier software support, and troubleshooting assistance available 24 x 7.

- Staffed functional product experts.

- Abundant documentation resources including over 800 pages of user guides (both technical and functional), numerous video tutorials, over a thousand knowledgebase articles, and formal training guides among other written resources.

- A commitment to push bug fixes, enhancements, and other issues that are discovered and resolved through the normal course of rSmart's ongoing support services back into the community code base.

Because rSmart sells support and not product licenses, it is highly motivated to provide the best support experience possible.

Easy to try

With rSmart's goal of making Sakai easy to "consume" for all types of intuitions, the first order of business is to make it easy to try. For this purpose, rSmart offers a free, hosted instance of Sakai called mySakai (`http://mysakai.rsmart.com`) where users can try Sakai in a real-world environment. Here users can set up their own Sakai course, portfolio and group sites. Users also have access to documentation, tutorials, support forums, and other resources. With thousands of users and hundreds of course sites, mySakai makes trying Sakai easy.

Given rSmart's origins as a consulting firm, the company still provides the typical consulting services one would expect from a full service provider, such as, installation, configuration, customization, and training. In addition, roughly 60% of rSmart's customers utilize its hosting services. Also worth noting are recent innovations in making Sakai adoption easy. Most of rSmart's customers now get started with Sakai using rSmart's new Sakai Adoption Package. Born out of the company's years of experience configuring, customizing, and installing Sakai dozens of times around the world, the Adoption Package is a repeatable methodology for adopting Sakai that includes all the necessary services, training, hosting, and ongoing support to quickly and reliably get started with Sakai.

Crossing the border into research: Students' engagement with a Virtual Research Environment, a case study

The VRE is used as an information hub; students requiring information will have need of the site as will those who use it for peer support and collaboration.

About the authors

Dr. Claire Cassidy: Claire is a lecturer in the Faculty of Education at the University of Strathclyde. She is course director for the PG Certificate in Philosophy with Children and is Programme Coordinator for the B.Ed. Educational Studies and Major Project. Claire is also a member of the Applied Educational Research Scheme, Learners, Learning and Teaching Network 1. Her research interests include Philosophy with Children, philosophical concepts of child and communities of enquiry—both philosophical and educational.

Sanna Rimpiläinen: Sanna worked as an administrator and a researcher in the Virtual Research Environment of the Applied Educational Research Scheme of Scotland at the University of Strathclyde in 2004-2008. Like Claire, she is a member of the Learners, Learning and Teaching Network 1. Currently, she is doing a full-time PhD at the University of Stirling attached to a project studying the use of semantic technologies for enhancing case-based learning in higher education.

Background

The Virtual Research Environment (VRE) was set up for fourth year B.Ed. students working on their Major Project—the undergraduate dissertation. In Scotland, the expectation that teachers should be practitioner researchers is well recognized in the Standards for Initial Teacher Education and later for Chartered Teacher Status. The Major Project is the first experience the teaching students have of conducting their own piece of action research.

The first VRE for this group of students was set up for the 2006-07 year and had three intended purposes. In the first instance, the module leader was a member of a research team belonging to the Applied Educational Research Scheme (AERS), who were investigating building Communities of Educational Enquiry (Cassidy, et al., 2007). Although the students were working on individual, independent projects, there appeared to be an opportunity to try to foster a community of enquiry approach in relation to this particular group of students. Further, the network within AERS that the module leader belongs to, Learners, Learning and Teaching Network 1 (LLT1), were extending their work on Communities of Educational Enquiry to consider the facilitation of collaborative groups using the VRE tool (Wilson, et al., 2007). These two factors provided the opportunity to provide support in the form of a VRE for the B.Ed. students, and this support mechanism for the students working on their Major Projects was the third purpose in the initiative. These three facets of this research project have remained constant and this case study considers how the final year Major Project students engaged with the VRE.

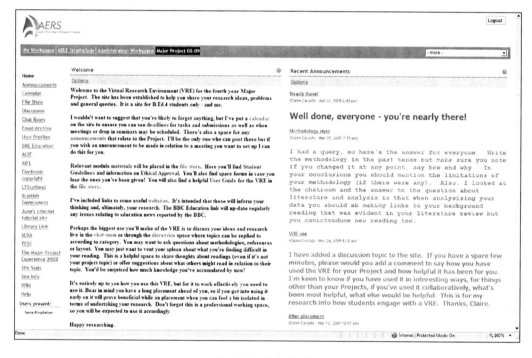

The Major Projects site

The VRE has not been made compulsory for the students but over the three sessions — 2006-07, 2007-08, and 2008-now — its use has been increasingly encouraged. The set of tools contains a file store, chatroom, discussion space, announcements, weblinks, and a calendar. The VRE is used as an information hub; students requiring information will have need of the site as well will those who use it for peer support and collaboration. The other feature that has evolved over the three years is the use of a drop-in surgery where the module leader has made time available for students to meet with her in the chatroom to discuss issues surrounding their research projects. As students are heavily time-tabled and also spend a large proportion of their time on a school placement, the drop-in surgeries are held in the evenings.

Tutor engagement

Interestingly, Somekh (2007) discusses a six-stage model of engagement with innovation in new technologies: orientation, preparation, routine, refinement, integration, and creative integration. Orientation relates the participants at the very early stages amassing information about the innovation before moving on to preparation, when they are ready to engage with the new technology. The third stage in the process, routine, is established with the participants employing the new technology in a fairly low-level manner before they begin to refine and improve their usage in the fourth stage of the process. Once the participants have refined and begun to adapt or improve their use of the technology, they begin to integrate the innovation more readily and ultimately they look to ways of using the innovation more effectively and in ways that others have not — this is the creative integration of the innovative technology. It would appear that the participants Somekh is referring to would be the students in this study. However, what is worth noting is that it was the module leader who went through these six stages. The students themselves did not have any need to engage at levels one or two and began at stage three in some instances but in others, they did not engage in a stage process such as suggested here but they became immersed and creative with the innovation from the beginning. This said, their engagement was facilitated considerably by the module leader having gone through this process.

Data collection

In order to gauge students' engagement with the VRE, several approaches to collecting this information were employed. As with all modules on the course, students complete a module evaluation. Supplementing the general module evaluations, some questions were included relating specifically to students' use of the VRE. This allowed for some very open-ended responses. At the end of session 2007-08, an online survey was issued to students. This had a response rate of 28% where 44 of the 155 returned the survey. There was a problem with this, however, as the Survey Monkey tool that was used crashed on the day it was announced to students. This resulted in some students failing to complete the survey and notifying the module leader that they had tried, failed, and did not try again. The online activity could be monitored as could the user logs. The "site stats" tool on the VRE allowed specific use by specific students to be seen. In other words, it was possible to see what exactly had been accessed by which students, when, and how often. The final approach that was used, and perhaps the most revealing, was semi-structured focus group interviews. Random groups of between six and eight students met with the authors to discuss their use of the VRE. During the interviews, students spoke very freely about whether they had used the VRE or not, how they had used it, what had been helpful, and if they had not used it, why not.

Student engagement

Already, in this third session of use, the VRE is being used more and by more students than in the entire sessions of 2006-07 and 2007-08. With user groups of almost 90% of potential users, this is very encouraging at the early stages. This may be for reasons such as students being more familiar with other technologies or that their course has, since they began, made greater use of virtual environments. However, one factor that cannot be denied is the development of the VRE because of the module leader's knowledge and experience. Drawing on previous evaluations and experience, the VRE has evolved. By creating web links that students would find not only helpful but necessary, there was a place where students could go immediately without having to trawl other Internet sites to find what they needed. Students have been increasingly "sold" the idea of the VRE as a tool to support the fledgling teacher researcher. Although it was not a compulsory component of undertaking the Major Project, its use was held to be valuable in undertaking the work. The module leader had ways of helping the students to see its relevance and potential. Initially when announcements were posted on the VRE, an email alert was sent to all students. Over the three sessions this element has been completely phased out and students now realize that if they have need of information or want to be kept up-to-date with Major Project news, then it is in their interests to log on. In the interviews students tended not to engage particularly well with the discussion space as they did not like the idea of putting up ideas for others to see in case they were thought silly. Instead, what they suggested was that the module leader initiates topics for discussion and the students then create messages under these headings. This appears to have been extremely successful so far in the new session.

Key themes

Some key themes emerged from the data. While some students claimed to be technophobes and to not want to learn another technology, others frequently used other social networking software. There was some interesting use of the VRE and its tools that could not be seen by looking at the "site stats". Some students talked about minimising the site at the bottom of their page when working on other assignments so they could access the web links. Others said they worked on the VRE with several friends around the one computer; this meant that the module leader might only see one person logged on in the chatroom when she was in the surgery but in reality, four or five students were on the opposite side of the exchange.

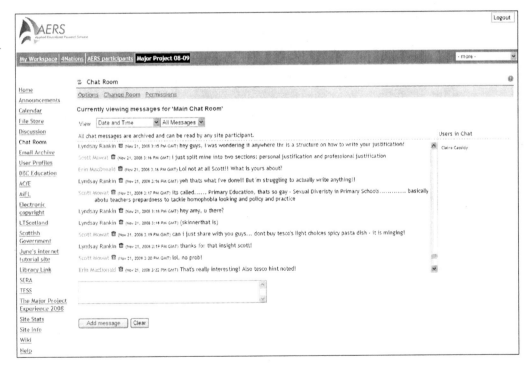

The VRE chat tool

Key to non-participation in the first two sessions was students' "risk" of online participation. They were uncertain about sharing their ideas and many were keen simply to read comments from others that assured them they were not alone in their worries about the Project. This support aspect was the main factor in the students' engagement in the VRE in sessions 2006-07 and 2007-08. While students were extremely clear that the support from the module leader was vital and that this was appreciated throughout the whole process, what was even more striking was the way in which students viewed peer support. Moore and Chae (2008) emphasize the importance of emotional support: the idea that participants can see that others are experiencing the same problems, issues, or worries. Additionally, they recognized the isolation that might be felt when working on an independent piece of work, particularly at a time when they were off campus on placement and the security of peers and the module leader was very important. Most certainly the two earliest cohorts were keen to stress this function of the VRE. Indeed, the students in the interviews suggested that the opportunity to use a VRE in their Probationary year in teaching, the subsequent August, would be helpful—this was subsequently established and used by a number of students. Indeed, students who had not used the VRE for the Major Project were keen, after listening to the views of their peers, to emphasize that they wished retrospectively that they had used it.

The current group of students seem to have engaged much more quickly and more fully than either of the two previous cohorts. Looking at the "site stats" user logs and online activity at the end of the first semester, the students are contributing much more to discussion: they are initiating discussions of their own, posting messages asking for advice, offering suggestions for reading, or considering methodological approaches to their topics. Similarly, the chatroom has been utilized much more widely and freely. Unlike previous years, the students from session 2008-09 are chatting about their projects at times when the module leader is not online in a surgery. Of course, the surgeries are still available and these have been even better "attended" than in the previous sessions. While there have been no interviews, module evaluations, or online surveys undertaken with the most recent group of students, initial observations would suggest that the VRE has a more central role than before. In fact, students appear to be very comfortable with this technology and the peer support for this group is more in line with the intended Community of Enquiry purpose as initially intended. Although the students have clear parameters that the VRE is to be used for discussing Major Project-related issues, they have managed to personalize what previous students called bland or boring; they leave informal messages or sign their contributions using emoticons.

Conclusions and recommendations

What can be gleaned from this study? Certainly the VRE has proved useful in the context of a final undergraduate dissertation module when students are embarking on their first stage of being practitioner researchers. The students, in the first instance, have to recognize the purpose and parameters of the VRE and recognize its potential. While the module leader has responsibility for this, students can also shape its use. Presenting the VRE as an additional extra but creating an element of "non-optionality" around it enabled students to see that the VRE was vital to their work and for keeping them up-to-date. The facilitator's role is one that involves many tasks. The module leader in this study performed a range of functions: reminding, guiding, urging, encouraging, and supporting were all facets of the role, but all that evolved in the last two to three years to help create a VRE that students view as helpful and beneficial to their work. In conclusion, therefore, all participants need to be clear about what the VRE is and can do for them, but also that it can evolve over time. In this instance, the evolution of the VRE for the Major Project students has been successful partly because the module leader is more confident in her use of the tool and the students are convinced of its worth.

References

Cassidy, C.; Christie, D.; Coutts, N.; Dunne, J.; Sinclair, C.; Skinner D.; Wilson, A. (2008) *Building Communities of Educational Enquiry*. Oxford Review of Education, 34 (2), 1-19

Moore, J.A. & Chae, B. (2007) *Beginning Teachers' Use of On-line resources and Communities*. Technology, Pedagogy and Education, 16 (2), 215-224

Somekh, B. (2007) *Pedagogy and Learning with ICT: Researching the art of innovation*. Oxon: Routledge

Wilson, A.; Rimpiläinen, S.; Skinner, D.; Cassidy, C.; Christie, D.; Coutts, N. & Sinclair, C. (2007) *Using a Virtual Research Environment to support new models of collaborative and participative research in Scottish education*. Technology, Pedagogy and Education, Vol. 16 (3), 289-304

SOLO—Taking e-learning offline

The solution was an offline client that enabled students to seamlessly switch from working through an offline study guide to participating in an online group discussion.

About the author

Louis Botha holds a master's degree in statistics from North-West University where he worked on computer-based simulation models and taught statistics to engineering students. He has been involved in distance e-learning since 1999 from both the teacher and developer perspective. As the technical lead developer for Psybergate Cape Town, he leads the development team building Sakai tools for the local community in South Africa.

Background

Solo (http://confluence.sakaiproject.org/confluence/display/SOLO), an offline tool for viewing Sakai content, needs to be considered in terms of the value it can add as well as the possibilities that it offers to the future of elearning. Using Solo, students do not have to be constantly connected to Sakai while studying. There is a significant saving of connection costs and time lost due to slow connections, particularly in developing countries where the bandwidth cannot be taken for granted. However, the possibilities go much further. Users can take their Sakai content with them while travelling or commuting and synchronize their learning content when they have Internet access. Future versions of Solo could allow lecturers to post announcements, create lessons, and add resources while working offline. The next synchronization will then upload the necessary data to Sakai. The current version of Solo makes announcements, resources, and Melete lessons available offline.

Solo is based on the concept of an email client: downloading email messages and reading them while disconnected. The idea is to implement familiar concepts like "download now", "work offline", and "send later".

Internet bandwidth and cost

If we look at a map representing international bandwidth in 2004 (Map source: `http://www.aptivate.org/webguidelines/attach/Summary/World_Bandwidth_Wiki.png`), it is clear that there is a large portion of the world that faces huge challenges. The situation has improved since 2004, but it will remain an issue for many years to come. Dial-up (<56 kbits) users tend to spend as little time online as possible by downloading information for offline reading. It therefore makes sense to keep these users offline for as long as possible. Conversely, keeping them online could degrade their learning experience and could have an impact on their final results. A factor is the cost of internet access. Although it has come down over the past few years in South Africa, it is still high compared to 1st world countries. This cost is an additional financial burden on students and one that they normally do not budget for.

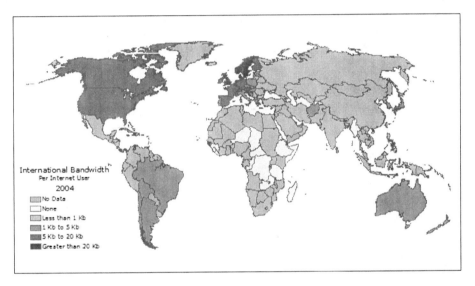

International bandwidth in 2004

North-West University (South Africa)

The academic program that initiated the development of Solo is the Honours B.Sc. Program in Pharmacology called Pharmacological Principles of Drug Therapy. This is a distance-learning programme, allowing learning wherever and whenever you have access to a PC and the Internet. It provides medical practitioners, pharmacists, and dentists with an insight into basic pharmacological and ethical principles, enabling them to practice more effective pharmacotherapy in community medicine. Sound basic computer and internet skills are therefore essential for this program.

The program was developed during the late 1990s. At that time, most students only had dial-up connections and the cost of Internet access was high. In an effort to assist students, the static study material was made available offline via a CD-ROM and students only had to go online for interactive learning activities such as reading announcements, taking part in discussion forums, sending email, and so on. A more sophisticated solution was required to manage this dual mode of study so that content could be updated and fairly computer illiterate users could easily find their way in this online/offline environment. The solution was an offline client that enabled students to seamlessly switch from working through an offline study guide, to participating in an online group discussion. This was accomplished by providing a single, user-friendly interface from which all relevant study resources can be accessed. An indicator in the interface shows whether the student is working online or offline. It also shows when content is possibly out-of-date, requiring synchronisation. The students also received a CD-ROM containing large files like electronic handbooks and video clips. Solo synchronizes with the CD-ROM content. This content will not be fetched from the Sakai server, further reducing download costs and time.

To enable students to make use of Solo, a normal Sakai course was created by the instructional designers. The Pharmacology program course site makes use of the following tools:

- Announcements (offline)
- Resources (offline)
- Melete lessons (offline)
- Schedule
- Assignments
- Forums
- Tasks, tests, and surveys

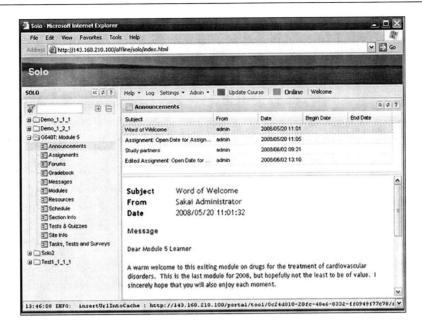

Sakai Announcements in Solo: The navigation tree on the left shows sites and tools that the user has access to. The main window shows a list of announcements. The selected announcement is highlighted.

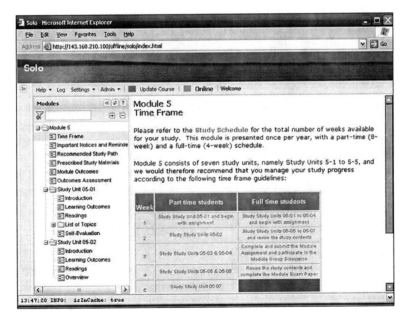

Melete lessons in Solo: The tree on the left shows the lesson structure. The tree is collapsible and can be filtered and searched. The main window shows the lesson content. Any images or links to resources will display without requiring an online connection.

To get access to Solo, a special Sakai URL is used. From there the user will be prompted to install the Solo interface. This is 4Mb download. Installation instructions are sent to students after registration. The normal online Pharmacology site is still available.

Once installed (`http://confluence.sakaiproject.org/confluence/download/attachments/40566886/installation_manual.doc`), the student will be prompted to download all relevant content by making use of the synchronization feature. The initial sync will fetch all content from the Sakai server or from a CD-ROM. A download can be aborted at any time and resumed later. After the first full sync, only new or changed content will be downloaded. All non-offline Pharmacology content is also accessible from Solo, but will require an online connection.

How Solo works

New tools like Google Gears (`http://gears.google.com`) combined with Google Web Toolkit (GWT) (`http://code.google.com/webtoolkit`, `http://www.gwt-ext.com/demo`) make it possible to develop rich web-based applications with the ability to cache online files and synchronize database content to a local database. The Sakai web interface is replaced with a rich Google Web Toolkit interface. This Windows-like interface is more familiar to users and eliminates browser refreshes. The user is notified when site content is possibly outdated and it is only changed and new content is downloaded during the synchronization process. A local SQLite database stores user profile and caching information. This database is part of the Google Gears browser plug-in.

One of the requirements was an option to distribute large files via CD-ROM instead of downloading them to the offline environment. These files are saved directly into the Google Gears cache and the appropriate entries are made in the Google Gears SQLite database. When the import is complete, Google Gears will pick up the new files as if they were simply synchronized from the online Sakai server. A Java Swing application was also developed to automate the CD-ROM sync. It reads an XML file and copies the required files to the relevant Google Gear cache location. An export function in Sakai generates the XML file and zips up the resources in the specific Sakai site.

The Google Gears cache will not be cleared if the browser cache is cleared or if the browser is upgraded. It is a separate persistent cache. The browsers that have been tested are FireFox 2.0+ on Windows/Linux/Mac and Internet Explorer 6+.

The entire offline user interface will also be upgraded using the normal synchronization when a new version is available.

The LAMP Consortium—Like a bundle of sticks

A genuinely collaborative model for colleges and universities with limited resources to provide low-cost, high-quality access to Sakai

About the author

Martin Ramsay is Managing Director of CEATH Company, a consulting firm he co-founded in 1979. CEATH Company (http://www.ceath.com) is an international consulting firm focusing on institutional effectiveness. In his role as Managing Director, Martin was featured in Fortune magazine as "an expert on the organizational impact of new information systems" who impresses clients with his "preparedness and clarity". The Center for Digital Education presented him with their "In the Spotlight" Award, calling him one of the "most innovative, hard-working, trend-setting IT leaders in the nation". His ongoing project for the Appalachian College Association, the Learning Asset Management Project (LAMP), won the Mellon Award for Technology Collaboration (http://matc.mellon.org/press-release) in 2008. As a consultant, Martin has worked in eleven countries (and counting) on three continents in his quest to help organizations.

Introducing the project

For this project, Ramsay focused on building a community of learners using a single instance of Sakai. The most remarkable aspect of the project is that sixteen colleges and universities collaborate to share a single Sakai instance; doing so allows the schools to share best practices, to collaborate on course development and delivery, and to work together like "a bundle of sticks". Ramsay notes, "Individually these schools are small and somewhat vulnerable. Sometimes, like an individual stick, they are strained almost to the breaking point. By joining together as the LAMP consortium, these schools are like a bundle of sticks—mutually supportive and collectively strong". Vint Cerf, Chief Internet Evangelist for Google, Inc. agrees, noting, "LAMP demonstrates a genuine collaborative support model, which has drawn interest from other consortia looking to support open source projects."

The Appalachian College Association (www.acaweb.org) is a consortium of small private, liberal arts colleges in five states in the Central Appalachian Mountain region of the United States. Sixteen of its members have joined together to form LAMP (lamp.acaweb.org) under Ramsay's leadership; LAMP went live on April 28, 2006. The group uses a single instance of Sakai hosted by The Longsight Group LLC (www.longsight.com). As of early 2009, the instance was hosting well over 14,000 users. It is entirely member supported, not depending on any grant or other external funding.

Award winning

In recognition for its success, LAMP received the Mellon Award for Technology Collaboration (matc.mellon.org) at a ceremony in Washington, DC on December 8, 2008. Along with the $50,000 prize given to award winners, the committee recognized "the LAMP project as a thought-leader around questions of adoption and sustainability of community source software in smaller institutions".

Martin Ramsay (l), Director of the LAMP Consortium, receives the Mellon Award for Technology Collaboration from Vint Cerf, Vice President for Internet Evangelism for Google, Inc. and representative of the Mellon Award for Technology Collaboration selection committee.

Winning factors

When questioned about how the LAMP group has achieved such remarkable success, Ramsay notes that the technology, while critical, is not the main focus. "LAMP is about building a community of learners", he says. "We try never to let the technological tail wag the pedagogical dog." He cites several critical success factors:

- **Quality of Sakai** — An earlier attempt to build a smaller consortium based on a commercial course management system failed, even with external funding support. The ease of use of Sakai, the quality of each subsequent release, and the easy learning curve all contribute to LAMP's success.

- **Hosted Technology** — Partnering with The Longsight Group has been critical. Longsight only works with open source systems and focuses on higher education. As such, their experience and advice kept the group from making poor decisions. Longsight has become a trusted partner in the LAMP consortium.

- **Support Model** — Each member campus has one or more coordinators that serve as the bridge between the local campus community and the larger LAMP group. Ramsay and CEATH Company provide oversight of the overall project, and are backed up for technical issues by The Longsight Group. Ultimately, LAMP has the entire Sakai community as its backup. "But", adds Ramsay, "we never forget that the students and faculty we serve are our most important concern."

- **Monthly Community Conferences** — The group holds monthly web conferences, facilitated by CEATH Company and The Longsight Group, with member campus coordinators in attendance. These meetings are used for issue resolution, training, decision making, and to generally keep the community cohesive.

- **Transparent Governance** — "We make decisions based on consensus", says Ramsay. "You can't build a community if members don't have a stake in the outcomes. Thus decisions from when to install an upgrade to our policy about guest accounts all come from the community." Most of the governance decisions are made during the monthly web conferences.

- **Annual Faculty Development Workshops** — Each summer, LAMP sponsors a week-long faculty workshop. The workshops focus on a variety of topics, with the constant theme of improving teaching and learning permeating the workshop activities. Sessions are offered on diverse topics, from introductions to Sakai for new faculty to the subtle aspects of new provisional tools. The workshops follow a very hands-on pedagogical approach; participants are encouraged to put their skills to use immediately. Each day of the workshop also includes some kind of experiential community-building activity, often conducted outdoors and always tied to the day's content. These summer workshops have been critical in linking the large LAMP virtual community together.

Workshops: This activity emphasizes working toward a common objective, even if the way to achieve the objective isn't clear.

- **Financial Sustainability** — LAMP receives no external financial support. Costs of the program (helped, in no small measure, by the open source license agreement for Sakai) are divided among member schools in an equitable way based on user activity. At the beginning of each academic year, each school pays dues; those dues cover expenses with the goal of maintaining a break-even budget. Schools save thirty to fifty percent of their costs compared to licensing and supporting a commercial system.

- **Membership Flexibility** — LAMP offers several levels of membership, based on member schools' needs. For schools that are just beginning to explore Sakai, a low-cost membership with a small number of user accounts is available. Other schools, where Sakai is the mission-critical course management system, select a scalable membership tailored to the number of users needed.

- **Trust** — "If there is one word I would choose to define how LAMP works", notes Ramsay, "It would be trust". The sixteen member schools of LAMP trust each other. Since we share a single instance of Sakai, the local campus coordinators have some administrative rights in the system that can be used across the instance — that doesn't work if we can't trust each other. We emphasize that in our monthly web conference and in our summer workshops. Without trust, the LAMP goes out."

Several other aspects of LAMP are worth mentioning. Longsight has built a sophisticated authentication system that allows each member school to have its own individualized access tied to its local campus authentication system. This allows member schools to optionally provide single signon capabilities to their local users. Euphemistically called GAS (for the "gnarly authentication system"), the system has facilitated the sharing of a single Sakai instance.

Longsight has also built a set of data mining and reporting tools for the LAMP consortium. These tools mine a data warehouse of transactions as well as other Sakai data sources, allowing member school coordinators to explore usage patterns and statistics for their own campus. The tool builds a wide array of charts, graphs, and tables based on various input parameters that provide local campuses with the culture of evidence needed to support Sakai's widespread usage throughout the consortium.

Finally, the group has included Turnitin (`http://turnitin.com`), the plagiarism prevention system into its system. Through integration between Turnitin and Sakai, instructors in LAMP can have student submissions analyzed for text matching and potential plagiarism detection from within their courses in Sakai.

The LAMP experience

Ramsay summarizes the LAMP experience this way: "While LAMP is not doing anything particularly new with the technology (although the GAS authentication system and Longsight's data mining tools are remarkable technological innovations), it is doing something quite unique with the softer side of Sakai. In the realm of collaboration, I couldn't agree more with the Mellon Award for Technology Collaboration. We have discovered a genuinely collaborative model that we think is replicable in many other situations in the open-source community".

Criminology—A distance course in Sakai

Since this is the only criminology department in Sweden, it was very important to facilitate ways for students living outside Stockholm to study criminology.

About the authors

The authors are Johan Kardell, Lotta Pettersson (Department of Criminology, Stockholm University, SE-10691 Stockholm, Sweden), and Magnus Tagesson (IT Services, Stockholm University, SE-106 91 Stockholm, Sweden).

Introduction

This case study describes a distance learning course given in Sakai at the Department of Criminology at Stockholm University.

Stockholm University started to observe the Sakai project in 2004 and is currently a member of the Sakai Foundation. In May 2007, the university released its implementation of Sakai, named Mondo (meaning World in Esperanto). A year later, the university upgraded to Sakai 2.5, which is the current version (`http://mondo.su.se/`).

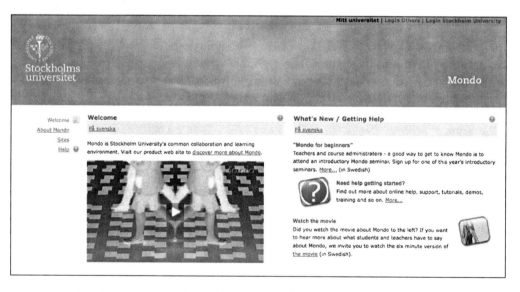

The front page of Stockholm University's Sakai implementation, named Mondo.

IT Services (representing the technical side) works closely with the Center for Learning and Teaching (the university pedagogical side), giving introductory courses, workshops and support. Together, documentation was written and requirements workshops held. A special committee with staff from both groups is working on prioritizing requirements for the upcoming Mondo releases.

The Department of Criminology

In the year 2002, the Department of Criminology at Stockholm University in Sweden began to offer a distance course in Criminology. Since this is the only criminology department in Sweden, it was very important to facilitate ways for students living outside of Stockholm to study criminology.

The Department of Criminology registers approximately 700 undergraduate students every year. 120 students are registered in the distance course, and about 50% of those complete their studies. Mondo is the third course platform used by the department for the distance course.

Description of the distance course

The course has been structured based on three main principles. First we aim to create a high degree of flexibility in order to allow people to participate regardless of their situation. Therefore, our students often work or attend other courses in Sweden or other parts of the world besides their criminology studies. For instance, some of the students did military service in Afghanistan, some studied in the United States and Thailand, and others were working in prisons. The different backgrounds and experiences of the students increases the diversity of the group compared with the "regular" students.

Secondly, the intention was to create as much social activity and interaction as possible. This implies that the students are expected to contribute frequently with different written assignments and group discussions. The main tools used for this were:

- Roster, a tool that facilitates the socialization in the student groups. Students are encouraged to update their profile with a short description and a photo as well.
- Discussion forums serve an important role both for the whole group with general topics, and forums for the small student groups, discussing explicit questions.
- Chat is used to ask general questions not only about the course itself, but also about difficulties with understanding Mondo's structure.

Thirdly, the students are expected to work independently without traditional lectures, seminars or other types of synchronous communication. Communication (discussions, feedback, and so on) in Mondo is mostly asynchronous. There are only a few optional seminars and lectures at campus. Instead, the students work in groups on a group-specific site. During different periods of the course, the students read the literature and write reflective blogs on their learning, publish the web log to their group, and comment on other students' logs. The students are also expected to discuss different topics in their groups. Both the web logs and group discussions are individually submitted to the teachers. An assignment (web log, discussion, or exam) lasts approximately a week.

In addition to the web logs, discussions, and the exam, the students use Test & Quizzes both for self-tests, to support the their individual learning process, and as a part of the formal examination.

Experiences—Lessons learned

Clarifying the structure of a course

One student with experience of one of the earlier platforms that was used by the Department of Criminology thought that Mondo was harder to learn. First and foremost, the issue was the effort required figuring out where to find relevant information. This was a shortcoming due to the fact that folders in Modules (Melete) were used to build up the structure of the course.

- **Solution [1]:** Since the autumn of 2008, the Wiki has been configured as read-only to the students and it serves its purpose well, which is to deliver directed information to the students about the course, the syllabus, and other related information.

- **Solution [2]:** Another strategy to delivering a clear overview of the course is to keep the number of tools to a minimum, with the ones used clearly explained.

The importance of the group

One student talked about the high degree of dropouts and that a relative small group meant a lower degree of group activity. Another missed the face-to-face interaction with other students and mentioned the motivating effect of spontaneous small talk in the breaks during a lecture. But still others emphasize the positive experience of having to learn to communicate in a different way and of enhancing their writing skills. Another student concluded that by following the discussions in the forums she had seen the subtle complexities of the subject and realized that other students might have different views and opinions.

One of the fundaments of the course, as mentioned, is that the group dynamic is an important factor. The dynamic is partly about a social context and partly about a forum that gives peer input and feedback. As a policy, dropouts are always made up for through the merging of groups to keep a minimum of 5-6 active students. However, there will always be groups that are more active than others.

The social space

If there is a sense of belonging to a group of peers, the feeling of social context supplies an extra boost to student commitment. In the first version of Sakai used by the Department of Criminology, the students were critical of the forum tool. Both students and teachers felt it was impossible to get a grasp of the discussions just by browsing the forums. In addition to that, the forum did not feel like a social meeting place. After discussion with the IT Services, extra functionality was added to the forums, and pictures from the Profile tool were added to the posts. This made the forum tool more user friendly and stimulated use. The following figure shows a thread in the forum, where the pictures is picked up from the users' profiles.

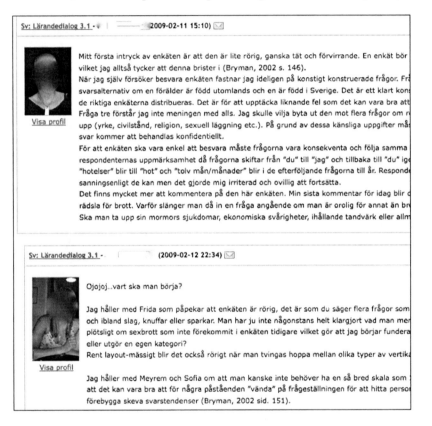

The chat tool is used on the main site as a social forum as well as for addressing general questions about the course.

The absence of feedback

A theme that frequently recurs in comments from the students is the lack of feedback. They want more feedback from the teachers. This has been an issue since the web-based distance course started, and from a teacher's perspective it is about keeping a balance between the time allowed for a task and how much time is budgeted for the course. The feedback is given at a group or course level. To make up for the missing individual feedback, there are usually extensive guidelines (about 10-12 A4 pages) about how the examination is graded. There are also scheduled meetings in the chat for discussions with the teachers about the reading and questions from the students; these discussions have tended to be about technical issues or more general discussions about criminology.

The need of support

Stockholm University decided to upgrade Sakai in May 2008, during the end of the spring term. The Department of Criminology and the IT Services had some discussions concerning a release during the course.

Due to technical issues after the release, staff from the IT Services made themselves available in the chat at certain hours. This saved time and diminished disruption, as it avoided having students reporting to the teachers, who would then have to contact the support at the university. This more direct approach accelerated responses and in some cases delivered instant solutions.

To minimize further disruption, the Department of Criminology and the IT Services now discuss the date for the next release and how to implement it in a mutually beneficial way.

Future development

One of the challenges for the future is how to include the students in the process of developing Mondo. One way is to actively use student evaluations of the course and its different parts. Presently, the course uses an external tool for course evaluations that is added as web content in the menu bar.

Another way of creating a social space would be to create multiple chat rooms. This would make it possible to dedicate, for example, one chat room to socializing, one for questions about the literature, and one for technical issues, and the owners of the site should be able to choose which one to feature at the homepage of the site at any given time.

Conclusion

Getting used to working together in an open source project and understanding the process takes time. There is no counterpart that takes responsibility for the product in the same way as a commercial company would do. The departments of the university ideally will work closely with the IT Services and the Center for Learning and Teaching not only when it comes to support and reporting bugs and problems, but also suggesting future requirements and new features. Specifically, in the autumn of 2008, the Department of Criminology hosted a workshop collecting requirements. This does not imply that we always agree upon everything, but shows the importance and need for ongoing discussion. We see this communication and mutual interest as a prerequisite for the creation of a good educational platform.

Summary

Coming next, in Chapter 15, *Innovating Teaching and Learning with Sakai*, we look at what makes an award-winning courses award winning.

15

Innovating Teaching and Learning with Sakai

By Mr. Josh Baron, Marist College with
Dr. Aileen Huang-Saad, University of Michigan and
Mr. Salim A Nakhjavani, University of Cape Town (South Africa)

Hitting a student upon the head with a textbook generally does not result in improved student learning yet this same instructional tool, when used by a knowledgeable teacher, is often considered the cornerstone of the educational process. Why? Clearly, the value of an instructional tool, whether it be a textbook or technology, is entirely dependent on how it is used.

With hundreds of institutions, thousands of instructors, and millions of students having now used Sakai, we have an endless number of examples of how this collaborative learning environment is being deployed in education today. Although few instructors are likely using Sakai to inflict physical pain on their students, the instructional approaches taken vary enormously, from traditional (for example posting lecture slides online) to extremely inventive (for example real-world simulations). Looking across this continuum of instructional applications, it is evident that those on the "inventive" end exhibit the potential Sakai holds to transform the traditional educational experience into something more engaging, richer, and more meaningful for the learner.

It was from a desire among the Sakai Teaching and Learning interest group to highlight and share these more inventive applications that the *Teaching with Sakai Innovation Award* Program, initially sponsored by IBM and the Sakai Foundation, was born. The program is not aimed at identifying technically complex uses of Sakai, rather to find those uses of the technology, even very simple ones, which are driving true innovation in how instructors are teaching and students are learning. In this chapter, we will discuss the award process itself and highlight the winners of the 2008 *Teaching with Sakai Innovation Award* as a means to provide concrete examples of how Sakai is facilitating truly inventive instruction.

The Teaching with Sakai Innovation Award

Although there are many ways in which instructional technology, and in particular Sakai, can make the teaching process more efficient or productive, truly innovative applications go further by fundamentally transforming the educational experience in ways that improve student learning. The intent of the Teaching with Sakai Innovation Award is to highlight examples of educational applications of Sakai that fall into this innovative or transformative category. To further this objective, the Award Committee established an application process that asked instructors to self-assess their course as well as provide evidence of how Sakai has facilitated a Foundational shift in their instructional strategy.

The self-assessment process required the applicant to use a Course Evaluation Rubric, developed by the Award Committee, to reflect on their course design and delivery methodology with respect to the degree to which it adhered to research-based best practices and aligned with the current understanding of effective pedagogy. The rubric covers five categories:

- *Communication and Collaboration* — examines the degree to which instructor-student and student-student communication and collaboration are facilitated, enhanced, and encouraged as part of the course.

- *Learning Material* – examines the structure, sequencing, and presentation of course content and materials.

- *Learning Outcomes & Assessment* – explores the degree to which recognized best practices in pedagogy and assessment have been followed (for example. *Seven Principles for Good Practice in Undergraduate Education* (Chickering & Gamson, 1987)).

- *Look & Feel and Usability* – determines the degree to which the course site is easy to use and navigate as well as the degree to which accessibility issues have been addressed.

- *Learner Support* — assesses how well learners are supported, with regards to technical as well as instructional issues.

Each of these categories has criteria that allow a course to be classified in one of three levels: "Not Evident", "Effective", and "Excellent" based on the criteria detailed in the rubric. The complete Course Evaluation Rubric appears at the end of this chapter.

In addition to the self-assessment, applicants were asked to explain, through an open-ended question, how their use of Sakai represented instructional innovation and to provide evidence of how Sakai had transformed the educational experience of their students. The intent of this question was to seek out those instructors who had leveraged the Sakai collaborative learning environment to create new and powerful learning experiences for their students — experiences that would not have been possible without the technology.

Once this was completed, applicants were subjected to a two-phase evaluation process. In the first phase, the Award Committee conducted an initial review of all of the applications using the Course Evaluation Rubric and rank-ordered them. From this initial phase, a group of finalists were identified for a second phase of evaluation. In the second phase, finalists were interviewed via web-conferences, by a three-member panel of experts with extensive knowledge of instructional technology and teaching and learning theory. Based on these interviews, which included course "walkthroughs" with the instructor, the judging panel selected a first and second place winner.

The OpenEdPractices.org repository

All of the past award-winning applications as well examples of other uses of Sakai, such as the Open Source Portfolio, can be found on the OpenEdPractices.org web site. The site is a community of practice for teaching and learning with open/community-source tools supported in part by rSmart, the Association of American Colleges and Universities, and Marist College. This is also where instructors can apply for future Teaching with Sakai Innovation Awards.

Case studies from the winner's circle

The first and second place winners of the 2008 Teaching with Sakai Innovation Award, Dr. Aileen Huang-Saad from the University of Michigan and Mr. Salim A Nakhjavani from the University of Cape Town (South Africa) respectively will be showcased in this section. Although there are many inventive aspects unique to how each instructor used Sakai to enrich their student's learning experience, both shared a common theme of shifting from a more passive teacher-centered instructional method to a more active student-centered approach.

1st Place Winner: Biomedical Engineering (University of Michigan, USA)

The first place winner was a Biomedical Engineering course run by Dr. Aileen Huang-Saad from the University of Michigan. A specific selection of Sakai tools was chosen to create a dynamic online experience.

Course description

This interactive graduate-level course, which spans two semesters, encourages innovative design in biomedical engineering by stimulating students to explore their own solutions to biomedical challenges. Students experience the entire spectrum of design, from concept inception to prototyping, thus allowing them to explore the entire innovation value chain in the context of biomedical engineering. The course challenges students to learn about the current state of the art in the field of biomedical engineering, explore current technical challenges, and brainstorm new solutions with members of the medical community. This experience provides students with the necessary skill sets to become innovative and adaptive learners beyond the University environment as they go on to new challenges in their research and professional careers.

"The Sakai platform was critical to the success of my class, and I am grateful to have had such a diverse platform readily available. In particular, the Wiki tool was crucial for developing class-based concept design documents, challenging students to evolve their ideas in and outside of class." – *Dr. Aileen Huang-Saad, University of Michigan*

The first semester of the course is dedicated to understanding the current state of biomedical technology, and formulation of ideas and design teams. This is facilitated through a series of lectures by guest clinical specialists who discuss current biomedical challenges and then brainstorm with students as to potential solutions. As the semester progresses, a range of potential projects are identified and students self-select into teams to work on specific projects. The second semester is dedicated to the actual development of the prototype device. Students are encouraged to participate in national and local design and business competitions throughout the year. Successful designs compete to represent the University of Michigan in a national design competition by the end of the second semester.

Course development and delivery

As a graduate-level engineering design course, the instructor felt it was paramount that it provide students with an authentic problem-solving experience that involved undefined and novel challenges. To achieve this goal, it was important that the course be student driven rather than something she structured and dictated. To facilitate this, she deployed particular tools from the **Sakai Toolkit** with the goal of creating a dynamic classroom environment in which the students, working both in teams and as a whole class, were at the center of the teaching process.

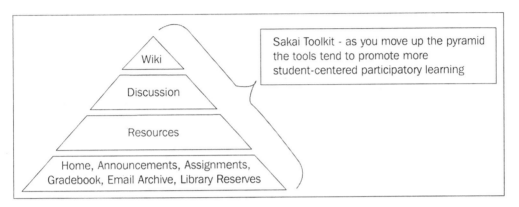

As the course was delivered, it became clear that certain tools naturally promoted student-centered instruction because of the ways in which they facilitated peer-to-peer communication and collaboration. For example, the Wiki tool provided students with a collaborative writing space where they could construct, individually and in teams, their own knowledge of the design challenges being studied. This collaboration was enhanced by the Discussion tool, which facilitated interactions among students, the instructor, and subject-matter experts outside of regular class time.

In order to understand in more detail how Sakai was used in the context of this course, it is useful to review the course using each of the five categories from the Course Evaluation Rubric.

Collaboration and Communication—Much of this course involved large and small group collaboration and communication, facilitated, and in many cases enhanced, through the use of Sakai tools. Of particular note, is the way in which Sakai allowed group collaboration and communication to continue outside of each class, removing the traditional time barrier that can often restrict group work and learning to individual class periods. A range of Sakai tools were used to support these types of interactions, including:

- Wiki—Each week during the first semester, after brainstorming with medical faculty, the students spent time contributing to a "Class Concept Design Wiki", which identified the biomedical problems discussed in class and potential solutions. This collaborative exercise actively engaged students in the problem solving process. The clinical faculty also had access to the Wiki, which allowed them to see how the students' initial ideas evolved after the class met face-to-face. Towards the end of the semester, students implemented a class voting process using a table within the Wiki to decide which proposed solutions were the most viable to pursue.

"The course structure incorporated a number of innovative class techniques that I have not encountered in any other course. These include scheduled brainstorming sessions in small groups to try to generate ideas to solve the medical problems presented, Wiki documents on Ctools [Sakai] where all class members participated and recorded everything learned and brainstormed on each topic presented... The design experience and biomedical engineering knowledge I gained from this course have given me a confidence in my abilities that no other course has." – BioMed 599 Student

- Discussion Forum—During the first semester an "Ask the Physician" Forum was used by clinical faculty to provide feedback to students on the prototype ideas evolving in the Wiki. It was also a central "teaming" tool as students used it to share their interests in particular projects and the expertise they would be able to bring to a particular project, thus helping to facilitate the formation of well balanced teams. Finally, an "Ask the Professor" Forum was used to maintain regular contact between the instructor and students outside of class.

- Project Sites—During the second semester, most of the teams opted to set up their own Project Sites, which provided them with private areas for group collaboration. As site "organizers", they had similar permissions to those the instructor had in the primary course site, allowing them to decide which tools to deploy based on their groups' collaboration needs. Although in most cases the teams used the sites for storing files and schedule coordination, some also took advantage of more collaborative tools such as the Wiki.

- Test Center — Regular surveys, initially using a basic web-based tool and then later on Test Center, were given to students to collect feedback on the course throughout each semester. The instructor would then adjust the course based on this feedback. For example, students were surveyed after each clinician brainstorming session regarding the format of the session and its outcomes. Student feedback then informed changes to the approach taken with subsequent guest experts. Creating this type of instructional "feedback loop" helped ensure that the approach matched the students' particular learning and collaboration styles.

 "As we saw needs, based on student feedback, the Sakai platform allowed us to make changes even on a daily basis."
– Dr. Aileen Huang-Saad, University of Michigan

- Announcements and Email Archive — It was important that the students understand the decisions the instructor was making as she adjusted the course throughout the semester and that they also saw that their suggestions were being taken seriously. The Announcement and Email Archive tool were used to communicate these decisions to students. In subsequent years, the Messages Tool was also deployed, which allowed for more targeted communication with particular groups (for example specific teams, groups of clinicians, and so on).

Learning Materials — The instructional content and activities associated with this course were well structured and sequenced so as to guide students through the two semesters, taking them from basic idea development to a final prototype. Several key Sakai tools were used to support these objectives, including:

- Resources — Every effort was made to ensure that students were prepared for each guest lecture by clinicians from the University of Michigan Hospital so as to maximize the limited class time available to work with these subject matter experts. To accomplish this, two or three scientific articles were posted to Resource folders for each speaker and assigned as pre-class readings. In addition, after each brainstorming session, the instructor would post digital representations (for example scanned-in diagrams) of what was discussed during the session. These materials helped form the basis for the Class Design Wiki mentioned earlier. Finally, a great deal of supplemental content (for example lecture materials, background information on the design process, FDA guidelines, and so on) in a range of formats was also uploaded to Resources for reference by students throughout the course.

- Drop Box—After reading their "pre-class" articles, students were also required to submit at least five questions to the Drop Box ahead of the clinical speaker's visit to make sure they were fully prepared. In subsequent years, the Forums Tool was used, which permitted students to see the questions others had submitted and also allowed students to interact with the clinicians around these questions before and after class.

Learning Outcomes and Assessment—Given the nature of the course, critical thinking and problem solving skills were primary learning outcomes. Sakai helped facilitate a peer-to-peer feedback and evaluation process and supported individual self-reflection as part of the assessment process. Some of the Sakai tools used to further these goals were:

- Resources—During the second semester, each team gave weekly design presentations on the status of their project. Besides verbal feedback during these sessions, individual students also provided written feedback using a standardized template. This helped those students who were less comfortable giving critical feedback in public or who wanted time to think through their comments. This written feedback was scanned and then posted to Resources for future reference.

- Wiki—The Class Design Wiki provided students with an authoring tool that supported powerful peer-to-peer interactions. For example, students often challenged each other's assumptions, posted probing questions or provided assistance to each other in addressing technical problems or gaining knowledge in a particular subject all via the Wiki tool.

- Assignments—Individual members self-assessed the overall team and each other as part of a mid-semester review. Each team member was then able to see the average rating given to them by their colleagues using the Assignment tool.

- Messages—Private feedback was also provided to students on each deliverable via the Messages tool (regular email was used during the first run of the course). This offered students a sense of privacy, allowing them to work on specific objectives without feeling singled out in the class.

Course Look & Feel, Web Usability—Sakai provided a "dynamic toolkit" that allowed the instructor to easily create a customized and aesthetically pleasing course site that was easy to navigate.

- Site Editor—The Site Editor provided the instructor with control over which tools to deploy as well as some of the content that would be displayed on the Course Site home page. In subsequent years, the instructor was even able to add capabilities that allowed student biographical sketches to be randomly displayed in the Worksite Information area of the course home page. This allowed students to get to know something about each other's backgrounds every time they accessed the course site.

- Wiki—The Wiki provided a flexible collaborative content creation tool that, over time, allowed students to evolve working draft content into a well organized and presentable document. The "history" option in the Wiki allowed students to look back over time to see how the materials as well as their thoughts and ideas had evolved. They were also able to upload images to a Resource folder and then incorporate these into the Wiki to enhance its visual appeal.

Learner Support—The course site included an extensive list of web-based as well as on-campus resources located in one central location. Because of the size of the University of Michigan having all of these support materials in one location was useful. The information was continually updated based on the needs of each project as well as input from students via regular class surveys.

- Syllabus—Students were provided with a detailed syllabus that provided standard course information such as grading information as well as how to get technical support.

- Resources—At the end of the course students uploaded their own information regarding University of Michigan resources, such as machine shops where tools could be made, for future classes to use.

Teaching innovation

Although this biomedical engineering course deployed many Sakai tools effectively, there were several that facilitated a transformation from what could have been a traditional capstone design course into one that embraced and leveraged a culture of participatory learning that was student-centered and active in nature.

"This course has been unlike any other course I've taken, and ten times the experience that [past] senior design courses have been…This class has given us much more freedom than the senior design classes to create teams and select projects that best match our interests, and the projects offered were far more involved and the results far more impactful. – BioMed 599 Student

These transformative uses of Sakai resulted in a truly innovative learning experience for the students in which they became active contributors to the course rather than simply passive recipients of information and instruction. In this role, students working collaboratively with their peers, instructor, and subject matter experts constructed their own knowledge of the design innovation process, leaving them with an innate understanding that would have been difficult to obtain through other more traditional instructional means. These transformative applications of Sakai can be categorized by how they facilitated new and meaningful "instructional interactions".

Interactions with Subject Matter Experts—Bringing in clinicians to brainstorm with the students allowed for rich exchanges between expert and novice. By using Wikis, Email, and Discussion Forums, the instructor extended these interactions well outside the confines of the classroom walls. Without Sakai, these interactions would have been isolated in time and place and would not have benefited from the iterative "give and take" process that is so central to brainstorming.

"In the 1st semester this year, students met with different UM clinical faculty. Students used this time to brainstorm with the faculty with regard to clinical state of the art and challenges. While these opportunities were critical, as with any class time, time is limited. Sakai maintained communication outside of the classroom, enabling constant momentum in idea generation." – Dr. Aileen Huang-Saad, University of Michigan

Interactions with the Instructor and Curriculum—Through regular student surveys and communication, the instructor was able to create a real-time curricular feedback loop that gave students real and meaningful control over how the course was run. Not only did this empower the students and facilitate a culture of participatory learning, it allowed the instructor to customize the educational experience to the learning styles of the students.

Interactions with Content—In a more traditional course, the instructor may have opted to provide students with well-defined design case studies. Such constrained and contrived approaches to teaching problem solving often leave students without the expert-level reasoning skills necessary to solve novel problems. By using the Wiki tool to facilitate a process in which students collaboratively worked on and refined concept design documents, they were compelled to actively engage in the problem solving process rather than simply reading about it. This "surfacing" to students of the cognitive process used to derive a solution is central in the development of tacit knowledge or "know-how". By shifting the interactions with content from passive absorption to active construction, students are much more likely to develop this type of tacit knowledge and be able to apply the problem-solving techniques they have learned in class to real-world situations.

"The evolution of the Wiki is a result of the collective mind set. By providing students with the opportunity to drive the process, the results were remarkable. This year, students used the Wiki to brainstorm new ideas, challenge proposed solutions, and even vote on the most likely viable solutions." – Dr. Aileen Huang-Saad, University of Michigan

Interactions with Peers—Shifting from traditional teacher-centered instruction to a student-centered model is challenging in part because of the importance of engaging in team-based collaborative activities. In this course, a range of Sakai tools including the Wiki, Forums, and Project Sites, were used to facilitate team formation, small and large group interactions, and peer-to-peer and group knowledge generation, much of which took place outside of the physical classroom. Without Sakai, the logistical barriers associated with implementing these approaches to peer-to-peer learning would have been significant and likely a limiting factor in their use.

"We engaged our peers, physicians, and instructor in meaningful discussions both in and out of the classroom, as well as in an online Wiki where we continued to brainstorm and filter ideas. I often found myself continuing these discussions with people not associated with the class. – BiomedE 599 Student

Today's students are growing up in an age of interaction and participation. Whereas their parents listened to music and watched television, the new generation lives in a participatory culture where they are no longer consumers of information but creators and authors—commenting on blogs, tagging pictures on Facebook, or remixing content to create something new and unique. In this age of interaction, it is increasingly important that instructors employ teaching tools that speak to this generation and empower them to participate in the learning process as meaningful contributors rather than sponges whose only role is to absorb information. In doing so, students, as evident from this Sakai-based course, do not just become more engaged in the learning process but in fact develop a deeper, richer, and more long lasting understanding of the subject matter.

2nd Place Winner: International Law (University of Cape Town, South Africa)

The second place winner of the 2008 Teaching with Sakai Innovation Award was Mr. Salim A Nakhjavani from the University of Cape Town (South Africa) with a course teaching international law.

Course description

Under South Africa's democratic, constitutional order, training in international law is as vital for domestic legal practice as it is for work with international and regional organizations such as the United Nations or the African Union. Because of the importance of this legal topic, students are required in the preliminary year of the Bachelor of Laws degree (LLB), to complete a compulsory, introductory course in international law. This course is animated by the tension between the classical, state-centered model of the international legal system and concepts such as international human rights, individual criminal responsibility, and the common heritage of humanity that are challenging and reshaping the international legal landscape. Topics covered include the sources of international law; international legal personality; the relationship between domestic law and international law; rights to territory, water, air and space; state jurisdiction; the regime of state responsibility; the settlement of disputes; the use of force; the United Nations; the African Union; and the influence of international human rights on South African constitutional interpretation.

The course is accompanied by an innovative tutorial simulation, supported by Sakai, known as Inkundla yeHlabathi (a phrase in isiXhosa, the predominant African language in the Western Cape, which translates as "World Forum") in which students learn to apply the rules and methods of international law by simulating the work of legal advisers to ten African States. Each week, a one-hour doctrinal lecture aims to develop frameworks and critical approaches to the law. In the second hour, students, who are seated by State as part of the Inkundla yeHlabathi (World Forum), learn to apply legal rules to complex facts to arrive at a State position, which may be negotiated with other States, and present views to the plenary. These real-world legal power struggles between "States" continue online in the Sakai-based Inkundla yeHlabathi (World Forum) simulation.

"This simulation connects African students with both the theory and practice of international law, helping the voices and insights of the next generation of African lawyers to be heard with confidence on the international stage." – Mr. Salim A Nakhjavani, University of Cape Town

Course development and delivery

By 2006, instructors found that International Law was increasingly perceived by law students as an inaccessible subject, remote from legal practice and the needs of the African continent. To address these negative perceptions, a team of instructors and instructional technologists began to introduce changes to the course, with the aim of "bringing to life" the development and implementation of international law in an African context and helping students experience in practical ways the interplay of law, power, geo-politics, history, and culture. An optional, classroom-based simulation exercise had been a key highlight of the existing course design, and the thought was to capitalize on this strength.

"I think all courses, especially law courses, should go beyond just using Vula [Sakai] as an electronic noticeboard or a place to download lecture overheads. So much more can be done through the interactive capabilities of Vula to bring the law to life!" – Shihaam Donnelly, a final year LLB student who helped in the development of the Inkundla yeHlabathi site.

In reflecting back on this effort to enhance the course, the instructor and technologists have identified three instructional stages that they progressed through as they began to use and pilot Sakai. These three stages, which are outlined below, show a progression from using Sakai to simply "automate" the instructional process (that is, making it more productive or efficient) to inventive applications that helped facilitate a shift from passive modes of instruction, such as lecturing, to much more active learning.

- Stage #1: Sakai as a Filling Cabinet—At this stage, Sakai was simply used for the storage and retrieval of information. Although this made it cheaper and faster for the instructor and students to access course materials, it did not facilitate collaboration or interactions among them.

- Stage #2: Sakai as a Dynamic Classroom—Sakai is used as an online classroom in which students and faculty could interact as a means to share knowledge.

- Stage #3: Sakai as a Living World—Sakai became a space where students actively constructed their own knowledge, not just shared it, thereby generating learning.

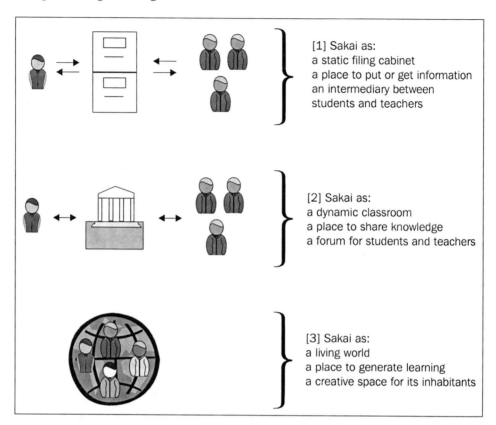

[1] Sakai as:
a static filing cabinet
a place to put or get information
an intermediary between
students and teachers

[2] Sakai as:
a dynamic classroom
a place to share knowledge
a forum for students and teachers

[3] Sakai as:
a living world
a place to generate learning
a creative space for its inhabitants

"Sakai provides a digital repository for information and research, a meeting place to exchange ideas, and a living world within which to generate new knowledge and harness learning."
– Mr. Salim A Nakhjavani, University of Cape Town

This concept of "Sakai as a living world" led to the transformation of what was once a traditional lecture-based course into an active learning experience that engaged students through a real-world simulation. A review of each of the five Course Evaluation Rubric categories will help reveal how Sakai facilitated this transformation.

Collaboration and Communication—Collaborative dynamics were integral to this course as evidenced by the many opportunities for students to establish and strengthen group identity and engage in peer-to-peer learning. A range of Sakai tools were used that facilitated this cooperative learning approach, including:

- Chatroom—Each State-specific team was provided with its own Chatroom (called the "Chatzone") to complement regular face-to-face meetings and support internal discussion between group members. In addition, a general Chatroom was used by students, teaching assistants, and the instructor to answer questions and debate current issues.

International Espionage!—The Case of the Teachable Moment

During one of the classes an "international incident" developed when one State was caught "spying" on another State in the Chatroom. Rather than dismissing this as a technical problem, the situation was turned into a "teachable moment" through the creation of the following scenario-based activity:

A dispute has arisen regarding the inviolability of State-specific chat rooms—that is, whether representatives of the receiving State or any other State may infiltrate another State's chat room in order to gather information. The Vienna Convention on Diplomatic Relations was drafted many years before the advent of the Internet or other forms of online electronic communication and does not specifically envisage confidentiality of electronic communications. Both the Ministers of Foreign Affairs and Information seek your advice (but unfortunately without doubling your meager salary)…

Learners, who now saw themselves more as real lawyers than students, had to research the law, interpret the applicable treaty and provide their recommendations. This "teachable moment" demonstrates how a simulation such as this one can encourage more authentic learning than would generally occur in a more traditional lecture-based class.

- Forums—The Forums tool, which was re-titled "International Actions" (2008) and "State Actions" (2009) for the purpose of the simulation, was used to support "formal" interactions between State-specific groups. For example, representatives of one State in the simulation might notify another State of objections they had over an existing treaty they were negotiating. The Forums tool was also used to collect feedback from students on the course itself as means to make improvements as it was run.

Learning Materials—One of the challenges faced by the design team was the escalating costs associated with course materials. In particular, the costs associated with purchasing the course's casebook, which contained primary source materials such as treaties, had increased to levels above the average monthly food budget for many students. To address this, the Wiki and Resources tools were used to reduce the costly paper-based learning materials in the following ways:

- Wiki—Over 1 GB of required readings, including over 90 treaties, were digitized and hyperlinked together in the course Wiki. Using the Wiki as the "delivery" tool for the materials, rather than Resources, helped make it easy for students to navigate to the materials they needed at any one time. This content was also distributed via a CD-ROM (2008) and Faculty-sponsored flashdisk (2009) as many students do not have easy or inexpensive access to broadband connections off campus.
- Resources—Acted as a "back-end" storage area or filing cabinet for the digitized materials. It remained hidden to students so as to reduce confusion over how to access the course materials.

Delivery of the course materials through Sakai had several major advantages, including:

1. Supported ecological sustainability by reducing the amount of paper, toner, and other consumables used.
2. Created more equity of access to the course materials, ensuring that all students, regardless of socio-economic status, could participate in the course.
3. Reduced course material costs by 80%.
4. Helped develop professional skills needed to search and use electronic materials, something that is increasingly important as many courts and law firms now only use digital materials.

Learning Outcomes and Assessment—A range of instructional strategies were deployed in this course to foster active learning and facilitate authentic assessment, such as group presentations, debates, and "mooting" (that is, a hypothetical legal case argued by students in a mock court setting). Sakai tools were deployed in creative ways to help meet these objectives. These included:

- Tests & Quizzes—Students were required to answer questions ahead of face-to-face seminar meetings, which were then reviewed by tutors prior to the sessions. This allowed for "targeted tutoring" in which the tutor is able to customize their feedback and instruction to address misconceptions or knowledge gaps evident from the student's initial answers.

- Assignments — Regular seminar assignments were posted as part of the course work. Generally, a choice of "baskets" of assignments were provided each semester that included learning activities aimed at developing higher-order thinking skills, such as "mooting" exercises, as well as more traditional assignments whose goal was basic skill development. By providing students with choices, it allowed them to select the more time-consuming types of assignments during parts of the semester when they had less to do for other classes. This helped ensure that students had the time needed to prepare for the more complex assignments, such as those requiring moots, without having to deal with the logistics associated with coordinating assignment due dates with other courses and instructors. The use of a digital tool for managing assignments also allowed for more efficient student feedback and recording of grades over what had been previously possible using a paper-based approach.

- Forums — As noted earlier, each State would post to the "International Action" Forum regarding decisions to sign or treaties to be modified. State teams would then receive feedback on their work in class, often by the instructor or a guest expert. For example, in one case regarding refugee rights, States posted their planned modifications to the definition of "refugee" and their rationale for the changes, which were then reviewed by a practicing refugee Attorney. The attorney then gave a guest lecture critiquing the student's work but did so in a "simulated" role playing the part of a representative from the United Nations. This allowed for a creative approach for student evaluations that mirrored how lawyers might be assessed in the real world.

Course Look & Feel, Web Usability — A project logo was designed and used on the Sakai site, departmental web site, PowerPoint slides, and print materials to create a feeling of identity and consistency across all of the different mediums. Images, which included real-life pictures and graphics, were used to enhance learning and helped to make the site serious and engaging without being tired or stuffy. In addition, text was resizable according to user preferences and content was generally provided in PDF format rather than MS Word documents in order to make it more accessible.

- Course Site — As already noted, some tools were re-titled to customize the course site and help immerse the students in the simulation. For example, the Forums tool was changed to "International Actions" and the Chatroom to "ChatZone".

- Wiki—Each State selected one or two Special Representatives to represent them in the International Actions Forum. Profiles for each representative were posted to a Wiki page, which included a biography of the student.

Learner Support—Sakai allowed for a level of student support outside of the regular classroom time that would have been impossible to achieve without the technology. This support included both instructional assistance and technical help in using the system.

- Chatroom, Forums, and Email—These tools were used frequently by students who had subject matter or technical questions. Lecturers and teaching assistants would monitor these areas several times per day and at late hours ahead of exams and major assignments. In general, student questions were responded to within 12 hours.

- Announcements—Regular announcements about events in the simulated world were posted as "Newsflashes" and also distributed to student email addresses as means to provide feedback and maintain regular contact with students. Doing so established a "teaching presence" in the online environment, which also helped the students feel supported regardless of whether they were in class or in Sakai.

Teaching innovation

Through the creation of the Inkundla yeHlabathi (World Forum) a traditional lecture-based course has been transformed into an authentic learning environment in which students were no longer passive receivers of information but instead actively constructing their own knowledge based on real-world experiences. As a result, students were more engaged in the learning process as they better understood the implications of what they were learning for their careers as well as for the nation and continent on which they live. In addition, to facilitate this fundamental shift in instructional methodology, Sakai significantly improved the delivery of course content by allowing for distribution of digital, rather than paper-based instructional materials. This has not only created a more ecologically friendly model, it has also reduced the cost to students to almost zero thereby allowing socio-economically disadvantaged students to participate in the course without incurring a major financial burden. To understand all of these innovations in more detail, it helps to view them through the lens of "learning interactions":

Interactions with Subject-Matter Experts—Traditional lecture-based classes tend to support "one way" interactions between students and subject-matter experts (that is, instructor, guest speakers, and so on) in which the expert transmits information for the student to passively absorb. The introduction of the Sakai-based Inkundla yeHlabathi (World Forum) simulation altered this traditional method by replacing the "one way" approach with a more active learning experience. The instructor was no longer at the center of the teaching process but off to the side facilitating learning. Rather than telling the students what they needed to learn through a series of lectures, the instructor directed the simulation (for example developing scenarios, creating challenges, and so on) as a means to guide the students through an educational journey.

Interactions with Peers—The shift facilitated by the simulation towards a more student-centered learning experience also resulted in a significant increase in peer-to-peer interactions over what would normally take place in a traditional lecture course. Students were no longer simply reading and hearing about international treaties but actively engaged in negotiations over them with other member states of the Inkundla yeHlabathi (World Forum). Even more significantly, student-based State teams were allowed to rewrite treaties, based on negotiations with other States in class and in Sakai, giving students the chance to construct new international law based on what they are learning in the course. Purely lecture-based classes rarely allow students to take center stage in the learning process, thus missing the opportunity for students to build their own knowledge of the subject matter.

"Inkundla yeHlabathi/World Forum offers students the opportunity to examine firsthand the current and emerging legal challenges facing the continent and the world. In a legal system that recognizes scholarship as a source of law, students grasp the potential to become an active part of shaping the law rather than passive observers of the law."
– Mr. Salim A Nakhjavani, University of Cape Town

Interactions with Content—Clearly, the use of digital content had a major impact on the ability of socio-economically disadvantaged students to enroll in the course. Beyond this, the use of electronic course content provided students with the opportunity to learn how to work with digital materials, something that is increasingly prevalent at most major law firms and international legal agencies who are increasingly relying on online databases and digital repositories over traditional libraries.

In summary, the Inkundla yeHlabathi (World Forum) simulation truly transformed the instructional methodology of this International Law course from a passive teacher-centered approach to one that created a dynamic, interactive, and engaging learning environment. This is a powerful example of the role that the Sakai Collaborative Learning Environment can play in facilitating the adoption of more active instructional strategies that promote knowledge construction over information absorption as the primary means of learning.

Want more examples of teaching and learning innovations?

The 2008 Teaching with Sakai Innovation Awards included two Honorable Mentions, one to Dr. Fred Hofstetter, University of Deleware, for his online graduate course on Web Design and the other to Mr. Michael Burns, Minisink Valley Central School District (K-12) for his Advanced Placement English Literature and Language course. These, along with all of the 2008 and soon to be added 2009 award submissions, can be found on the OpenEdPractices.org web site.

Conclusions and lessons learned

Although the work of the Teaching with Sakai Innovation Award Program does not represent rigorous research, several important and powerful conclusions can be drawn from observations of the work of the two award winners. As one looks at both courses and their uses of Sakai, one overarching truth seems evident: these are not traditional classes based on time-honored lecture-style instructional practices. Instead, both instructors have used technology to create dynamic educational environments in which their students are active participants engaged in authentic learning activities. Rather than passively absorbing information and regurgitating it back to the instructor, students apply their new knowledge to real-world problems and situations, making it feel more like the workplace than the classroom. To better understand the role Sakai can play in facilitating a transformation of this nature, it is helpful to generalize some of the instructional approaches taken by these two innovative educators.

Today's literature on pedagogy is rich in theories and concepts related to how students learn most effectively and associated teaching methods that support them. In examining the work of the award-winning instructors and the role technology played in transforming the educational experience of their students, one could identify many such methodologies (for example constructivism, experiential learning, and so on) at work. Although viewing these courses through the filter of specific learning theory would be interesting, taking a broader perspective allows for generalization to different educational contexts. Two such broad instructional concepts are those of "active learning" and "student-centered instruction", both of which are evident in the work of these two instructors and their courses.

Active learning sits on a continuum on which "passive learning" lies at the opposite end, see table next. One can define active learning as involving "students in doing things and thinking about the things they are doing" (Bonwell and Eison, page 2) as opposed to simply listening and absorbing information. Although passive learning, such as what occurs when listening to a lecture, can be effective in mastering a set of facts, it generally does not result in the development of higher-order thinking skills (for example problem solving, critical thinking, and so on) and is associated with low levels of student motivation and engagement. Active learning, on the other hand, encourages students to analyze, synthesize, and evaluate the information they are receiving through the educational process and apply it in new settings. This approach can result in a deeper understanding of the subject matter and inspire students to become self-directed, life-long learners.

Passive versus Active learning

Passive learning	Active learning
Students listen to a lecture	Students participate in a simulation
Students work by themselves	Students work in groups
Students take multiple choice tests	Students give class presentations
Students listen to a podcast	Students create a podcast
Students read a book chapter	Students write an article

Whereas "active – passive" learning relates to the types of instructional activities students are engaged in, "teacher versus student-centered" instruction addresses the role that the learner and instructor play in the educational experience. In the student-centered mode of instruction, unlike teacher-centered methodologies (next table), the focus is on the student's needs, abilities, interests, and preferred learning styles and tends to be very participatory in nature. In this approach, the instructor's role is that of "learning facilitator" guiding the students through an educational journey rather than attempting to prescribe precisely what the participants will learn and how they will learn it, as is often the case in traditional lecture-based classrooms.

Teacher-centered versus Student-centered learning

Teacher-centered	Student-centered
Professor's role is to be primary information giver and primary evaluator	Professor's role is to coach and facilitate, Professor and students evaluate learning together
Knowledge is acquired outside the context in which it will be used	Emphasis is on using and communicating knowledge effectively to address enduring and emerging issues and problems in real-life contexts
Emphasis is on right answers	Emphasis is on generating better questions and learning from errors
Focus is on a single discipline	Approach is compatible with interdisciplinary investigation
Only students are viewed as learners	Professor and students learn together

Reflecting on the two award winners' works, it is clear that they both used Sakai in ways that facilitated a shift from passive to active learning and from a teacher- to student-centered educational environment. For example, Dr. Huang-Saad, used the Wiki tool to support her students in actively constructing Class Design documents rather than taking a more passive approach such as providing the students with pre-determined case studies. Similarly, Mr. Nakhjavani used Sakai to create a real-world simulation that replaced time that had been spent on traditional lectures, shifting from a passive teacher-centered to an active student-centered model of instruction.

In reviewing these two courses, it is important to recognize that the innovation for which they won awards was not driven by the types of tools they used as much as how the instructors opted to deploy these tools. For example, if Dr. Huang-Saad had only used the Wiki tool to post her lecture notes, little instructional innovation would have likely been realized just because she chose to use a Wiki. This brings us back to the concept that was introduced at the start of this chapter: how the tools available in Sakai are used is much more important than which tools are used.

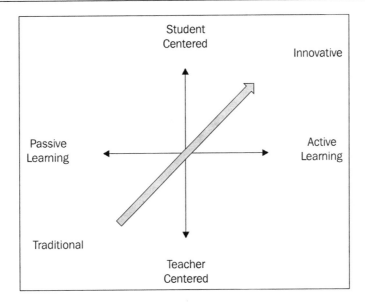

Less innovative versus More innovative uses of tools

	Less innovative	More innovative
Wiki	Instructor posts unit review notes to help students study	Students work in groups to create a their own course review guide
Forums	Instructor answers questions about homework	Student groups debate key concepts and issues raised in class
Tests & Quizzes	Instructor gives weekly tests to assess students	Teacher assess student understanding prior to instruction as means to inform the content and approach taken with each lesson

Traditional approaches to teaching and learning, such as lecturing, may be effective for meeting certain types of learning objectives but are seriously lacking when attempting to develop skills such as problem solving and critical thinking. Given the importance placed on these types of high-order thinking skills in today's workplace, it seems imperative that institutions of education seek out new instructional methods aimed at developing them. This posses a significant challenge as moving from a more traditional form of teaching to more innovative models requires a fundamental paradigm shift on the part of instructor and student. Technologies, such as Sakai, cannot drive this transformation in and of themselves but they can provide a new pallet of teaching tools that can help facilitate the change process.

As educators begin to use Sakai it is important to look at how rather than how much, the technology is being used. Is it simply making traditional teaching methods more efficient or is it creating new and innovative learning opportunities for students? As you and your institution begin to implement Sakai, challenge yourself to seek new and inventive ways of teaching and learning with the technology. Constantly ask yourself how Sakai's tools can be used to facilitate a more student-centered and active learning environment rather than simply deploying it in ways that support traditional forms of instruction. In doing so, you will see your teaching trending towards the "innovation quadrant" (see the previous figure, the Sakai Innovation Chart) where the most powerful educational experiences lie. Only by shifting instruction in this direction will the true potential of Sakai to innovate teaching and learning be realized.

The following tables provide the criteria for the three levels for all five categories for the Course Evaluation Rubric.

Communication and collaboration criteria

Level	Criteria
Not evident	The course offers limited or no opportunity for communication student to student, student to instructor, and student to contact.
Effective	The course provides an opportunity for student introductions, exchange of personal information. It fosters student collaboration in informal and/or graded contexts. Technologies and strategies are clearly identified to facilitate the collaborative, learning community environment.
Excellent	Multiple technology options are provided for collaboration and community building throughout the course, as a requirement of participation and excelling in the course. Instructional activities focus on learner input and reward paired or group interaction both inside and outside the course. Student reflection on their learning and the collaborative dynamic is encouraged.

Learning material criteria

Level	Criteria
Not evident	The course provides few structural or easily identifiable learning components, and/or navigation is difficult such that the components are not easily found. Learning activities are absent or unclear.
Effective	Key components of the course content are identified and easily accessible. These include items such as the Syllabus, a reading list, assignments and due dates, basic contact information. Instructions as to sequencing and expectations are provided. Basic resources are provided to meaningfully enhance the content.
Excellent	Via the visual design, as well as written material, students can clearly understand all components, structure, sequencing, and expectations. Roles are clearly delineated both in written and visual form.
	Resources are provided to address the content in multiple ways, taking into account student learning styles or abilities and levels.

Learning outcomes & assessment

Level	Criteria
Not evident	Learning objectives/outcomes are vague or incomplete. Course provides limited or no activities to help students develop critical thinking/judgment, problem solving skills, and digital literacy. Course has limited activities to assess student learning. Opportunities for students to receive feedback about their own performance are infrequent and sporadic.
Effective	Course goals/outcomes are clearly defined and aligned with content. Course offers some activities based on some of the 7 principles for good practice in undergraduate education (http://www.tltgroup.org/programs/seven.html). Provides several activities to develop critical thinking/ judgment, problem solving skills, and digital literacy. Assessment strategies are used to measure content, knowledge, attitudes, and skills. Opportunity is provided for student feedback about their own performance. Students are encouraged to share their knowledge with others.

Level	Criteria
Excellent	Course goals/outcomes are clearly defined and aligned with content. Course provides ample activities based on all of the 7 principles for good practice in undergraduate education (`http://www.tltgroup.org/programs/seven.html`). Interaction and communication between students, peers, faculty, and content are provided in a variety of ways with choices sometimes available.
	Activities to help students gain critical thinking/judgment and problem-solving skills are integrated into every aspect of the course. Multiple assessment strategies, including ones that attend to student styles and needs, are used to measure content knowledge, attitudes, and skills. Feedback about student performance is frequent and timely throughout the course, and provides clear opportunities for improvement and encouragement to excel. Students are required to become self-reflective learners and are given feedback on their reflection. Other forms of feedback such as peer review or feedback from experts is encouraged. Students are encouraged to generate course content using traditional or new media.

Course look & feel and Web usability

Level	Criteria
Not evident	Much or some of the course is under construction, or key components are missing. Aesthetic design does not present and communicate course information clearly. Accessibility issues are not addressed.
Effective	Appropriate tools are selected and identified for student navigation. There are no major usability issues. Different media are used to present information to students. Accessibility issues are briefly addressed.
Excellent	Course is well organized and easy to navigate. Aesthetic design enhances both the presentation and the communication of key information throughout the course. All web pages are visually, functionally, and aesthetically consistent to aid in course navigation. Different types of media are used to suit best the nature of the content to be communicated. Accessibility issues are addressed throughout the course.

Learner support

Level	Criteria
Not evident	Course contains limited or no information for online support and/or links to campus resources.
Effective	Course contains basic information for online support and links to campus and/or course-specific resources.
Excellent	Course contains extensive information about the online and/or campus environment and requirements for this particular course. A variety of resources and contact information is clearly presented. On-the-fly support material is developed throughout the semester if needed.

Summary

The intent of the Teaching with Sakai Innovation Award is to highlight innovative or transformative Sakai-based learning experiences. What makes excellent courses is discussed. Rubrics are given to measure against. A significant conclusion is that new tools can support a shift towards more student-centered active learning, moving our educational practices from the traditional status quo to something new and innovative.

Coming next, Chapter 16, *A Crib Sheet for Selling Sakai to Traditional Management*, discusses motivations for deploying open source applications in higher education environments such as at the University of Amsterdam.

References

Chickering, A., & Gamson, Z. (1987). *Seven principles of good practice in undergraduate education.* AAHE Bulletin, 39, 3-7.

Bonwell, C.C. & Eison, J.A. (1991). *Active Learning: Creating Excitement in the Classroom.* ASHE-ERIC Higher Education Report No. 1. Washington, D.C.: School of Education and Human Development, George Washington University.

16

A Crib Sheet for Selling Sakai to Traditional Management

Open source, community source, closed source — software must do the job.

– Hans Nederlof Managing Director Central Computing Services, Universiteit van Amsterdam (UvA)

David Jan Donner graduated with a Doctorate of Philosophy in 1987 from the Universiteit van Amsterdam. He works as an applications and functional administrator in the Education and Research Services group, where he monitors the requirements for a portfolio system based on Sakai, the portal for students, and Blackboard. Since 2006, David Jan has been a member of the ondernemingsraad — the staff's corporate council.

Léon Raijmann is the manager of the Education and Research Services Group at the Central Computing Services of UvA. The Education and Research Services group consists of 25 people and is responsible for developing new IT systems to facilitate learning and teaching. Léon trained as a scientist with hands-on experience in e-learning and e-research (he holds a PhD in Biology); he now finds himself between e-learning front runners. This chapter discusses the challenges and great advantages of Sakai as a community source project at the Universiteit van Amsterdam (UvA, http://www.uva.nl). Like all universities, this is not a standard company with standard requirements. Students, teachers, and departments all have their own unique demands.

No student is an island. The competitiveness of modern universities is measured by the value of their online services. Online courses offered 24x7 are the norm and not the exception. The current Learning Management System (LMS) at UvA is designated mission critical. If the LMS fails, the daily lives of the students and of the authors of this chapter are significantly affected.

LMS, CMS, VLE, VRE, CLE

When you read the international journals you can see some nearly interchangeable terms that mean roughly the same thing; Learning Management System (LMS), Course Management System (CMS), Virtual Learning Environment (VLE), and if you are a researcher, Virtual Research Environment (VRE). Sakai is a Collaborative Learning Environment (CLE), which is an LMS with extra features that support ad hoc collaboration.

Mission-critical systems impact our lives. If the payroll system, time tracking or mail fail, expect a flood of career altering messages from the director. This global importance is reflected in the money spent and the care taken in product deployment and daily support. Redundant server parts, platinum-level support contracts, consultants wearing expensive suits, and constant system and application monitoring are the daily luxuries you can expect pampered on a mission critical system. If significant money is spent, services must work or your career ends. You can't afford to make mistakes, so whenever it can the university introduces services slowly to a wider audience in parallel to the older legacy service.

Sakai is growing in popularity in Amsterdam. It is used for ad hoc site creation for anyone who wishes and is also ePortfolio server. It is implied that it will one day supplant in demand the current LMS.

At UvA, sometimes unnoticed by the wider organization, the Central Computing Services have deployed open source products. For the last four years the student portal and central authentication services have run continuously. On any given day, as many as 10,000-20,000 Students log into uPortal for the student portal and Yale CAS for authentication. This is approximately 300,000 online student hours per year spent interacting with open source products, and we expect a doubling in demand every two years. For UvA's closed source LMS, Blackboard (http://www.blackboard.com), students spend a cool half million online hours per year, and that immense number will be a million hours per year before 2011. If the LMS has even a low level of bugs, then hundreds or thousands of student hours are wasted. As a potential replacement, Sakai has to be as near perfect as possible. Are we confident that community source is up to the job?

The next chapter mentions the ongoing Patent lawsuits by Blackboard.

Context

The UvA has its own unique culture, location, and way of working. This section explains the structure and situation its central IT department finds itself.

The University's IT department

The UvA has more than 28,000 full time students and over 5,500 employees. They work in over 100 buildings distributed in roughly five major clusters throughout Amsterdam, as shown in the Google Map.

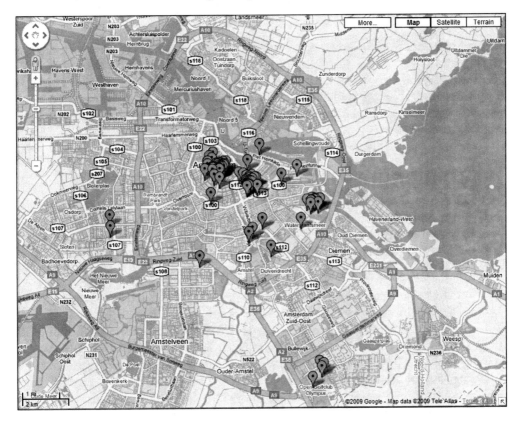

The UvA is independent in its ethos and also independent in infrastructure; it even owns the data network cables between the buildings.

The university has a centralized IT department, known as the Central Computing Service; in Dutch it is called the Informatiseringscentrum (IC `http://ic.uva.nl`). The IC has to manage a lot of assets: the network, all the servers, the information systems, and the central services for communication—email and Content Management system (CMS)—and most importantly for the future online education.

The 250 employees of the IC are divided into three groups. The infrastructure group, Information Systems, and the group for education and research support. The IC is one of seven joint service units, centrally organized to service the primary processes of the university.

The dispersed nature of the physical locations implies that online services have a critical role to play in every student's life. Traditional services such as email, home pages, and a portal to the students' information play a binding role, making for a cohesive student-wide community.

As the Internet matures and new competitive, socially-aware services are brought to the attention of students, the demand for online interactivity is increasing. Opportunities exist for greater and more flexible interrelationships. We are going through a period of online social dislocation driven by Darwinian competition between companies such as Microsoft and Google and a legion of other almost-free social service providers.

The challenges of a shared service center

When taking into account the software requirements, a university is not like a standard company. True, it needs a standard administration, however, its primary processes are education and research and both require a range of different media to support learning. Learning tools just don't fit within the standard notion of a generic application.

Education at UvA is at best a standard process for a third of the time. The students bring into the organization their own frame of reference, such as the use of online social networks and unduly high expectations. Teachers bring in the course material and also their ideas of guidance and support (not always Internet related). The two models of the Universe need to live within one application; both students and teachers need to be comfortable with the way their LMS responds. The application needs to feel responsive and be able to adapt to changing needs without continued relearning by the teacher or rewriting of previous course material.

Accommodating large classes and student-centered training demand a flexible online system such as Sakai. Project sites are particularly adjustable to changing requirements. Scientific researchers take their pick from the tools available and will demand more as they get to know the online environment better. The gratification of making sites stimulates the development of more tools.

UvA chose Sakai due to its promising possibilities. Packages for educational support need to deal with rosters, homework, workgroup communication, class preparation, and have the ability to test and then store grades. Sakai has these tools and more.

Every university in the Netherlands has departments like Economy, Medicine, Humanities, or Sciences that are by law independent. They derive their budget from the success they make, or go bankrupt due to their failures. Therefore, at UvA, educational tools need to support up to seven different departmental policies within the same license and software.

In 2006, the board of the UvA made each department's budget dependent on the success of the department's policies. At the same time the board took the support for IT, administration, library, and facilities out of the departmental organization and placed them into shared service centers (SSCs). The university model is that student influx and research grants pay the departments, and the departments pay the SSCs for their services but can also look for needed support elsewhere or buy it in. Departments are not allowed to sabotage central administration by buying their own systems alone. There are provisions for central concern systems and core facilities, but money for educational systems depends on how the departments perceive their quality. This means that an SSC will have problems implementing within the departmental boundaries if the applications they deploy are inflexible to change and do not offer a wide range of functionality.

The IC is the shared service center responsible for the whole of the university's IT services. Economies of scale force the IC to make standardized services with an organized control of quality. Without quality control, some of the services will be good and some will be bad, but more services will fail in the long run. Quality control does not always improve on the excellent, but rather ensures that a minimum level of quality has been reached and dubious projects are terminated early, thus limiting budgetary risks. Not only do the educational services of the IC use quality control, but thanks to the Sakai Foundation, Sakai is evaluated by skilled testers through every release cycle, implying that a minimum standard has been defended, which reduces our own efforts.

Central IT management would like to be less dependent on proprietarily licensed software for mission-critical systems. Historically, these systems have been expensive and risked vendor lock-in. Alternative open source products have the potential for flexibly dealing with departmental requirements, thereby securing customer relationships with positive evaluations, and increasing income.

Sakai is not only a learning environment. It has been designed from the bottom up to make tool building and interconnection from central administration through web services easy. The easy implementation of interconnectivity through web services meets a lot of requirements in the context of a shared service center as at UvA.

Departments are fiercely independent. Sakai is an online platform that supports different kinds of tools—each tool installed with its own configuration. This promises to offer a solution by enabling configurations tailored to each department. Such flexibility is not easily obtained in a standard application. By participating in the Sakai project, the UvA helps to make sure that the tools it wants become reality.

Research is a core aspect of any serious university's efforts and it demands a flexible approach from central services. The IC's expert groups need to determine and then support requirements that their various departmental customers expect. The requirements (we need x) are turned into services by software teams (IC produces an application to support x). These services are not easy to define (what are the specifics of x?) and then organize (what do we need to maintain x throughout its lifecycle?). The SSC has the challenge of accommodating and still managing costs in times of reducing budgets. Sakai helps by supplying a standard structure to build on that is relatively easy to learn.

Educational systems and administrative systems

The university administration systems are based on SAP (http://www.sap.com/). SAP is used for Human Resource Management (HRM) and Customer Relationship Management (CRM) and is a commercial heavyweight with a heavyweight price tag. Kuali (http://www.kuali.org/) is the open source equivalent and drop-in replacement of some of the functionality. Kuali learned its lessons from Sakai, copying its governance model. It is unlikely that Kuali will replace SAP, but healthy competition pushes prices down and drives innovation. In the future as Kuali matures, expect marketing pressure to be felt by SAP and other commercial providers in the Higher Education arena.

The soon-to-be-launched student registration is being built as a joint venture with several universities and relies on a turnkey adaptation of a commercial Peoplesoft application (`http://www.oracle.com/applications/peoplesoft-information-portal.html`). It will be interesting to see if community source can supply a competitor here as well.

Like most universities, UvA has a wide range of applications from commercial, through self-built to open source. Other large-scale applications include the University's web site (`http://www.uva.nl`). The web site is driven by a UvA-built database-centric application. The application is a CMS (Content Management System) written in ColdFusion that runs on Windows. The CMS has matured successfully over a period of ten years. Other applications include document archiving and administration of ongoing research projects. The IC has an online course catalogue that supports the publication of a paper version of the same information.

UvA decided nine years ago to use one educational environment, which is Blackboard (`http://www.blackboard.com`), a system dominant in the American K12 sector. It is well known by teachers and students alike, making it difficult to replace. Like it or hate it, most students use it during the course of their studies. A replacement would not only have to be better; it would have to be significantly better to motivate management to change. Further, the education support group is now working hard to set up a service for building questionnaires. A number of systems are being evaluated, including Questionmark (`http://www.questionmark.com`), features in Blackboard, and tools in Sakai. It is too early to tell which product will be chosen—we only know that there is a lot of pent up demand and a lot of future possibilities in this direction. It is vital to choose correctly or the end user might get used to a particular choice, making it difficult later to change to a produced that is a better fit.

Open source at the IC

The IC works with both open and closed source products. The organization's main goal is to keep its customers satisfied at the right cost levels. This section explores the IC's history with open source in mass education.

Introduction

A typical university environment requires IT support for mass education where licensed software and a stable infrastructure are primary prerequisites. Most commercial programs are not scalable and are inflexible, suited to only specific well-defined situations. Software needs to be abstract enough to be applicable in different educational settings. Ideally, IT support should focus on bug free software and secure network communication and not on bypassing known limitations. Can open source deliver?

Success with uPortal & CAS

The IC started working with open source in 2004 when it chose uPortal for the student portal (`http://my.uva.nl`). The portal influences the daily workflow of students and is the main online contact point for the students to other applications, such as email and course event notifications. Choosing an open source rather than a commercial product was the right choice, but a brave policy for management at that time. Development of the connections from uPortal to other systems was done in-house. Helpdesk support and training material resulted in systems to get a central view of what is going on in their daily university life. Portals were a new concept for the IT organization: one online student logon opens connections to services such as email that would normally require their own logon, but now were opened by the portal from the experiences gained.

As of spring, 2009, the original service has run reliably for four years with little change, partly due to the protective attention from key personal and partially due to the original architectural design, which included a load balancer.

The uPortal application, shown in the next figure, was the first encounter of the IC with an open source product as a mission-critical system. It is a web portal that contains a student's aggregate information.

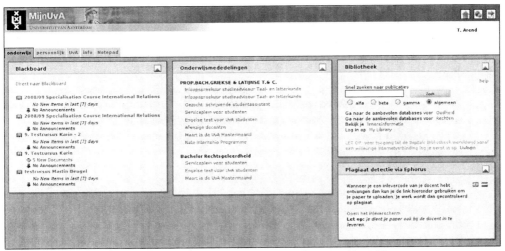

uPortal image courtesy of Bas Toeter, software architect IC.

The uPortal work was promising enough to broaden our open source efforts. Motivated by the uPortal success, starting in summer of 2006 the IC became interested in Sakai. Sakai played well with uPortal, had a clear roadmap, and its legality was defended by a central Foundation. As a significant bonus, Sakai had a central QA process and a clear stated preference for the use of open standards. With configurable tools, enabling flexibility in policy, and solutions tailored to departments, management became interested.

Sakai on the fringes

Sakai was first brought into production as a platform for the Portfolio tool (OSP). The Portfolio tool holds the means to make presentations and a matrix for students to develop skills and ask their mentor or teacher to review or evaluate their progress. Sakai is therefore not immediately replacing Blackboard. The ability of the university community to make open project sites is the second Sakai-related package that is being offered as a service at the UvA. Interest groups form communities. Allowing anyone to build project sites in Sakai empowers people to start an online community. This driving force is leading the demand. Humans, by their very nature, want to build communities. In life-threatening environments where mankind has lived in for most of its history, individuals fare better as part of a community than alone. This instinctive outreach has a positive impact on learning. Allowing full freedom to build online communities plays well to these instinctive drives. On an average, individuals learn better when motivated and working with others.

Sakai at UvA

There are a number of practical differences between community source and closed source at UvA. You should consider these as strong selling points for management. They include:

- **More influence** — There is great opportunity for future collaboration between different organizations within the community, whereas with commercial software you have an asymmetrical relationship where you have very little influence on the product's roadmap.

- **Empowerment** — Traditionally management at UvA arranged the responsibility for the IC along three tiers: 1, hardware and software; 2, at the applications level; and 3, defining functionality. The sources for these three are the IC, supplier, and the user. This shows the checks and balances the three-tier division is building into the traditional management style. Hardware maintenance and software distribution are available in house, whereas the software suppliers are accountable for the applications. The users will make a complaint when nothing works as it should, but what changes with open source is the relation with the supplier: part of the previous work moves to developers within the IC. The other change is the relation with the user who now specifies the required development. The responsibility of the user becomes therefore productive and with a well-defined service agreement that secures the IC funds. Both the organization and the representatives of the end user are happy, as they are both more empowered to influence the future roadmap.

- **Insourcing knowledge** — Using Sakai within the IC also requires the defining of new roles. A functional analyst is needed to understand the requirements of the user and translate those for the code writer. The IC also actively participates in the open source community to make sure that the requested changes are implemented as part of the software's standard release. The IC will also now have to be able to read the code and have significant software development expertise on the payroll. Influence and knowledge move away from commercial companies and reside more within the university. You may not save money in the end, but you do regain an element of control over the product, and insource knowledge rather than outsource it.

- **Licensing**—The License does not consist of a fee and restriction for copying, unlike traditional commercial licenses. Open source licenses can take many structures but they always involve the preservation of copyright. In the open source community, there are many variations. For example, the Sakai community source license has the Foundation as the legal home of Sakai. However, anyone is free to use the code or modify it. If a commercial company decides to sue individuals because they dare to use an open source variant, they now have to deal with a community with a well-defined and motivated central Foundation with well funded legal resources.

- **Control of rising licensing costs**—The yearly costs of licensing a commercial LMS rise above inflation. You are at times held hostage to unpredictable increases based on what the commercial company perceives the market can take. Buying into community source removes this unpredictable budgetary risk. Though the costs are elsewhere, you have more control over the unforeseen.

- **More control over requirements**—Traditionally, the supplier will make a note and add it to the pile of feature requests. In some cases, users can hand in homemade improvements or extra functionalities, and the producing software company will integrate this software enhancement into its product and own it. The motives for decision are mostly marketability of the product. Occasionally, requested changes at extra cost can be made, but the support does not guarantee compatibility of the changes for each product upgrade. You are going to put a lot of effort and cost and in return you may end up giving your improvements away with very little to show in return.

- **Participation**—The open source community is aimed at improving a product to fit the collective need. Its participants are not only the companies and universities, but also the individual code contributors. Members of the community can build their own improvements. Such improvements can be added to the software package and as a result become a standard part of the application. One can participate in a community process where new requirements are collected. Others may end up doing the work. The community decides not upon marketability or the bottom line, but on focusing on building the best. If you have a winning idea that you can sensibly debate, then others will build it.

At UvA, organizational change, the shift from corporate service station to a multi-department supporting shared service center made it necessary to rethink the strong points of what an LMS should have or what a collaboration system should be capable of. The rigor of propriety code should be combined with adjustability to a wide scope of multidimensional demands, and because this is still a research university with international ambitions, that scope should also include the unknown or room for innovation that is scalable. Blackboard also has the capacity to support the scope and innovation, but it leaves that to consulting vendors. It is very much a question of what a department is willing to pay for such development and lag time. For the same investment, Sakai moves faster.

Proprietary licensing is expensive, but to have developers within the company is not cheap. As far as the IC at the UvA is concerned, the transition from proprietary LMS to the community source of Sakai brought with it the investment in Java programmer's time, setting up a three-tier development street infrastructure, and still, yet to come, to manage the flow from building to line organization. The change to community source also makes for a shift in the culture of IT support: developers are too often treated as application managers by the call center, and system operators are usually mistaken to be the voice of the users by the requirements officer. Formality and dynamic exchange are difficult to spontaneously mix, and management has to overcome the divide. This may sound abstract, but working with community source allows us to engage the end user more directly. What is bought from the supplier is now paid for in the participation in the open source community. The dependencies do differ. Traditionally, the supplier and its support needed to be available, but the quality of its support was part of the license fee. To support open source development requires a reorganization of structures within and an investment in people's knowledge.

You are spending your money on training people rather than licenses.

An interview with the Director

 Hans Nederlof is a "Certified Management Accountant" (CMA) and "(Executive) Master of Finance and Control" (MFC) and currently is the Managing Director of the Central Computing Services, Universiteit van Amsterdam (UvA).

Hans Nederlof became managing director of the Central Computing Services in 2008. He is educated in finance. With experience at managerial positions in several non-profit organizations, the work at an educational organization was definitely new and therefore very attractive to him. It was time to explore other fields of work. "At a university, one expects to work with highly motivated people, driven by concern for content, and to work for a lively student population", Hans says. "The Universiteit van Amsterdam has it all".

What is Hans' managerial experience with closed and open source, or, as in the case of the Sakai framework, community software?

"What I know about open source or community software is what was told to me in the last couple of months," he replies with a smile. That is to say, "The group Education and Research Services has the experience at the central level of the university. It feeds me the first information. However, for sure there is a lot to gain from the projects and experiments at the different faculties. In particular, the science faculty has a long tradition and experience with the use of open source software. But this really is a new field for me. The open source software involvement is an interesting one and definitely a field of work that turns out to be one of the reasons to apply for my current position. So far, the organizations I worked for built their IT services on proprietary software, and there was no time for change since the services worked the way they should."

What are his concerns about implementing projects with community source software?

To Hans the answer is as simple as it can be, "Open source, community source, closed source—software must do the job. The IT governance of your IT infrastructure, and the IT services built on this infrastructure, have to go with the character of your organization. At the central IT department, we supply the departments with service of good quality and at a low cost. This university, however, is made up of diverse groups—departments, institutes—with each having separate needs and varied population, from IT-wise and very skilled people, to those who consider IT a commodity and on rare occasions even the enemy. The challenge for us at the central computing department is to service all the needs to work in the field of education and research. Community source-based tools with a variety of functionality have the potential to serve these groups best."

How can a community source project diminish his concerns?

Hans starts talking about the split between operational excellence and customer intimacy. "The value of a centralized IT department at a university must be found in the close interaction between supply and demand. In this case, that means for me that our IT services have to be as close with the user as is needed. The *UvA-Community* web site, based on the Sakai framework, though still in a pilot phase, seems to be spot on: the IT department delivers the infrastructure and a variety of tools, but in the end the course creator or researcher decides which tools he or she will use in practice. This model of offering as the supply seems to fit the demand of this organization and fit to the working attitude of the scientific staff. The upside is that support staff, in general without any advanced skills or needs, can provide support by means of commodity services."

What are his main causes of concern about proprietary software? Does he have any?

His main concern is not using proprietary software for what it's good at, or, so to speak, an inappropriate way of using proprietary software. "Use it the way the producer prescribes then the out-of-the-box means will not incorporate custom made solutions." That makes proprietary software in an organization as demanding as it is in the university, with skilled users, and with a tradition of 'openness' not the best option. And being a financial officer by trade Hans' other concern is the ever-rising license costs.

How can we take advantage of particular projects in the open source community?

If we can look at issues mentioned in the previous answer—license costs and facilitating your organization—"then that's where open source-based solutions and standards should excel. Use solutions based on proprietary software for standard services and explore the possibilities for open source in processes linked to the primary goal of an educational organization: teaching and doing research. And we should also mention the spin-off you can expect if you advertise yourself as an innovative, open department. That definitely suits a university. At this moment, however, we are in the midst of a discussion about open versus closed software so we still need some time to have our position clear. Having said that, we—as we did in the past—are eager to explore the possibilities of open and community source products in the educational environment. We have deployed Sakai for our Student Portfolio system and are piloting it for a community web site."

Does recession bias decisions towards one type of software or another?

"That's an interesting question, especially since we are not sure yet how the current economic situation will work out. The storm is coming but what will be hurt most? In general, management tends to focus in a period of a recession on one issue only and that is money. This means that the board lowers the costs as much as possible to match reduced margins, but also has to predict the development of costs for now and the nearby future as well as it can." And when it comes to predicting future costs, building your services on proprietary software from reliable and viable companies has an advantage over software built with open source. And yes, companies can increase the price of licenses or consultation, and even worse, can go bankrupt, but Hans believes conservatism will rule and therefore, open source being labeled as more adventurous, has to expect hard times. Though, on the other hand, he agrees that you can think of a scenario in which companies will seek open sourced-based solutions because of the lack of license costs. "But your support must still be organized and the IT employees must be ready for it." For the university business, the central computing service's main goal stays the same: support the university as well as possible.

Which roadmap does Hans believe is the most viable: Sakai or a commercial VLE?

"The experience we have with our current VLE, Blackboard or Sakai or other educational systems we provide for the university shows that the teacher has a crucial role in the making or so-to-speak breaking of their teaching and student satisfaction. And for students in the first year we see that the less adjustable systems in terms of functionality do the job perfectly. But later on in their curriculum teaching becomes more complex. That's a situation where more flexible systems are more beneficial. But only when the course instructors know how to press the buttons correctly."

Summary

Open Source projects such as CAS and uPortal affect the daily lives of nearly every student at UvA.

Sakai has to compete against Blackboard and deliver considerable value beyond the current choice to be worth adopting.

To sell Sakai to management not only requires an investment plan for skills, procedures, and process management. It also requires that we move software development to within the IT department. You are spending your money on training people and their time rather than licenses. Planning requires a thorough look at the Sakai community to judge the product's durability.

The next chapter discusses how to successfully interact with the Sakai community.

17
Participating in the Sakai Community

This chapter discusses what the Sakai community is and how to participate in it.

The Sakai ecosphere is structured around a community source model (`http://en.wikipedia.org/wiki/Community_source`). Sakai is distributed with an open source license whose legal home is the Sakai Foundation. The Foundation centrally coordinates project management for core features and sets date-driven targets for development. The core, enterprise-ready code has a well-defined software life cycle with a fully integrated Quality Assurance process. The combination of vigorous project management, a legal home for the source code, and a clearly identifiable Foundation enables large organizations to confidently donate resources to the collective whole. There is also room for individuals to do well and have a significant impact.

You can read an excellent article on the subject of community source by Brad Wheeler (Indiana University) at `http://connect.educause.edu/Library/ EDUCAUSE+Review/OpenSource2010Reflections/40682`.

The community includes the Sakai Foundation, individuals, teams within universities, commercial affiliates, consortiums, and diverse interest groups. The community interacts at conferences, via distribution lists, a central Wiki, conference calls, via Google docs, and directly through the addition to and modification of the Sakai source code. It is driven by the central overwhelming motivation to deploy and improve an online environment for communication and learning, and the exploration of new functional needs. It is not only about bashing code, but also consensus building about best practices and the evolution of functionality as the high education market for learning changes.

The community has its own unique and creative atmosphere driven by a willingness to get things done. Efficiency in achieving goals is fed by transparency of information, be it technical documents or meeting notes. It communicates in the open enabling individuals to decide where they can best help. The community is composed of individual free thinkers who have a wide range of ideas and opinions. This diversity brings with it long-term strength and staying power for Sakai, as debates look at issues from many angles. If you have one central view and much less debate then it is more likely that you will go in the wrong direction faster than with this more meritocratic approaches.

Sakai planet (`http://www.planetsakai.org/`) is a web site that aggregates the blogs from around 40-50 Sakai key players. Here, you can feel the heartbeat of the community and get a snapshot of current thinking.

The newcomers FAQ (`http://confluence.sakaiproject.org/confluence/pages/viewpage.action?pageId=27807`) quickly details the most common initial questions.

The Sakai Foundation

The Sakai Foundation supports the health of Sakai as a product and as a community through a number of coordinated processes. This section discusses these processes.

Consensus building

The Foundation supports consensus building within the community using a transparent communication strategy. All the important decisions are discussed in the open. The community is not chaotic; the Sakai Foundation supplies the central infrastructure for communication such as the community web site, Wiki, bug tracking database, and source code repository, and takes responsibility for delivering timely information. The newsletter from Sakai is sent out twice a month and contains a summary of important announcements and is a great shortcut for keeping up with what is important and playing in the community at any specific time. The Foundation also manages the International Sakai Conference.

Legal home

The Foundation provides a legal home for Sakai. This is vital for confidence in long-term investment by organizations that adopt Sakai. One reason for this is that a small minority of commercial companies have aggressively used the legal system against their competitors. A number of recent cases have the potential to disrupt confidence in open source products or at least products without a clearly defined legal home. For example, SCO questioned the ownership of the Intellectual Property (IP) rights of Linux. Groklaw is an excellent resource site on this subject (`http://www.groklaw.net`). Recession has the potential to aggravate this type of marketplace behavior. Luckily, the Foundation has the resources and willpower to defend.

Although not in the same negative category as the SCO adventure, Blackboard's effort to sue Desire2Learn generated a considerable negative reaction within the Higher Education community. There was a vigorous debate in blog space over acceptable borderlines in the use of patent infringement lawsuits.

Whatever the strength of the lawsuit, Blackboard risked the perception that it was prepared to sue its own customers and stifle innovation, thus damaging its own reputation and marketing campaign.

EDUCAUSE (`http://www.educause.edu`), a nonprofit association whose mission is to advance higher education by promoting the intelligent use of information technology, sent a message to Blackboard explaining fully the feelings some of its members were having at the end of 2006 due to the lawsuit (`http://www.educause.edu/October82006/12077` attachment A). "One of our concerns is that you may not fully appreciate the depth of the consternation this action has caused for key members of our community. Among those who have been most directly involved in the development and evolution of course management systems, customers whom Blackboard has relied upon for ideas and advice, these concerns are most pronounced. Their anger over the lawsuit is so intense that many are simply not communicating with Blackboard. We have seen this intensity of anger only a few times before. In those cases, the corporations involved were unaware of what was happening outside their official channels. Please do not underestimate this consternation which we believe will impact Blackboard in both the short- and the long-term."

The Software Freedom Law Center (`http://www.softwarefreedom.org/`) filed the re-examination request on behalf of Sakai, Moodle, and ATutor.

Blackboard received a negative legal ruling, which triggered an official response by the Sakai Foundation. "This hopefully marks the beginning of the end of this unfortunate and distracting chapter in the evolution of learning and collaboration software. In 2005, multiple companies and open source communities were productively innovating and competing to provide a range of educational tools. It is widely believed that the patent lawsuit impeded this healthy marketplace. At a time when there is considerable public pressure on the cost of education, this multi-million dollar patent distraction is not helpful. ATutor, Moodle, and Sakai all urge a definitive end to this distraction that has been harmful to the free expression of ideas and tools for education. We believe the USPTO non-final ruling provides a basis to put this patent matter behind us and resume productive work without distraction. We urge all involved to make that so."

At the time of writing, the law case was ongoing with Blackboard appealing. You will find the most current information on this ongoing saga at `http://www.desire2learn.com/PatentInfo`.

Partnering up

The Foundation generates its income through the Sakai Partners Program (SPP), where individual commercial and non-commercial organizations pay around 10,000 dollars per year to participate, and each year vote for members of the board of directors. The partners also provide the labor needed to improve Sakai. One of the motivations for becoming a partner is economy of scale. Well-focused, shared effort is cheaper than doing things alone, and you end up with a better-quality product. You also diminish your risks as knowledge is spread more evenly over the whole community and the negative aspects of local mindsets, such as "it was not invented here" syndrome, cancel each other out.

An important aspect of being a partner is that you have some control over the future of Sakai. The community is predominantly made out of universities, with a communal vision that you can influence with well-formed arguments. You do not get this degree of influence on a commercial product. Thus, you can consider being a Sakai partner as *enlightened self-interest*.

The official partner agreement states: "SPP provides the institutional and organizational base for the Sakai community. Sakai partners are dues-paying members who provide the intellectual, human, and financial capital necessary to support both the Sakai Foundation and the work of the community. Sakai partners participate in Foundation governance; help determine priorities for the community; and work cooperatively in every phase of Sakai's software production process. Membership in the Sakai partners program is open to academic institutions, non-profits and commercial organizations committed to Sakai's community-source vision of open-source software development and distribution."

Paying to become a Sakai partner is optional. For organizations that have deployed Sakai, especially for large-scale deployments, being a partner states to the community that you are committed and gives you voting rights to elect the Foundation's board. This governance model brings the Foundation into close contact with the requirements of a broad range of interested parties and ensures that the Foundation stays true to the needs of the organizations that fund it. If the Foundation moves away from the overall community consensus and fails to deliver a supportive environment for continued change, then the partner program stagnates and commercial revenues diminish. If the Foundation fails to response to those needs, it will not stay financially healthy. If a significant part of the community is disenfranchised, as Sakai is open sourced the disenfranchised can simply take the current code, make a new code branch, and enhance it in any way they see fit.

A starting point for background reading is the Sakai Foundation's home page (`http://sakaiproject.org`). Here, you will find the most current list of events and pointers to the most important documents. The home page represents the Sakai Foundation's official view.

The Foundation also supplies a project coordinator and community liaison officer. The enterprise core of Sakai has a clear roadmap (`http://bugs.sakaiproject.org/confluence/display/MGT/Sakai+Roadmap`) with tight time planning and a fully fledged QA process.

The Foundation comprises members whose roles include Executive Director, Administrative Coordinator, Project Coordinator and Bug Manager, QA Director, and Community Liaison.

The community

The following figure displays the dynamic of support be it financial or human for the Foundation. This figure was kindly contributed by Anthony Whyte.

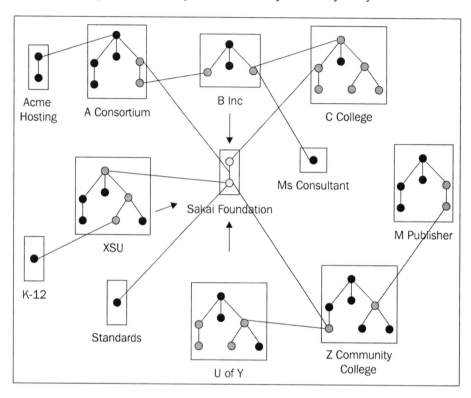

Non-commercial, and to a lesser extent commercial, organizations pay annual fees and donate human resources. The central pillar of the community is individual universities that collectively work towards their common goals. Many individual universities are involved such as the University of Michigan, Indiana University, Cambridge, Berkeley, Amsterdam, Cape Town, Hull, Paris, Texas State, University of Florida, and apologies to the large number of other universities not mentioned but that deserve mentioning.

Non-profit consortiums host or support Sakai for a wide set of small- and medium-sized organizations. Shining examples include CampusEAI (http://www.campuseai.org) and the Etudes consortiums.

CampusEAI recently won a significant contract to implement Sakai for the Northern Buckeye Education Council (NBEC), a not-for-profit Council of Governments organized to provide Northern Ohio K-12 educational entities with low-cost administrative services.

Etudes offers centralized hosting, support, site and account management, and training and professional development opportunities to institutions and organizations that need a turnkey, fully-managed course management solution. As an Application Services Provider, Etudes supports over 94,000 student enrollments across twenty five client institutions.

The use of open standards is important for the interaction between the Sakai source code and commercial companies. Open standards allow an even playing field where no particular organization can gain control of parts of Sakai via obscuring data formats or use of proprietary protocols.

There is a significant learning barrier to initial deployment of Sakai, especially for smaller organizations that do not have the manpower to invest. Commercial companies (http://sakaiproject.org/portal/site/sakai-support) such as Unitech, Netspot, Serensoft, rSmart, Unicon, and Edia provide the services needed. These companies can bundle their hosting or consultancy efforts for a number of small organizations and gain by economies of scale.

A number of talented individuals in the community provide freelance consultancy. These individuals, such as Zach Thomas and Mark Norton, have contributed in the past significantly to the code base and have invested their own time in helping build up fundamental core services within the Sakai framework or tools.

There are all kinds of relationships between the organizations. These relationships are dynamically changing as the community size increases. Working with Sakai is a great opportunity for teams to meet up and work towards common goals. This permeating commonality enhances opportunities to work on projects outside Sakai later.

As the community matures further, expect a positive cycle with more funding for the Foundation, better centrally supplied infrastructure, and a greater range of tools and documented best practices. Life is good, yet still it improves.

DoOcracy

The community is tied together by the common interest of building and using Sakai to its best possible extent. No one owns Sakai and its future is dependent on the efforts of a large number of individuals. The Sakai community is a DoOcracy (http://www.communitywiki.org/en/DoOcracy). Individuals see something that they think needs to be done and help. A DoOcracy can only exist if communication between individuals is honest and polite. If the community is too critical, it will demotivate those who are actually doing the hard work. If you do not like what is happening, time to pull your sleeves up, get your hands dirty, and lead by example.

DoOcracies depend critically on good information being transparently available in a timely and structured manner.

The quality of decision making within international communities such as Sakai is based on multiple cultures and organizational mindsets. It is critically dependent on information transparency. Without transparent communication, efforts will be duplicated, contradictory approaches applied, the time to establish a consensus long, and the general organization of labor inefficient.

Transparent communication

Without transparency, the community runs the significant risk of forming cliques, where local groups have a specific way of thinking or doing business and find it hard to imagine a Universe outside their own environment. Cliques are efficient for specific goals; however, they do not scale, and their effectiveness diminishes as the number of things to do increases. In practice, the transparent democratic dissemination of information is vital for the community's productivity. This section explores the issue.

Conferences

The Foundation sits like a spider in the community web of interaction. The Foundation publishes events in its twice-a-month newsletter and arranges the international conference. The conferences were originally held twice a year in America and are now settling to once a year in different countries, with more specific regional conferences. Previous locations include Amsterdam, Paris, New Orleans, Austin, Texas, and Vancouver, and the conference has now passed its tenth incarnation.

The conferences act as vital synchronization points, where the organizers reserve two days before the conference for project planning, discussions on high-priority topics, board meetings, and the running of the programmer's cafés. Even with the most current technologies, face-to-face communication is still the most efficient method to debate and move opinions.

Free meals

Sakai has a reputation for being technically daunting for teams that are trying to deploy it for the first time. Conferences act as an excellent place to ask difficult questions and learn from others' experiences. You get to meet the people that have either already deployed and have learned the ins and outs of the technologies, or those who have been active in building. Do not be afraid to make contact. *Bribing with a meal is always welcome.*

At the conference, presenter awards are given out, such as the Fellows award. To quote the Foundation's web site: "The Sakai Fellows program seeks to foster community leadership by recognizing and supporting outstanding Sakai volunteer contributors. Sakai Fellows bring a wealth of expertise to the community in the areas of software design and development, pedagogical and teaching practices and community advocacy."

In practice, the recognition given by the fellowship reinforces the fellow's position within the community and helps them influence decisions within their specific problem domain. Fellowships are rotated every year and past fellows are still very active and influential — once a fellow always a fellow.

During the conference, the Sakai Fellow awards and Teaching with Sakai Innovation Award (TWSIA) (http://openedpractices.org/tag/twsia) are also handed out. In the final analysis, the core business of Sakai is to support collaboration and teaching. The TWSIA award highlights pedagogical best practices. The intent of this award is to highlight examples of educational applications of Sakai that fall into this innovative or transformative category. The reward is relatively new, having been presented for the first time at the 9th International conference (http://openedpractices.org/twsia-2008-award-winners). Sakai has the ability to influence teaching practice. Therefore, expect the reward to have a positive influence over mindset.

Ego forces me to admit that there is also an Alan Berg Award for the most bug reports cleaned up by a given person. However, the award's survival is in doubt, as the champagne prize may not be enough incentive for programmers to keep track of their skillful efforts. This humble author may end up in a corner of the conference somewhere forced to drink the prize.

The conferences also include BOFs (Bird of a Feather) meetings, where people with similar interests meet, discuss, and agree to work together. Anyone is welcome to arrange a BOF. A number of the popular BOFs act as starting points that later grow into Work Groups.

If your organization is interested in involving itself with Sakai, the conference is an excellent place to kick off that relationship.

Local interest groups communicate their existence through Confluence (`http://confluence.sakaiproject.org/confluence/x/jAfJAg`) and arrange regional conferences (`http://confluence.sakaiproject.org/confluence/display/CNF/Conferences`) and meetings. For example, the European Sakai community has recently started up and will have had its first conference in Stockholm in June 2009. The Australian has a more-established yearly conference known as AuSakai.

Regional conferences, naturally lead to specific focus over regional issues. In Europe, you can expect greater discussion on Internationalization than at a regional conference at, for example, Virginia Tech. A local conference in America may have more BOFs for K-12 deployments and the Europeans are currently more focused on ePortfolios.

There are also events tailored for specific purposes. For example, Cambridge University provided a hackathon (`http://en.wikipedia.org/wiki/Hackathon`), where a group of developers got to grips with building and using new features, with a bias towards client-side widgets and improving the Graphical User Interface (GUI). As the community grows, expect more diversity in topics and locations of conferences.

Collab

Collab Failure March 2009

Collab failed in March 2009 due to hosting issues. The Foundation acted promptly and temporarily migrated the discussion lists to a traditional listserver. At the time of writing, it was not certain what the plans are. There is a discussion about migrating the lists to a Sakai server or back to a Sakai. This implies that at the time you read this book, the specifics of how to join a particular list are potentially incorrect. However, the choice of lists to join should not have changed radically and the ability to send email to the lists will definitely continue to exist in one form or another.

The Collab server `https://collab.sakaiproject.org` is a central support in the communication strategy of the Foundation. Anyone can create an account on the server and then join sites within via the membership tool, shown next. Each site has its own email address and if you write to that email address, every member of the site receives the message. To stop receiving messages, you simply need to unjoin the specific site.

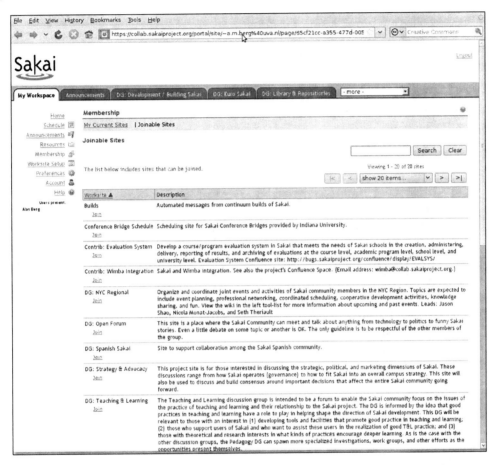

Email is an excellent way of communicating. It allows for thoughtful discussion between interested parties scattered across many time zones. The email archive acts as a historical reference and allows others to see how decision-making processes occurred. The email archives also represent a good place to trawl for generating FAQs for your helpdesk.

Although Collab sites are primarily used for email routing, the site maintainer has the power to add other tools as well. Examples include the use of the Resources tool to enable uploading of documentation, presentations, and videos. Using the scheduling tool to mark times for synchronous online meetings is another.

There are two types of groups to communicate with. The first is the Discussion Group (DG) and the second is the Work Group (WG). A DG is a place for transparent discussion on a common theme, such as development or teaching and learning. The Work Groups are for getting actionable pieces of work done, like dealing with release management, QA, or internationalization issues. Work Groups are mirrored onto spaces in Confluence to help with coordination and documentation.

The DGs are the location where ideas are competively debated and improved. As such, the DGs can act as spawning grounds for Work Groups. The three DGs recommended on the Collab site to first join are Announcements, Development, and User.

1. Announcements is a DG everyone should join. As the name suggests, its role is to distribute announcements and news of the Sakai community. Resources include development documents, Sakai newsletters, videoconferences, presentations, and demonstrations. This is a low volume list sending out only couple of messages per week. To avoid chaos, moderators control the list. To send a message to the whole community requires getting in contact with the Foundation via the email address `sakai-Foundation-staff@umich.edu`.

2. Development is the most active list of them all. This is the best place to ask questions and participate in discussions relevant to all aspects of Sakai development. The membership includes nearly all of the developers who have worked or are actively working on Sakai. Therefore, before sending out a question to this list, make sure that you have done your research. Nabble is a great place to check that the question has not already been answered.

3. User is the place for the end users of Sakai—faculty, staff, students, researchers, instructional designers, and end-user support staff—to share and discuss best practices for using Sakai.

Occasionally, there is a cleanup by the Foundation's community liaison officer of the unused sites within Collab. It is possible that a number of unpopular sites are removed, but only after each site's membership is consulted.

If you cannot find a DG that suits your needs then it is worth getting in contact with the Sakai Foundation. They will probably make you the maintainer of a new DG site. If other people join, then there is opportunity to agree on combining efforts and getting your ideas improved and implemented. Perhaps even a specific Work Group is spawned. The long-term health of the community depends on the revitalization of purpose through debate.

Work Groups

The table below lists Work Groups. The WGs exist to get things done, from release management, QA, to collecting tutorial material for end-user support, and more. There is a lot of practical value in choosing the most appropriate WGs and joining.

Work Group	Description
Accessibility	The place for discussion, documentation and the posting of developments associated with Sakai Accessibility efforts.
Course Management	The Course Management Working Group's focus is twofold: understand and (re)design for users of Sakai's course management-related tools; and build a new framework for integrating institutional course data with Sakai.
Data Analysis	Easily-accessible information about usage is critical to the work of Sakai-related staff, including support staff, support staff, designers, researchers, developers, testers, and system administrators.
End-User Support	This is a place where the Sakai Community can: – share tutorials and documentation to support Sakai end-users – exchange Best Practices for training and consultation – discuss ideas and share end-user experiences – pose and answer questions
Google GWT	Advocacy group for the use of the Google GWT inside Sakai.
I18N & L10N	This group discusses Internationalization (I18N) and Localization (L10N) within Sakai.
K-12	This group is for those interested in K-12 applications of Sakai.
Licensing	The Sakai Licensing Working Group is responsible for: – documenting licensing requirements for all code and libraries used and distributed by the Sakai Foundation – maintaining a sustainable license management practice for the Sakai community
Migration	This site is focused on moving content in various ways in and out of Sakai.
Performance	The Performance Working Group is a team of interested organizations working collaboratively to improve Sakai framework and tool scalability, reliability, and performance times. Shared design, resources, results, and discussions of this working group will supplement the functionality testing of the QA Working Group.

Work Group	Description
Production	All about installing, implementing, configuring, and supporting Sakai. A place to find release documentation and learn.
Programmer's Café	This is the home of the Sakai Programmers Boot camp. The activities here are designed to introduce new members of the community to programming for Sakai.
QA	The home of the central Quality Assurance (QA) effort.
Release Management	Work Group focused on the coordination and documentation of the release process.
Sakai Community Practices	This workgroup is chartered by the Sakai Board in order to shape a common "Sakai World View" and a set of community practices that maximize the effectiveness of our community. The SCP conducts our work transparently with broad community input.
Sakai Foundation Web site	This space serves as a work space for community members working on the Sakai Foundation web site.
Scorecard	A Work Group formed to improve the current Core/ Provisional/Contrib Tool Status system.
User Experience (UX)	The Sakai User Experience (UX) Working Group conducts the research, design, and development that shapes the overall Sakai user experience. Its main focus is on core Sakai tools and services included in the Sakai release. Contrib projects are also strongly encouraged to consult with this group in their development efforts in order to help provide an appropriate, uniform user experience.

Asynchronous communication

Individual members of the community are scattered across numerous time zones. If you work in Amsterdam and want to talk with someone in Perth, you will find yourself eight hours behind their working day. If you arrange a conference call and the majority of the group live within one time zone then there is a natural bias against arranging suitable times for the minority. Therefore, to fight this bias, if you are setting up a new Work Group, you should leave as much evidence of events as you can on Confluence.

The most regular meetings are associated with new release management and Quality Assurance. As part of the release cycle, there are synchronous online meetings once a week. The organizers arrange the timing of the event so that those on the East Coast do not have to get up too early and those in Europe and South Africa do not have to work too late. The meeting notes are kept up-to-date and are online for all to read (see figure for an example for the QA work group). The conference bridge is open to use by all interested parties.

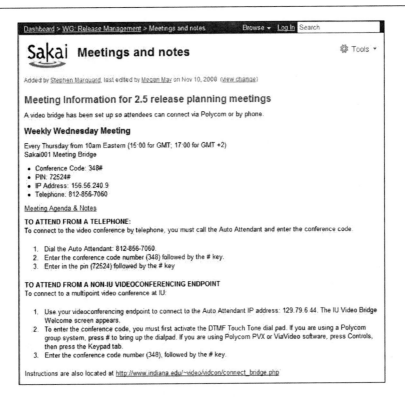

The meeting notes are not verbose; they contain brief and honest summaries of the main themes. The notes also contain the list of promised actions and the period of enactment.

The Foundation also keeps notes on board meetings and budgetary information on Confluence (`http://bugs.sakaiproject.org/confluence/display/SBCO/Sakai+Board+---+Communications`).

Open code, Open Standards

Transparency of information does not only reside at the level of documentation and meeting notes. Transparency also resides in the availability of source code and the use of Open Standards.

Open Standards are important in order to avoid vendor lock-in and they help you keep your options open for future events, planned or unexpected. If you choose proprietary standards, then you force yourself to follow the same path as a vendor. If the vendor changes course or discontinues support, you have bleak choices such as supporting the service yourself or discontinuing.

Example of Open Standards within Sakai include:

- The existence of multiple SCORM players (`http://bugs.sakaiproject.`
  `org/confluence/display/SCORMPLAYER`) that work within Sakai to play
  learning content. This allows reuse of material that you may have originally
  generated within another application.

- The ability to export Tests and Quizs via the IMS QTI standard (`http://www.`
  `imsproject.org/specifications.html`, `http://bugs.sakaiproject.`
  `org/confluence/display/SAM/Import-Export+Features`).

- SOAP and RESTful web services that make Sakai a malleable partner within
  the infrastructure of the enterprise.

- The consistent use of XML for configuration and defining features within
  tools, such as parts of portfolio templates in OSP.

- The use of the JCR standards for storing and retrieving content that you
  have generated via tools or files you have uploaded via the Resources tool
  (`http://en.wikipedia.org/wiki/Content_repository_API_for_Java`,
  `http://bugs.sakaiproject.org/confluence/display/CHS`).

The examples mentioned show that the community is concerned about decoupling
content as far as possible from the Sakai application. The coverage of import and
export options is not perfect. However, if you have a specific requirement that is not
covered, you can work with the community to build it.

Proprietary code does not come included as part of the source code. Commercial
licenses tend to be aggressive in their defense against reverse engineering. Sakai, like
many of its open source brethren, makes the source code and helpful documentation
available. This allows you to get your fingers into the code and form a studied
opinion about quality. If a bug appears in the code and it is important to resolve
the issue, you stand a good chance of being able to find and destroy the problem
yourself. If not, you can always send an email to the Dev list and ask for advice.

In the worst-case situation where specific functionality does not exist, you can
always build it yourself as a member of a group of interested organizations or with
the help of Sakai Commercial Affiliates. If you then commit the code into Contrib
and advertise it, other organizations may pick up the code and start to get involved
in improving it. In the end, if there is a demand for the feature, then you will save
yourself effort and get more back in results relative to your effort.

The Central Computer Services at the University of Amsterdam (`http://www.ic.uva.nl/organisatie`) take advantage of the instant availability of the code to scan the code base three times a day for known bug patterns. There is even a **what is new** section (`http://qa1-nl.sakaiproject.org/whatsnew`), reporting on any newly-found bug patterns. The figure displays one sample report. The HTML table contains information about potential bugs. The details include the specific project, the importance of the bug pattern and a link to an HTML version of the source code. If you click on the source code link, your web browser displays the offending lines of code.

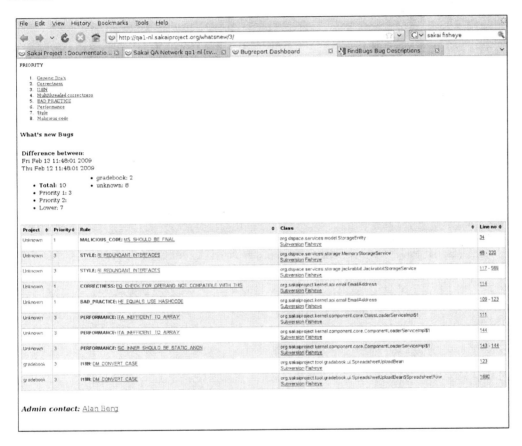

Without code transparency, this reporting would not have been possible, which would make it harder for individuals working on different parts of the code base to assess code quality.

Without code transparency, managing a multitude of simultaneous projects, each potentially influencing the others, would be troublesome and liable to unconsidered errors.

In combination with code transparency, the central high-level coordination of the development efforts by the Sakai Project Leader is vital. The Project Leader communicates, coordinates, and structures at the top level. If there is friction between the Project Leader and the community that he or she is involved with, then expect a significant lowering of overall productivity. Therefore, if you wish to donate coding time and effort and are not quite sure where to start, you can always get the Project Leader's opinion.

The best practices for participating as a developer are mentioned in the link `http://bugs.sakaiproject.org/confluence/display/SAKDEV/Sakai+Develope r+Practices`, and are:

- Every member of the Sakai community will respect the efforts and contributions of every other member of the community.

- No commit will blatantly rewrite the code of another developer without prior agreement.

- Code changes should aim to deliver the required purpose. For instance, wide-scale code reformatting of other people's code without agreement is not acceptable.

- If a committer needs to work in an area of code for which they are not responsible, they will contact the lead of that area of code and/or the Sakai-Dev Discussion Group to inform and discuss their intended actions.

- A committer that is responsible for an area of code, either as lead or as part of a team, should communicate regularly with the team of committers working on that code.

- Cross project changes require discussion on the Sakai-Dev list and may require the creation of a branch depending on the impact.

- You must take care in every commit not to impede the work of others.

To apply for your own source code location under Contrib, you will need to email `svn@collab.sakaiproject.org` and ask for commit permissions.

Once you have the right to modify code within Subversion, you will find that your mailbox receives lots of automatic email (similar to the one shown in the next figure). This is because you are automatically joined to the source DG. Collab sends one email per commit added to Contrib or trunk.

```
Details: http://source.sakaiproject.org/viewsvn/?view=rev&rev=57698

Author: jean-francois.leveque@upmc.fr
Date: 2009-02-19 09:13:00 -0500 (Thu, 19 Feb 2009)
New Revision: 57698

Modified:
sam/branches/sakai_2-5-x/samigo-app/src/java/org/sakaiproject/tool/assessment/ui/bean/author/ItemAuthorBean.java
Log:
svn log -r52561:52562 https://source.sakaiproject.org/svn/sam/trunk
------------------------------------------------------------------------
r52562 | ktsao@stanford.edu | 2008-09-22 19:18:00 +0200 (lun, 22 sep 2008) | 1 line

SAK-14151
------------------------------------------------------------------------
leveque@jfl149:~/sakaiBranchManagement/2.5.x$ svn merge -r52561:52562 https://source.sakaiproject.org/svn/sam/trunk sam/
U sam/samigo-app/src/java/org/sakaiproject/tool/assessment/ui/bean/author/ItemAuthorBean.java

This automatic notification message was sent by Sakai Collab (https://collab.sakaiproject.org//portal) from the Source site.
You can modify how you receive notifications at My Workspace > Preferences.
```

The subject headings have a specific structure, so it is easy to create a rule in your favorite mail client (mine is Thunderbird `http://www.mozilla-europe.org/en/products/thunderbird/`) to move the mail to its own folder and to not swamp your daily mail conversations.

The subject format starts with `[sakai]` for core Sakai code-related activity and `[contrib]` for contributed code.

The flow of email keeps you in intimate contact with what is going on in the code. If you start to see problems with your test servers, this is a rough indicator of who and where and when generated problems.

The source code also contains licensing information, such as headers, at the top of some of the code files and occasionally the full license text in separate files. Based on the open source tool known as arat (`http://code.google.com/p/arat/`), the Amsterdam QA server scans for this licensing information once a day and generates a detailed report.

The example reports show that having the whole of the source code available to you gives you a great opportunity to do clever things that benefit the whole community. Code transparency just begs you to be creative. For example, you can find some experiments in visualization commit data, including animations, on Confluence at (`http://bugs.sakaiproject.org/confluence/display/QA/Visualization`).

The QA network

Transparency of information also includes testing. The QA network is the place where the Sakai code base is tested during the release cycle. QA testers report any bugs triggered during testing through the bug database. A detailed FAQ on the correct way to write a Jira can be found at: `http://confluence.sakaiproject.org/confluence/display/QA/QA+How+To`.

The QA network currently comprises around ten servers, which the table below lists. Each server is intended to have a different hardware and software configuration. The motivation for this server diversity is that developers normally write their code in only one environment. There can at times be bugs, like errors due to the difference between forward and backslash representations of file pathnames, slightly different ways database drivers work, and a whole slew of character encoding issues due to Internationalization or web browser differences.

Location	Description
`qa1-nl.sakaiproject.org`	Linux/MySQL server located at the Universiteit van Amsterdam, Amsterdam, The Netherlands
`qa1-us.sakaiproject.org`	Linux/Oracle server located at Boston University, Boston, Mass., USA
`qa2-us.sakaiproject.org`	Solaris/Oracle server located at Columbia University, New York, N.Y., USA
`qa3-us.sakaiproject.org`	Linux/Oracle server located at Indiana University, Indianapolis, Ind., USA
`qa4-us.sakaiproject.org`	Linux/Oracle server located at the Georgia Institute of Technology, Atlanta, Ga., USA
`qa1-uk.sakaiproject.org`	Linux/MySQL server located at the University of Cambridge, Cambridge, UK
`qa1-za.sakaiproject.org`	Linux/MySQL server located at the University of Cape Town, Cape Town, South Africa
OSP QA servers	
`qa1-osp.sakaiproject.org`	Linux/MySQL server located at The rSmart Group, Phoenix, Ariz., USA
`qa2-osp.sakaiproject.org`	Linux/Oracle server located at Indiana University, Indianapolis, Ind., USA

For the hosting organization, there are advantages as well. The administrator that maintains the QA server gets to see Sakai at its worst. This excellent learning experience prepares new system administrators for the rigors of production life. Having a QA server within your organization allows you to understand which issues are playing out in the code and hints at when you should deploy the newest versions. Outside the release cycle you can always retask the QA server to other local needs. Further, being part of the QA network you get into contact with a rather intelligent crew of system administrators that can potentially help you solve Sakai-related glitches.

Anyone can create an account on a QA server and test for their own specific needs. However, it is better for the community as a whole if you act as part of a centrally coordinated effort, led by the Sakai Foundation's QA director. To sign up, you will need to add your name to a list maintained under the QA Work Groups home page (`http://bugs.sakaiproject.org/confluence/display/QA`). Every time there is a new release, there is a new signup process.

There is a QA FAQ that also includes information on how to get started with hosting an official QA server (`http://bugs.sakaiproject.org/confluence/display/QA/FAQ+QA`).

The risk of information loss

If the community is to remain open, then as much communication as possible needs to be captured in places that everyone in the community can access.

Documentation is not automatically generated for synchronous tools such as chat, Skype, on line, white boards, and video conferencing. However, you can keep track of these informal online conference calls and leave hints on Confluence so that others can join in.

Google is very good at making services that people want. It provides all kinds of interesting services, including a tool to peer-review code, a place to chat, a portal, and a way to share and collaborate on documents and presentations. A large proportion of the Sakai community is used to working daily with this freely accessible infrastructure. However, some of the services compete for attention with the supplied services from the Sakai Foundation. For example, at the time of writing the role of Google Docs within the Sakai community is ambiguous. Google Docs allow groups to update documents simultaneously online; however, you can argue that the same functionality exists within the Sakai Wiki. Google Docs do have an advantage in terms of user experience and a little better functionality, as they are included with the whole Google experience. However, if links do not exist to the specific Google Docs area in the Sakai Wiki and from Google to the Wiki, then information islands will start to appear and overall transparency and efficiency will then decay. The efficiency decay is not necessary felt by the interest group, but the wider community will find it harder to keep track of what is happening.

Despite a significant amount of effort and a solid first-level structure, a community issue is the continued effort required to keep information up-to-date on the Wiki. The front page of Confluence mentions the most current changes. It is clear from the activity that popular subjects, such as changing the User Experience (UX), have the full attention of a number of active writers; however, some other less popular sections of the Wiki are not updated per version of Sakai.

Confluence has other issues as well. Sometimes, it is slow to use and has multiple redundant entries. However, over time a vast amount of knowledge and wisdom has accumulated in the text. If you are logged on, you can export entries in Word or PDF format, but like most Wikis it requires work to synchronize between a local document and the Wiki entry. Confluence's built-in editor is the place where most people do their writing and the editor does not include the nice extras of a word processor, such as grammar checking. Thus, the quality of Confluence articles suffers.

You may also find some parts of the Wiki illogical; some of the information is reported in more than one place. The Foundation staff work hard to keep the top-level structure of the Wiki consistent, so that all Work Groups and projects have their own space. They also work hard to maintain the most critical documentation, such as the administrator's guide, the list of contributed tools, the production server data, and the release notes. However, there is a lot of documentation outside that scope and when community members work across a number of these spaces and migrate from one effort to another, expect inconsistencies and errors to naturally creep in.+

If you see any factual errors then you are welcome to update or comment on the Wiki page.

Google has the positive attribute of stimulating competition. When Google does something, then other big players like Microsoft try to follow. Therefore, you can expect free services that are more interesting on the Internet that in the future will channel information away from Confluence. To resist the negative impact of this trend requires a debate about best practices and a periodic look at what infrastructure supports the community's needs. Expect the Foundation to be sensitive to this and update the centrally supported infrastructure when needed.

The current wish list

Sakai is an ever-expanding masterpiece that will never be finished. It cannot be finished, as change is the only constant. The Internet is a dynamic, competitive place where new services emerge fully-grown in the collective conscious and others dissipate to vague memories. Netscape was once the king of browsers, later it was Internet Explorer. A long time ago web developers replaced sites based on static HTML with Perl CGI and later replaced Perl CGI with sites based on Web 2.0 technologies. University infrastructures more and more connect students who have telephones and laptops to course material through wireless networks. The builders of online educational services take advantage of the new to enrich their own offerings. For the Sakai community, there will always be the next piece of work—another way of delivering part of the learning experience.

 In Chapter 19, *Looking Ahead:Sakai 3*, Michael Korcuska mentions some of the planned changes for Sakai.

The current roadmap describes an aggressive date-driven development cycle. The current wish list mentioned in this section is for descriptive purposes only. What will always be valid is the need for competent managers, architects, developers and their counterparts working in Quality Assurance. There will always be room for new functionality, documentation, testing, and the creation of the definition of what is needed. If you want to do something for a large community, there is always something to do in Sakai.

There is a lot of space for you to add value to Sakai. The current roadmap details the dates when the core framework services are going to be replaced with a total top-down redesign known as Kernel 2. Ian Boston is taking the lead and his team is working at full capacity. The change from the current Kernel 1 to the planned Kernel 2 services requires human resources for developing and testing.

Less romantic is the cleanup of already-existing code. If your institute is deploying Sakai and is hitting a few issues, why not clean those issues up? The positive effects of cleaning the code up not only include an improved experience for the end user, but are also a good way to learn the inner workings of Sakai. The best approach to cleaning code is to write a patch (http://en.wikipedia.org/wiki/Patch_%28computing%29), then submit it as part of a bug report to JIRA. You should also include a description of how to trigger the bug so that once the code is patched a tester can verify that the issue has successfully been removed. At this point, the relevant branch manager will assign the testing of the patch to a responsible person.

 Being a branch manager is hard work. However, it is an advantage for an organization to donate a branch manager. The manager, through his or her work, has clear insight into the state of the code and which bugs the developers have fixed.

At the time of writing, the design of Sakai is under debate. This is a formative moment and you can influence the overall design with good arguments, ideas, and design patterns. Consistently reading the distribution groups and answering questions in areas in which you have experience takes time, but builds your knowledge up and at the same time supports others.

Internationalization is an ongoing task as the community adds or updates functionality and the associated text needs to be added or updated for each language. Currently, developers actively maintain Sakai in over ten languages: English (US, UK, AU and so on), Japanese, Korean, Dutch, Simplified Chinese, Spanish, French (France & Canada), Catalan, Swedish, Arabic, Russian, and Portuguese (Portugal & Brazil). As the number of deployments of Sakai increases, expect more languages to be supported. The Internationalization (I18N) & Localization (L10N) Work Group is a good starting point for reading up on this topic (http://confluence.sakaiproject.org/confluence/display/I18N).

Once you are a member of Confluence, you have the power to modify and update its pages. You are always welcome to add content.

Sakai is a target for evil doers and curious students. The Foundation has documented (http://bugs.sakaiproject.org/confluence/display/SEC/Security+Policy) how you can help your local organization as part of a security response process.

Tools are straightforward to write in Sakai. If you have a good idea, you are always welcome to float the idea on the Dev list and then write it.

If you would like to improve the performance of Sakai by writing stress-testing scripts, primarily Grinder (http://grinder.sourceforge.net) or JMeter, then the Performance work group needs you.

One of the daily problems for Sakai is the human cost in time of consistently testing the functionality. If you have skills that help automate functional testing, then the QA working group will welcome you very quickly indeed.

If you are good at writing high-quality course material, portfolio templates or best practices, then sharing via the opened practices site `http://openedpractices.org/` will help others refine their own practices.

The End-User Support Working Group (`http://bugs.sakaiproject.org/ confluence/display/ESUP`) is where you set links to tutorials or documentation that end users find useful during their daily work on Sakai. If after getting involved with the Distribution lists, you are looking for an opening, you are more than welcome to contact the Sakai Foundation at `http://www.sakaiproject.org/ portal/site/sakai-contactus`.

An interview with a member of the community

Who is Tom Kuipers and what is his relationship with Sakai?

> Ik ben ontwikkelaar en werk voor de Universiteit van Amsterdam. 4 jaar geleden ben ik aanraking gekomen met Sakai. Ik heb me voornamelijk bezig gehouden met de implementatie van OSP.

> I am a developer and work at the University of Amsterdam. Four years ago, I encountered Sakai. I kept myself mostly busy with the implementation of OSP.

How do you participate in the community?

> Ik probeer de mailinglijst bij te houden en hulp te bieden waar mogelijk. Verder lever ik patches voor issues die we tegenkomen. Nieuwe features die ik en mijn collega's zelf ontwikkelen koppelen we terug aan de community.

> I try to keep up with the mailing lists and help when it is needed with difficulties. Further, I make patches for issues that I come across and return to the community new features that my colleagues and I have developed.

Can you give any tips for new community members?

> Niet bang zijn om vragen te stellen op de verschillende mailinglijsten. Er is heel veel kennis, er is altijd wel iemand die je kan helpen.

> Do not be afraid to ask questions on different mailing lists. There is a lot of knowledge, and there is always someone who can help.

> Raadpleeg Confluence om meer te weten over het betreffende onderwerp.

> I would advise you to use Confluence to learn relevant subjects.

What are the strengths of the Sakai community?

> Het is een hechte community. Internationaal, maar ook regionaal actief. Verder bestaat de community niet enkel uit ontwikkelaars, maar zijn er ook 'faculty' en 'staff' actief.

> It is also a close community, international, but also regionally active. Further, the community is not only composed of developers, but local staff and members of university facilities.

Do you have more fun working with open source software?

> Ja, het mooiste is dat je invloed uit kan oefening over de richting die het product op gaat. Het is fin dat je niet alles zelf hoeft uit te vinden, maar kan terug vallen op een community van een heleboel slimme personen.

> Yes, the best is that you have influence over the direction of the product. It is nice that you do not have to discover everything for yourself. You can always fall back on a community with a large number of clever people.

Summary

A community source model governs Sakai where there is a centrally coordinated Foundation and the code is freely available to everyone.

The Sakai Foundation acts as a legal home for Sakai and supports transparent communication by building a supportive infrastructure including the bug database, the confluence Wiki, and distribution and work groups.

The community has a wide range of participants, from individuals and commercial organizations, to universities and consortiums. The universities are the main pillar of support.

The Foundation recommends that any new community members join the Announcements distribution list. This will give you an insight into current news and events.

There are many areas where you can constructively work on Sakai. These include developing, testing, documenting, discussing, and designing.

If you are not certain where you can help, you are welcome to contact the Foundation directly at `http://www.sakaiproject.org/portal/site/sakai-contactus`.

Chapter 18, *Rogues Gallery*, outlines the biographies of around 30 members of the Sakai community and is intended to give you a feeling for the strength, wealth, and vibrancy of the community's being.

18
Rogues Gallery

Sakai is a project where individuals have a large degree of influence. If you have a good idea and are prepared to spend your time discussing the details in the Distribution Groups, then you can influence change, redirect community effort, and help build a great product.

This chapter is a biographical list of some of the individuals that are influential. Due to the size of the community, it is inevitable that a number of significant contributors have been missed—for that my personal apologies. To those of you that are involved, well done and keep up the good work, without you Sakai would not be possible.

If the Sakai community were a person

If the community were a person then she would always be on time for planned events such as meetings, meals, and secret rendezvous at bars and sending in her work to her boss. She always meets her deadlines even if it means working in the weekends or late into the nights. Her friends call her Sakaigeress after a famed mythical stuffed toy (the Sakaiger) that she once received as an award for all her hard work.

Sakaigeress is fluent in many languages and is a renowned karaoke singer and chili eater. She likes to collect photos on her travels and share them through social networks with many dubious associates. She has flashes of inspiration that mean she is constantly discussing ways of changing the businesses she is involved in.

Sakaigeress is still young; however, she is growing up fast. She has travelled the world and is constantly looking for new challenges.

For more details visit `http://www.sakaiger.com`.

Sakai fellows

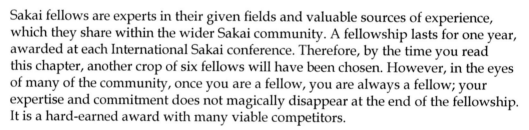

Well deserved *congratulations* to the Sakai Fellows for 2009:

Ian Boston, University of Cambridge

Jean-François Lévêque, Université Pierre et Marie Curie

Nicolaas Matthijs, University of Cambridge

Mathieu Plourde, University of Delaware

Janice Smith, Three Canoes Consulting

Steve Swinsburg, Lancaster University

Sakai fellows are experts in their given fields and valuable sources of experience, which they share within the wider Sakai community. A fellowship lasts for one year, awarded at each International Sakai conference. Therefore, by the time you read this chapter, another crop of six fellows will have been chosen. However, in the eyes of many of the community, once you are a fellow, you are always a fellow; your expertise and commitment does not magically disappear at the end of the fellowship. It is a hard-earned award with many viable competitors.

Sakai fellows fit across a broad range of categories such as developer, teacher, tester, administrator, with the boundaries blurred for most of the fellows.

Ian Boston has led the charge for greater architectural improvements and has been greatly influential in refactoring Sakai to be flexible for future needs. He has written chunks of the functionality within Sakai such as the Wiki and search functionality. It is no coincidence that he is the Chief Technical Officer (CTO) at Cambridge University, the skills and leadership he has clearly displayed with his work in Sakai are a match for such a role.

Aaron Zeckoski has supported new developers through his involvement in the programmer's café and has consistently shaped the debate on code quality. He has also written some of the core services. This author would also like to thank Aaron for his constant feedback during the writing of this book.

Stephen Marquard is not only a fellow, he has also been voted onto the board of directors of the Sakai Foundation. Many organizations voted for Stephen in part due to the respect for the knowledge he has built up supporting aggressive early adoption of new Sakai versions at the University of Cape Town.

A large proportion of the fellows mentioned have a bias towards coding and you can see their work every time you use Sakai. As Sakai is redesigned, expect this natural bias to change, as educators gain a greater community voice.

Dr Ian Boston

Ian has extensive experience in the field of highly distributed web applications. He is CTO at CARET at the University of Cambridge and for two other organizations: CBCL Ltd, a Medical Informatics Company delivering drugs information on a global scale, and Sybermedica Ltd, a Medical Diagnostics company providing telemedicine solutions on an international scale.

Prior to joining **CARET** he was CTO for an early leader in BPM and Activity-Based Workflow with customers including Bank of Scotland, New Opportunities Fund, UK Sport, UK Sports Institute, British Olympic Association, Magma Inc., British Telecom, Sema, and PwC.

Ian has been an active investor in twenty or more start-up companies in the Cambridge area over the past 15 years and sits on a number of advisory boards.

He holds a 1st Class Honours degree in Engineering and a PhD in Parallel Computing and he worked on a number of "Grand Challenge" grid problems in the 1990s.

Clay Fenlason

Clay Fenlason first became captivated by the role of technology in both communities and education while working as a volunteer in educational development in rural South Africa. There amidst schools without libraries and communities historically walled off from the world he discovered the power of the Web for leapfrogging a generation of infrastructure and lack of informational resources.

Upon returning to the States in 1999, he moved to Boston to enter a master's program in philosophy at Boston University, and he parlayed his experience doing computer modeling in gamma ray astronomy (he holds an M.S. in Astrophysics from Iowa State University) to acquire a job in the IT department—initially just for the tuition remission while he pursued his own studies. But a professional philosophical interest was once again eclipsed by a fascination with the computer as both a social tool and a medium for learning and collaboration. Late in 2003 he became the Associate Director for Academic Computing for Boston University's School of Management, and then spearheaded BU's entry into the Sakai partnership in early 2004. Since then he has been a vocal and active member of the community at a number of levels, and was named one of the inaugural Sakai fellows in May of 2006. In late 2006, Clay joined Georgia Tech as Director of Educational Technology. Throughout, his keenest interest has been in the nature and health of the organization and the community source model for higher education.

Nuno Fernandes

Nuno Fernandes is a Software Developer with eight years of Java experience. Currently working at University Fernando Pessoa, he has been involved with Sakai development and its local implementation (branded as UFPUV) since December 2005. His current responsibilities include UFPUV deployment, local QA, maintenance, support, localization, internal services integration, bug fixes, and implementation of new features and tools. Recent work with Sakai involves Java, Spring, Hibernate, JSF, Velocity, Apache Wicket, HTML, CSS, and JavaScript technologies.

In June 2008, he was awarded Sakai Fellow 2008 at the 9th Sakai Conference in Paris, an international acknowledgement of the quality of his contributions to the Sakai community.

He was previously a co-founder of BlueSpan, a software/hardware R&D company, and Software Developer at Multiwave, a fiber-optic R&D company, developing Eclipse RCP desktop applications for telecommunication device management and interoperability.

Steven Githens

Steve grew up in the Upper Peninsula of Michigan and since discovering the Open Source Movement in his freshmen year of college has been very passionate about creating a full stack of free software for education. He started hacking Sakai while working in a basement teaching lab in the Chemistry Department at Northwestern University, and has continued work on Sakai at the University of Cambridge, Indiana University, and other interesting places.

While primarily a Vim user, Steve hopes to someday finally get a grasp on Emacs. In his free time, he enjoys running, playing mandolin, progressive social activism, programming in Python, and tinkering with JVM languages other than Java.

David Howitz

David Horwitz has over ten years of experience in developing educational technology solutions for residential university courses. From his previous existence as a maritime archaeologist, David has cultivated an interest in integrating appropriate educational technology, both within the curriculum and with other university systems. In his spare time, he restores his Victorian house and studies traditional Okinawa karate.

Beth Kirschner

Beth Kirschner has over twenty years of experience in software development of online collaboration systems, grid computing, digital libraries, automation. For the past few years, she has been involved with the Sakai project's localization, ePortfolio, and research-oriented collaboration efforts. She was first introduced to Sakai when developing a collaboration portal for a grid computing project at the University of Michigan. In 2008, Beth was recognized as a Sakai Fellow.

Prior to working at the university, Beth worked mostly in embedded systems programming, as a manager of a systems software group developing proprietary hardware/software machine vision systems. Previous to that, she managed a group for an industrial control system used for final verification in the assembly of automotive engines and transmissions. In her spare moments, Beth will take any excuse to go flying in her Piper Archer airplane.

Dr. Maggie McVay Lynch

Dr. Maggie McVay Lynch has worked developing online instruction for the past two decades. She has developed over 150 online courses for colleges, universities, and private industry. Her university teaching includes both traditional and online courses in counseling, education, business Administration, and management information systems. She has also published widely, including four textbooks on e-learning. Lynch has served in e-learning management positions at three universities, most recently as the Director of Statewide Teaching and Learning Services for the Oregon Health and Sciences University School of Nursing, where she provides strategic direction and support for administrators, faculty, and students engaged in both classroom-based instruction and e-learning. She also teaches in the Master's in Nursing Education program at OHSU, and has created an e-learning certificate program in Education at Portland State University.

Lynch has been a part of the Sakai pedagogical effort since 2001, and has been a regular presenter at conferences around issues of Sakai implementation, faculty development, and pedagogical improvements to the Sakai. In 2007 she was named a Sakai Fellow, the first pedagogically-focused fellow in the history of the award.

Stephen Marquard

Stephen is responsible for co-coordinating the portfolio of learning technologies. These include a next-generation environment built on the Sakai framework, and other software and hardware technologies that support teaching and learning processes at the University of Cape Town. Stephen also pursues interests in online collaboration, open source software, and learning theory. He is currently a member of the board of directors of the Sakai Foundation.

Seth Theriault

Seth Theriault works on research, teaching, and learning systems at Columbia University and was named a Sakai Fellow in 2006. He has worked on the Kerberos provider, runs a Sakai Community QA server, and has contributed code for the Schedule tool's iCalendar import capability.

Zach A Thomas

Zach Thomas is a software engineer who has contributed to Sakai since its first public release in June of 2004. He is a Sakai Fellow, speaks at conferences on topics of Sakai adoption, and runs a Sakai consulting business called Aeroplane Software (http://aeroplanesoftware.com). In a previous life, he co-founded a modestly famous folk punk rock band called Okkervil River. He lives in San Marcos, Texas, with his wife and two little boys.

Aaron Zeckoski

Aaron Zeckoski is a Senior Research Engineer in CARET (Centre for Applied Research in Educational Technologies) at Cambridge University. He has been involved in many aspects of system development over the past six years including analysis, design, implementation, QA, deployment, and support. His current responsibilities include project analysis, system design, and system implementation for web application development. Recent work involves Java, Spring, Hibernate, RSF (Reasonable Server Faces), PHP, and Sakai.

He was previously the Manager of Application Development and Lead Developer in the Learning Technologies unit at Virginia Tech for five years.

Foundation members

There is a small team of dedicated staff belonging to the Foundation. The staff has to work efficiently and diplomatically with a wide range of interesting characters within the community. Staff roles include Project Coordinator, Community Liaison, Director of QA, and Administrative Coordinator.

Michael Korcuska

Michael Korcuska is the Executive Director of the Sakai Foundation and has nearly 20 years of experience in technology-enabled education and training. Prior to joining Sakai, Michael served as Chief Operating Officer for ELT, Inc., a leading compliance training provider. He has also held leadership positions at DigitalThink (now Convergys Learning Solutions) and Cognitive Arts, an award winning custom e-learning developer.

Michael got his start in technology-based learning at Stanford University's Courseware Authoring Tools Lab and Apple Computer's Multimedia Lab in the late 1980s. He holds an M.S. in Computer Science from Northwestern University (where he studied and worked at the Institute for the Learning Sciences) and B.S. in Symbolic Systems from Stanford University. He lives in Berkeley, California, with his wife and two children.

Peter Knoop

Peter Knoop is based at the University of Michigan. Peter has been involved with Sakai since its inception and collaborated on several of its predecessors, including CHEF, WorkTools, NEESgrid, and UARC/SPARC. In addition to his Sakai duties, he also teaches digital field mapping at the University of Michigan's Rocky Mountain Field Station during the summer, and maintains an active research role in technology in non-traditional classroom settings as the co-principle investigator of the GeoPad/GeoPocket projects and in Cenozoic paleoceanography and marine geochemistry.

Mary Miles

Mary provides support to the Sakai community and the Sakai Foundation Board of Directors and is the meeting planner for the Sakai Conferences. Mary has been with the University of Michigan for 9 years. She also serves as the Secretary to the Sakai Board. Prior to joining the Sakai Foundation, she worked for the Millennium Project, Michigan Virtual Automotive College, the National Center for Manufacturing Sciences, and St. Joseph Mercy Hospital. She holds a B.S. from Eastern Michigan University and has a strong background in meeting planning and other administrative responsibilities.

Pete Peterson

Pete has worked for the University of California, Davis, for the last 20 years. During his tenure there, he has worn many hats including support coordinator, technology trainer, and web designer. Pete sometimes refers to himself as a "4 Star Generalist". For the last several years, Pete has been deeply involved with the Sakai support, development, and implementation efforts at UC Davis where he served initially as the Tier 2 Support Coordinator and later as the QA Manager. Pete's diverse background provides him with both a programmer's and a user's perspective to the Sakai application development process.

Pete brings much knowledge, experience, and enthusiasm to his new role as the QA Director for the Sakai Foundation. As the Sakai QA Director, Pete's primary duty is to ensure that Sakai software exceeds industry norms for defects, reliability, and scalability as well as to coordinate the QA efforts of the Sakai community and staff.

Anthony Whyte

Anthony is the Community/Technical liaison for the Sakai Foundation and a Senior Applications Programmer/Analyst at the University of Michigan. Anthony is currently involved in release management, tool development, site administration, community relations, and advocacy. Prior to joining the Sakai Foundation, Anthony served as a developer, lead developer, and ultimately Director of Systems for Strategic Interactive and Novations Learning Technologies, where he helped design, build, and implement commercial learning management systems for Fortune 100 companies. A Fulbright scholar, Anthony was educated at Michigan State University and Princeton University. He is an avid cyclist and woodworker.

Developers

There are over 50 core developers committing code in any given month. People are working very hard on improving Sakai. Historically, many of the Sakai Fellows were developers; expect more to become so in the future.

Nicolaas Matthijs

Nicolaas has been involved with learning environments for some time, and first came to the University of Cambridge as a summer student. CARET's director, John Norman, asked him to do some "cool stuff" — like a FaceBook application for CamTools — and since then Nicolaas has been at the forefront of CARET's innovative user interface work, developing new things at a prodigious rate, and sharing what he has built with the wider community. He is now the lead developer at CARET for CamTools and Sakai user interfaces.

Nicolaas co-developed the new user interface for CamTools 2008, and after presenting his work at the Paris Sakai Conference in July 2008, has been leading development on the next generation interfaces for Sakai 3. As well as doing development himself, Nicolaas has been working on the vision for Sakai 3 and leading five developers around the world in frontend development for this exciting new system.

Working with Sakai is hugely rewarding for Nicolaas, and he enjoys engaging with such a bright community of people, who are open to changes and improvements.

Ray Davis

Since 1984, Ray Davis's jobs have included real-time EEG analysis and imaging, corporate consulting in Manhattan, operating system I/O libraries, visual authoring systems for games and interactive simulations, P2P clients, many web applications, a book on web publishing, and even a bit of teaching. He currently works for the University of California at Berkeley and contributes to the open source Sakai and Fluid projects.

Outside software engineering, he has published critical essays and short fiction in a number of venues, has more-or-less maintained a more-or-less literary blog since 1999, and produces online editions of others' writing at `http://www.pseudopodium.org/repress`.

Quality assurers

Vigorous, centrally-coordinated Quality Assurance is a crucial process that ensures a positive end-user experience. There are many community members busy with testing Sakai to find the bugs before you do.

Jean-François

Jean-François Lévêque is solely responsible for almost the whole of Sakai running at the Université Pierre et Marie Curie (UPMC). He has been able to slowly hand over documentation, training, and system administration, but still has to oversee support and localization efforts.

Jean-François has over ten years of experience covering database administration and design, software engineering, web hosting, network administration, and system administration. He has been working as a Software Engineer for six years at UPMC and has been involved in e-learning from the beginning. He likes to make things easier and deal with problems, from the smallest to the largest. He does his best to keep a balance between a sound mind and a sound body, enjoying the companionship of others from storytelling to climbing.

Jean-François has much experience with Sakai. He first heard about Sakai in 2004. He started to try it out in 2006 when the 2.2 release with the Canadian French locale was expected. He finally booted a production instance in September 2007 with the newest version of Sakai. He has contributed to the enhancement of processes for quality assurance, internationalization and localization, maintenance branch management, and release management.

Megan May

Megan is currently the quality assurance team lead/project planning coordinator of the local development team working on Sakai within University Information Technology Services (UITS) at Indiana University. Prior to this position she was the Quality Assurance (QA) Director for the Sakai Foundation from January 2006 to November 2008. Over the years, Megan has been responsible for tier-2 support, communication, coordination, data analysis, design, documentation, and directing the testing and shepherding implementation effort of IU's migration from the legacy CMS to Sakai. Megan earned her B.S. in Business from IU's Kelley School of Business with concentrations in information systems, operations management, and process management.

The rest

Consultants, driven leadership, inspirational ex-Foundation directors, hardworking newsletter editors — this section highlights them all.

Chris Coppola

Chris Coppola is a founder and the CEO of rSmart, a company that supports open source business applications for colleges, universities, schools, and districts globally. He is responsible for rSmart's open source community strategy and leads the rSmart team as they engage and support open source projects that offer great potential for global education. Working with leaders from Indiana University, Stanford, Cambridge, and other institutions, Chris and rSmart are helping to build a rapidly evolving ecosystem of open source software in the Education sector.

Chris recently completed a three-year term on the Sakai Foundation board of directors and is now serving on three Kuali Foundation boards. He writes and speaks frequently about open source and education.

Blog: http://coppola.rsmart.com/

John Leasia

John Leasia is currently the Director of the CTools Implementation Group at the University of Michigan. CTools is based on Sakai, and has evolved from the pre-Sakai CHEF days running four or five pilot classes, to a system now serving over 5000 classes per term on two campuses, with over 40,000 active users. John has been involved with Sakai planning from the beginning and continues to take an active role in the Sakai community, participating in the various email groups and planning groups. At the University of Michigan, John coordinates the integration of Sakai with the UM environment, and works with educators to tailor and configure Sakai to fit their needs.

John Norman

John is the Director of the Centre for Applied Research in Educational Technologies and "Head of e-Learning" at the University of Cambridge. CARET provides infrastructure and support to the campus for the use of technology in teaching, learning, and research, including the deployment of Sakai campus-wide. Prior to this he had experience as an engineer and medical devices entrepreneur on three continents. John chairs the advisory board for OSS-Watch and is an advocate for open standards and open source software in higher education. He is the current chair of the Sakai Board.

Mark Norton

Mark Norton is an independent consultant in the field of technology-based learning in higher education environments. He has participated as an architect and developer in the Sakai project since its inception, participating in and contributing to a variety of Sakai-related projects. Mark served as the Chairman of the Sakai Requirements Working Group in 2007 and served as Technical Liaison to the Sakai Educational Partnership Program in the early days of Sakai. He has been a contributor to the Open Knowledge Initiative providing technical feedback and guidance to the Open Service Interface Definitions (OSIDs). Mark was the Director of Specification Development at the IMS Global Learning Consortium and coordinated the development of several key industry standards including Simple Sequencing, Learning Design, and Digital Repositories. As chairman of the IMS Accessibility Group, he led the development of several specifications on support for accessibility in educational technology. He was a founding architect at TechOnLine (custom Internet architectures), and Avid Technology (digital video editing systems). Mark Norton has an MSCS from Boston University.

Charles Severance

Charles is currently a Clinical Assistant Professor in the School of Information at the University of Michigan. Charles also works with the IMS Global Learning Consortium as the IMS Developer Network Coordinator. Previously, he was the Executive Director of the Sakai Foundation and the Chief Architect of the Sakai project.

Charles is the Author of the book *High Performance Computing*, Second Edition, published by O'Reilly and Associates. Charles has a background in standards including serving as the vice-chair for the IEEE Posix P1003 standards effort and edited the Standards Column in *IEEE Computer Magazine* from 1995-1999.

Charles is currently teaching in the University of Michigan School of Information. Charles has also taught in Computer Science at the University of Michigan and Michigan State University.

Charles is active in television and radio as a hobby; he has co-hosted several television shows including "Nothin but Net" produced by MediaOne and a nationally televised program called Internet:TCI. Charles appeared for over 10 years as an expert on Internet and Technology on a call-in radio program on the local Public Radio affiliate (www.wkar.org).

Chuck's hobbies include off-road motorcycle riding, karaoke, and playing hockey.

Charles has a B.S., M.S., and Ph.D. in Computer Science from Michigan State University.

Margaret Wagner

Margaret Wagner is a senior technical writer at the University of Michigan. She has been involved with the Sakai project since its earliest predecessors, UM.CourseTools, UM.WorkTools, and CHEF, were developed, and she wrote the original help guides for these applications. Margaret is also the editor of the Sakai Newsletter, which is received by members of the Sakai Community around the world every two weeks.

Margaret attended Whitman College, University of Colorado, and University of Michigan, where she studied linguistics and piano performance.

19
Looking Ahead: Sakai 3

Sakai has been an extremely successful open source project as evidenced by the many top universities around the world installing it as their primary course management and academic collaboration system. Since the inception of the Sakai project in 2004, the Internet itself has changed dramatically with the popularization of so-called "Web 2.0" technologies and the explosion of social networking. The organizations and the individuals who work on Sakai are natural innovators. They experiment with cutting-edge technology and are continually thinking about how to apply it at their institution. The changes in Internet technology and their own experiences with these technologies have led a group of organizations to begin to think about what a next generation of Sakai might look like.

Indeed, the initial ideas are for a system that would look significantly different from the current Sakai. The most significant driver for a new version of Sakai is the recognition that the traditional role of Course Management Systems and ePortfolios is rapidly changing. There is broad recognition that the current platforms, including Sakai, need to evolve substantially to meet the long-term needs of users and institutions. Additional drivers of changes to Sakai include:

- Sakai end users, increasing familiar with "Web 2.0" technology, are demanding an environment that is extremely flexible and affords them substantial control.

- Uses of Sakai in research and administrative collaboration have proven extremely valuable and these users have demands that weren't envisioned when Sakai was started.

- The emergence of new standards and open source projects that Sakai can leverage and integrate with.

- The popularity and maturation of new models of web development that leverage client-side technology, significantly improving productivity and lowering the bar for meaningful contributions.

- Service Oriented Architecture has emerged as a design and deployment preference for institutional systems, again allowing integration opportunities that were previously unavailable.

At the same time, the Sakai community has also learned a great deal. Increased adoption has revealed the breadth and complexity of use cases. It has become increasingly clear that portions of the code would benefit from a substantial rewrite that lowers maintenance costs while retaining flexibility to meet local needs. The limitations of the "site" as the organizing principle of Sakai are increasingly felt as institutions use Sakai in more contexts and across many years. Areas of production stress in the code and database have been identified and substantially improved, but we are reaching the point of diminishing returns with the current architecture. Sakai's SOA implementation has proven extremely valuable in practice, and yet could be improved to adhere to current standards and make it maximally compatible with new projects like Kuali. And, finally, the relative scarcity of Java developers on campus makes it imperative to open the Sakai platform to a broader group of developers. This will also have great benefits for sustainability and the long-term health of the project.

Sakai 3 goals

The ambition for the next generation of Sakai, which we are calling Sakai 3, is not merely an incremental improvement of the current Sakai. Nor is it to copy Google applications, although we do take inspiration from their work. Similarly, our goal is not to create a better and cheaper version of Blackboard, the most popular commercial courseware management system. We should, in short, strive to create a different type of academic collaboration system. Institutions that choose Sakai 3 will be choosing to run a qualitatively different type of system. This is the kind choice we should provide to the educational community, not just a choice between open source and proprietary or between Java and PHP.

For all of these reasons, a group of institutions, led by the University of Cambridge, Georgia Institute of Technology and University of California at Davis and including Indiana University, University of Michigan and University of California at Berkeley, have begun to develop a vision and preliminary technology for a next generation Sakai. This Sakai will be based on a new set of core Sakai services (the *kernel*) that leverages best-of-breed open source technologies (for example. Jackrabbit, Shindig, and Google Guice) to enable development resources to focus on what is truly special about academic collaboration. It will showcase a new, user-centered interface that is both easy and enjoyable to use. And it will include new capabilities, like social networking and flexible content authoring, that today's users expect from a web application.

This core group has begun to make progress. The beginnings of a new kernel have emerged. Design work has started on a new user interface (see the figure next). New concepts for many aspects of Sakai are being discussed and analyzed. While many areas need further conceptual and technical work, the path forward is increasingly clear and achievable. The remainder of this chapter provides more detail on the proposed approach. By publication time, a prototype should be available at `http://3akai.sakaiproject.org`. We expect the transition of the community from Sakai 2 to Sakai 3 to take several years, with the Sakai 2 code base continuing to be supported through at least 2013.

Sakai 3 for users

There are a number of changes envisioned in the Sakai 3.0 user experience. From a look and feel perspective, the current design effort is already pointing the way to a more responsive, flexible, widget-based user experience. This work is resulting in significant improvements to the user experience, improvements that are critically important but by no means sufficient. Beyond this usability work, there are important conceptual changes that need to be made and many of these changes require a change to the core Sakai architecture. We highlight a few of these changes here: Moving beyond sites, Breaking tool silos, Social networking, and Content creation and organization.

Moving beyond sites

Sites are the primary organizing principle of today's Sakai. Site context is a deep and rigid assumption for nearly all functionality, and it stands in the way of activities that might extend across sites or operate independently of them. The notion of a group in Sakai stands as a particularly strong example of unnecessary site dependence. In Sakai 2, groups only exist within a site. If you want to address a particular group of individuals, they need to all be members of a single site. If the same group needs access to multiple sites then that group needs to be recreated. In Sakai 3, groups are treated as first class citizens. Users will be capable of managing groups independent of sites. They can create groups, referencing an external system as needed (for example, an SIS-like Banner perhaps through the IMS Enterprise Specification or via a more generic LDAP provider), and later worry about what that group has access to.

This line of thinking will be applied to other items in Sakai, including Users and Content (and Tags and Permissions). Content is another excellent example where the primacy of the site is more tyranny than convenience. While content can be made public, it exists inside a particular site context. Moving content between sites or referencing content from another site is cumbersome and unnatural. In Sakai 3, content will be a first class citizen as well. Content owners can organize content in a variety of ways and make it available to various users, groups, and sites as they see fit. Instead of the site's content, we will think about the user's content or a group's content, both content they own and content they have access to.

Breaking the tool silos

Tools are another important target for rethinking as part of building Sakai 3. Sakai's "tool silos" are well recognized as often creating unnecessary steps for users. A good example is an instructor who wants put an assignment into his or her syllabus for students to post something to the discussion forum. This interaction requires both instructor and students to visit four tools: Syllabus, Assignments, Forums, and Gradebook. Ideally, this type of interaction should be easy to complete without so much navigational overhead. For example, clicking the name of the assignment as it is listed in the syllabus could open a form for submitting a discussion post.

While more intuitive "cross tool" interactions are more and more common in Sakai 2, the underlying architecture and original technologies make this difficult at best. Sakai 3 will be constructed around smaller units of capability (in the form of true SOA services) that can be quickly stitched together to provide intuitive workflows. We need to think of the relevant items in Sakai (from discussion posts to assignment submissions to test questions to portfolio reflections) and the activities relevant to those items. These items and activities will surface in many different places depending on the context. Sakai 3 should respect the context and present the workflows that make sense inside them.

Social networking

Academic research and teaching are sometimes solitary experiences, but increasingly they are becoming collaborative endeavors. There is a trend towards greater openness in university teaching, and group activity often enhances learning. The emergence of 'Social Networking' web sites such as Facebook, LinkedIn, and MySpace has created a new standard of convenience for creating online spaces that can be used to collaborate in small groups and to present profile information to peers. Innovative features such as 'activity feeds' are proving addictive in sustaining online engagement and there is increasing openness of the social networking platforms through the Facebook APIs or the OpenSocial APIs promoted by Google that is being adopted by almost all social networking sites.

However, many social networking sites require the member to grant the site owner liberal licenses covering the member's work, thus limiting the security with which confidential research or teaching can be carried out on such platforms. Moreover, the interfaces and facilities of such sites are not well adapted to academic purposes (for example, LinkedIn profiles do not readily display publication lists).

The incorporation of Social Networking into Sakai, using the Apache Shindig project, will enable new models of interaction among users of the Collaboration and Learning Environment, in a manner suitable for academic work, but will also facilitate collaboration among Sakai institutions in which the members of a network at a trusted partner institution can be given access to the network(s) of a Sakai-adopting school for research, learning, and the formation of peer groups of many kinds. While we do not know exactly what direction this work will take, we believe it is critical that universities play a leading role in the development of social networking technology on campus.

Content creation and organization

Creating content is a lot of what academic work is about. Instructors create syllabi for their students. Students, working alone or in groups, complete homework assignments for submission to the instructor. Research groups share and elaborate ideas in Wikis and other collaborative writing software. Administrators write policy and procedure documents, and so on. In the meantime, web-based collaborative authoring tools like Google Docs/Sites/Groups have increased expectations about what is possible online.

Sakai 3 recognizes that content creation and organization is a primary activity of Sakai users, whether they are instructors or students or researchers or staff. Providing simple template-based authoring and flexible tools for organizing and presenting content will be a primary focus of Sakai 3. On the technology side, we will leverage industry standards (JCR) and open source technologies (Apache Jackrabbit) to support content storage. This will provide a significant improvement in capability (for example, versioning) and reduce the amount of code the Sakai community needs to support. And, of course, we are not talking about creating our own HTML editor. There are a few capable open source tools we can lean on for this purpose, the current leading candidate being TinyMCE because of its flexibility, extensibility, and focus on accessibility.

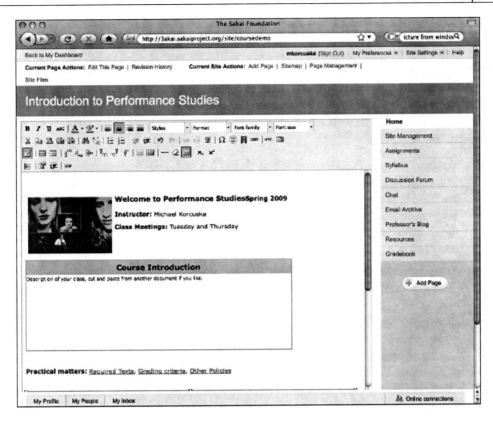

Finally, Sakai 3 recognizes that many things should be treated as content. Discussion forum and blog posts, assignment submissions, user profile information, and online test answers could all be usefully regarded as pieces of content. Taking an "everything is content" approach to Sakai 3 will allow much more flexibility in searching, organizing, tagging, and otherwise manipulating items in Sakai.

Sakai 3 for technologists

We have learned a great deal in the last several years and, at the same time, new technologies and techniques have emerged. Armed with the insight gained from the current experience, we are in an excellent position to establish backing technologies that both improve the product and reduce the maintenance burden on the community. The resulting Sakai 3 will deliver a variety of technical benefits, including the following:

- **Scalability and Resilience:** While Sakai has achieved impressive levels of scalability already with installations of over 200,000 users, achieving good performance at this scale has required a significant investment. With the knowledge we've gained about Sakai usage patterns and the inclusion of new "Internet scale" open-source technologies, Sakai 3 will both achieve new levels of scalability and make it simpler to run a smaller installation.

- **Developer Focus & Ease of Use:** Recent community efforts in client-side development have underscored just much more efficient Sakai development can be. Sakai 3 services will provide JSON data feeds allowing JavaScript developers to create user interfaces and, if desired, generally function independently of Java developers. This also frees Java developers to spend less time on user interface rendering and focus on the scalability and quality of the core services. The overall increase in the number of developers qualified to work on Sakai and the improvement in individual productivity should improve the rate at which feature development can occur.

- **Code Quality and Maintainability:** The maturity of other open source projects now allows us to consider swapping out whole regions of Sakai services with third-party code. By judicious incorporation of such services our overall quality can be improved, our APIs can be made more standard, and our maintenance burdens and risks lightened.

- **Installation and Maintenance:** Sakai can be difficult to deploy for staff that do not have sufficient experience with Java applications. A smaller, tighter kernel and a mechanism for easily adding/removing tools will allow new Sakai users, implementers, and developers have a more positive and productive initial experience. This is important to the growth and overall health of the community. A more efficient, easier to maintain installation has many benefits, most notably that staff can spend more time on innovation.

Interview with Sakai 3 chief architect

The following is an interview with Ian Boston, Chief Technology officer of the Centre for Applied Research in Educational Technologies at the University of Cambridge (CARET). Ian holds a first degree in Engineering and a PhD in parallel computing. As CTO at CARET, Ian has been deeply involved with Sakai, as well as other community source projects such as Kuali Student. He is leading development of the new kernel (K2) for Sakai 3. Ian was awarded one of the first Sakai Fellowships, and speaks regularly at open source conferences and events around the world.

In this interview, we ask him about his perspective on the evolution of Sakai.

Who are you and what is your role within the Sakai community?

> I became involved in Sakai at the start due to a research project at the University of Cambridge that needed to extend the capabilities of Sakai. Since then I have become more involved dealing with the build systems, performance, and optimization of content hosting, kernel1 and kernel2 work. I try to help lead the technical roadmap in these areas, but there are many stakeholders and we are an unusual community.

What does CARET bring into the Sakai community?

> CARET is leading research into the application of educational technologies at the University of Cambridge; one such technology is Sakai. The members of the University are harsh judges of almost everything, and expose cracks wherever there is weakness. Consequently, our campus drives us to improve the systems we have and offer more. This means that CARET is often at the bleeding edge of development and production in the Sakai Community, testing out multiple avenues down potential roadmap directions. Our struggle is to listen to the stockholders and take directions that the community will follow.

Can you give a little history behind the Kernel 1 and 2 efforts?

It became clear in the 2.3, 2.4, and 2.5 releases that the cost of development working in Sakai was sapping resources away from the production teams, QA teams for the release, and developers. If this trend continued, we would stagnate as a community and be unable to deliver any innovation. The development community started Kernel 1 as an effort to localize the core components of Sakai, and ensure a more robust and stable core for Sakai 2.6. Kernel 2 continues this effort but will radically alter the way in which Sakai works to embrace many of the concepts within initiatives like OpenSocial (`http://code.google.com/apis/opensocial`) and Cloud Computing.

How do you see Sakai evolving in the future?

While the progress of the Web accelerates and engages with new user experiences, applications that live in the Web, they either adapt or over time become extinct. Sakai operates within this environment. Many of its users come from a base that is constantly being refreshed with a generation that grew up with no knowledge of a time before "online".

- The development methodologies and the environment that those methodologies target are changing. Sakai 3 with Kernel 2 is adapting to capitalize on the opportunities. Online communities are becoming the size of nation states. MySpace has a population ranking fifth in the world, and the volume of transactions through eBay is greater than a basket of EU countries. These are communities focused on the expectations and needs of the user as a human being. Where radio took 38 years to reach a target audience of 50 million people, Facebook took less than a year. Proprietary silos typified phase one of this evolution. As with all ideas that take a hold, proprietary silos are overtaken by standards efforts. As I write, OpenSocial is nearing its first birthday, there is the realization that human beings are the users of the third generation of the Web, and that Web is a social organism. Those human beings interact with many systems, each system vying for their attention. The light shone by OpenSocial is that these applications can agree on how to support the human beings in their desire to form relationships and interact with one another.

- Strangely ignored by the rise of the social web is academia. At all levels, teaching, learning, and research are fundamentally driven by the desire to form relationships, establish trust, and communicate. In kindergarten, the kids look up to their teacher. They come home and tell their parents about the wonderful things they are being taught. Their parents close the circle communicating with the teachers. Within the rose-tinted world, the relationships have context and attributes. In higher academia, researchers build relationships with peers. Their progression is supported by the weight of acclaim, which drives their desire to generate output.

- Sakai 3 and Kernel 2 are adapting to become a first-class player in this world. We are designing a user experience in which Sakai focuses on the user as a human being. Early prototypes of this work are in production at the University of Cambridge as our local deployment of Sakai. The work of Sakai 3 is going much further than this, making Sakai a native of the Web, as ubiquitous as GMail and Google Apps. Under the covers, Kernel 2 focuses on cloud-like storage meeting the needs of the user. We are embedding OpenSocial into the core and enhancing it to make it capable of supporting the rich ecosystem of relationships within academia. We are adding OAuth (`http://oauth.net`) and other open standards that will make every Sakai installation a part of the Web. This adaption is part of our evolution.

Summary

In summary, the Sakai 3 effort is designed to bring a number of benefits to campuses around the world, including:

- Increased user satisfaction—A more fluid and flexible Sakai, one that is both pleasurable and efficient to work with, will allow users to focus energy on improving the quality of their work.

- Improved stability & quality—In addition to the obvious user satisfaction that comes with stability and quality, your campus IT and support staff will have more time for other activities.

- Increased scalability—The ability to support more users per application server will reduce the overall cost of ownership of Sakai and can let your organization serve additional customers (for example, a local school district) that might previously have been too expensive to consider.

- Fewer local customizations—As an open source product, customizing Sakai for your local needs should continue to be one of the main benefits of using Sakai. By ensuring that more use cases are covered "out of the box", however, your local customizations can really focus on what is unique to your organization.

- Simpler integration—Sakai already has a reputation for being an excellent application to integrate with other campus systems. By building on and improving Sakai's service-orientated architecture, these benefits will continue to accrue as more campus systems support SOA.

- Ease of development—Allowing a wider variety of developers to contribute to Sakai creates a wonderful virtuous circle. More participants can help the project and existing contributors will be more efficient. This means more staff time for local customizations and, more importantly, innovation.

All of these add up to a lower total cost of ownership and better value for the investment you make in Sakai. What your campus chooses to do with the additional resources—spend them on other project or increase the amount of innovation in the development and use of Sakai—is up to you.

Endwords

I'm writing these final words at a time of continued consolidation in the marketplace for courseware management systems. Just this week, in fact, Blackboard announced its intention to acquire Angel Learning. This acquisition comes three years after Blackboard acquired WebCT, at the time its largest rival. As is common in such circumstances, many WebCT customers were unhappy with the changes the merger inevitably brought with it and this merger is likely to be no different. At the same time the patent battle between Blackboard and Desire2Learn shows no signs of abating. While we believe Blackboard's patent is without merit, the continued legal cloud has frightened some institutions away from considering Desire2Learn as an alternative.

The result of this industry consolidation and the various legal actions is that the choice of commercial software platforms for teaching, learning, and academic collaboration has been severely curtailed. If it weren't for the open source software alternatives, most notably Sakai and Moodle, customers in Higher Education would really have very little choice about where to go for their courseware management software. In our view this would be an extremely negative development for education in general and higher education in particular. Robust competition drives companies to innovate and keeps the resulting solutions affordable.

If you've made it to this point you're undoubtedly familiar with installing, configuring, and using Sakai. You've seen that Sakai comes with a great deal of flexibility, giving each organization and each user a great deal of choice. This isn't an accident. The entire Sakai effort was created in order to provide more choice to the user, the organization, and the industry in general. This philosophy permeates all aspects of the software and the project, from how Sakai actually functions to the ways that members of the community can contribute. This emphasis on choice is one reason participants in the Sakai community often react negatively to events — like the patent lawsuits or industry mergers — that threaten to reduce the amount of choice their organizations have. As important as choice and competition are to any industry, there are two other reasons — more important reasons in our view — that Sakai is a critical open source effort in education.

The first reason of these additional reasons relates directly to one of the core missions of schools and universities around the world — teaching and learning. It is critical for organizations to invest in research and development in those areas that are core competencies. If they do not make these investments they will eventually be left behind by others that do. While schools, colleges and universities have other core missions, teaching and learning technology is one area of IT we cannot entirely hand over to commercial vendors. Some investment must be made directly by the educational institutions themselves.

Participating in Sakai isn't the only way to make an investment in innovation in teaching and learning, of course, but it is one excellent way to do so. Whether you're a faculty member or instructional designer who is helping articulate use cases or requirements from your institution, a user experience designer working on wireframes for a new set of features, or a software developer figuring out how to implement the user requirements in a secure, scalable, and reliable manner, you will find a community of expert practitioners in Sakai that will challenge you to see issues from a fresh perspective and help you find creative solutions. Innovation in Sakai is driven by people who work on campuses around the world, people who sit next to the end users on a daily basis. This is the reason that Sakai works so well today and why it will be even better tomorrow.

The final reason we believe Sakai is important is because, as a community-driven open source software project, it embodies the value of openness in education. Education is one of those domains where it is important, critical even, to provide the highest quality to the highest number of people. Quality education is not something that should be reserved for the privileged few and open software and open content are key components to realizing the full potential of education worldwide. The following excerpt from The Cape Town Declaration on Open Education articulates this extremely well:

We are on the cusp of a global revolution in teaching and learning. Educators worldwide are developing a vast pool of educational resources on the Internet, open and free for all to use. These educators are creating a world where each and every person on earth can access and contribute to the sum of all human knowledge. They are also planting the seeds of a new pedagogy where educators and learners create, shape and evolve knowledge together, deepening their skills and understanding as they go.

This emerging open education movement combines the established tradition of sharing good ideas with fellow educators and the collaborative, interactive culture of the Internet. It is built on the belief that everyone should have the freedom to use, customize, improve and redistribute educational resources without constraint. Educators, learners and others who share this belief are gathering together as part of a worldwide effort to make education both more accessible and more effective.

The expanding global collection of open educational resources has created fertile ground for this effort. These resources include openly licensed course materials, lesson plans, textbooks, games, software and other materials that support teaching and learning. They contribute to making education more accessible, especially where money for learning materials is scarce. They also nourish the kind of participatory culture of learning, creating, sharing and cooperation that rapidly changing knowledge societies need...

These strategies represent more than just the right thing to do. They constitute a wise investment in teaching and learning for the 21st century. They will make it possible to redirect funds from expensive textbooks towards better learning. They will help teachers excel in their work and provide new opportunities for visibility and global impact. They will accelerate innovation in teaching. They will give more control over learning to the learners themselves. These are strategies that make sense for everyone.

It is worth reading the entire declaration, which you can find at http://www.capetowndeclaration.org. This declaration has been signed by thousands of individuals and hundreds of organizations around the world, including the Sakai Foundation. We encourage you to read and sign it yourself.

Sakai is open source and free of charge. This means that ideas can come from anywhere and can be distributed everywhere. While it takes money and skill to operate any enterprise software platform, license fees are not be a barrier to having a feature available. There is no "platinum edition" of Sakai that only wealthy institutions can have. Sakai is also open to contribution for anyone with the skill and time to participate. This means that the software can meet even unusual requirements, requirements that might not make "commercial sense" to include in a proprietary product.

So, for all of these reasons, we are extremely gratified that you've purchased and taken the time to read this book. The author's royalties will be directed to the Sakai Foundation and that will help advance the effort. Your participation in Sakai is far more important than any royalties. So please do get involved. Read the lists. File a bug report or feature request. Write some code. Attend a conference. We hope to see you around!

A
Glossary

Sakai is a place where teaching practice, technologies, architectural structures, development frameworks, and hardware maintenance intersect. This soap of relationships leads to a rich set of concepts and an overflow of terminology. This glossary defines some of that glorious richness.

Admin user: The admin user is a user within Sakai who has all the online administrative rights needed to maintain a running instance.

In the demonstration version, a user with the name **admin** is automatically added as a member of every new site.

Aggregation: The creation of a web page out of parts. Within the Sakai framework, there can be different aggregators for different views of the same information.

API (Application Programmers Interface): An API is an agreed-upon set of functions and method calls that programmers can use to build parts of an application.

Architectural best practices: Commonly-used practices for designing applications.

Authentication: The ability to prove that someone (or something) is who they say they are. You authenticate by logging on to Sakai.

3akai: The next version of Sakai created in parallel to version 2. 3akai is a radical rethink and update.

CAS (Central Authentication Service): An example of a server that provides authentication services.

See: Authentication

Collab: A Sakai server (`https://collab.sakaiproject.org/portal`) where , you can become a member of specific discussion groups, such as the development or end user lists, by creating an account and joining specific sites.

See: Discussion Group

Collaboration and Learning Environment (CLE): An online place of learning that supports ad hoc collaboration. Note that Sakai project sites are a means for supporting ad hoc collaboration needs, whereas the course sites are tailored to offer courses.

Commit: To add, delete, or modify code in a source code repository.

Committer: Anyone who commits code.

See: Commit

Common Name: The Sakai application's internal name for a tool.

Community Source: An open source model where a strong central Foundation supports the activity of a wider open source community.

See: Open Source

Confluence: The central Wiki for the Sakai project (`http://bugs.sakai-project.org/confluence`). Confluence is named after the software it runs on. It has extra features for integration with the Sakai bug-tracking database known as Jira.

See: Jira

Continuous build server: A piece of software that periodically compiles source code. Its purpose is to catch early code that breaks compilation.

Contrib: The location within Subversion where contributed code to Sakai is stored (`https://source.sakaiproject.org/contrib`).

Contrib tools: Tools that have not gone through the Foundation-coordinated QA process. The tools can sit in Contrib, or externally within the developer's own source code repository.

See: Contrib

Core tools: *See:* Enterprise bundle tools.

Deadlocked: Processes are deadlocked when they are waiting on each other and never complete their work.

Discussion Group: A group of community members who discuss a particular theme (such as development or end user needs) through the means of a distribution list.

See: Distribution List

Distribution List: An email address passes your message on to a group of other addresses. A moderator chooses whether the message should be distributed to the whole group.

DoOcracy: A community in which if an individual sees work that needs to be done, he or she does it. A DoOcracy can only work efficiently if the community is polite and supportive. The mentality is best summed up by the phrase, "If you think that you can do it better then please do so".

Document Object Model (DOM): A model of an XML structure stored in memory for easy programmatic manipulation.

Enterprise Bundle Tools: Tools that the Sakai community feels are ready for enterprise deployment in large installations, having gone through a formal QA process. Enterprise Bundle tools are also known as core tools.

Environment variable: A variable set in a user's command-line shell that tells programs how to behave. The behavior of Java is modified by the `JAVA_OPTS` variable.

Entitybroker: A specific service manager in Sakai that helps manage data and provide extra utility functionality. It is exposed via RESTful web services.

See: Service manager, Web services

Exception handling: An error handling mechanism in Java that deals with exceptional situations, such as when a program runs out of memory.

Front-end server: A server that a user interacts with directly. A load balancer can distribute user requests across a number of frontend servers. Conversely, a backend server is a server such as a database or Network Attached Storage (NAS) that users do not interact with directly.

Garbage Collector: The part of the Java Virtual Machine that manages its memory.

Graphic User Interface (GUI): Allows for human interaction with an application via windows and menus. The web pages of the Sakai application rendered in a web browser are an example of a GUI.

Hardware encryption: The process of using hardware, such as a load balancer, to encrypt plain text.

Headless: A server with no monitor or keyboard attached. Administration is normally done over the network.

Hot Swappable: The ability to replace a component of a server, such as a hard disk, while the server is still running.

IDE (Integrated Development Environment): A GUI for developers that allows them to do many of their daily development tasks such as writing and checking code, compiling, and debugging. Note that Eclipse is the recommended IDE for Sakai.

IT Infrastructure Library (ITIL): A documented set of best practices for structuring an organization.

JAVA_OPTS: An environment variable that modifies how the Java Virtual machine behaves.

See: Environment variable

Java Management Extensions (JMX): A set of extensions and tools within Java that enable the monitoring and management of devices, applications, and service-driven networks. Note that you can use JMX-aware tools to monitor the JVM that Sakai runs on.

See: JVM

Java Virtual Machine (JVM): A Java application runs within the Java Virtual Machine. A virtual machine hides differences between various hardware and operating systems so that programmers have a uniform way of writing code.

Java DataBase Connectivity (JDBC): A Java API allowing a program to talk with many different types of databases.

Java Development Kit (JDK): A Java software development environment from Sun, which includes the runtime environment plus a number of extra tools.

JavaDoc: A standardized way of writing documentation in Java. The data for documentation and the code sit in the same file. A tool can then transverse the source code to generate PDF, HTML, or other documentation types.

Java Object: An object in Java is a programming construct that can have methods and store data about itself.

Jira: The Sakai bug-tracking database (`http://jira.sakaiproject.org/jira`) named after the software it runs on.

A common term for a bug report.

Join/unjoin: To become a member of a worksite. You can unjoin to remove yourself from the membership of a site.

License: Sakai is published under the open source ECL2 license (`http://opensource.org/licenses/ecl2.php`). Note that the Sakai Foundation is the legal home for the Sakai license.

Linking out: A link within content stored in Sakai that points to resources outside Sakai.

ListServer: A server that allows individuals to send emails to a group. The server includes mechanisms for subscribing and unsubscribing, moderating, and maintaining the mail groups. The original listserver was first developed by Eric Thomas in the mid-eighties, but the term is now used generically for all servers that fulfil this functionality.

See: Distribution list

Load balancer: A network device that divides web requests between a number of servers.

See: Frontend server

Maven: A tool that is used to build a Sakai binary from its source code.

Network File System (NFS): A protocol that allows a file system on one server to be used by the network on another.

Open Source Portfolio (OSP): A robust, non-proprietary, open source electronic portfolio application that is an integral part of Sakai.

Patch: Code in a text file that, when added to source code (via the process of patching), removes a bug. A patch follows a specific format that describes the difference between the old and new code.

Page: A rendered area within Sakai with a specific URL that can contain one or more tools.

Password wallet: An application in which you can safely store, retrieve, and manage multiple passwords.

Persists: A process where data stored in memory is saved to a database so that if an application is restarted, the data can be retrieved. Examples of persisted data include user accounts, sites, and user preferences.

Planet Sakai: A Sakai-specific news aggregator (`http://www.planetsakai.org/`).

Programmer's Café: A workshop introducing developers to the basic programming concepts needed for creating tools in Sakai. The Programmers Café is traditionally run for two days just before the international conference.

Provider: A piece of Java code that you can plug into Sakai by changing a configuration file. The provider performs a specific duty, such as authorizing a user, adding to the membership of a group, or returning course details.

Provisional Tools: Tools that are in the process of being accepted by the Sakai community. Provisional tools normally start their lives as contrib tools, and then pass through a formal QA process. Provisional tools are part of the binary version of Sakai, but are hidden (stealthed) from the end user.

See: Stealthing

Pseudo byte code: Compilers change code from text source code into byte code that can be run by specific processor types. Java compiles source code to "pseudo" byte code that can run in the JVM and is not dependent on the underlying processor of the computer it is running on.

Publish: The act of making a site visible to members of that site. Conversely, to unpublish is to remove a site from the view of its members.

QA network: A ready-to-be-tested set of servers, distributed throughout the world, running the most current version of Sakai.

Realm: A set of roles and permissions. An instance of a realm is used to control who can do what.

Role: A role is a group with a set of permissions in a site. Roles can include student, instructor, maintainer, and so on.

Sakai.properties: Sakai's global configuration file.

Sakai Commercial Affiliates (SCA): Sakai Commercial Affiliates (SCA) are commercial firms offering for-fee support and expertise for the Sakai community source software.

Sakaiger: A handmade stuffed creature of unknown, possibly alien origin that is awarded to community members that have significantly contributed to the Quality Assurance (http://www.sakaiger.com/).

Sakai Educational Partner Program: The source of funding for the Foundation, which involves an annual fee plus a three-year commitment. It enables the Foundation to support the community in numerous ways, including maintaining central infrastructure.

Sakai Fellowship award: An annual award whose purpose is to foster community leadership and contribution through recognizing and supporting active contributors.

Sakai Foundation: The Sakai Foundation is a non-profit corporation with a small staff and modest budget. Activities include managing the intellectual property of Sakai, organizing conferences, planning meetings, and maintaining the Sakai technology infrastructure.

Sakai Gateway page: The front page of Sakai.

Sakai Instance: A running Sakai deployment. The instance includes all the hardware and software on the application side that is needed for a student to log in and use Sakai.

Sakai Library: Example pieces of code found under the references/library directory in the source code that show how to make the GUI of a Sakai tool.

Sakai Style Guide: A guide for interface designers that explains how to make consistent-looking tools.

SAX: A programmatic API to process XML.

Section: Course sites can be divided into sections. Each section can be assigned memberships and announcements, and resources can set up so that they are seen only by specific sections.

Service manager: Pieces of running code within Sakai that manage services such as adding, deleting, or modifying courses, users, groups.

Site: By default, there are three types of site within Sakai—course, project, and OSP. Course sites are designed to support traditional learning structures such as university courses or workshops. Project sites are intended for ad hoc collaboration between peers. Portfolio sites are intended to keep a track of individuals' portfolios. Each site has a set of roles associated with it, such as instructor and student. The choice of site member roles depends on the site type. The set of tools to choose from also depends on the site type.

Single Sign On (SSO): The ability to log on once and then use many applications without having to log on to each application separately.

Spring: A Java framework that decreases development effort.

Static analysis: The process of checking code that's not running for patterns that indicate programming faults.

Static content: Content that does not change, such as ordinary web pages and images. Conversely, dynamic content does change, such as a web page generated by looking up information in a database.

Stealthing: The ability to hide tools from the tool choice list when a site is created.

Sticky Session: A load balancer remembers which server a user request should go to via a cookie. A session (such as when a user logs in, does something, and then logs out) using this method is known as a sticky session.

Stop the world process: A process that stops an application from running while it is executing. The JVM sometimes performs a stop the world process when it cleans up memory.

See: JVM

Subversion: The Revision Control System (RCS) for the Sakai source code, named after the software it runs on.

Teaching with Sakai Innovation Award (TWSIA): An annual award that seeks to highlight Sakai-related innovative teaching practices.

Tool: A small piece of functionality within Sakai that you can add to a site either during site creation or afterwards. Tools include Wikis, blogs, and the ability to make announcements.

Tomcat: It's the application server that Sakai runs on. (`http://tomcat.apache.org/`). Note that Sakai can also run on the JBoss application server, but there are few real examples of this.

Trunk: The main location within Subversion for developers to store their code related to the core Sakai features (`https://source.sakaiproject.org/svn/sakai/trunk/`).

Unhide: The process of changing the permissions of a resource, such as a file, so that others can see the resource. Conversely, hide is the process of hiding a resource from others.

Uninterruptible Power Supply (UPS): A device that supplies electricity even when the main supply is disrupted. This allows system administrators to safely turn servers off during power failures.

Work Group: A group of interested people working towards a common goal. The group is in communication with the Foundation and has its own moderated location on Confluence and distribution group. Common work groups include Internationalization, user experience, Quality Assurance.

See: Distribution group

Web services: Services available over the Network based on standards such as SOAP and the RESTful architectural pattern. Through web services, Sakai exposes its own internal services to the world.

Wicket: A framework for writing reusable parts in Java (`http://wicket.apache.org/`).

B
Resources

With so many people using Sakai daily for learning, it is natural to have diverse sources of helpful information available over the Internet. This Appendix points to some of them. There are links to information about the central infrastructure that the Sakai Foundation fosters, pointers to documents that help you understand the Sakai community a little better, best practices, training materials, and finally links to tools that are used provide a better Sakai experience and to develop Sakai.

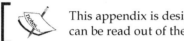 This appendix is designed as a quick start and can be read out of the context of the rest of the book.

Sakai Foundation support

The Sakai Foundation is the legal home for Sakai, and provides a central infrastructure and coordination point for the whole community. The infrastructure is periodically reviewed by the Foundation for its fitness for community use. Therefore, over time, you can expect improvements and additions.

The links in this section direct you to the Foundation-sponsored infrastructure:

- `http://sakaiproject.org`: The home page of the Sakai Foundation. It is a good jumping-off point for beginners. The site is updated daily.

- `https://collab.sakaiproject.org`: The collab server is where you activate your membership in distribution and work groups. Currently, collab is being replaced. However, there is talk about reinstating the same features, but based on 3akai. If the link does not work, the Foundation home page will have a reference to the new infrastructure and information on how to subscribe.

- `http://bugs.sakaiproject.org/confluence`: Confluence is an enhanced Wiki where a large amount of information resides. Similar in editorial freedom as Wikipedia, you can create your own account, and add and modify content.

- `http://bugs.sakaiproject.org/confluence/display/MGT/ Sakai+Roadmap`: A Wiki page with the current Sakai Roadmap.

- `http://bugs.sakaiproject.org/jira`: This is the bug database known as Jira, which keeps track of all currently unresolved Sakai-related issues, historic bugs that have been removed, feature requests, and a list of the configurations of many production servers around the world.

- `http://www.sakaiproject.org/portal/site/sakai-downloads`: The location for downloading the current version of Sakai.

- `https://source.sakaiproject.org/svn/sakai`: The source code. Note that you can see the code via a web browser.

- `https://source.sakaiproject.org/contrib`: Location of the contributed source code. There are over 168 individual directories with lots of extra tools, experiments, and new features that may one day make it into the main code base.

- `http://opensource.org/licenses/ecl2.php`: Sakai's license.

The community

This section provides links to places that provide information on what the community is thinking and doing, and includes examples of reliable commercial vendors. Commercial support gives planners confidence in investing in the long-term future of Sakai because they know they can always buy in help if needed.

- `http://www.planetsakai.org/`: SakaiPlanet is a news aggregator that keeps track of changes in the blogs of at least 40 active community members. If you want to know the buzz, this is the place to go.

- `http://www.nabble.com`: Nabble keeps a searchable HTML version of the Sakai Distribution groups. Distribution groups are an excellent source of expert advice. Being able to search through nabble allows you to do research quickly.

- `http://openedpractices.org/`: OpenEd practices is a web site for sharing community best practices and resources with a emphasis on Sakai-related material.

- `http://www.rsmart.com/`: rSmart is one of the lead commercial companies involved with Sakai. It has also generously donated three case studies to this book.

- `http://www.unicon.net/services/sakai/evaluation`: Unicon is a respected commercial company that provides a Sakai test drive that you can log onto to evaluate Sakai quickly.

- `http://www.edia.nl`: Edia is a Dutch homegrown company. It has donated more than five tools to contrib, and supports turnkey and hosting solutions.

- `http://www.serensoft.com`: Serensoft, another example of a respected company with solutions based on Sakai.

Best practices

Mentioned here are a number of best-practice guides and links to infrastructure that supports these best practices:

- `http://bugs.sakaiproject.org/confluence/display/DOC/Install+Guide+(2.5)`: The Install Guide for version 2.5 of Sakai, which is designed for those installing Sakai from scratch. Both good and bad practices are mentioned. You may have to update the number 2.5 in the URL if you want a guide for another version.

- `http://bugs.sakaiproject.org/confluence/display/DOC/Sys+Admin+Guide`: The System admin guide, which gives you more detailed advice about configuration and tuning Sakai than the install guide does.

- `http://bugs.sakaiproject.org/confluence/display/BOOT/Programmer%27s+Cafe`: The home page of the Programmer's Café. It links to a programmers guide and best-practice advice.

- `http://qa1-nl.sakaiproject.org/codereview`: The home page of automatically-generated daily reports on the current state of the Sakai source code. The reports are particularly interesting for project coordinators and programmers.

- `http://source.caret.cam.ac.uk/continuum`: An example of a continuous build server that regularly compiles the Sakai source code and reports on any difficulties. Having a build server is considered a best practice; if code gets broken, the error is found and repaired early.

- `http://nightly2.sakaiproject.org`: The official nightly build server for a number of Sakai-related projects.

- `http://nightly2.sakaiproject.org/javadoc/sakai-javadoc/index.html`: The most up-to-date Java documentation (JavaDoc) for Sakai.

Training material

Large organizations that have deployed Sakai need to train their staff and students. Universities such as Indiana have kindly placed their training material online, and the material is available to review and potential reuse.

- `http://www.freesoftwaremagazine.com/articles/create_your_online_project_site_with_sakai`: An online article published at the FreeSoftware magazine's web site about how to run Sakai for the first time.

- `http://bugs.sakaiproject.org/confluence/display/ESUP/End-User+Support+Working+Group`: The Sakai End User Support Work Group home page. Many tutorials and other training materials are cataloged and linked to from here.

- `http://www.ohsu.edu/edcomm/academictech/sakai/help/tutorials.shtml`: Tutorials and video presentations from the Oregon Health & Science University. They include the dos and don'ts of starting with Sakai, using the Rich Text Editor efficiently, how to manage resources, and a plethora of other interesting topics.

- `http://www.udel.edu/sakai/training/printable/wiki/TipsTricksSakaiWiki.pdf`: Written by Mathieu Plourde from the University of Delaware, the document describes a number of educational approaches to using the in-built Wiki tool.

- `http://bspacehelp.berkeley.edu`: A help site at UC Berkeley. It includes how-tos, FAQs, videos, support, and a workshop schedule.

- `https://oncourse.iu.edu/portal/site/!gateway/page/!gateway-500`: Indiana's online support for its instance of Sakai known as Oncourse. The material includes quick starts and how-tos.

- `http://confluence.sakaiproject.org/confluence/x/UkI`: An example of commercial support for tailored trainings. The confluence page includes a list of training material that the consultant, Mark J. Norton (see entry in *Rogues gallery* chapter) can teach you.

- `http://www.unicon.net/training/sakai`: The training services page of Unicon, which offers standardized workshops for functional training and specific trainings for system administrators or developers.

Tools

The links mentioned in this section point to tools that developers use daily. The password wallet and flashcard tool mentioned are also generally useful.

- `http://www.eclipse.com`: Eclipse is the programmers' open source IDE (Integrated Development Environment) of choice when working with Sakai. Eclipse functionality can be expanded by third-party plugins.

- `http://source.sakaiproject.org/appbuilder/update`: Home of App builder, a Sakai-specific plug-in for Eclipse, which takes a lot of the drudgery out of building new Sakai tools.

- `http://subclipse.tigris.org/install.html`: Subclipse is an Eclipse plugin that enhances its ability to talk with Sakai's source code repository.

- `http://findbugs.cs.umd.edu/eclipse`: Findbugs is a plugin that searches for around 400 types of coding bad practices.

- `http://pmd.sf.net/eclipse`: PMD is an Eclipse plugin that finds specific programming errors. Findbugs and PMD compliment each other's analyses and generally find different bug types.

- `http://www.freesoftwaremagazine.com/columns/destroy_annoying_bugs_part_2`: A magazine article on bug removal with Eclipse, Findbugs, and PMD.

- `http://openjdk.java.net/tools/svc/jconsole/`: Jconsole allows you to monitor the resource utilization of Sakai live.

- `http://ws.apache.org/commons/tcpmon/`: TCPMON is a handy tool for debugging interactions with web services. It allows you to watch the requests that are sent from web browsers to a server and the returned responses.

- `http://subversion.tigris.org/`: Subversion is the program that stores the Sakai source code. This URL not only points to Subversion, but also the associated client-side tools.

- `http://maven.apache.org/`: Maven is the command-line tool that developers use to build Sakai from source code.

- `http://www.mysql.com/`: The open source database MySQL is a supported Sakai database type. The link points to its home page where you can find not only the binaries, but also a full set of documentation and client-side tools, such as a visual database browser.

- `http://keepass.info`: A password wallet that can store multiple passwords in an encrypted format that is ready for use when you need to log on to many different services on the Internet.

- `http://flashcards.sourceforge.net`: Flashcards are an excellent way to help you remember things. Jflash was used in this book for learning about the specifics of Sakai tools.

Index

DG
about 450
announcements 396
development 396
user 396
digital portfolio
use case 295
Discussion Group. *See* DG
distribution list 451
DNS 39
documentation
need for 89
Document Object Model. *See* DOM
DOM 229, 451
Domain Name Service. *See* DNS
DoOcracry 392, 451
drop box tool 164
drop box tool, course tools 108

E

Eclipse 138
Eclipse, URL 461
Edia
about 143
Fedora tool 146
Sakai maps 145
section author 143
skin manager tool 144
URL 293, 459
web course tool 147, 148
Edia tools 122
EDUCASE
URL 387
EID 181
Elluminate tool 122
email archive tool 98, 158
end-user support working group
URL 410
Enterprise Bundle Tools 451
Enterprise Data Integration
about 43, 44
brute force anti-pattern 43
commercial offerings 43
Enterprise ID. *See* EID
enterprise-level quality
automated testing 87- 89

automatic code analysis 90- 93
maintenance releases 86, 87
Quality Assurance (QA) 83, 84
Quality Assurance (QA) process 84
entity broker
about 201, 216, 21, 4517
authenticating 219
client side coding, example 219, 220
interview, with author Aaron Zeckoski 220, 221
services descriptions, finding 217- 219
Environment variable 451
eportfolio 110
error messages
class not found 275
database 271, 272
file permissions 275
Java version 267
Out of memory 268-270
portal 270, 271
port issues 267, 268
Sakai.properties 273, 274
search 272, 273
errors, policy
production systems 262, 263
Quality Assurance analysis 261, 262
reporting 259, 260
evaluations, portfolio toolset 112
evaluation system tool 122
evaluation tool 128, 130
Excalibur 231
exception handling 451

F

fckeditor, URL 54
feed tool 122
fedora tool 146
filter 36
Findbugs tools, URL 90, 461
flashcard activity 97
flashcard tool, URL 461
Fluid project, URL 33
FOP 231
Formbuilder 131
form builder tool 122
forms, portfolio toolset 112

Mod_deflate 240
modules tool 165
more innovative uses of tools
  versus less innovative 363
MOTD (Message of the day) tool, adminis-
    tration workspace 175
MRTG 235
Multi Router Traffic Grapher. *See* MRTG
MyFaces
  about 231
  URL 208
MySakai tool 122
MySakai URL 119
MySQL, URL 461
My Workspace, Sakai site structure 155

N

Nabble
  NabbleURL 458
netcraft
  URL 238
Network File System. *See* NFS
newcomers FAQ
  URL 386
news feeds tool 122
newsfeed tool 131
news tool 53, 98, 168
NFS 453

O

object-orientated
  URL 185
official Sakai FAQ 11
Ohloh web site 78
Oncourse
  URL 460
online article
  URL 460
online help tool
  about 46
  URL 65
online tool, administration workspace 176
open code 399-404
OpenEd 195, 196
OpenEd practices
  URL 458

OpenEdPractices.org repository 343
OpenEd site, URL 113
open source community, Sakai 10
Open Source Portfolio. *See* OSP
open standards, example 399, 400
Open Syllabus
  about 151
  Alpha version interface 150
  members 148
  section author 148
  syllabi or course web sites authoring, solu-
    tions for 149
OSP 14, 51, 110, 111, 453
OSyl. *See* Open Syllabus
out of memory 268-270

P

packages
  binary 18
  demonstration 18
  source code 18
Page 453
passive learning
  versus active learning 361
password wallet,
  about 453
  URL 461
Patch 453
Peoplesoft application
  URL 375
permissions, realms
  all.groups permission 187
  delete.any permission 187
  delete.own permission 187
  new permission 187
  read.drafts permission 187
  read permission 187
  revise.any permission 187
  revise.own permission 187
permission tool 104
Persists 453
Planet Sakai 453
Pluto 231
PMD tools, URL 90, 461
podcast tool 96, 99, 166
polls tool 99, 166

Moodle 1.9 Multimedia
Create and share multimedia learning materials in your Moodle courses

João Pedro Soares Fernandes

PACKT

Moodle 1.9 Multimedia

ISBN: 978-1-847195-90-6   Paperback: 272 pages

Create and share multimedia learning materials in your Moodle courses.

1. Ideas and best practices for teachers and trainers on using multimedia effectively in Moodle

2. Ample screenshots and clear explanations to facilitate learning

3. Covers working with TeacherTube, embedding interactive Flash games, podcasting, and more

Moodle Course Conversion
Get your existing teaching material online quickly and easily

Beginner's Guide

Ian Wild

Moodle Course Conversion: Beginner's Guide

ISBN: 978-1-847195-24-1   Paperback: 316 pages

Taking existing classes online quickly with the Moodle LMS

1. No need to start from scratch! This book shows you the quickest way to start using Moodle and e-learning, by bringing your existing lesson materials into Moodle.

2. Move your existing course notes, worksheets, and resources into Moodle quickly then improve your course, taking advantage of multimedia and collaboration.

3. Moving marking online – no more backbreaking boxes of assignments to lug to and from school or college.

Please check **www.PacktPub.com** for information on our titles

Moodle 1.9 E-Learning Course Development

ISBN: 978-1-847193-53-7   Paperback: 384 pages

A complete guide to successful learning
using Moodle

1. Updated for Moodle version 1.9

2. Straightforward coverage of installing and
   using the Moodle system

3. Working with Moodle features in all learning
   environments

4. A unique course-based approach focuses
   your attention on designing well-structured,
   interactive, and successful courses

Moodle Teaching Techniques

ISBN: 978-1-847192-84-4   Paperback: 192 pages

Creative Ways to Use Moodle for Constructing
Online Learning Solutions

1. Applying your teaching techniques
   through Moodle

2. Creative uses for Moodle's standard features

3. Workarounds, providing alternative solutions

4. Abundantly illustrated with screenshots
   of the solutions you'll build

Please check **www.PacktPub.com** for information on our titles

Printed in the United States
219782BV00001B/1/P